P9-DVP-832

MARY McCARTHY

Also by Carol Gelderman

Henry Ford: The Wayward Capitalist

MARY McCARTHY

A LIFE

c. 1

CAROL GELDERMAN

ST. MARTIN'S PRESS

NEW YORK

B
MCCARTHY, M

Design by Jaya Dayal.

LIBRARY OF CONGRESS
Library of Congress Cataloging-in-Publication Data

Gelderman, Carol W.
    Mary McCarthy : a life / by Carol Gelderman
        p.   cm.
    ISBN 0-312-00565-2 : $24.95 (est.)
    1. McCarthy, Mary, 1912–   —Biography. 2. Authors,
American—20th century—Biography. I. Title.
PS3525.A1435Z64   1988
818'.5209—dc19   87-27953
                                                          CIP

First Edition

10 9 8 7 6 5 4 3 2 1

Contents

PART FOUR

PART FIVE

PART SIX

Acknowledgments

Several years ago, I happened to mention to Elaine Markson, my agent, that *Memories of a Catholic Girlhood* was one of my favorite books. I, too, had been a Sacred Heart pupil, I told her, and I found Mary McCarthy's descriptions of her life in a Sacred Heart convent evocative of my own school days. "Why don't you write a biography of McCarthy," Elaine suggested. "Certainly not," I protested. "She's very much alive, and I can't write the biography of a living person."

Elaine persisted, and before long, I was on my way from my home in New Orleans to Castine, Maine, where, uninvited, I hoped to meet Mary McCarthy. Although I did not know it at the time, her unfailing courtesy was my ally, for when I phoned her from the Pentagoët Inn, only a few doors from her own house on Main Street, she invited me for tea, a civilized ritual she observes late every afternoon. She, too, was uneasy with the idea of a biography of a living subject. But she was sympathetic to my argument that I wanted to speak to the "principals" of her story while it was still possible; indeed, the two people she admired most, Nicola Chiaromonte and Hannah Arendt, had already died.

After reading the galleys of my previous biography, she agreed to cooperate; she gave me introductions to friends and access to much of her correspondence, as well as her willingness to answer a host of personal questions. So, first and foremost, I want to thank Mary McCarthy, not only for her cooperation, which in no way should be construed as approval of what I have written, but also for an opportunity to get to know her and her work, which has changed my own way of viewing the world.

Next, I want to thank Mary McCarthy's publisher, William Jovanovich, who not only gave generously of his time, but who saw to it that thirty years of their correspondence was photocopied, put in chronological order, and sent to me in New Orleans. Others who provided copies of McCarthy's letters are: Carmen Angleton, Arthur Schlesinger, Jr., David and Eleanor DuVivier, Ulrich Middeldorf, William Phillips, Jess Rosenberg, Kevin McCarthy, Frani Blough Muser, and Cynthia McCarthy Sandberg, who also photocopied diaries, baptismal and marriage records, and who introduced me to members of the McCarthy family in Minneapolis.

I am grateful also to the John Simon Guggenheim Memorial Foundation, to *The New Yorker,* to *Partisan Review,* to I Tatti Archives, to Vassar College, to Annie Wright Seminary, to Sacred Heart Academy (Forest Ridge), and to Saint Stephen's School, for access to files and copies of relevant correspondence; to Mrs. Richard Rovere for the prospectus of *Critic;* to Miriam Chiaromonte for the statement of purpose of Europe-America Groups; to Roger Straus for relevant portions of his oral history; to the Sterling Library, and the Beinecke Library of Yale University, to the Houghton Library, Harvard University, to the Butler Library, Columbia University, to the Tamiment Library, New York University, to the Berg Collection of the New York Public Library, to Special Collections, Vassar College Library, and Lisa Browar, archivist, to the Library of Congress, to the Pierpont Morgan Library, to the libraries of the Universities of Pennsylvania, Texas, Virginia, and Norwich University, and to Maurice F. Neville Rare Books; at the University of New Orleans, to Evelyn Chandler, Director of Interlibrary Loan, to the Graduate Research Council and the College of Liberal Arts for research grants, and to Elizabeth Penfield, Chairman of the Department of English for a reduction in my teaching load; to the National Endowment for the Humanities for a one-year research fellowship; to Sherli Goldman for her excellent published bibliography of McCarthy's work through the middle 1960s; and to Anne Giovingo and Patricia Sorrell, who typed the manuscript.

I wish to thank the following people for interviews: Lionel Abel, Sir Harold Acton, Carmen Angleton, R. W. Apple, James Atlas, William Barrett, Signora Luigi Biso, Professor and Mrs. Walter Blair, Mary Brady, Irma Brandeis, Tom Buckley, William Buell, Francis Casavetti, Dick Cavett, Miriam Chiaromonte, Countess Anna Maria Cicogna, William Corson, Barbara Anderson Dupee, David and Elinor DuVivier, Donald Finn, Philippe Franchine, Joseph Frank, Eleanor Perkins Frazier, Stanley Geist, Brendan Gill, Robert Giroux, Alan Glyn, Walter Goldwater, Hester Green, Elizabeth Morgenstern Greenebaum, Miriam Gross, Doris Grumbach, Mark Hamilton, Elizabeth Hardwick, Francis Haskell, Mathilda Rosenberg Hbishman, Rudolph Hertzberg, Minna Newberger Hiller, Mrs. Herbert Hirsch, Mary McCarthy Hooper, David Jackson, Kot Jelenski, Eunice Clark Jessup, C. Colton Johnson, Molly Johnsrud, Gloria Jones, William Jovanovich, Harold Kaplan, Mr. and Mrs. Terence Kilmartin, Nicholas King, Judy McCarthy Knickerbocker, Lotte Kohler, William Koppelmann, Angélique Levi, Frances Lindley,

Lady Caroline Lowell, Dwight Macdonald, Nancy Macdonald, Charles McCarthy, Eleanor McCarthy, Flip McCarthy, James McCarthy, Kate McCarthy, Kevin McCarthy, Mary Dabney McCarthy, Preston Mc-Carthy, Mrs. Sheridan McCarthy, Hazel Guggenheim McKinley, Mary Lou McCarthy McKissick, James Merrill, Blanche McCarthy Michaels, Professor and Mrs. Ulrich Middeldorf, Karl Miller, Herbert Mitgang, Gaia Servadio Mostyn-Owen, William Mostyn-Owen, Frani Blough Muser, John Bernard Myers, Cees Nooteboom, Ellen Adler Oppen-heim, Benjamin O'Sullivan, Cleo Paturis, Eleanor Perényi, William Phil-lips, Frank and Myrtle Preston, Augusta Dabney Prince, Jonathan Randal, John Richardson, Yale Richmond, Jess Rosenberg, Mrs. Rich-ard Rovere, Countess Cristina Rucellai, John Russell, Rosamond Bernier Russell, Cynthia McCarthy Sandberg, Emilia Sartori, Arthur Schles-inger, Jr., Charles Schlessiger, Laurence Schwabacher, Reverend F. Q. Shafer, Margaret Shafer, William Shawn, Elizabeth Niebuhr Sifton, Robert Silvers, Eileen Simpson, Werner Stemens, Eve Gassler Stwertka, Fiorella Superbi, William Tuohy, Niccolò Tucci, Margo Viscusi, Ade-laide Walker, Lord George Weidenfeld, Alison West, Mrs. Harold Wil-liams, Reuel Wilson, Cecylia Wojewoda, Daniel Woolsey, Francis Wyndham, and Barry Zorthian.

My agent, Elaine Markson, and her associate, Geri Thoma, were sources of never-ending encouragement and help. My editor, Peter Ginna, was insightful, demanding, and enormously helpful to me during the revision of this manuscript. Thanks also to Robert Daniels, an unusu-ally observant copyeditor, and to Amit Shah and Amelie Littell, the production editors.

And finally, I want to acknowledge my debt to my daughter, Irene Gelderman, who accompanied me on many of my interviews, making those trips memorable and fun, and who, because she was a lot like the younger Mary McCarthy, gave me insight into McCarthy's personality and character. Irene was killed trying to land a disabled airplane on a foggy November 2, 1985. I dedicate this book to her memory.

During the six years I have been working on this biography of Mary McCarthy, I have found that when I mention my subject to others, their reactions usually fall into one of two categories: "How interesting for you to be dealing with such a fascinating subject," and "How can you stand to read that dreadful woman's work?" I have rarely encountered indifference. What seemed surprising at first was that otherwise restrained people, who had never met Mary McCarthy, would attack her as a person. But for the past fifty years, critics, too, have seemed to be either captivated or outraged by McCarthy as a person as much as as a writer.

From the time she first appeared on the literary scene in the pages of the *New Republic* in the mid-1930s until the present day, she has drawn the ire of commentators. John Aldridge has depicted her as strident and shrewish and her novels as "crammed with cerebration and bitchiness." Paul Schlueter has described "her approach to writing as reflective of the modern American bitch." Norman Mailer, less overtly hostile to McCarthy, nonetheless opened a review of one of her novels by portraying her as a virago: "Mary, our saint, our umpire, our lit arbiter, our broadsword, our Barrymore (Ethel), our Dame (dowager), our mistress (Head), our Joan of Arc, the only Joan of Arc to travel up and down our raddled literary world, our poor damp kingdom, her sword breathing fire." After Alfred Kazin criticized McCarthy as harsh-tongued and snobbish in his *Starting Out in the Thirties*—she set out to remind readers, he said, "of the classical learning they had despised, the social lapses they could no longer overlook"—he told Dwight Macdonald that dozens of people had written him, saying, "God bless you Mr. K., for speaking out on THAT woman." The recurring sameness of the criticism prompted a Ph.D. candidate, preparing to write a dissertation on the critical reception of McCarthy's work, to ask if in a hundred years textbooks on American literature will still be using words like "knives, stilettos, switch-blades, cold, heartless, clever, cerebral, cutting, acid, or acidulous" in discussions of Mary McCarthy.

McCarthy is accustomed to such attacks by now, though she does not claim to be able to ignore them. She wrote a friend in 1974 that she disliked "being on the receiving line of so much hostility. Well, it would be better, clearly, if I didn't mind, but I do and I find it deeply discouraging. The sense that one is not 'getting through' to one's imagined listeners; it is like making a transatlantic call with a bad connection. The fact that this *keeps* happening to me . . . adds a ghostly element of repetition, as if I were condemned to this punishment throughout eternity. . . . And the punishment is somehow mysteriously, arcanely, related to my eternal self: the bars of the cell are, so to speak, my own ribs."

Her friend and publisher, William Jovanovich, once attributed some of the bad reviews to her having "dared too early—it's apparently allowed to women now—to speak as a person, as an intellectual, and a woman, *without distinguishing those roles*." But the principal reason for the hostility, he felt sure, was the laziness of reviewers "who will go back, time and time again, to what was said before. Striking or forceful figures in public life carry with them the stereotype that first put them in print. This applies to writers, actors, politicians, hedonists, tycoons." It is true that Mary McCarthy, beginning with her first published series of articles, "Our Critics, Right or Wrong" (which took America's book reviewers to task for their mediocrity), has helped to make her own reputation as a literary duelist. Just two samples from her twenty-five years as theater critic for *Partisan Review* illustrate her talent for dishing out punishment. Eugene O'Neill, she wrote in 1946, "belongs to that group of American authors, which includes Farrell and Dreiser, whose choice of vocation was a kind of triumphant catastrophe; none of these men possessed the slightest ear for the word, the sentence, the paragraph; all of them, however, have, so to speak, enforced the career they decreed for themselves by a relentless policing of the beat." And of Tennessee Williams's *A Streetcar Named Desire*—which she characterized as a play about a man's difficulty in getting into his bathroom because his sister-in-law is always occupying it—she wrote, "if art, as Mr. Williams appears to believe, is a lie, then anything goes, but Mr. Williams' lies, like Blanche's, are so old and shopworn that the very truth upon which he rests them becomes garish and ugly. . . . His work reeks of literary ambition as the apartment reeks of cheap perfume." Forty years after they were written, these words still provoke angry responses.

In her fiction, too, she is ruthless in exposing the failings of her characters. Yet Mary McCarthy, for all her sharpness as a writer, is not the "cold, cutting" person that so many critics and readers have presumed her to be. Her close friend Hannah Arendt once told her that "the discrepancy between public image and actual person is greater in your case than in any other I know of." This biography attempts to probe that discrepancy.

When people first meet Mary McCarthy they often remark on the contrast between her reputation and her real self. William Tuohy, who met her in Saigon when he was bureau chief there for the *Los Angeles Times,* expected her to be serious, even grim. "I had heard about McCarthy's being able to cut up someone verbally, and she wasn't like that at all. She was pleasant, witty, charming, gossipy in the best sense of the word—chatty about people and about things. Obviously she's a brilliant person with a wit that can be acid and biting, but she is not the kind of person who relies on that." Countess Anna Maria Cicogna, at whose Libyan villa McCarthy worked on her novel *The Group,* says, "Mary is full of life and amusement and fun—wonderful company, she is." Lifelong friends, as well as new acquaintances, appreciate McCarthy's gregarious nature. "Mary had a good time in Rome," Italian writer Nicola Chiaromonte wrote Dwight Macdonald. "We, and the Roman literary circles as well, managed to have her entertained and feted all the time. She loves that, as you know, and her pleasure is communicative."

Her devotion to her friends is strong. She is known for having an eventful love life—she has been married four times, and acknowledges several affairs besides—but nonromantic friendships have been of equal importance to her. Her closest friends have been those with whom she has an intellectual rapport. "I would date my own life more by friendship than by love affairs on the whole," she has said. "Friends and teachers—for me, it has often been the same thing."

Those who know her well point to the perfectionism she brings to everything in her life. "The care she takes is at the heart of her charac-ter," according to one friend. She is an indefatigable student of lan-guages—she has learned French and Italian and continues to take German lessons; and of art—she visits and revisits churches, monuments, and museums, insisting on knowing every detail and looking into every corner. She sets aside a solid week each year to work on her extremely complicated income tax, trusting no accountant to be as thorough as herself. A dedicated cook who makes everything from scratch, McCarthy still chops parsley with a big knife and makes crumbs with a rolling pin. She refuses to own a food processor. She will not even grind coffee electrically. Nor does she have a word processor; she prefers her old manual typewriter. "I like labor-intensive implements and practices," she told an audience at the MacDowell Colony. "In word production, housekeeping, gardening, reading, I actually believe that the amount of labor that goes into human manufacture determines the success of the enterprise. Whether it's pushing a fruit or vegetable through a sieve or cranking by hand an ice cream freezer, or going to trouble over a party or a paragraph, the more labor, the better."

"Mary's so tenacious, so pure: no jam with pectin," says her sister-in-law Kate McCarthy. "Yes," agrees Mary's brother Kevin. "Pure in her food, her opinions, her life; uncompromising and . . . always ready to take up arms." That McCarthy is "ready to take up arms" is not in doubt. Even those who have never met her can tell from her two memoirs, *Memories of a Catholic Girlhood* and *How I Grew,* that competitiveness is deeply rooted in McCarthy's character. "Winning is the key to her nature," her French translator has pointed out. McCarthy herself once laughingly told Hannah Arendt that she was taking an inordinate amount of time reading the page proofs of one of her stories from *The New Yorker* because "a normal person cooperates with the checkers or uses them as a convenience, but I cannot help competing with them."

Often Mary McCarthy will turn an odious task or a sacrifice into a challenge for herself. When a doctor told her to quit smoking, she asked him if two cigarettes a day would be permissible. Yes, he replied, but cautioned that no lifelong smoker could stop at two. "Well, that's all Mary needs—'no one can do it,' " an acquaintance observed. And she was right: Mary McCarthy has been smoking two Lucky Strikes a day for five years.

Coupled with her competitiveness, McCarthy's memoirs acknowledge, is her "wish to play a part and attract notice." Disappointed at getting only a minor role in an elementary school play, the young Mary McCarthy compensated by memorizing the entire script and reciting every line along with the other actors. Something of the same impulse motivates Martha Sinnott, the protagonist of McCarthy's novel *A Charmed Life*: " 'I like your shells,' " Martha tells Dolly Lamb, "examining an arrangement of graduated seashells that Dolly had picked up on the beach. 'You did it for pleasure, I imagine. If it were I, I would do it to make somebody admire my ingenuity.' "

Given Mary McCarthy's outspokenness, her compulsion to say what she thinks—even when it is damaging to herself—she has had little trouble attracting notice. Her quick tongue has gotten her into trouble again and again. "I do not seem to live and learn," she told Edmund Wilson after an unpleasant article about her, by an author with whom she had cooperated, appeared in *Esquire.* She echoed herself a few years later in a letter to Doris Grumbach, after reading the galleys of Grumbach's critical biography *The Company She Kept.* "Unfortunately,"

McCarthy wrote, "I am not discreet, and I do not seem to learn. I enjoy talking." The book included several cutting remarks about people and events that McCarthy had made in a taped interview.

McCarthy rarely appears on television, but when she does, she is liable to say something unexpected. In a televised interview with Edwin Newman, she told him that the controversial Pullman-berth seduction scene in her story "The Man in the Brooks Brothers Shirt" was autobiographical, down to the detail of the missing button on the protagonist's underpants. On the "Today" show she blurted out that she had had several abortions. On "The Dick Cavett Show," in a fateful aside, she called Lillian Hellman a liar. Her friend Stanley Geist believes that "honesty is her absolute rule, even if it hurts others and herself."

In her writing, too, McCarthy has never held back with an ironic remark or a damning observation, whether directed at herself, her foes, or her friends and acquaintances. Her novel *The Oasis* caricatured the circle of intellectuals, including herself, around *Partisan Review*. After its publication, McCarthy and her husband moved away from New York because, she recalled, "no one was speaking to us." Later novels shone an equally relentless light on other groups McCarthy had been part of: Vassar women *(The Group)*, college faculties *(The Groves of Academe)*, the New England towns of Wellfleet *(A Charmed Life)* and Stonington *(Birds of America)*. When *Birds of America* appeared, McCarthy wrote her publisher that her husband was "checking off Stonington on the map as another place we can never go back to."

She has been just as hard on herself, both in her memoirs, where she has pictured herself as constantly playing "deliberately, to the gallery," and in her fiction, which is almost as strongly autobiographical as her memoirs. In *The Company She Keeps,* her first and still finest book of fiction, she portrays the protagonist, whose escapades are based on McCarthy's own, as playing a series of roles in order to set herself "apart from the run of people."

Some reviewers, in fact, have devoted their efforts to identifying the real-life models for the characters in McCarthy's fiction. But Mary McCarthy objects to this literal approach to her work, saying it detracts from what she is "trying to do in the novel." At least the reviewers are in agreement on one thing: the unflagging elegance of her prose style. William Barrett says it is "a pity this woman was not born into a time when style was the essence of life itself, like the court of Versailles or a salon of the 18th century." He believes McCarthy's work will not last because it is "all style" and nothing else. McCarthy, for her part, dislikes the word "style," but believes the only writers who will last are those who care about language. She is passionate about language, and is most critical of those writers who compose carelessly. (Her own composition is scrupulous, as her editors have attested: Rarely so much as a comma needs to be changed in a McCarthy manuscript.)

This concern for language has been the common thread in a very diverse body of work. In the age of the specialist she is its antithesis: In the past half century Mary McCarthy has been a critic, short story writer, essayist, novelist, journalist, and art historian. Millions of copies of her books, most of which are still in print, have been sold in America, as well as a great number of other English-speaking countries, especially the United Kingdom. In addition, her books have been translated into Catalan, Danish, Dutch, Finnish, French, German, Hebrew, Hungarian, Icelandic, Italian, Japanese, Norwegian, Polish, Portuguese, Rumanian, Serbo-Croat, Slovak, Slovene, Spanish, and Swedish. Not surprisingly, she thinks that what is notable about her life is her writing, and not her biography. "I think," she has said, "that what one has written takes precedence over what has happened."

Nonetheless there is a strong relationship between her life and her work: her evolution as a writer has paralleled her evolution as a person. As Irvin Stock, McCarthy's most perceptive critic, has said, she belongs among those writers whose exploration of their own nature becomes a way of understanding the world.

MARY MCCARTHY

PROLOGUE

KEVIN McCARTHY: Do you think that our lives have anything to do with trying to readjust the imbalance that took place when our parents died?

MARY McCARTHY: I think that it is natural that orphan children, rather looked down on in their family, and different from the little children they were growing up among, would try to distinguish themselves. And instead of being distinguished unfavorably, would try to distinguish themselves favorably, on the whole. I know that I have a great, still have, alas, a great attention-getting business, seeking to call attention to myself. And I had it very strongly when I was younger, as a child, and from then on. . . . I would say you could see a connection.

T HE THIRD of the three most devastating epidemics to attack mankind struck in 1918. Only the affliction brought by the Plague of Justinian in the sixth century and the Black Death in the fourteenth matched the severity of the twentieth-century influenza outbreak that killed 22 million people, infected over a billion more—half the world's population—and, within a few weeks of autumn, covered the globe. Mistakenly thought to have arisen in Spain, the cataclysm was popularly known as the Spanish flu; but, in fact, it broke out almost simultaneously in all European nations, spreading rapidly because of the movement of troops through war-torn Europe.

In America, half a million died. Among this number were thirty-eight-year-old Roy McCarthy and his twenty-nine-year-old wife, Tess.

The McCarthys, with their children—Mary, six; Kevin, four; Preston, three; and Sheridan, one—had boarded the North Coast Limited, a Northern Pacific train bound for Minneapolis, on the evening of October 30, 1918. They had just vacated their home in Seattle, where they had lived since their marriage, in 1911, to move to Minneapolis, the city where Roy had spent most of his boyhood. His brother Harry and sister-in-law Zula, who had just crossed the country to help in the move, entrained with them. During the three-day journey they crossed three mountain ranges, endless prairies, and the two mightiest rivers in America.

Yet most of the McCarthy party paid little attention to the spectacular scenery. Mary, not yet six and a half, remembered that "waving good-bye in the Seattle depot, we had not known that we had carried the flu with us into our drawing rooms, along with presents and flowers, but, one after another, we had been struck down as the train proceeded eastward. We children did not understand whether the chattering of our teeth and mama's lying torpid in the berth were not somehow a part of the trip."

Roy and Harry's parents, faces covered by masks, met their sick family. Amid the confusion of stretchers, wheelchairs, redcaps, and four tired, sick children, the McCarthys left the depot for home. All hospitals in the area were full.

Mary's Uncle Harry and Aunt Zula recovered. Their parents worsened despite the unceasing care of Emily Fifield, the family doctor, who spent several nights at the McCarthys' house, and Marie Macdonald, a next-door neighbor, who had been a nurse before her marriage. Roy died on November 6. Tess succumbed the next day. No one told the children.

PART ONE

CHAPTER I

FOREBEARS
(1821–1912)

MARY MCCARTHY'S heritage on her father's side is midwestern and Irish Catholic; on her mother's, New England Protestant and eastern-European Jewish. From the McCarthys she inherited Irish good looks and a fervent Catholicism; from the Prestons and Morgensterns, clearheadedness and candor. She herself has always believed her McCarthy legacy was a natural rebelliousness, and her Preston endowment a sensitivity to justice. She first wrote about the antithesis between her McCarthy and Preston inheritances in an early 1950s memoir. In "The Figures in the Clock," which later became a chapter in *Memories of a Catholic Girlhood,* she depicts the Prestons as exemplary, high-minded, and reticent, representing duty and always doing the right thing; and the McCarthys, who had been traders made rich by their own adroitness and hard work, as adventurous and a touch iconoclastic. Thirty years later she still saw herself as the embodiment of these two different attitudes toward life: "I was a natural rebel who was also in love with law. This was my autobiography, and it was not going to change."

In the introduction to *Memories of a Catholic Girlhood,* she attributes "a wild streak" to the McCarthy side of her family. This judgment was based on her mistaken notion that her paternal forebears had been "wreckers," a term applied to nineteenth-century land pirates who hung lanterns along the rocky cliffs of the Nova Scotia coast to lure ships to their destruction for plunder. Although there was no obvious "wildness" in the Sheridan and McCarthy sides of her father's family, there was a decided trait of risk-taking in both. Mary McCarthy's paternal great-grandfathers, adventurers both, emigrated to the New World before the 1845 potato famine forced one out of every seven persons to leave Ireland. John McCarthy, whose father had been a successful contractor and builder in Kilmacow, county Kilkenny, was only fourteen when he left Ireland in 1837. He supported himself in Saint John's, Newfoundland, as a cod fisherman and a hunter of seals and whales, treacherous occupations in the rough North Atlantic. Within ten years he had earned enough money to marry Mary Brennan, another Irish immigrant, whose family had owned a stone quarry and lime kiln in County Tipperary, and to buy his own trawler. His fishing and hunting expeditions, some lasting several months, took him far from Newfoundland. Mary dreaded these long and dangerous trips, begging him to give up the sea. Only after he was shipwrecked did he agree to quit. When his trawler sank, he and his crew drifted for several days in a small lifeboat until they were picked up by a Norwegian fishing craft on its homeward voyage. Dropped off at a port in northern Scotland, they made their way to England, where they boarded a ship bound for Newfoundland. By the time they reached Saint John's, they had been gone a year.

Mary, already the mother of four children—one of them James Henry, Mary McCarthy's grandfather—persuaded John to move to the rich farming area of northern Illinois, where they had friends. They set sail for Boston and from there took the train to Illinois, finally settling in Sycamore, where they remained for the rest of their lives. John, restless and bored away from the sea, hired local Swedes to farm while he entertained himself with an occasional trip to Tennessee to see the famed walking horses and with regular visits to the Sycamore tavern. His forty-year marriage to Mary Brennan produced ten children, who remembered John as a heavy drinker and stern disciplinarian and Mary as a quiet and gentle mother who imparted to her offspring serenity and an ardent Catholicism.

Great-grandfather William Sheridan had emigrated from Ireland to Montreal, where he operated a general store. For half a dozen years after the potato blight struck Ireland, he exhibited something of the "wild streak" as a member of an underground network that helped Irish soldiers desert from the British colonial army and make their way to America. (Many Irishmen enlisted in the British army hoping to be sent to Canada and thus get a free passage across the Atlantic.) Late one night William got word that the authorities had discovered he was part of the illegal network and that he would be arrested the next day. He and his wife, Catherine McDonald, escaped, making their way to Chicago, where he went to work for a hotel. All five of the Sheridan children were born in Chicago: Alice Elizabeth (Mary McCarthy's grandmother), Catherine, William Francis, Mary, and Margaret. Half a century later Mary and Margaret would become surrogate parents for Roy and Tess McCarthy's four orphaned children.

Alice Elizabeth Sheridan, known as Lizzie to her family, married John and Mary McCarthy's second child, James Henry McCarthy, in 1875. J. H. had left the Sycamore farm after high school to work on the Chicago Canal. When he met Lizzie, he was a streetcar conductor, but after marriage he moved back to Sycamore and opened a grocery store. In 1879 he and Lizzie and one-year-old Esther moved to Sterling, a few miles west of Sycamore, and once again opened a grocery store. In 1880 Roy Winfield McCarthy, Mary's father, was born in the family living quarters above the store.

Meanwhile, J. H.'s brothers, Thomas and John, who had left Sycamore to settle in the Dakota Territory, were prospering as owners of a general store and as salesmen of farm machinery. J. H., impressed by stories of his brothers' successes, sold his grocery store in Sterling and opened a hardware store next door to their general store, in Altoona. He built a house for his family behind the store. Here, in 1885, James Harry was born, the same Harry who would go to Seattle to help Roy and Tess transport their four youngsters across the Great Plains to Minneapolis during the Spanish flu epidemic of 1918.

Besides operating their retail businesses, the McCarthy brothers filed land claims for homesteads outside of Altoona across the James River. The federal government required that homesteaders build homes, occupy them for a minimum time, and till the land. Since the men were busy in town, it fell to the women and children to fulfill occupancy prerequisites. Their houses, not much more than shacks, provided inadequate protection against the violence of nature on the Dakota plains. Winters were severe, with heavy snows and subzero weather; and summers were hot, with the temperature staying over one hundred degrees for days at a time. Worse, dust storms and tornadoes were common. Yet this harsh land, with its rich soil capable of yielding all varieties of grain, provided the very opportunity the three McCarthy brothers were seeking. They bought grain from farmers, then loaded it into railroad boxcars and shipped it to terminal markets to be sold. In 1887 John moved to what is now Oakes, North Dakota, to supervise the construction of the McCarthys' first modern grain elevator.

South Dakota, that part of the Dakota Territory where Altoona was located, became the fortieth state in 1889. Although by this time the McCarthys were among the new state's most prominent citizens, they decided to leave. Realizing that the grain side of their business was the most dynamic, they left Altoona for Minneapolis, which was already the cash grain market and milling center of the world. There was more storage of grain there than anywhere else. They planned to buy grain from Dakota farmers, ship it to Minneapolis, and sell it to millers. Accordingly, in 1890 J. H. and Thomas started a grain commission business by setting themselves up as terminal representatives for country grain buyers. A year later their brother John left Oakes, North Dakota, for Duluth, Minnesota, to open a branch office of the firm, by now called McCarthy Brothers. In a few years they built a four-million-bushel elevator in Duluth. Capitol Elevator, as they called this side of the business, eventually became the big money-maker for the family, its profits used to help educate and buy houses for scores of the brothers' children and grandchildren, Mary McCarthy among them.

James Henry McCarthy settled in Minneapolis on the west bank of the Mississippi. The house he purchased had an inside bathroom, the family's first. Esther, twelve, and Roy, ten, were enrolled at the local public school as second graders, not having been given full credit for their Dakota education. Harry, five, was too young for the classroom. The last McCarthy child, Louis, was born in 1895, the twentieth year of J. H. and Lizzie's marriage. When he turned three, the family moved for the final time. They built a more spacious home at 2214 Blaisdell Avenue, the house in which Roy and Tess would die twenty years later. It was an unpretentious three-story white clapboard dwelling with a wide porch across its front and adequate space for four children, a cook, and a coachman. The residence, set back from the street and hedged by empty lots on three sides, was approached from the street side by a carriage driveway that led past the house to a two-story barn where the McCarthys kept their horses and carriages, soon to be replaced by two motorcars, a Pierce-Arrow and a canvas-topped Locomobile.

Lizzie and J. H. McCarthy had come a long way from the ramshackle quarters of their Dakota homesteading days to their present residence. Old family photographs show a large living room adorned with Italian country scenes in heavy gilt frames, a library furnished in leather and mahogany, a dining room equipped with an amplitude of newly purchased Irish linens and sterling flatware, a music room with the latest in player pianos, a sewing room equipped with modern machine and mannequin, a sun porch filled with wicker furniture, and, most wonderful of all, a bathroom with a porcelain bathtub—a genuine luxury compared to the tin one in their first Minneapolis house.

Yet life for the McCarthys remained essentially the same in each succeeding house. Neither J. H. nor Lizzie was sociable; J. H., basically sweet-natured, was often distant and always reserved; Lizzie, bossy and busty, with a bulldog jaw and singsong voice, lacked warmth. Neither felt comfortable with people, and so almost never entertained anyone other than family or an occasional priest. When they did receive visitors, they relied on a few well-worn topics of conversation: appreciation for the pope, disparagement of Protestants, and anecdotes about local tradespeople were Lizzie's favorites; the grain business was her husband's sphere. According to daughter-in-law Eleanor McCarthy, "Lizzie talked all the time but didn't have much to say. J. H. didn't have much to talk about either. All he knew was the grain business." It rarely occurred to Lizzie to offer refreshments to her infrequent guests. Grandchildren remember that when their grandfather wanted a drink, he excused himself, retired to the library, opened a small mahogany cabinet, poured a shot glass of whiskey that he downed in a swig, then returned to the company. When the McCarthys' invitations included dinner, as they did in later years every Sunday for their married children, the food was excellent and admirably prepared and served by the cook, whom Lizzie referred to as "the girl." Many years later Eleanor McCarthy, who dreaded these obligatory occasions, remembered spending hours after dinner sitting on her in-laws' screened porch in summer and fern-filled sun porch in winter. She summed them up as "a dull couple."

Their social isolation was partly self-imposed and partly a result of the relationship between the Catholic and Protestant populations of the time, a relationship marked by hostility and intolerance on both sides. By the time the McCarthys had moved to Minneapolis, the potato famine had created an influx of the poor and ignorant from Ireland, who soon outnumbered the more educated American Catholics of English and French extraction.

Conflict between Protestants and America's newest Catholics developed almost immediately. All public school children were made to read the King James version of the Bible (the Irish-Americans who refused were whipped), recite Protestant prayers, and sing Protestant hymns. Moreover, the teachers, almost invariably Protestant, tried to rescue the Irish children from what they considered to be the ignorance of Catholicism. One of Roy McCarthy's first cousins, Blanche Michaels, remembered the day he quarreled with a history teacher who praised Henry VIII's renunciation of the pope. "Roy was defending the Faith," she said with pride during a 1981 interview. Even the textbooks propagated an anti-Catholicism with passages like:

Abbeys and monasteries became seats of voluptuousness.

If any person denied the pope's authority he was burned alive.

To this day [the Irish] consider Saint Patrick as in Heaven, watching over the interest of Ireland. They pray to him, and do to him honor, set apart one day in a year for going to church, drinking whiskey, and breaking each other's heads with clubs.

Catholics suffered prolonged prejudice and discrimination, and in many cases responded with militancy and belligerence. Lizzie McCarthy, far more than her husband—who associated with Protestants at the grain exchange and at the posh Minneapolis Club, to which he belonged as a leading businessman—was such a militant. Confining herself to mass-produced Catholic literature like *Our Sunday Visitor, Ave Maria,* and *Sacred Heart Messenger,* she sustained a stern and almost fanatical Catholicism her whole life. Her granddaughter made the point in *Memories of a Catholic Girlhood* that her own Catholic heritage consisted of two distinct strains. One was "a religion of beauty and goodness," represented by her mother and the nuns she encountered in school, and the other "a sour baleful doctrine in which old hates and rancors had been stewing for generations, with ignorance proudly stirring the pot," represented by Lizzie McCarthy. Lizzie's "bloodcurdling Catholicism" did, however, give rise to considerable storytelling skill. "It gave me a thrill to hear her go on about 'the Protestants' and the outrages of the Ku Klux Klan; . . . in her way," recalled Mary, she was "a spellbinder."

Lizzie McCarthy was not so much combative as she was inflexible, a trait that showed up in her granddaughter too. She was always good to her children, but it was her husband who seemed to enjoy them more. In fact, J. H. adored them. He loved nothing more than to take them for rides in the country and, when they got older, on trips throughout the Midwest. Occasionally he took them to visit his brother John McCarthy in Duluth, and every summer to various resorts in northern Minnesota. In 1893 he and Esther and Roy traveled to Chicago for the Columbian Exposition, and in 1901 all four children went to Buffalo for the Pan-American Exposition. (Once, after the other children were married, he took Louis out of school for an entire year for a trip around the world.) He attended all the children's school events; having been athletic as a younger man, he was especially interested in Roy's considerable football prowess. Roy became both center and captain of his high school team. When he entered the University of Minnesota in 1902, however, he discovered that he would no longer be able to play football. A medical examination revealed that his heart was severely damaged; when campus doctors discovered that he had had rheumatic fever eight years earlier, they blamed that for his trouble. He dropped out of school, and before long had established a reputation as a problem drinker.

Mary McCarthy was in her late thirties when she first heard about her father's drinking. Her uncle Harry, annoyed by her portrait of Lizzie McCarthy (his mother) that had appeared in *The New Yorker* in 1948, told her that her father "was a periodical drunkard." Although she recorded his charge in *Memories of a Catholic Girlhood,* she thought it improbable. "I refuse to believe it. Uncle Harry's derelict brother, Roy, is not the same person as my father. I simply do not recognize him."

Harry McCarthy had, however, told the truth. Roy's serious drinking started when he joined the family firm, working first in Minneapolis and then in Kasota, Minnesota, until 1908. Even though he was the president's son, he was well liked by other employees and often joined them for a drink after work. Innocent tippling soon gave way to serious drinking. Before long the whole family—cousins, aunts, uncles, as well as parents and siblings—were aware of his on-again, off-again bouts with the bottle. Most of his relatives, at one time or other, were called to fetch him from some hangout in town. Years later when his sons Kevin and Preston were grown, an old manager of a Minneapolis bar famous for its bock beer spotted the boys at a table. "My God, I'll bet you're McCarthys," he said. "I threw your father out of here many a time."

Proprietors all over Minneapolis looked after Roy because they liked him. Charming, convivial, gentle, he was a favorite of his family too, and his long-suffering father consistently covered the overdrafts Roy drew on his account to pay for his revels. Roy McCarthy was an all-or-nothing drinker; he could abstain for long periods of time, but once he started drinking, he could not stop before blacking out. His Minneapolis friends were heavy drinkers, and all the social gatherings he attended were drinking occasions. To separate himself from these friends, he and his mother established residence at the Hotel Menger in San Antonio, Texas, for the winter of 1907. Roy was twenty-seven years old. Unluckily, the Menger was a favorite rendezvous for officers from nearby Fort Sam Houston. It took no time for Roy to discover new drinking companions.

Roy did stop drinking for a while, after he and his mother returned to Minneapolis. A cousin remembered talking to him at his sister's wedding in June. "Guess we're the only two here not drinking," he told sixteen-year-old Blanche McCarthy. She recalled that conversation and Roy's exact appearance more than seventy years later: "He was a handsome man with a mass of prematurely grey hair that fell into a natural pompadour; he had thick dark lashes, bright green eyes, wide brow, long thin nose. Oh, I loved him! Everybody did. He was a big jolly, funny Irishman. No one could resist him."

The drinking, however, resumed shortly after his sister's wedding and even worsened, at least to the extent that Roy exported his carousing to Milwaukee, Chicago, Omaha, and Kansas City, making it more difficult for his family to keep track of him. His father committed him twice, once to a hospital in Chicago (where he fell in love with his nurse) and once to a sanatorium in Dwight, Illinois (run by a doctor who claimed to be able to cure alcoholism with bichloride of gold). Neither stay did any good.

Hoping that a fresh start elsewhere might induce Roy to stay sober, J. H. McCarthy arranged for his son to enter the timber brokerage business in Portland, Oregon. Roy left Minneapolis for his new job in March 1909. His father continued to send him regular checks. As Roy made friends easily, it was not long before he had a new coterie of drinking comrades. He must have wanted to stop drinking, though, because early in 1910 he checked himself into Mercy Hospital. After discharge, he continued to see his nurse, Sister Rita, who his family hoped could effect a cure.

During a period of sobriety in the summer, Roy joined Portland friends at the Breakers, an old family hotel on the Oregon coast near the Washington border. It was there that he met Therese Preston of Seattle.

It is not known when the first of Mary McCarthy's maternal relations arrived in America. Her great-grandfather Simon Manly Preston, son of Warner Preston and Esther Brown, was born in Strafford, Vermont, in 1821. Because he lived almost a century, he knew his great-granddaughter Mary. Roy and Tess frequently took toddlers Mary and Kevin to visit him, and once J. H. and Lizzie McCarthy, in Seattle to see their grandchildren, gave a birthday dinner for Preston at a downtown hotel.

Simon Preston was almost seventy when he moved to Seattle. He had grown up in Vermont, graduating from Norwich University in 1845 with bachelor's and master's degrees in engineering. (Norwich University had been founded in 1819 by Alden Partridge, former superintendent of West Point, to train students for army service in the event of national need, but not, like West Point, to produce professional soldiers.) After four years of residence in two military academies in Raleigh, North Carolina, where he taught mathematics and military tactics to men who later became distinguished officers of the Confederate Army, some actually fighting against Union regiments he commanded, he returned to Norwich to be acting superintendent for a year.

When the Civil War did erupt, Simon Preston was living with his wife, Martha Sargent (whose surname Mary McCarthy used later for the protagonist of her first novel, *The Company She Keeps*), in Illinois. Simon Manly Preston answered the Union call at once. He became drill master for the Fifteenth, Sixteenth, and Fifty-second Regiments, Illinois Volunteers, with the rank of first lieutenant. For the next three years he served

on the staffs of Generals Halleck, Hurlbut, and Wright, but when the tide of the war turned—in July of 1863 Vicksburg surrendered and the whole of the Mississippi Valley passed into Union control—Colonel Preston was sent to Natchez, Mississippi, to command a Negro regiment. He did a good job; when he was mustered out of the Volunteer Army at the end of the war, he held the rank of brigadier general, having been given a field promotion on December 30, 1865, "for long and faithful service."

Simon Preston liked life in Natchez and was happy to accept President Grant's appointment as Collector of Internal Revenue for the First District of Mississippi. He was paid $2,500 a year to tax exported cotton. But every year on the job (1869–1873), tax collections dropped precipitously; from $500,000 in 1868, they went to less than $17,000 in 1872. These figures, of course, reflected the downward spiral of cotton prices that began in the late 1860s, but they also accounted for Preston's disappointment with life in postwar Natchez. He wrote to a Norwich friend, "While Collector of Internal Revenue in the south I met with heavy losses by defalcations of deputies which impoverished me. My nose has been on the grindstone ever since. I was not able to carry out my purpose in educating my children." This misfortune revealed Preston's true colors: he accepted responsibility for the funds misappropriated by his own deputies. After he had repaid every cent of the ill-gotten funds, he resigned as Collector of Internal Revenue. His scrupulous honesty was a trait that showed up in his son, Harold, Mary McCarthy's grandfather, and eventually in Mary herself. (C. T. Conover, a Seattle lawyer who knew Harold Preston all his adult life, never got over the fact that his friend turned down fees because he thought they were too high. One such case involved the estate of a client for whom the Seattle Trust Company was trustee. When final settlement came due, Preston, who was out of town, was represented by a clerk, and the trust company by one of its officers. The court granted the usual statutory fees to the trustee and the attorney, which came to $4,000 for each of them. Preston insisted that they were reasonably entitled to $500 each. At his suggestion, he and the officer surrendered $7,000 legally awarded them.)

For the next seventeen years, fourteen of them in Iowa, Simon Preston supervised the construction of various railroads. In 1890 he moved to Seattle because his four children lived there. Apparently needing to keep his "nose on the grindstone," he managed the Seattle National Bank Building until he was nearly eighty. He lived to be ninety-eight.

*   *   *

Harold Preston was the first of Simon's children to head for the Northwest. After finishing college at Grinnell, he clerked for a law firm in Newton Center, Iowa. At twenty-five, he left Iowa for Seattle, where he worked two years for a lawyer before setting up his own practice. A few years later one of his brothers and a brother-in-law joined his firm.

Not long after Harold moved to Seattle, he met Augusta Morgenstern, Mary McCarthy's grandmother. Gussie, as she was known to her family, had been born in San Francisco, the daughter of Therese and Abraham Morgenstern, who had emigrated to California from Germany in 1849. Abraham was the son of a rabbi. Therese and Abraham died young, leaving three teenage children, Augusta, Rose, and Elkan. The oldest child, Eva, was married to a well-to-do Seattle fur importer named Aronson. She brought her orphaned sisters to live with her; Elkan stayed in San Francisco to finish high school and later moved to Seattle himself. Harold Preston and Augusta Morgenstern were married in 1888, and their first child, Therese, was born at the end of the year.

After the Prestons' boys, Frank and Harold, were born, the family started spending part of every summer in Oregon at the Breakers. Tess, as Therese was called, was twenty-one the summer she met Roy McCarthy there. Roy was twenty-nine. Zella Steele, Tess's closest friend, described their courtship in a letter to Mary McCarthy: "Roy was quite a bit older than the college boys your mother had been dating, but she liked that, and the Prestons liked Roy. He was a charming man. Before he met Tess, he was quite a gay blade, but he never looked at another girl after he found Tess." Tess was a dark-haired beauty with a husky speaking voice and a lovely contralto singing voice. According to Zella Steele, she was "charming, attractive, kind, thoughtful, witty. . . . She was one of the most popular girls who ever attended the University of Washington. . . . She had more clothes, more trips, more fun than any of us and no one minded. Truly she was a darling." Roy and Tess were engaged by Christmas and married in April 1911 in the Preston house, a large frame edifice on a sloping lot overlooking Lake Washington.

They moved to Minneapolis, as Roy was expected to work for McCarthy Brothers again. They rented an apartment in the Maryland Hotel. J. H. McCarthy believed that his son had finally stopped drinking, but he was bitterly disappointed. Enticed by old friends, Roy was almost continuously inebriated. Utterly defeated by his son's condition, which he now called incurable, J. H. urged Tess to leave Roy and return to Seattle. Instead, she persuaded Roy to move to Seattle. By mid-November they were living in the Frontenac Apartments, where they stayed until their first child, Mary Therese, was born, on June 21, 1912.

J. H. McCarthy continued to support his wayward son; Roy's bank books indicate that during the next seven years his father sent $41,700 for his and his family's maintenance. No matter how reckless Roy's behavior became, and it is possible his overindulgent father prolonged this irresponsibility, the fact remains that everyone who met Roy liked him. He was unfailingly thoughtful, kind, generous, an entertaining companion, and despite the recurrent drinking, he made Tess very happy. She never tried to change him. Perhaps her absolute acceptance enabled him finally to stop drinking forever, or possibly it was the birth of his first child; but whatever it was, Roy McCarthy was never seen to touch another drop after Mary's birth.

CHAPTER II

PARENTS
(1912–1918)

THREE MONTHS after Mary's birth, Roy McCarthy entered the University of Washington law school. He was thirty-two. His parents, euphoric about their son's transformation, journeyed across the country for his graduation three years later. It was a time of reunion, not only with their son and daughter-in-law but with their two grandchildren (Kevin had been born on February 15, 1914) and their son Louis, who had been living with the younger McCarthys while attending the University of Washington as an undergraduate.

No sooner had Roy passed the bar examination than he signed a lease for an office in the Hoge Building in the central business district. Although he continued to rent this space until the end of April 1918, he used it only occasionally. According to his desk calendar, a dozen appearances before local judges, a case argued before the state supreme court, and an election to the Seattle Bar Association constituted the substance of his legal activity. Deteriorating health was the reason. Digitalis, plus monthly checks from his father, sustained him, as well as the pure pleasure he took in his children. By 1917 he was the father of four, all under five years of age. Preston had been born on September 5, 1915, and Sheridan twenty months later, on April 26, 1917.

Because Roy was confined to bed a good deal of the time, he entertained his children all day, reading to and playing with them. His calendar pad, on which he made daily entries from October 1914 until his death four years later, reveals the depth of his concern and love. He entered their weight, height, temperature (on one occasion Mary's was chronicled every hour), dates of haircuts, Mary's first manicure, birthday parties with guest lists (on December 21, 1917, he noted, Mary turned five and a half), rides in the Buick (Tess learned to drive in 1916; Roy in 1917), and the loss of every baby tooth in the family ("Pulled Mary's upper front tooth, at her request, this evening. This is the fifth of her first teeth to go"). He recorded the date Mary's sweet peas bloomed, the night she switched from pajamas to a nightgown, and the morning she awakened crying because she had been dreaming of giants.

No circumstance of their daily life was too trivial to be commemorated: that " 'Pomps' [a nickname for Preston] was weaned from the bottle a year ago this evening," that Sheridan stood for the first time by holding on to the footrail of his father's bed, that the older children wanted to peer into Sheridan's crib all day, that "Mary woke up at 4:30 A.M. to watch the fairies bring May baskets and then stayed awake." He relished the joy the children took in each other and reported every instance—"Kevin and Mary kissing Preston's little toes this evening while he just squealed with laughter"; "The babes all tired out from play [are] peacefully sleeping, although I heard Kevin still whistling in bed about 15 minutes ago. The rascal tries to wake up Pomps, so they can have a romp and a visit." Roy never made entries of the treats with which he delighted his offspring—plates full of plump peaches arranged around a mound of fine sugar shaped to look like Mount Rainier; baskets filled with dogwood, Japanese maple, hyacinths, and lilacs that he hung on each child's bedroom door for May 1; an ermine muff and neckpiece for Mary when she was two—but they have remembered them all their lives.

Tess, too, cherished her children. She and Roy were enthusiastic parents who thrived on excursions designed to please their four: downtown on the streetcar for lunch at Frederick and Nelson; uptown to visit Great-grandpa Preston, still vigorous in his nineties; out of town for picnics at Lakes Sammamish and Overlake and for day trips to nearby Tacoma. And there were yearly jaunts to the circus and the Fourth of July fireworks display. Tess was not above issuing reprimands, but Roy always responded with a gentle "Now Tess," and called whoever had been disciplined to his bed to be read to. The only "discipline" these sweet-natured parents consistently exercised was their gentle insistence on nightly recitation of prayers.

Roy's daily calendar documented their devout Catholicism. Important liturgical feasts (the Purification, Palm Sunday, Easter, Ascension Thursday, Pentecost, Trinity Sunday, Corpus Christi, the Assumption), days they received communion, and places where the children were baptized (Mary at the cathedral, the boys at a Jesuit church) were marked down. Even their magazine subscriptions—*America, Catholic Mind,* and *Missionary Monthly*—and club memberships—the Newman Club, the Knights of Columbus, and the Holy Name Society for Roy, and the Child of Mary sodality for Tess—illustrate the central role Catholicism played in their lives. Tess, who was proud to be a convert, often took Mary to early Mass at the nearby Sacred Heart Convent, while her husband, an usher for the 11:30 A.M. Mass in their parish, always attended Sunday services at Saint Joseph's.

Roy and Tess stayed close to both sides of the family. Most holidays were spent with the Prestons, who lived nearby, but the senior McCarthys came to Seattle often. Louis McCarthy, who had been part of the household for two years, corresponded frequently from MIT, where he had transferred from the University of Washington, and later from France, where he had gone as a volunteer in the Norton-Harjes Ambulance Corps. After the United States Army took over the administration of the civilian drivers, Louis returned home to take a commission in the Naval Aviation Service. Frank Preston, the older of Tess's two younger brothers, who was the same age as Louis, entered the Army Officers Reserve School early in 1918. Roy avidly followed their service careers as well as those of five McCarthy cousins, and so apparently did the children. Roy wrote Louis that "the young rascals go around here with sticks and clubs beating the Kaiser."

By the spring of 1918 Roy's health had declined dangerously. His calendar entry for April 29, the first to mention his suffering, stated, "Nitro-glycerine raises havoc with me; gave me severe pains in legs, thighs, back of neck. Shooting, sinking pain in heart; at 2 A.M. couldn't get to sleep from little convulsive pains or spasms running along spine which made me want to scream. Was unable to get to sleep before 6 A.M. Had great difficulty in breathing also." The pain continued for the next week and a half. On May 12 Tess summoned his family. Harry arrived on the fifteenth, Roy's parents and sister on the sixteenth; Louis, who had to obtain sick leave, came from Pensacola, Florida, on the nineteenth. Roy's close friends Jim Cooke and his wife came from Portland. By June 3 they had all left Seattle, although Roy had not improved. Not until Mary's sixth birthday, on June 21, did Roy get out of bed, and then only for a few hours. During July and August he was too weak to receive visitors, but toward the end of the month he was well enough to sit up in bed, writing on August 24, "Most beautiful view I ever noticed on Lake Washington I had from my bedroom window at 11:15 P.M. last night. The lake looked smooth as glass with the moon shining upon it. Mount Rainier was visible all afternoon and evening." By September he was allowed to go downstairs; on September 4 he left the house, his first outing since mid-March.

Mary was to have started first grade on September 10, 1918. She was enrolled at Forest Ridge, a private girls' school run by the Religious of the Sacred Heart of Jesus. Only a dozen years old, it was part of an international network of Sacred Heart schools founded in 1800 in France. Tess, who had become acquainted with the Sacred Heart nuns from her monthly sodality meetings at the convent, decided that her daughter must have a Sacred Heart education. Mary, however, had contracted chicken pox shortly before the first day of school. By the end of September she was well enough to begin, but eight days later, when the mayor of Seattle closed all schools because of the flu epidemic, she left Sacred Heart, not to return for five years.

It is odd that Mary went at all. On September 15 her Minneapolis grandfather had wired her father that he had bought a house down the street from his own for Roy and Tess and the children. No one now knows the reason for the move East, but it appears to have been a desire on the senior McCarthys' part to keep the family they supported close at hand. In any case, the wire indicates that the decision to move had been made long before Mary set off for first grade.

The last month of Tess and Roy McCarthy's lives was chaotic. Tess came down with the flu on October 7. The next day the nursemaid, Gertrude, was fired. The girl who replaced Gertrude quit when Tess was hospitalized on October 11. Augusta Preston and her youngest child, Harold, were obliged to come and take charge of the household. During their first day at the McCarthy house, three-year-old Preston hammered out the glass in both headlights of his grandmother's "electric," unloaded the car's inside pockets onto the street, and lost the ignition key. Kevin, then Preston, and finally Sheridan, came down with chicken pox. Roy kept himself going with prodigious amounts of digitalis. The laundress, frightened by the prevailing invalidism, quit. Finally, on October 16, a nursemaid was hired, and the Prestons left, altogether worn out. Tess came home from the hospital on the twenty-second. Two days later Harry McCarthy and his wife, Zula, left Minneapolis for Seattle to help in the imminent move, arriving on the twenty-seventh. Roy and Tess and the children vacated their house and joined Harry and Zula at the New Washington Hotel. The day the entourage left Seattle for Minneapolis, Mary filled her mother's perfume bottles with ink and Kevin started a fire.

Roy's last calendar entry, a reminder to pick up shirts and gloves, was written on October 28. The calendar came with Roy's and Tess's other effects on the train to Minneapolis. The final entry on the pad, in Lizzie McCarthy's handwriting, acknowledged abruptly:

November 6 Roy's death 2:30 P.M.
          7 Therese died 11 P.M.
          9 Mr. and Mrs. Preston arrived; Frank arrived.
       11 Funeral Mass for two at St. Stephen's Church.

The caskets were stored in a vault until the spring of 1919, when the ground at Saint Mary's Cemetery in south Minneapolis had thawed sufficiently for burial.

CHAPTER III

ORPHANS
(1918–1923)

SHORTLY after the funeral, Roy's brother Louis returned to the naval air base at Pensacola, where he was stationed, and Tess's family to Seattle. Zella Steele, Tess McCarthy's good friend, wrote Mary McCarthy in the 1950s that the Prestons wanted to take all four children with them. Frank Preston, Tess's brother, disputed this in a later interview. His parents felt they were too old, he said, to be able to take care of four children, the oldest of whom was six. The senior McCarthys and Roy's sister, Esther (his brother Harry was still convalescing from the flu), deliberated about the children's future. Mary McCarthy says she and her three brothers were kept in Minneapolis to make sure the Protestants would not "get some of us."

The most likely explanation is that a house had already been purchased, the children were in Minneapolis, and J. H. McCarthy was willing to continue supporting them; so they stayed. The house he had bought for Roy and Tess was two blocks from his own. He had arranged for their furniture, shipped on ahead from Seattle, to be moved in, and he had hired a carpenter to make a screened-in sandbox and wooden swing.

The house was ready, but there appeared to be no appropriate foster parents. Esther, pregnant with her third child, must have eliminated herself as a candidate. If Harry had adopted his brother's offspring, he would have been the father of seven children under the age of seven. Lizzie McCarthy at sixty-three and J. H. McCarthy at sixty-eight were too old. Yet the guardians they settled on—chosen, no doubt, for their availability—were not much younger. Margaret Sheridan, Lizzie McCarthy's youngest sister, after years as a store clerk, had recently married for the first time; she was in her mid-fifties. Her middle-aged bridegroom was a pickle buyer from Elkhart, Indiana, named Myers Shriver. Margaret and Myers Shriver, and later the last of the unmarried Sheridan sisters, Mary, became guardians to Roy and Tess's orphans.

Maintenance of the household was assumed by J. H. McCarthy, yet Margaret and Myers held no sinecure. In advanced middle age, they had accepted responsibility for children aged six, four, three, and one. Added to this was Lizzie McCarthy's odd behavior toward her sister and brother-in-law. No family member can recall the Shrivers' having ever been invited into the McCarthy home, nor can Mary or Kevin remember Lizzie's having ever entered the Shriver household. They were treated more like servants than relatives. When Mary Sheridan came to live with them, they in turn treated her as a maid. A painfully shy white-haired spinster with gnarled fingers, Mary remained hidden in her room most of every day, reading Catholic fiction in *Extension,* and emerged only to serve meals or dust furniture. She was, however, a godsend for her grandniece, with whom she passed many hours, teaching young Mary to sew and allowing her to read magazines. She gave the child a refuge from the repressive home life that Margaret and Myers served up.

The Shrivers scrupulously discharged their duties, but they were unimaginative and ignorant, expecting perfect behavior from the children, for whom they designed odious and often meaningless rules and to whom they meted out harsh and sometimes brutal discipline. And certainly Lizzie McCarthy's disdainful attitude toward her sister and brother-in-law did nothing to encourage their familial sentiment for their charges.

The children could not associate with other children, leave their backyard except for school, go to movies, slide in Fairoaks Park (when Mary ripped her coat sliding down an icy hill there, she begged a neighbor to repair the tear, knowing Myers would thrash her for disobedience), read anything other than "edifying" religious books, or play with the elegant French dolls, baseball mitts, and games the Prestons sent for Christmas (permissible toys included a beat-up electric train that did not work and had no tracks, a pair of rusty roller skates, and a few marbles); and they could not touch candy, an especially onerous prohibition, since Myers frequently made his own, turning out sheet after sheet of cooked white confections. Kevin and Preston remember sitting for hours in their cold, dark cellar, pungent with the odor of stored potatoes, peeling the raw peanuts Myers used for his candy, but neither can recall tasting a single piece of the finished product.

The candy taboo might have originated with Margaret, whose idea of raising healthy children did not include serving pleasant-tasting food. Ice cream, cake, pie, even butter, were banished from her larder in favor of plain food like turnips, parsnips, rutabagas, and carrots. Boiling and stewing summed up Margaret's cooking style: boiled potatoes, boiled cabbage, boiled onions, stewed prunes, stewed rhubarb, stewed peaches, stewed pears, even stewed plums, were common fare along with nearly meatless stews, rice puddings, and overcooked custards. Myers, perhaps because he weighed more than two hundred pounds, got special food (fresh fruits, for example), which he shared with Sheridan, the only one of his charges he seemed to love. Mary, Kevin, and Preston, by contrast, were made to sit at the dining room table until the last morsel of their tasteless food was eaten.

Fresh air, too, was forced upon the children. Often they were locked outside on Saturdays and Sundays for several hours at a stretch, no matter how low the temperature, and they were made to take regular five-mile hikes. But no one taught them games or sports. Mary eventually learned to swim from an elderly bachelor in the neighborhood. Pillows and mouth-breathing, thought to be unwholesome during sleep, were forbidden. Every night Margaret or Myers sealed the children's mouths with tape, removing it each morning with ether. (Kevin is certain that only his mouth was taped shut each night, but Mary and Preston vividly remember similar treatment.)

Margaret supervised the smallest detail of her charges' lives, checking their homework, their letters to the Prestons, which she dictated, their nightly prayers, their morning bowel movements. But it was Myers who dominated the household. A boorish and cruel man, he often beat the children, especially Mary and Kevin, sometimes for real offenses, occasionally for preventive medicine, such as the time Mary won a city- and statewide contest at age ten for her essay "The Irish in American History." Not only did he appropriate her twenty-five-dollar prize, but he whipped her with a razor strop lest she get "stuck-up." Perhaps Myers could never forget the impertinent taunt Mary had once flung at him: "My father was a gentleman, and you are not." A composite of Margaret and Myers was the model for Aunt Clara in "Ghostly Father, I Confess," the last section of Mary McCarthy's first novel, *The Company She Keeps.*

> Up to the time her mother had died she had been such an elegant little girl. She remembered her ermine neckpiece and the ermine muff that went with it, her two baby rings with diamonds in them, the necklace of seed pearls. . . . Then, after the flu was over, and her mamma did not come home from the hospital, Aunt Clara had moved in, the rings were put in the vault (to keep for you until you're older), the ermine set wore out, the velocipede broke, the white sand darkened in the sandpile, and there were prunes and pudding on the table.

The description of her guardian's reaction to the winning essay is spoken by the protagonist: "My aunt, having just beaten me for my error in winning the prize ('you are too stuck-up already'), is at home in her bedroom having hysterics."

Part of Myers's unpleasantness stemmed from not having enough to do. He worked a short time for McCarthy Brothers, soliciting grain shipments in western South Dakota, North Dakota, and eastern Montana, but was let go because it cost too much to feed him on the road. A nonchurchgoing Protestant, he took no part in the religious observances of the household—daily prayers, attendance at Sunday Mass, preparations for First Communions, study of pious literature. Nor did he read secular matter. Neither he nor Margaret had friends, so he expended no time being sociable. Besides candy-making, his only activities consisted of listening to the phonograph or to a crystal radio set, of reading Uncle Remus stories aloud over and over, and of taking the children on outings.

He regularly took them for streetcar rides that cost a nickel; to free concerts at Donaldson's, a local department store, or to its provisions department for complimentary samples of ham and cheese; to the Minneapolis Millers' baseball games—but only after the seventh inning, when everyone was let in for nothing; to the zoo to watch other children ride the ponies; to the cemetery to visit their parents' graves (their deaths had finally been acknowledged); and to every parade in town—the Fourth of July parade, the Labor Day parade, the circus parade, even a doll-carriage parade staged once a year in a nearby park. It was recreation on the dole, demeaning to a perceptive child like Mary, and she chronicled it all in "Yonder Peasant, Who Is He?" and "A Tin Butterfly," which became the first two chapters of *Memories of a Catholic Girlhood.*

What protected Mary from Myers's parsimony and hardness of heart, as she later wrote of the five years in the Shriver household, was religion. "Our ugly church and parochial school provided me with my only aesthetic outlet, in the words of the Mass and the litanies and the old Latin hymns, in the Easter lilies around the altar, rosaries, ornamented prayer books, votive lamps, holy cards stamped in gold and decorated with flower wreaths and a saint's picture. This side of Catholicism, much of it cheapened and debased by mass production, was for me, nevertheless, the equivalent of Gothic cathedrals and illuminated manuscripts and mystery plays. I threw myself into it with ardor."

Saint Stephen's, an old brown-brick church with a copper spire that could be seen from blocks away, was the parish primarily for the poorer immigrants of the neighborhood. Mary and her brothers attended the parish school, while Esther and Harry's children went to private academies like Saint Margaret's and Notre Dame. Even so, the nuns at Saint Stephen's were able to impart to Mary some sense of the majesty and mystery of the Catholic Church that she experienced in its rituals—in the

ashes on the forehead at the beginning of Lent; in the purple coverings
for church statues during Passiontide; in the Latin hymns, the lighted
candles, the ringing of bells during the most sacred times of the Mass;
in the incense at Benediction and during solemn High Mass; in the
priest's variegated vestments, a different color for each feast and for
various times of the liturgical year; in the confessionals, the holy water
fonts; in the sign of the cross.

Besides kindling an aesthetic sense, Saint Stephen's fostered Mary's
natural competitiveness, her determination to win and to be first. So
much at the parochial school was a contest: spelling bees, arithmetic
competitions, debates on every subject, and sports rivalries on the play-
ground. Each child at Saint Stephen's was graded not only in the usual
subjects—reading, spelling, arithmetic, grammar, geography, and history—but also in deportment, Christian doctrine, music, Bible, penman-
ship, drawing, and hygiene.

Mary's grandparents, Lizzie and J. H. McCarthy, among the more
well-to-do parishioners of Saint Stephen's, often heard from the pastor
how well their granddaughter performed at school. Occasionally their
chauffeur drove the Pierce-Arrow to the church to pick up Mary and her
brothers for Sunday dinner, leaving the Shrivers and Mary Sheridan
behind. At their grandparents' house the four orphans mingled with
Aunt Esther and Uncle Harry's children. Mary always noted how well
dressed they were compared with herself and her brothers, just as she
reflected on the difference between the food the orphans were made to
eat at home and the beef tenderloin, green vegetables, and fresh fruits
her grandmother served. Mary often spoke of her sense of injustice to
her cousins, who grew weary of her complaints, but at least one, Judy
McCarthy, argued Mary's case before her mother. Zula always responded by sighing that she knew it was true, that she felt sorry for Roy's
children, but that she had her own problems too. Few of the McCarthys,
though, ever investigated the situation firsthand. Mary never saw her
cousins on her home ground, but always as a guest in their homes for
Halloween, birthday parties, and Christmas dinners, at their summer
places at Gull Lake or Lake Minnetonka, or at family reunions in Frontenac or in Alexandria, northern Minnesota resorts. Her cousins liked
her for the gripping ghost stories she loved to tell, but they did consider
her peculiar for her habitual reading. "Mary's always got her nose in a
book," they frequently chanted.

The only agreeable memory Mary McCarthy has of "family" during
her time in Minneapolis is of pleasant summer afternoons visiting her
grandmother, who did needlework and let Mary read the *Ave Maria*

magazine. When Mary got bored, she went out to the garage to ride the turntable, a metal plate which rotated on a pivot so that the family cars never had to be put in reverse. Once she went with her grandmother to Breezy Point, a resort in northern Minnesota owned by Billy Fawcett, publisher of the popular *Captain Billy's Whiz Bang.* On the way home in the Locomobile, they visited her great-uncle John McCarthy in Duluth. Despite dreadful roads, especially trying for Mrs. McCarthy, who, with her hair piled high under a straw hat, repeatedly grazed the canvas top of the car as they bumped along, and despite getting lost and having to stop and urinate by the side of the road, they had a happy time together, Mary McCarthy remembers today. Yet in the recently published memoir *How I Grew,* she obviously regards her grandmother's omissions (not investigating the conditions of her everyday life, not inviting Mary to live with her) as seriously as Margaret and Myers's commissions (beatings with the hairbrush and razor strop, forcing the children to remain outdoors in brutally cold weather). "Uncle Myers and Aunt Margaret, my grandmother, too, in her own style, amuse me by their capacity for being awful. . . . To the extent that my memory has been able to do justice to that talent in them, they have been immortalized."

Nevertheless, at the time, she enjoyed being with her grandmother. Perhaps such respites from the Shriver household heightened the sense of entrapment she felt there, because when she got older, she ran away twice. She spent a night in the confessional at Saint Stephen's and a day behind the statue of Laocoön at the Art Institute. Kevin also fled the dismal foster home, looking for an orphanage he had spotted once from a streetcar. Their desperation forced their grandparents to acknowledge Myers's shortcomings. The older McCarthys responded by providing temporary shelter (each runaway was allowed to sleep in Lizzie McCarthy's sewing room for a few nights) and by forbidding reprisals up the street. The breakup of the Shriver-Sheridan household was imminent. During the summer of 1923 Lizzie McCarthy, with Mary, looked at an Ursuline boarding school. They must not have liked it, for Mary reentered Saint Stephen's in September, remaining there less than a month.

Precisely what happened then no living member of the McCarthy or Preston families can determine. Evidence points to a McCarthy resolve to change their grandchildren's living situation, but a crisis seems to have diverted their attention. Harry had "borrowed" $200,000, it was discovered, to cover losses he had incurred in commodity speculation. Two clerks had altered McCarthy Brothers books for him until he could repay the "loan"; Harry and the clerks were fired. In addition, his father repossessed Harry's house, which he had previously purchased, gave it to Esther, banished Harry to Florida, and replaced every cent of the missing money.

At this inauspicious time, Harold Preston appeared in Minneapolis to see his grandchildren. (Mary's uncle Louis McCarthy had probably summoned him.) Mary and Kevin, left alone with this grandfather, described the unhappy atmosphere of their home. Mary was ensconced at her grandmother's house, where she remembers hearing from upstairs an excited conference between the two sides of the family. Shortly after, the three elderly guardians moved to Elkhart, Myers's hometown, taking six-year-old Sheridan with them. Kevin and Preston were moved into their grandmother McCarthy's sewing room until places could be secured for them at Saint Benedict's, a boarding school, and Mary was whisked off to Seattle by her Protestant grandfather. "I was sitting in a compartment with him on the train," she recalled in *Memories of a Catholic Girlhood*, "watching the Missouri River go westward to its source, wearing my white-gold wrist watch and garish red hat, a highly nervous child, fanatical against the Protestants," yet reassured by the cache of Catholic literature she carried in her suitcase—pious reading matter her grandmother had given her to plant in the Preston household.

CHAPTER IV
CAESAR AND
CATILINE
(1923–1929)

I T WAS IN October of 1923 that Mary McCarthy took up residence in her maternal grandparents' house overlooking Lake Washington. For the second time in her scant eleven years, her life underwent a stunning metamorphosis. No longer crammed into a house that she later described as "a crude box in which to stow furniture, and lives, like a warehouse," she moved into a spacious and attractive home, luxuriant with such trappings as grass wallpaper and silk curtains, crystal, silver, fine china, and fresh flowers in every room, cut and arranged every day by her grandmother. The first floor had a large entrance hall and living room, a good-size parlor with a bay window, and a small library stocked with Dickens, Frank Stockton, Bulwer-Lytton, and the Elsie Dinsmore books that had belonged to her mother. The rooms upstairs were partitioned into two generous suites—one for her grandparents, the other for Harold, her seventeen-year-old uncle—and there was a bedroom, newly decorated in greens and violets, for Mary. The third floor provided sleeping quarters for the maid. The stable out back had already become a garage for her grandmother's "electric."

No longer sentenced to Margaret's unappetizing food, Mary now ate meals she enjoyed. Everyday fare for the Prestons included delicacies like Olympia oyster cocktail, deviled Dungeness crabs, salmon in a sherry sauce with oysters and baby shrimp, and eggs stuffed with chicken livers; the freshest of vegetables, grown in the backyard; fruits from the Preston's currant bushes and crab apple, apricot, and cherry trees; and homemade ice cream, mayonnaise, and salad dressings. No longer subjected to cut-rate recreation, Mary now got an allowance that she could spend as frivolously as she wished; and no longer branded by Margaret and Myers's dowdiness, she became fashion-conscious. Her Seattle grandmother dressed smartly, preferring dark dresses and suits, their skirt lengths just so; hats with veils pulled tightly across her longish face; leather shoes with "Louis" heels; gloves; and jewelry like a single strand of pearls, with matching earrings for her pierced ears, and an onyx-and-diamond lorgnette. The refined scroll of her monogram, AMP, which adorned her silver, brushes, combs, and automobile, expressed her understated style. She had five fur coats, and several fur pieces that she wore with suits in autumn and spring.

Not surprisingly, Augusta Preston's chief diversion lay in daily trips to I. Magnin or Frederick and Nelson. Every afternoon except Sunday, in every season of the year, she drove downtown to survey the latest in fashion. In the days of her electric car, the Prestons' Chesapeake retriever trailed after, content to wait outside whatever store his mistress entered. Promptly at five-thirty she called for her husband at the Rainier Club, where he had been playing bridge since four. They drove home, ate dinner at six, read or played cards until ten, and went to bed, only to repeat the same inflexible cycle the next day. Thursday nights they might have dinner at the club, and occasionally they took in a play or a movie. Every winter they went to California, staying at the best hotels. The distance between the life-styles of the Shrivers and the Prestons made an indelible impression on the eleven-year-old child. Mary McCarthy inherited her grandmother's fondness for fine living. Like Augusta Preston, she is meticulous in selecting her clothes and furnishings, and she, too, sets a good table and travels in style.

Yet despite the improvement in her everyday life, Mary felt alone in this household. As she wrote in *Memories of a Catholic Girlhood,* her strongest memory of the place was the shut doors and the silence. Even when everyone was at home, the house seemed empty, for the adults kept to themselves in the upstairs apartments. The downstairs rooms were seldom used in the daytime except by Mary, who amused herself by reading and by playing the Victrola. Visitors of any kind were rare in the Preston house. Since Augusta and Harold Preston were themselves exceedingly taciturn, any caller felt he should tiptoe and whisper. Young Harold's friends always made a beeline for his private apartment. One of them said the Preston house "should have been lit with gaslights and become the scene of a famous murder." The family was far too reserved for Mary; only Aunt Rosie Gottstein, Augusta Preston's favorite sister, seemed like Mary—excitable, talkative, opinionated, and sociable.

Augusta, by contrast, was so reserved that many people called her austere. One of young Harold's friends, who was often at the Preston home, said that he did not "recall that she ever spoke to me, but nodded very stiffly." Zella Steele, who spent several nights a week at the Preston home during Tess's college days, wrote Mary McCarthy that "Mrs. Preston was a very reserved person, and she used to frighten me at first. I thought she disapproved of me." Frank Preston, Augusta's older son, claimed his mother was shy. The only time Mary can remember her grandmother's entertaining anyone for dinner, other than Frank and his wife, Isabel, who were expected every Sunday night for a supper the cook had prepared in advance, was a dinner party for a local judge. Augusta Preston never asked her sisters and brother and their families or any of her husband's siblings for a meal, yet she got along with them all. She made exceptions for her sister, Eva Aronson, and Harold's sister, Alice Carr, only after they were widowed. As a young girl, Mary always wondered what her grandmother thought about the various family members and especially about herself. And she was always trying to find out about her grandmother's past. "All those old things, Mary," Augusta would reply, "why do you keep asking me all those old things?"

Although Augusta Preston was a kind woman, no one seemed able to penetrate her aloofness. She had a loving and attentive husband and two sons, two sisters to whom she talked on the phone every day, and a granddaughter who was eager to please her, but she was altogether unemotional and undemonstrative. She was a striking and vain woman who, her granddaughter remembers, worked hard to preserve her looks with ointments and special lotions, with mascara, eye shadow, rouge, and powders, with pencils, brushes, and tweezers, and with numerous jars of Elizabeth Arden, Dorothy Gray, Helena Rubinstein, and Harriet Hubbard Ayer. When Tess married, Zella Steele noted that Augusta Preston "looked almost as young as her daughter." Even so, two years before Tess died, Augusta had a face-lift, one that turned out disastrously. In the early days of plastic surgery, the doctor routinely pumped a patient's face full of hot wax to remove wrinkles. In Augusta's case, either the paraffin had been injected improperly or it had shifted afterward, for big lumps settled at the bottom of her cheeks. Worse, disfiguring scars ran from the cheeks to her neck. When Harry McCarthy first met her, he thought "those big lumps at the bottom of the cheeks were really startling," but by the time Mary came to live with her grandmother, the botched face-lift simply gave her cheeks a flushed, swollen look. In fact, Mary knew nothing about the face-lift, and only learned of it in adulthood, and then from outsiders, for no one in the family ever mentioned it. She realized then why her grandmother never permitted anyone to photograph her. The face-lift, too, probably accounted for Augusta Preston's absence from the family's annual summer trips to Singer's Tavern on Lake Crescent, a resort in the Olympic Mountains. Her husband took Harold, Jr., with a friend, and Mary, leaving Augusta in Seattle. Unquestionably, the shock of her altered appearance reinforced her natural tendency to solitariness.

Harold Preston was reserved too, but certainly not so withdrawn as his wife. Actually, he was one of Seattle's best-known lawyers, having been elected president of the state and city bar associations as well as a

state senator. While serving in Spokane, he distinguished himself as the
strongest advocate for a railroad commission. This advocacy cost him a
Republican seat in the U.S. Senate, for which he ran in 1903. When his
law partner, Henry McBride, ran for governor in 1904, the railroad
commission was the principal issue of the campaign. The formation of
the commission finally became law in 1908, almost entirely through
Harold Preston's efforts. It set standard shipping rates to stop the railroads' unfair practice of giving rebates to favored customers. Harold
Preston had also been responsible for the drafting of a workman's com-
pensation act, which became a model statute for other states. His reputation for uprightness and fair play was so widespread that he was asked
to run for a judgeship and for mayor, but he chose to return to his private
law practice.

It was Harold Preston's finely tuned sense of justice that captivated
his granddaughter. She wrote in *Memories of a Catholic Girlhood* that "the
injustices my brothers and I suffered in our childhood had made me
rebel against authority, but they had also prepared me to fall in love with
justice, the first time I encountered it. I loved my grandfather from the
beginning." Her admiration of him, coupled with her playing the rebel
Catiline in *Marcus Tullius,* a play put on by her high school Latin club,
and her reading of Caesar's *Commentaries,* illuminated for her the two
sides of her own nature. Her interpretation of Caesar and Catiline made
her own life "readable":

> Caesar, of course, was my grandfather: just, laconic, severe, magnani-
> mous, detached. These are the very adjectives I might use to describe
> Lawyer Preston, who was bald into the bargain. Catiline was my McCarthy
> ancestors—the wild streak in my heredity. . . . To my surprise, I chose
> Caesar and the rule of law. This does not mean the seesaw between these
> two opposed forces terminated; one might say, in fact, that it only began
> . . . when I recognized the beauty . . . of a rigorous code of conduct.

She paid the ultimate compliment to her grandfather by adopting his
conduct for her own. With uncustomary praise, longtime friend Dwight
Macdonald attested to her success: "I think one of Mary's greatest qualities . . . is her character. She really tries to do the right thing (and often
succeeds)."

Harold Preston was fair-minded in his public life, in business, and at
home, so it is puzzling that he more or less ignored his grandchildren
from the time of his daughter's death, in 1918, until he fetched Mary
in 1923, and that he did not take on more of the financial obligation for

Tess's family. Mary McCarthy says she is certain that her grandfather contributed money to the Seattle household while her parents were alive, and he paid her bills at private schools and Vassar, including expenses for clothes and travel that the McCarthy trust money did not cover. But, according to the McCarthy relatives, from the time of Tess's death in 1918 until the children left Minneapolis in 1923, the only financial assistance he offered was $300, and that was after being prodded. Yet the McCarthys, from the time of the children's births until the final disposition of proceeds from Capitol Elevator, spent close to $200,000. Moreover, Harold Preston, after rescuing Mary, continued to neglect Kevin, Preston, and Sheridan, showing no more interest in them than to send perfunctory birthday and Christmas checks. Kevin and Preston, and eventually Sheridan, lived at Saint Benedict's, spending Christmas and Easter vacations in the care of the Benedictine nuns; during summers they either visited their McCarthy cousins or went to camp. After Mary's Uncle Louis got married, he had the boys live with him.

The apparent contradiction between Harold Preston's demonstrable sense of fair play and his behavior regarding his grandsons did not occur to Mary McCarthy when she was living with him. Only later did she wonder about how differently her grandfather had treated her and her brothers, most particularly at the time she wrote the two memoirs about her life as an orphan in Minneapolis. The first, "Yonder Peasant, Who Is He?" was published in 1948 and the second, "A Tin Butterfly," in 1951. Three months after the second appeared, her uncle Harry McCarthy, who had accompanied his doomed brother and sister-in-law on their last train trip across the country, wrote his niece to complain about her depiction of the McCarthy family, especially his mother, Lizzie McCarthy. His letter and Mary's reply demonstrate firsthand his niece's unchangeable attitude toward, and strong feelings for, Harold Preston as well as her McCarthy relatives. Although her memoirs make it clear that she admires very little about the McCarthys, she was surprised by the literary merit of her uncle's letter, and she told him so: "I think you have a wonderful gift of expression. Your letter is full of literary talent that many a writer would envy." Harry McCarthy's unconventional letter-writing style is lively and in some parts witty:

> old arthritics do not die, they just ache away, as i have always been some what amused and critical of people attempting to move the calender back, i make a special effort to be my age, which is 66, . . . fortunately living in beautiful coral gables meets the requirements of contentment for such

quiet peaceful existence and i am very happy with the care of my lawn, flowers and shrubbery, intermingled with daily walks accompanied by my welch terrier, all of this was disrupted.

A few weeks past the barefoot mailman delivered a copy of the new yorker to which i do not subscribe and opening it i found what i expected, some bird brained individual had red pencilled the title ["A Tin Butter-fly"] in the index, underlined many phrases and thruout the article had made remarks in the margin which he or she figured would really tear me apart.

it has never been said about me, "he has not an enemy in the world" so why even start to puzzle who sent it, i have hesitated for some time as i dislike writing this letter very much, but i could no more avoid it than i could stop the sunrise tomorrow. . . .

one glance at the title and author, i told zula, another scream of persecution for profit by our niece, she replied "it could'nt be, mary promised me in new york the peasants was her last on that subject, furthermore she was sorry she wrote that." . . .

you definately are a throw back to the maternal side of your breeding which explains your inability to resist this urge, particularly as you apparently have a ready market, many jews have told me and it is recognized by all who stop to wonder, why all this race creed and color lament, it is because they most of all owe their present position of advancement to the constant cry of persecution. . . .

remember the nite you and i got drunk in that cold water walk up where you lived in new york. . . . we probably both talked at the same time but my recollection was that you questioned the amount of money furnished your family thruout the years, you insisted that mr preston most certainly furnished a good share.

When i returned to minneapolis i asked my brother lou to check the accounts and diary for me, he has all the records, he confirmed the figures i gave you but i decided to forget the whole matter, we liked you so why start the bitterness again, it would lead no place in fact would turn back on itself, it is the eternal cul de sac. you ripped it open again and i have to answer.

father advanced $41,700 during those years, each year would write preston and inquire if he could not spare a bob or so for his grandchildren and preston sure did open up the purse strings, he sent two checks for one hundred and fifty each from 1918 to 1923, i would inquire if any funds ever arrived from seattle, father would say, he is probably hard up, besides father was very fond of tess and roy and could afford it. . . .

this figure you were absolutely positive was wrong, maybe he did not tell you or you just wanted to forget it, from 1927 to 1938 my brother as executor mailed to mary mccarthy in care of her grandpa preston, $11,200.00 no wonder you questioned it, probably took care of vassar. to complete the picture when we sold the capitol elevator in 1947 you received $23,250.00 add those up and remember if my mother had raised her little finger in opposition to those funds, preston would have really needed all his legal talent to get you any of it. that my friend is what your mccarthy grandparents did for you and you have the nerve to try and look down your subversive schnabel at them. . . .

did you ever stop to think what would have been the picture if your mother and father had lived, you would have probably attended a convent instead of vassar, you would have missed all those tender agnostic teachings of grandpa preston and the communism of vassar, my heavens what could you write about.

in case you have any doubt in your mind about me, before i take up your maternal grandparents and uncle frank let say i am what is called a beligerent catholic, the greatest thing in my life is that i was born into the catholic faith, i am also one of the usual sort of irish lads, who just naturally has the greatest inherent respect and love for my mother and if any one tosses a slur at an irishman's mother, he dont cry persecution or police, he licks them or gets licked trying.

this should interest you but also your brothers, on nov 10, 1919 the following letter was written, to frank preston.

my dear son.
i have this day had the proper papers executed making you the beneficiary under policy of life insurance number 500797 in the mutual life insurance company of new york, for the principal sum of five thousand dollars, it being my will and desire that in case of my death that you should use the proceeds of this policy for the benefit of the children of your sister. . . .

another letter, this one was written by frank preston to lou and he calls attention to the letter you wrote him in which you said kevin was destitute in new york and he adds mrs morganstein preston just opened wide her heart and purse strings and sent twenty five dollars to mary to be advanced to kevin, then he made a bad mistake, he explained how this could all be handled very nicely out of the mccarthy trust fund. which trust fund had been handled very capably by my brother lou and to my knowledge there has not been a grunt of appreciation for the handling of it.

lou's last paragraph in reply to frank preston is what pleases me no end, quote, however in so far as the trust fund is unable to give further aid to kevin at this time, i am reminded of a certain life insurance policy which made you the beneficiary, but at the same time a letter accompanied it, directing you what to do with the proceeds of said policy, to refresh your memory the policy number is 500797 written by the mutual life insurance of new york, possibly considering kevin's destitution, you could do something about it. signed l.a.mccarthy

looks to me as though uncle frank reached out and got his paws burned. . . .

you have gone into such detail about my father and mother, its about time we looked into harold and augusta morganstein preston, your mother told me her father was an agnostic so there is no trouble figuring where you received the hatred training for the catholic church, that is his doubtful priveledge, there will always be agnostics i presume just like there will always be guys who wear white sox or bow ties. its his cheapness that stands out to me. . . .

i feel sorry for you and like you as does zula and if you are in florida at any time you will be very welcome, but you had to be answered.

Mary replied four weeks later:

I don't remember "promising" Zula not to write any more about the family. But I probably did say, in a less categorical form, that I didn't intend to write further about it; I felt through with the subject at the time. . . .

Perhaps my grandfather Preston felt that the sums he had expended on me absolved him of responsibility; certainly, they must have amounted to a good deal more than $5000. The $11,000 you mention spread over eleven years did not by any means cover an expensive education. The tuition at the boarding school I went to was $1200, exclusive of extras, dentists, doctors, riding lessons, summer vacations, expensive dresses, and so on. At Vassar, the tuition was $1000 a year, plus the usual extras, plus the railroad fares back and forth, plus an allowance of $100 a month, plus a new wardrobe every fall, plus a furcoat, books, doctors and dentists, and all the rest, which, having brought up three daughters, you must know about. You may think that I should not have had such an expensive education, that I should have been brought up like an orphan, more in the style of my brothers, but, except for the injustice to my brothers, this is beside the point of whether my grandfather Preston did or did not contribute. He did. Why he sent so little during our years in Minneapolis is difficult to understand; he may have felt guilty afterwards when he saw my peaked condition and learned about our life there and tried to make it up to me later. I don't know. One excuse for him is that he had an extravagant wife who kept him very close to the margin. As for Frank's letter, about Kevin, it seems to me pretty bad, even if the insurance policy had already been cashed in by my grandfather, which I suspect now may have happened when my school bills began to pour in.

In any case, I feel no inclination to condemn him, since in all his dealings with me he was kind, generous, and just. He was well known for these qualities all over Seattle and is still remembered for his integrity by lawyers and business men and judges. He did not turn me against the Church; in fact, he insisted on my going to church long after I had stopped believing in it. He always had it on his conscience that I had lost my faith in his household, though this happened independently of his influence and

in fact counter to it. He thought he had a duty to your family to see that
I was raised in the church, and he only let me follow my own way when
he thought I had reached the age of individual judgement. And he always
spoke highly of your mother, for whom he had great respect; he regarded
her as "a fine woman." Any criticism I have ever heard between the
families always came from the other direction. No doubt, your own feeling for your mother has the same basis as mine for him; it is a case of direct
experience which no argument will budge.

However, as far as I am concerned, those years in Minneapolis remain
a hard fact—what do you expect me to do, be grateful for them? No one
wishes to be blamed and you feel blame attaching to yourself for them;
I don't blame you now for that—you weren't directly involved and no
doubt had only the dimmest guess as to what was happening there. What
I do blame you for is your trying to shift the blame now suddenly onto
me, as if I, by writing about it, were responsible for the whole thing, as
if I, somehow by a persecution complex, had invented Uncle Myers. Don't
deceive yourself; he was real, as Kevin and I both can well attest.

I'm sorry that all this upsets you, sorry that you have anonymous
correspondents who want to bedevil you. I'm sorry also, as I told you in
New York, that you can't rid yourself of that terrible anti-Semitism. As
I said to you that night, rather drunkenly, "God will not forgive you for
that, Uncle Harry." It is true; such sentiments are unChristian and unCath-
olic; any priest will tell you so. It's just a frenzy you lash yourself with and
unworthy of you; if there is an after-life, you will have to account for it
there. . . . In any case, Uncle Harry, in some strange way, it was a pleasure
to get your letter; perhaps just because of your vitality, which I admire.
Don't treasure this grudge up against me. I think of you and Zula with
affection, despite all this. My grandfather, by the way, was not an agnostic,
but some mild form of old-fashioned deist. And my grandmother's name
was *Morgenstern,* not Morganstein.

In spite of Harold Preston's unequal treatment of the McCarthy children and his niggardly financial support of them, Mary McCarthy still
considers him "much more admirable than all [her] Catholic relations.
He was scrupulous, with a very active conscience, but he was also remarkably tolerant and unbigoted." Her McCarthy relatives, by contrast,
seemed to her very bigoted, given to anti-Semitic epithets and fulmina-
tions against the IWW and Communism. What irritated her the most
about Harry McCarthy's letter, though, was his contention that she had
lost her faith owing to Harold Preston's influence. In fact, he had insisted
on her practicing her mother's religion, at least at first. Every Sunday the
gardener drove Mary to Immaculate Conception Church for Mass.
Once, arriving to pick her up a few minutes early, he spied her flying
in one door, then emerging one minute later from another, pretending

to have been in church all along. When her grandfather learned that she had been skipping Mass to visit nearby friends, he directed the gardener to wait outside the church for the entire service to make certain Mary stayed inside. And he sent her to the Sacred Heart Convent, where she had begun first grade five years earlier, before moving to Minneapolis.

When Mary returned to Sacred Heart as a five-day boarder, she was eleven years old and in the seventh grade. This particular Sacred Heart Convent (there are convents run by the Sacred Heart nuns all over the world) was aptly called Forest Ridge, located as it was on acres of woodland three hundred feet above the waters of Lake Union. It was nothing like the school she had been going to:

> I was fresh from a Minneapolis parochial school, where a crude "citizen-ship" had been the rule, where we pledged allegiance to the flag every morning, warbled "My Country, 'Tis of Thee," said "grievious" instead of "grievous," competed in paper drives and citywide spelling contests, drew hatchets for Washington's Birthday and log cabins for Lincoln's, gave to foreign missions for our brown and yellow brothers, feared the Ku Klux Klan, sold chances and subscriptions to periodicals, were taken on tours of flour mills and water works; I looked upon my religion as a branch of civics and conformity, and the select Sacred Heart atmosphere took my breath away. The very austerities of our life had a mysterious aristocratic punctilio. . . . I felt as though I stood on the outskirts and observed a ritual of a cult, a cult of fashion and elegance in the sphere of religion.

Here the students, all girls, curtsied and spoke French; wore uniforms; practiced perfect posture by sitting erect, spines independent of the backs of chairs, knees together, and feet flat on the floor; assisted at Mass every morning and benediction every evening; made retreats every year during which no one could talk for three days; sang hymns familiar to every Sacred Heart girl all over the world, "Oui, je le crois," "Donne nous un bon jour," "Les enfants du Sacré-Coeur"; enjoyed afternoon snacks called *goûter* and played *cache-cache* (hide-and-seek in teams) on *congés,* special holidays given to the school by the Reverend Mother. Here education was not just a matter of mastering skills, although intel-lectual discipline was rigorous: the nuns of the Society of the Sacred Heart taught by a syllabus adopted in 1805, which aimed at the forma-tion of character. A Sacred Heart girl learned that things must not just be done—they must be done in a certain way.

The Sacred Heart nuns, too, were different from the nuns Mary had known at Saint Stephen's. Here the nuns kept their own surnames— Mother Coakley or Mother Bourneuf—unlike the parochial school nuns, who dropped their family names for saints' names—Sister Agatha or Sister Bridget. Here the nuns were cloistered, giving them an interesting and mysterious air, whereas the parochial school sisters rode buses in pairs to shop at the dime store or to visit the dentist. Although the boarding pupils lived side by side with the nuns, they knew little about them. They often woke up in the morning and fell asleep at night to the sounds of the Gregorian chant—the nuns singing their daily office. But they never saw the nuns eat or drink. They speculated whether they used mirrors, whether their hair was shaved off or just cut short to fit under the fluted white caps that enclosed their faces. These nuns moved with a graceful dignity, their slightest gesture made significant by their prevailing stillness. They could bring a classroom to silence by standing motionless. They were not severe, however, nor were they all alike. It was fitting that these nuns were called Mother, for firm as they were, Mary remembers them as kind. In spite of their silence and rules, they made the convent a happy place. The life they provided had allure and stateliness. That Mary McCarthy devoted three of eight chapters in *Memories of a Catholic Girlhood* to that life, though she spent less than two years with these nuns, is a measure of its influence on her.

At the time, however, Mary McCarthy was not especially happy at the convent. Like any new girl in school, she felt like an outsider. But she had more obstacles to overcome than did most new girls. As she writes in *How I Grew* (1987), she had few terms of reference in common with her classmates. "Unlike them, at the age of eleven, I had never seen a movie (not counting *The Seal of the Confessional*); the children's books I *had* read dated back to my parents' childhoods. . . . I arrived among my Sacred Heart contemporaries like a dropped stitch in time and in some ways I never caught up—I was twice married and driving a car before I could ride a bicycle."

Wanting to be not only accepted but more than accepted, seen as a star, she devoted her considerable energies to getting noticed. When shaving off half her eyebrows did not attract attention, she decided to lose her faith, a move guaranteed to attract attention in a convent. The discussions that followed upon her announcement, not only with the Mistress General of the convent but also with two Jesuits, produced the realization "that there was no belief inside me." She told her grandfather, who asked only that she continue going to Mass on Sundays until she was older.

Although her separation from the Church occurred early, the legacy of her childhood Catholicism lasted a lifetime. From it she gained an intense identification with the past, and a sense of the mystery and wonder of life. More than forty years later she said, "I don't believe in God—that's just a fact, it's not an act of will. . . . But ethics came to me in the frame of Christian teaching, and even though I don't believe in an afterlife, I'm still concerned with the salvation of my soul."

Her struggle to get herself recognized "at whatever price" was unnecessary. According to Sacred Heart contemporaries, Mary was already conspicuous for her classroom performance, for the reading she had done, uncommon in one so young, and for her grown-up air. At the opening of a routine instruction during the annual retreat, the Jesuit retreat master asked the students, who filled every pew in the chapel, which biblical figure had said, "From the rising of the sun, even to its setting, my name is great among the nations; and everywhere they bring sacrifice to my name, and a pure offering; for great is my name among the nations, says the Lord of hosts." Up went Mary McCarthy's hand. "Malachi," she answered. The priest, astounded not only to have received the correct response but to have heard it from one of the youngest students present, told the assembly that he had asked that question at every retreat he had given and had never before received the right answer.

Mary was also known for her storytelling. One of her tales brought a Christian doctrine class to a standstill. After a nun had related several stories about miracles, Mary asked for permission to speak. She explained how she had persuaded her grandfather, who was not a Catholic and who was suffering from a leg injury, to visit the shrine of Saint Anne-de-Beaupré in Quebec. After a great buildup, she told how he went into the church, and how when he came out—she paused here—he fell down and broke his other leg. The story illustrates inventiveness (her grandfather McCarthy did sustain a fractured hip in a carriage accident in Quebec, and he had been to Sainte Anne-de-Beaupré; he was, however, Catholic, and he did not injure his good leg), a sly sense of humor (the story was germane, in an ironical way, to miracles), and a sense of narrative.

Although Mary eventually liked the nuns and the girls at the convent, she really wanted to attend a coeducational school. She left the convent permanently in June of 1925 to attend Garfield High School, which she knew all about from young Harold Preston, her uncle, who was a recent graduate. She entered Garfield as a freshman; she was thirteen.

Garfield was closer to what Mary McCarthy had known in Minneapolis at Saint Stephen's, except that here there was no discipline. Like a camp follower, she was able to follow the football and basketball teams all over the city, prompting her grandfather to forbid her to date. This may have saved her grades, though the standards of the school were not high enough for them to mean much: 85 in English and drama and 90 in algebra, French, and history. What was special about her one year at Garfield was her meeting the Rosenberg family, thereby becoming "conscious for the first time of a type of person that we would now call an intellectual." Mr. Rosenberg, a Jewish tailor, held regular open house every Monday night for people who wanted to discuss politics and literature. He had four children. Dan, the oldest, who was interested in theater, was a graduate student in the speech department at the University of Washington. Seattle, with its Women's Century Club, Cornish School, Seattle Repertory Theater, University Theater, and Penthouse Theatre, provided him with ample opportunity to see a dozen or so shows each year. The second oldest child was Mathilda, called Till. She never liked Mary, calling her too self-centered. ("It was I, I, I, all the time.") Till had a younger sister, Ethel (called Ted), who was a class ahead of Mary at Garfield, and a younger brother, Jess, who often played tennis with Mary's Uncle Harold and who once made a formal call at the Preston house bringing a copy of Rupert Brooke to read to Mary, who "allowed as to how she had a strong preference for Edward Arlington Robinson." It was Mary and Ted who became good friends. The bond between them was books. Ted introduced her to authors like W. H. Hudson, Aubrey Beardsley, Lord Dunsany, and Vachel Lindsay. She was an aesthete whose taste ran to *The Rubáiyát* or Rabindranath Tagore. Today, Mary McCarthy considers herself fortunate that one of her uncle's friends, Mark Sullivan, provided an antidote by recommending authors of a different stripe, such as H. L. Mencken, George Jean Nathan, Theodore Dreiser, and Ben Hecht.

Mary expressed no desire to leave Garfield, but her grandparents must have decided it was not the right school for her, for she was sent to Annie Wright Seminary in nearby Tacoma for the next three years of high school. The private Episcopal school sat on a lovely ten-acre site in Tacoma's historic North End, overlooking Commencement Bay, Puget Sound, and the snowcapped Olympic Mountains to the west. This choice of school turned out to be of great importance to Mary McCarthy, since it was at Annie Wright that she got the idea of going to Vassar.

Captivated by the mind and style of her sophomore English teacher, a Vassar woman by the name of Dorothy Atkinson, Mary decided that she, too, must go to Vassar. She later recalled that "Miss Atkinson symbolized to me the critical spirit, wit, cool learning, detachment—

everything I suddenly wished to have and to be—from the moment I first heard her light, precise, cutting voice score some pretension, slatternly phrase or construction." A strange-looking person with blond buns over each ear, a queenly pince-nez, and a decided severity to her features that made her appear older than she was, Dorothy Atkinson was a witty and inspired teacher who brought to "Sir Roger de Coverley Papers," *Silas Marner,* and *The Merchant of Venice* her special insights and enthusiasm. Mary began begging her family to send her East instead of to the University of Washington. By the end of her sophomore year, her grandfather had written to Vassar asking for application papers.

Despite her enjoyment of English class, Mary was once again marked as an outsider. As one of the few Catholics in an Episcopal school and as a nonathletic girl at a place where basketball, track, and tennis were important, she stood out. But it was her reading, precocious for a fourteen-year-old, and her sexual experiments that really set her apart. As she herself has written, "I was an intellectual by the time I reached Annie Wright. And no one else was." It was true that Mary McCarthy was reading books like James Branch Cabell's *Jurgen* (which did much to crack the taboo on sex in early twentieth-century American fiction) while her contemporaries were still enthralled by *Molly Brown's School Days.* She was also reading all of Tolstoy and Hugh Walpole. She confessed to sexual adventures, mostly invented, that startled her classmates. No one knew whether or not to believe her. "Mary was pretty shocking," says Jean Eagleson today. "I'd pretend not to be shocked, but I was shocked out of my skin." Another classmate remembers that "she was involved in escapades all through school and tried to give the impression that she knew all about boys." "She was a braggart; always the boys were in love with her," states a third. That Mary McCarthy told "all" to her classmates is doubtful, but what she did tell them they remembered, whether or not they believed her.

She lost her virginity during her first year at Annie Wright. During the summer that she turned fourteen, she met Forrest Crosby, a man in his twenties, at Singer's Tavern, the Lake Crescent resort her grandfather took her to every summer. As she tells it in *How I Grew,* one night Crosby asked her to dance on the hotel porch to the resort's two-piece female "band." Her grandfather, who was close by playing cards, seemed to pay little attention. Later, however, when the young man spirited Mary away to a secluded place, her grandfather ran after them. She was "saved" this time, but the next time she and Crosby found a secluded spot, the front seat of his Marmon roadster the following November, her grandfather was not around. Had he ever found out, he would have been horrified, not only that his young granddaughter had lost her virginity, but that she had done so with a man nearly twice her age. In *How I Grew* she describes the deflowering in minute detail, including the condom Crosby used, "a transparent little pouch resembling isinglass that has whitish greenish gray stuff in the bottom that I recognize as 'jism.' " She made a "date" with Crosby to meet him again at a certain street corner during Christmas vacation, but he never showed up. The waiting scene she describes— going into a drugstore to pretend to look at magazines and into a Piggly Wiggly to look at the fruit, walking up and down the sidewalk and watching streetcars, counting to a thousand again and again, and finally giving up and going home—is reminiscent of a similar scene in *The Group,* when Dottie, who at her lover's bidding, has just been to a doctor for a pessary, waits futilely for him on a park bench in Washington Square.

The summer after the Crosby "affair," Mary (now just fifteen) met, through Ted Rosenberg, Seattle's most gossiped-about woman, Czerna Wilson, and her pseudointellectual lesbian friends. At one of Czerna's at-homes, Mary was introduced to Kenneth Callahan, who later became a well-known painter. Although Callahan was older than Forrest Crosby, Mary readily accepted his invitation to pose for him at his studio. As she tells it in *How I Grew:*

> He did not invite me to pose nude, but naturally we "went the limit" when he set down his brushes. Some of the things he did in bed made me cringe with shame to think of afterwards. It was those sexual practices of his— now common, cf. John Updike—that taught me . . . how to deal with shame and guilt. When you have committed an action that you cannot bear to think about, that causes you to writhe in retrospect, do not seek to evade the memory: *make* yourself relive it, confront it repeatedly over and over till finally, you will discover through sheer repetition it loses its power to pain you.

She asks herself now if, by overcoming self-disgust, she had not killed a moral nerve. She concludes that she was a true girl of her generation, "bent on taking the last trace of sin out of sex." Besides, she was getting herself "in training" for her adult " 'career of crime.' "

Back at school, she turned her Seattle experiences with Crosby and Callahan and a White Russian named Baron Elshin, who had a greeting card business and used a drawing of Mary for a line of Christmas cards, into much milder escapades to tell her less rebellious classmates. They were shocked, even so. For Annie Wright girls, a typical outing was a chaperoned cultural trip into Tacoma to see a play like *Rose Marie* or *The Desert Song,* or best of all, the Canadian Stratford-on-Avon players doing Shaw's *You Never Can Tell.*

Though Mary "regarded Annie Wright as a more or less unworthy place of confinement" for her rebellious spirit, "it was school that was the predominant, the most powerful influence." School was predominant because of Dorothy Atkinson, not only because she influenced Mary to go to Vassar, but also because she encouraged her writing. Impressed by her star pupil's initial efforts—though today Mary McCarthy cannot see why—Miss Atkinson persuaded Mary to send a story entitled "Wife and Mother" to H. L. Mencken for criticism. (He never replied.) Other stories Mary wrote were for Miss Atkinson's eyes only. One was about a "prostitute with ideals" by the name of Gracia Poldock, who sells cosmetics in a department store, and her "prince-charming," Moses Nordstrom, a "small, stout Jewish gentleman with a heavy jaw, and a flabby, dissatisfied face with great pouches under hard bright eyes." Gracia, who pretends that the men who buy her favors are in love with her, comes to a bad end. The point, Mary McCarthy says today, is to show the danger of self-deception. Even now she feels that self-deception is a major vice.

She was already developing into a perceptive reader. She received an A for this paper on *Wuthering Heights*:

> It is difficult to write of "Wuthering Heights"; it is such a queer book. If one took the plot and certain characters by themselves, one would say that it was a monstrosity. Certainly the devilishness and malignity of the chief characters is absurd.
>
> It is not an artistic book at all, but it is a powerful one. Emily's imagination was even greater than that of her sister, Charlotte; her characters regrettably do not show the same human traits that are the charm of "Jane Eyre." "Wuthering Heights" is as far from realism as a book may be.
>
> The atmosphere of the wild Yorkshire heaths broods over the whole novel. The soul[s] of the people in it are as strange and incomprehensible as the country around them. The principal character, Heathcliff, has been a gypsy waif, found on the street by the kind father of one of the local families. He comes out of the void. He lives, hating and hated by his fellowmen, and, in the end, he returns to the void.
>
> Whenever she brings Heathcliff into the story Brontë loses her normality. When she is treating one of the minor characters, on the other hand, she can be humorous and mildly ironical. But the character of Heathcliff seems to fascinate her; she revels in an air of weirdness and mystery. One cannot say that this atmosphere spoils the book, for without it there could have been no book.

Dorothy Atkinson was not the only teacher at Annie Wright who impressed Mary McCarthy. There was also Ethel Mackay, a Scot in her late thirties, who taught Latin. In her sophomore year Mary had taken cooking instead of a more academic course; by the time she decided to go to Vassar, which required three years of Latin, it was too late to start Latin. Since Miss Mackay planned to rent a furnished room in the university section of Seattle during the summer, she agreed to tutor Mary in Caesar so that she could join the regular Cicero class at school in the fall. Miss Mackay became Miss Gowrie in *Memories of a Catholic Girlhood,* an introverted and rigid woman who brought to Latin a real passion for Caesar and his era. This she passed on to Mary, who continued taking Latin courses at Vassar. Miss Mackay thought highly of her student and praised Mary's aptitude for languages in a college recommendation for her. No doubt she would have been pleased to know that nearly sixty years later Mary McCarthy still studies languages, presently German.

Scholastically, Mary was at the head of her class. In her three years at Annie Wright Seminary, her lowest grade was 84 in cooking, ironical in view of her later proficiency as a cook. Her teachers respected her; a few feared her. Mary herself admits that she "made Miss Marjorie Atkinson [Dorothy's sister] cry in class with my well-aimed satirical shafts." A classmate later recalled Mary as "a girl with a terrific I.Q., an unbelievable brain, intolerant, sarcastic and wilful, who used her intellect as a weapon," words that sound a note to be heard again from many other critics throughout McCarthy's career. Another classmate still remembers how Mary shocked everyone with a comment she made in front of the class about a teacher's wig.

It was probably this willfulness that Adelaide Preston, the principal of Annie Wright, alluded to in filling out a Vassar form. In the space after "Spirit of loyalty and cooperation; sense of community responsibility," she wrote, "Sometimes lacking in these qualities, but her home life in early years was unfortunate. Lost both father and mother in the flu of 1918. She is somewhat temperamental due partly to her heritage. Her grandfather on one side of the family is of old New England stock and the other middlewest Irish, and I think there is a strain of Jewish, a peculiar combination." On another form she wrote, "Miss McCarthy is an orphan, having lost both father and mother during the flu epidemic of 1918. At present she is living with her grandfather, a prominent attorney of Seattle. Her life has been a sad one for so young a girl. One needs to know something of her history in order to understand her."

The principal was remarkably tolerant toward Mary, who frequently ran afoul of school authorities. Even when Mary was caught smoking on the fire escape, and another time leaving the school grounds without permission, she let her off with a reprimand. This tolerance stemmed partly from the principal's understanding of Mary and respect for her grandfather, and partly from the desire to keep the brilliant student who would shine at Vassar and reflect glory on Annie Wright.

In June, shortly before her seventeenth birthday, Mary McCarthy and fifteen classmates, in white caps and gowns, received their diplomas and gold crosses. A friend of her grandfather's wrote to "Dr. H. N. Mac-Cracken, President of Vassar," that Mary McCarthy "just graduated from Annie Wright's Seminary, Tacoma, with highest honors and as valedictorian. From my knowledge of her character and industry she will make a very creditable scholar."

The graduate, however, having taken part in several plays, wanted to be an actress. Her acting "career" at Annie Wright began with recitations of "The Fall of the House of Usher" and "The Cask of Amontillado," which delighted the children in the lower school. Soon she was being cast as the star in whatever play the elocution teacher decided to put on. Mary's favorites were the parts of the motherless daughter in David Belasco's hit play *The Son-Daughter* and Catiline in Ethel Mackay's *Marcus Tullius.* Miss Mackay thought that she had "considerable dramatic ability." With this commendation, Mary convinced her grandparents to send her to Seattle's famous Cornish School for the summer.

The school's curriculum reflected Nelly Cornish's belief that every student should study all the arts, not just the single art that might be his or her chief interest. An actress, for example, would be a better performer if her background included music, the dance, and the graphic arts in addition to the technical knowledge involved in the writing, producing, and acting of plays. Thus, Mary McCarthy studied under the beautiful young dancer Louise Soelberg and the well-known drama teacher Ellen Van Volkenburg, who, with her husband, Maurice Browne, directed Cornish's repertory company. Mary learned "standard English pronunciation" as part of the theater course, and took a class in eurhythmics, the art of interpreting in graceful bodily movements the rhythm of musical compositions. Although the school had an international reputation, McCarthy's summer there was a disappointment. "We wanted Cornish to let us *act,*" she recalls in *How I Grew,* "rather than teach us the principles of acting." Undaunted, she set off for Vassar still nurturing dreams of an acting career.

PART TWO

CHAPTER V

VASSAR
(1929–1933)

IN THE LATE spring of her senior year at Annie Wright, Mary McCarthy wrote a letter to the secretary of the admissions committee of Vassar outlining her plans for college study. Remarkably, her principal interests at sixteen—literature, language, and theater—turned out to be lifetime pursuits.

> I should like to center my interest in either literature or dramatics, or both. I am not sure, now, which of these two interests I should like to pursue when out of college. One can never get a good perspective of oneself in high school. At present, I know that I should like to write or to act, but I do not know whether, judged by harsher standards than those of boarding school, I could do either of these things even passably. That is one of the things I expect to learn in college. In connection with literature, I should like to study as many languages as possible. I should like to continue from Latin and French to Greek, Italian, German, Russian and later Chinese. . . .
>
> These plans seem real to me now. Some of them I shall, in all probability, never fulfill. But it seems to me that to fulfill as many of them as possible, I should go to Vassar; and I hope that it may be my good fortune to do so.

When Vassar received her college board scores—low 70s in math, middle 80s in French and Latin, and middle 90s in English—her good fortune was assured. In the fall of 1929, just weeks before the Wall Street crash, she walked through Vassar's Main Gate with 1,150 other undergraduates, certain that she was on the "threshold to possibility" and that Vassar was "a cornucopia overflowing with promise." The dean congratulated the new freshmen, telling them they were the most highly selected class to have been admitted to Vassar in its history and that, therefore, certain responsibilities fell on them; "but to this part I hardly listened," Mary McCarthy wrote later, "being so filled with the pride and glory of belonging to the very best class in the very best college in America. This feeling did not really leave me during four years in college."

Vassar College had been founded in 1861 by an English-born beer baron named Matthew Vassar, who declared that he would finance a

college to give women a liberal arts education equal to that offered by
the best men's colleges of the day. In 1865, four years after the original
charter, Vassar's great Main Building, where Mary McCarthy lived in
her senior year, was completed, and the college opened with 353 students. Matthew Vassar had given his college two hundred acres and
almost $800,000. By the time Mary McCarthy arrived sixty-eight years
later, there were nine hundred acres of campus and farm, the latter
consisting of vegetable gardens and a dairy operated for the benefit of
the college dining rooms. Other than a magnificent Gothic entrance
gate, a fieldstone Gothic euthenics building, a Gothic library, and a
chapel in the Norman style, the buildings at Vassar were undistinguished
red-brick edifices, yet the campus as a whole was lovely owing to its
natural setting—though for Mary it took some getting used to. "The
scenery is nice in a way," she wrote Ted Rosenberg, "but it's much too
pastoral. . . . Nice little rounded hills, and short fat trees. It looks like
an English countryside. It's too domesticated. I am homesick for geomet-
ric lines, points, and angles." The hazy outlines of the Catskills, visible
from all over Poughkeepsie, looked insignificant to a westerner who had
grown up near Mount Rainier, and the elms, maples, oaks, lindens,
pines, ginkoes, and magnolias that grew in profusion on the campus
appeared stout by comparison to the tall pines of the Olympic and
Cascade Mountains. But for most people the campus was beautiful, and
so it became for Mary McCarthy as she became accustomed to the
Dutchess County landscape. Long after her initial impression, she described the campus as "bucolically set in rolling orchard country just
outside the town of Poughkeepsie, with the prospect of long walks and
rides along curving back roads and cold red apples to bite; framed by
two mirrorlike lakes."

Mary McCarthy liked little about her freshman year. She wrote Ted
Rosenberg that "there is too much talk, too many labels for things, too
much pseudo-cleverness. I suppose I'll get that way, too, though I'm
doing my best to avoid it." Most of her classes bored her. Philosophy,
"a ridiculous subject . . . so delightfully purposeful and serious-minded,"
was taught by "a very aesthetic creature, much like some kind of large
bird," who "just vapored on" for a whole year. Chemistry did not
interest her either, though she liked the teacher. French was no better
than philosophy or chemistry. The instructor was "a timid little bird"
who taught from mediocre textbooks.

Anna Kitchel's English 105 saved the year. "The English teacher is
a joy," McCarthy wrote home. "She's homely, raw-boned and middle-

aged, . . . but she's real . . . ; she's sincere, and she has a good, hearty sense of humor. I enjoy the class tremendously; it usually turns into long conversations between her and me. She has read practically everything, and what's more, knows what she's reading. It's a composition class, but at present we're reading Irish literature on the side." They also read Croce, Tolstoy's "What is Art," and Max Eastman on poetry. McCarthy took an extra hour in English 105, an independent study for which she read Turgenev, and then submitted a paper to Miss Kitchel. One of her class papers was printed in *The Sampler,* a faculty publication in which the best themes from the various sections of English 105 were collected.

Contrasts

I.

The House of God

The church was quiet with reverence, and dim with holiness. Far down at the altar, tall tapers burned ardently, but they did not disturb the still twilight of God's house. There a priest moved slowly back and forth, repeating the solemn words of the most sacred Mass. His voice was low, and rightly so, but now and again a phrase drifted down from the altar. "Dominus vobiscum." One could feel the Divine Presence hovering over the altar, enveloping it and the intent worshippers. The priest and the altar boys were feeling it and chanting of it; their dark red robes were symbolic of the richness of God's grace; the incense they burned, of the sweetness of His love.

Near the front of the church, a window was open. Beyond it was a patch of blue sky, and the green branch of an apple tree waving in the wind. They, too, were expressing the ineffable goodness of God. All life, human and inanimate, bowed down to Him, and was bathed in His peace.

II.

A Survival

Outside the open church window there is spring. The sky is an intense blue. The green branch of an apple tree waves gently in the wind.

Inside there is gloom and unreality; inside, there is a priest. Around a shadowy altar, a few feeble tapers burn. Grey wisps of incense salute a God, old beyond human understanding. A book is moved back and forth on the altar by small, puzzled boys. Their robes are like those of the priest, dark red, the red of old blood and time-worn sacrifices. A few Latin words drift down toward the worshippers, dead ritual, in a dead language to a dead God. A thin piece of whitish bread is raised; and the believers bow their heads and beat their breasts in fear and adoration.

The spring and the sky and the apple tree seem more breathtakingly

real as the grotesque mummery is enacted far in the front of the church.
But one notices that the spring shrinks from the open window; it remains
very definitely outside, as the weary mutterings of a sacred Mass go on.

Recalling the course half a century later, Mary McCarthy remarked
that "the best thing that I ever got out of Vassar was Kitchel in 105. If
the whole thing could have been like that!" Because Miss Kitchel was
her faculty advisor, Mary saw a great deal of her during the next four
years. She memorialized Kitchel in *The Group,* her best-selling novel
based on Vassar. "Miss Kitchel had noticed her [Libby MacAusland, one
of the group] immediately in English 105 as 'the artistic young lady with
the fine Italian hand.' Her 'effusions,' as Miss Kitchel, who was a hearty
soul, used to call them, had been printed in the freshman *Sampler.*"

In her sophomore year, another good English teacher made a course
come alive for McCarthy. Helen Sandison, who also happened to be
chairman of the department, was a pretty, slight, gray-haired woman with
a gentle manner and a will of iron. She taught English 165, a yearlong
course in Shakespeare. "If there was any single course at Vassar that I
would say was formative for me, I would say it was that one," McCarthy
said in an interview. "It has really stayed with me ever since and such
ethic as I have is really Shakespeare's ethic that I learned in English 165."
She explained this view of "Shakespeare's ethic" in another interview.

> Aside from Christian doctrine, the thing that has most formed my cast
> of mind has probably been Shakespeare. Whether the two are connected
> in some way I'm not sure, but it seems to me that throughout Shakespeare
> there is a deep rejection of the will. The will naturally allies itself with
> abstractions, and abstractions in Shakespeare are always wrong. In comedy
> they simply lead to comic conclusions, beginning with *Love's Labour's Lost*
> where the young men make their absurd vow and try to stick to it. And
> anyone who thinks that he embodies what Ibsen called "the claim of the
> ideal" is shown to be wrong in Shakespeare, like Angelo in *Measure for
> Measure* or Lear or Coriolanus or Shylock with his insistent idea of a pound
> of flesh—a bloodless abstraction, evidently.
>
> Shakespeare's view of the will and its capacity for abstractions, as op-
> posed to the things of nature, to the instinctive and the concrete, spoke
> to me very young and still speaks to me. I believe in humility, in a certain
> modesty towards what is outside, towards what is not I. . . . The assertion
> of any absolute idea is really a claim on the part of the mind to control
> the world, to control reality. It's a proclamation of sovereignty, and I don't
> want that. I don't believe in it; I think one must respect the created world
> which has its own laws, including unjust laws, and its own harmony. We

must listen to messages from that world, and this comes over very strongly in Shakespeare where the rustics are always right; they have the last word. The rustics and the clowns and even the fools. That corresponds to my sense of the way things ought to be.

This ethic has carried over into her writing. The character who most nearly speaks for the author in a McCarthy novel is the one guided by the sensory world rather than by ideas. When Rosamund, a character in *Birds of America,* tells her son, "I love reality, Peter. I hope you will, too," and when the Dutch deputy in *Cannibals and Missionaries* tells the chief hijacker, "You have only your will on your side, Jeroen. Den Uyl has reality, the power of circumstances. *His* individual will does not count," McCarthy is giving voice to her own basic belief about life. Despite a wide iconoclastic streak, she has always had an unshakable respect for the natural order of things, a respect that comes, partly, from taking Miss Sandison's Shakespeare course. Those characters in a McCarthy novel who find ideas more true than the data of reality are depicted as foolish and deluded, none more so than the members of Vassar's class of 1933 who show up in *The Group.*

Miss Sandison, who wrote two books on grammar, one with Henry Noble MacCracken, Vassar's president, was a stickler for the proper mechanics of language. Her abhorrence of sloppiness influenced McCarthy, who told an interviewer recently, "I still punctuate according to Sandison." Miss Sandison's precision and clarity of style were partly responsible for Mary McCarthy's choice of Vassar inasmuch as she had written Vassar's catalog, which Mary had admired. As a senior at Annie Wright, she had written the college admissions committee explaining why she had chosen Vassar. "My family sent for catalogs from several of the women's colleges. Of all of them, Vassar's was the least complicated, the most clear. I liked that."

Despite her having taken seventeen semesters of English during her college years, only one other English course had any noticeable influence on McCarthy. In Rose Peebles's Contemporary Prose Fiction she read John Dos Passos's *The 42nd Parallel.* She says today the book "turned her around politically"; it "radicalized" her. In "Politics and the Novel," an essay she wrote for *The New York Times Book Review,* she explains how:

> I fell madly in love with that book. . . . I went to the library and looked up every line that Dos Passos had published that was in the card catalogue. I read them all. The last was a pamphlet on the Sacco-Vanzetti case, which

I found and read in the library basement, feeling tremendously stirred by Vanzetti's famous words, brand-new, of course, to me, and by the whole story. . . . I was moved to read up on the Tom Mooney case too . . . and to become aware of the *New Republic.* One thing leading to another, soon after graduation, I was writing little book reviews for the *New Republic,* then for the *Nation,* and I never looked back. Like a Japanese paper flower dropped into a glass of water, my political persona unfolded, magically, from Dos Passos, though he would have been saddened in later years to hear what his energy, enthusiasm, and sheer unwary talent had brought about.

It was not only Rose Peebles's course that awakened Mary McCarthy politically. Events outside Vassar—worsening depression at home (Mary had considered applying for a scholarship for senior year but finally did not) and rampant fascism abroad—awakened in most students a political awareness. Moreover, senior year was an election year. When Franklin Delano Roosevelt, a Vassar trustee, was elected president, a member of the economics department was asked to serve on a presidential commit-tee and President MacCracken of Vassar was invited to lunch with Roosevelt at the White House. The undergraduates "felt more than ever that Vassar was at the center of everything." Radicals on campus tried unsuccessfully to abolish the senior prom so that the money could be used to help the poor. It was in this environment that Mary McCarthy discovered Dos Passos.

Though a newfound zeal for politics swept the college in the years 1932–33, during McCarthy's first few years at Vassar, the outside world, at least beyond New York City, rarely impinged on students' lives. Mary did spend a good deal of time in New York as a result of a chance encounter on her first visit to the city.

At the start of her freshman year, she and her grandmother and Aunt Isabel (her uncle Frank Preston's wife) were spending three days in New York before going up to Poughkeepsie. Mrs. Preston and Isabel were at the Metropolitan Museum when Mary, walking back to the Roosevelt Hotel, ran into the only person she knew in New York. Harold Johns-rud, an actor and aspiring playwright nine years her senior, had worked for the Seattle Repertory Theater. Mary had first seen him, in a pageant celebrating the Magna Carta, when she was sixteen. His striking appear-ance—the combination of a tight-skinned, bony face with a receding hairline, expressive Mephistophelean eyebrows, and a neatly trimmed mustache—attracted her attention. When she learned that he knew the

Rosenbergs, she asked her friend Ted Rosenberg to arrange a meeting. Ted persuaded her mother to invite Johnsrud and Mary to lunch. When Mary arrived at the Rosenberg's house, Johnsrud and Dan Rosenberg were fencing in the small backyard. Johnsrud made a marvelous figure— tall, high-shouldered, narrow-waisted, slender—unnerving Mary, who had worn, to her regret, a white tennis dress, which she had made herself. The skirt barely reached her knees, making her feel like a child. In fact, the next time she saw Johnsrud, three months later in his dressing room after a performance of *The Wild Duck*, he said, "Ah. So this is the child Mary." Mary saw him act once more in Seattle, in a melodrama called *The Jest*. She did not see him again until after graduating from Annie Wright. At the Cornish School, where she spent the summer before Vassar studying theater, she learned that Johnsrud was having an affair with the dance teacher, Louise Soelberg. At the end of the summer, when Cornish staged a farewell dance, Mary learned that he was going to New York to look for work on Broadway, and that he, too, had a Minnesota background. So when they met by chance in September 1929, they already knew a little about each other.

The next day, Johnsrud and Mary rode the subway downtown to the Provincetown Playhouse to see a play by Mike Gold, a writer for *The Daily Worker*. In mid-October, Mary used her first off-campus weekend to go down to see Johnsrud in *The Channel Road*, a George S. Kaufman and Alexander Woollcott adaptation of a de Maupassant story. By the winter of her freshman year she was sleeping with Johnsrud. Their affair lasted the four years of college, culminating in marriage immediately after graduation.

Johnsrud, Mary soon realized, was a born pedagogue, and he proved to be an apt guide to New York. Whenever she could come down from Poughkeepsie, he took her to museums, the theater, and the opera, awakening in her, it would seem in retrospect, a real love for the arts that resulted, much later, in two books on Renaissance art, many dozens of theater reviews, and a new story adaptation of Giuseppe Verdi's *La Traviata* for the Metropolitan Opera Classics Library. Nor did Johnsrud neglect lighter pursuits, introducing her to the Staten Island Ferry, rides on bus tops up and down Fifth Avenue, and, best of all, popular restaurants, nightclubs, and speakeasies. Every so often he took her to visit Albert Parker Fitch, pastor of the Park Avenue Presbyterian Church, who enjoyed reading aloud with Johnsrud. Mary liked their *Tamburlaine* and *Doctor Faustus* best. When Dr. Fitch, who was a well-known preacher, delivered a sermon at Vassar, Mary was proud of knowing him—and "I a 'lowly' freshman." A Vassar classmate remembers that

Johnsrud enjoyed impressing Mary with his sophistication, and that she
was fascinated by him.

The summer before Mary's senior year, Johnsrud got a job directing
a summer theater at Scarborough, about midway between New York
and Poughkeepsie. Although he had never directed a play before, he put
on eight new plays in an eight-week season. The company (Lloyd Nolan
was one of its members) had to rehearse one play while performing
another. Mary had stayed in New York that summer to be near Johnsrud, but until the season ended, she saw little of him. When they moved
into a furnished apartment a month before Vassar's school year resumed,
they discovered they did not get along. Mary remembers the time as the
worst month of her life. Johnsrud, apparently regretting the move, was
sarcastic and nasty, denouncing Mary every chance he got. When she
finally returned to college and he went to Hollywood to work as a
two-hundred-dollar-a-week scriptwriter, she assumed their love affair
was over.

To her surprise, he wrote often, yet his letters contained no word of
love, not even a hint as to his feelings about her. Instead, he described
in detail the sexual adventures of several screenwriters, studio execu-
tives, and stars. McCarthy has remembered the content of these letters
all her life. "I knew some of the names or came to know them—Thal-
berg, Harry Cohn—but all those men sounded like characters in Krafft-
Ebing ('He was first immoral with a hen at the age of eight'), whose
Psychopathia Sexualis, at John's [her name for Johnsrud] recommendation, I had just bought. John did not say that he took part in the incessant
Saturnalia he described, but he did not say that he didn't. I was left to
draw my own conclusions."

When Johnsrud returned to New York in late spring (shortly after
Mary had ended a brief affair with Alan Barth, later to become the chief
editorial writer at *The Washington Post*), she was not so sure she wanted
him back. But when she made Phi Beta Kappa and he gave her the key
he had earned at Carleton College, she considered herself engaged. She
knew she did not love him, but she felt vindicated in the eyes of her
friends who thought Johnsrud had "thrown her over." Besides, she was
in awe of him, believing him to be a budding George Bernard Shaw. In
May he came up to Vassar to see her play Leontes in *The Winter's Tale.*
He declared she had no acting talent and should abandon any idea of
becoming an actress. She accepted his verdict without a second thought,
so sure was she of his theatrical genius.

Owing to the attractions of New York and of Johnsrud (at least most
of the time), Mary McCarthy lost interest in many of the friends she had

made in her dormitory, nor was she absorbed with weekends at men's colleges, as most undergraduates were. She did go to Yale a couple of times, but when she got a free weekend, she usually preferred going to New York. Since her real interests were literary, it is not surprising that the few extracurricular activities she took part in—debating team in freshman year; Philaletheis, the student dramatic society, in junior and senior years; *Miscellany News,* the college newspaper, in senior year— were also literary, at least in some measure. So, too, were the friends she kept.

Her friendship with Frani Blough of Pittsburgh went back to her freshman year and extends to the present day. Frani impressed Mary with her knowledge of Botticelli and Fra Filippo Lippi, of Shelley (whose personality, she told Mary, was "over-prominent in his poetry"), of Hemingway (whom she did not like, nor did Mary), and of the classics. Frani Blough had gone to the same preparatory school (Walnut Hill) as Elizabeth Bishop, who, because of severe asthma, did not arrive at Vassar until 1930. Like Mary McCarthy, Bishop (as her classmates and teachers called her) was an orphan, her father having died when she was a baby and her mother having been committed to a mental hospital when she was five. Besides their common background, the two classmates shared an intense interest in literature. Bishop introduced Mary to the works of Dorothy Richardson, Wyndham Lewis, Gerard Manley Hopkins, Sarah Orne Jewett, and Gertrude Stein.

Frani Blough, Elizabeth Bishop, and Mary McCarthy were soon talking about starting a rebel literary magazine (Mary suggested calling it *The Battleaxe*) to protest *The Vassar Review,* the official college literary magazine, which "no longer represented Vassar writing but had become an inheritance of a 'pallid' literary clique," as McCarthy wrote in *The Group.* Frani Blough remembers that it was not only the review's stodginess and conservatism that bothered them but, above all, the fact that it ignored contemporary writing. Elizabeth Bishop thought their motivation was more practical than theoretical. "Most of us submitted things to the *Vassar Review* and had been turned down," she said in a 1974 interview. "We were all rather put out, so we thought we'll start our own magazine." Not until senior year did they organize a group—Margaret Miller, Muriel Rukeyser, and the Clark sisters, Eunice and Eleanor, besides Blough, Bishop, and McCarthy—to produce their review, christened *Con Spirito* by Elizabeth Bishop. There were two issues in 1933, in February and April, and a third the following fall, by which time Mary McCarthy, Eunice Clark, and Frani Blough had graduated. Eunice Clark, who had been editor of the college newspaper, *Miscellany News,* took charge of all practical aspects: she found a printer in Roxbury, Connecticut; she directed that posters be nailed to trees announcing *Con Spirito*'s inauguration; she arranged for the bookstore to sell it for fifteen cents a copy; and she sent a copy of the first issue to Lewis Gannett of the *Herald Tribune,* who reviewed it favorably. On campus it caused quite a stir, chiefly because no one knew who the editors were or who wrote the articles, poems, and stories. That the conspirators managed to keep their enterprise secret—only Miss Kitchel and Miss Sandison were let in on their identity—was a wonder, because at Vassar all the seniors lived together in Main Hall. Mary McCarthy roomed in South Tower, Frani Blough in North Tower, and Eunice Clark somewhere in between, yet no one breathed a word.

Mary McCarthy wrote a review of Aldous Huxley's *Brave New World* and Harold Nicolson's *Public Faces* for the first issue. With a perversity critics would later deem characteristic of McCarthy's criticism, she accused Huxley of "easy mechanical production of Wellsian prophecies," D. H. Lawrence of "sentimental mysticism," James Joyce of "comfortable unintelligibility," Virginia Woolf of "a pretense of acute feeling," and Ernest Hemingway of "romantic and conceited morbidities." She showed the review to Malcolm Cowley, the book editor of *The New Republic,* during spring break, hoping for review assignments. He said she would have to be a genius or starving before he would give her a book to review. "I'm not starving," she shot back. (After graduation he did assign her three books, but that was all.) For the second issue of *Con Spirito,* McCarthy wrote a prose poem, ironically entitled "In Pace Requiescamus," that "had come out of my interior without much sense of order just the way automatic writing was supposed to do." It dealt ("in a mixed-up way," she later admitted) with the Polish Corridor, Jews, Hitler, Mussolini, and the Pope's birth-control encyclicals.

> The Vatican doors open and the Pope steps out. But the Pope is an ex-mountain climber of seventy-odd, who composes new encyclicals on birth control, and sets new red hats on his prelates' bald heads, while the Italians increase and multiply as the Lord commanded them, and the Nazis, Poland looking, test their clubs on Communist pates.

Although Mary McCarthy may have preferred her literary friends, she was by nature gregarious, and "she had a group of very nice friends, socially very presentable," according to Eunice Clark. Like any friendly western or midwestern girl who goes East to college, she was invited to winter and summer homes up and down the Eastern Seaboard. In fact, except for the first two summers of her Vassar years, she never went home during her college vacations. This was partly because of the four-day train trip between New York and Seattle and partly because of Johnsrud. For her first Thanksgiving in the East, she stayed at Elinor Coleman's on West End Avenue, which was then, she relates in *How I Grew,* "at the height of its fashion among better-off Jews," and went to several coming-out parties at the Plaza. "Thousands and thousands of dollars spent on glamour in the first winter of the depression—in Seattle we had never even imagined anything like it." The men she met there went to Yale, but they did not look like, or have names like, the Yale men she had met through Virginia Johnston of Waterbury, Connecticut. Those men thought "it was a rich joke that a girl named Mary McCarthy should be drinking cocktails with them at the Country Club: Irish were mill workers." All this came as a surprise to her, because "in Minneapolis and Seattle, to be Irish was to be among 'gentles,' entitled to look down on Swedes, Norwegians, and Finns."

She visited the Bloughs in Pittsburgh in winter and in Osterville on Cape Cod in summer, noting that they lived on "the income of their income," and that Mrs. Blough washed her breakfast china in a bowl of hot water at the table. She spent a Thanksgiving at Cape Elizabeth, Maine, with the Denisons, an aristocratic family that had lost its money, though no one seemed to mind. She enjoyed weekends in New York with the Swan family (Mrs. Swan had been a co-founder of the Junior League), who lived in the East Eighties. At Rokeby, a country house on the Hudson, she was the guest of Margaret Chandler Astor Aldrich, known as Maddie to her friends. As McCarthy gadded about, mastering the finer points of class distinction, which she stored away for later use in her fiction, she recalled "all those mornings spent poring over *Vogue* opposite my grandmother with her mending in the upstairs bay window," when she had yearned to be part of the New York society she read about, yet knowing this was impossible for her. "There was never a word in *Vogue* about what happened socially in Seattle, scarcely even about San Francisco, unless it happened to be a Spreckels." When she saw her girlhood wishes "come improbably true," she found that "it delighted me to be staying not merely with rich society people but with old-family patricians unable to afford central heating."

Still, all the glamour in the world did not compensate for the loneliness of not having a "normal" family like her friends, especially at Christmas. Her cavalier descriptions of two of those Christmases, the first sent to Ted Rosenberg and the second to Frani Blough, do not mask the hurt she must have experienced.

I spent Christmas and the days just before and after it with a girl who lived in Poughkeepsie. I did this foolish thing for sentimental reasons. I wanted to be in somebody's house at Christmas time. The thought of waking up Christmas morning in the Vassar Club in New York was too much for me. The rest of the time, however, I spent in New York. I saw John there in case it might interest you.

Two years later she spent Christmas with Johnsrud, but he had to leave New York early Christmas morning to rehearse a play scheduled to open in Washington. She wrote Frani Blough:

I haven't minded particularly all day, for I did nothing more than lie about reading books; but when I had to wander about the Village this evening, looking for an inexpensive restaurant to eat my Christmas dinner, and then ate it, and read a good book; well, on my return from that adventure, the situation got a bit too much for me; and I have been indulging in some good old self-pity. . . . The vacation has buzzed along merrily enough, what with the usual amount of alcoholism, and several daily battles with John. Once I walked out on him altogether which, if I may say so, was rather effective. Last night, for the first time in many a weary month, John didn't have to work, so we had a bit of a party . . . beginning with gin, continuing with Irish and rye whiskey, on through sour red wine, and sherry, and back to gin again. There was an excellent duck, and a plum pudding, which had been made in May in England, and a whiskey sauce for that. We exchanged tokens of affection, and even sang a Christmas carol or two. And then, of course, for no reason at all, I wept. . . . For once John and I desisted from our usual mongoose-and-cobra act, and enjoyed each other's company. Which makes today all the worse. . . . I might as well go back to college. And that's one of the purposes of this letter, i.e., to find out when you are going back, and to offer you my charming companionship on the way back, if you go early enough.

The only other time Mary spent a school vacation with Johnsrud was that miserable summer when she decided she did not love him. The first two months, while he was in Scarborough directing summer theater, she lived with three classmates in a brownstone that belonged to the family of one of the girls. She regaled them with accounts of the doings of Emmanuel J. Rousuck, for whom she typed at the Carleton Gallery. He became the model for Mr. Sheer in "Rogue's Gallery," a chapter in her first book, *The Company She Keeps.* Mannie Rousuck, as he was known then, was a "nice, sweet battered soul who spends his time skulking about, avoiding the sheriff," McCarthy wrote Frani Blough. "He now owes me eighteen dollars, and there is very little prospect of collecting it, unless I enlist my grandfather's services and join the ranks of the vultures who are hovering about the poor man ready to pounce." Besides "reading the want ads every day in a threatening manner under [Rousuck's] very nose," she read Proust and detective stories, and occasionally went up to Scarborough, "to have a look at the theatre." She also spent time with Phil Huget, a young man who had shared an apartment on Bank Street with Johnsrud. "I have been having a great deal of Phil's society, that is, if you can call long and detailed soliloquies concerning his fascinating inner nature, his purposes and his capabilities, society. I am afraid Phil has a good deal of Hamlet in him." When the season closed at Scarborough, she moved into a furnished apartment with Johnsrud, but was relieved when he left for California and she returned to Poughkeepsie for her final year at Vassar.

This was Mary McCarthy's happiest year in college. She was one of a group of six who lived in the nicest suite in Main, the South Tower suite, whence comes the title for *The Group.* She took a senior seminar in non-Shakespearean Elizabethan literature with Helen Sandison, writing a sixteen-page research paper about Sir John Harington. He was a godson of Queen Elizabeth, a minor poet, translator of Ariosto, and inventor of the water closet. The paper, "Touchstone Ambitions," published in Vassar's *Journal of Undergraduate Studies*, foreshadows, with its elegant parallel structure, faultless transitions, and Latinist construction, the fine prose style of her mature work. The second half of her senior thesis was on the poet Robert Greene.

That year she also took a course in advanced composition, her last writing course. Narrative writing in her sophomore year had disappointed her and turned her against creative writing courses for the rest of her life. "I just couldn't stand my narrative writing class at Vassar," she remembered some fifty years later. "It was so boring. We all wrote the same thing and then had to read what each other wrote. I think we hadn't enough experience to write a story—our experience was too fragmentary." Nonetheless, the critical judgments she made at the time inspired Jean Anderson, a classmate who also took the narrative writing course, to create a cartoon that has become familiar to every Vassar undergraduate. In it a scowling girl is asked, "Miss Abbott, would you care to reply to Miss McCarthy's criticism of your story?"

Mary McCarthy graduated in June, having taken seventeen English courses, ten Latin, eight French, four philosophy, and "a dab of this, and a dab of that," as she once described a few miscellaneous courses in a letter to the dean. She had immersed herself in classical and Elizabethan writers because she loved them, not because she thought they might be useful to her. They were, however, very useful, definitive for her writing style and system of values, yet "the idea of *using* what you were learning seldom entered your head," she told a 1976 Vassar commencement class. "My roomate was a mathematics major, though her chief interests outside the classroom were men, clothes, and smart cars. It happened that she was intelligent, and her brain enjoyed calculus, and she never asked herself what she should *do* with it—such a question would have appeared vulgar or else senseless."

As it turned out, however, Mary McCarthy was able to use everything—academically, emotionally, and, above all, socially—that she learned at Vassar. The lesson she took away from Miss Kitchel was to pursue her own native ability. According to Johnsrud, it was not acting, and according to her English teachers, it was not creative; she left Vassar convinced that hers was a critical talent. From Miss Sandison she assimilated the principle that whatever one does, one must do it as perfectly as possible. Emotionally, she seems to have decided, if only subconsciously, never to live alone again, never to be without some sort of family, even if "family" consisted only of a husband or lover. And socially, she gained a world of fact, which she later called "the staple ingredient" of all great novels. Not only *The Group,* with its vivid reproduction of Vassar College and the 1930s, but all of McCarthy's novels exemplify what is to her the very definition of the novel: "its concern with the actual world of fact, of the verifiable, of figures, even, statistics."

Vassar left its mark. References to it abound in her writing, not only in *The Group.* She still sees the exemplary Vassar undergraduate as pursuing excellence and possessing "a wistful respect for the unorthodox," yet her portrayal of Vassar girls in *The Group* is uncomplimentary, because, Mary McCarthy has said in several interviews, she was not depicting exemplary girls in her 1963 novel.

The raw western girl who arrived in the sophisticated East in 1929, sexually adventuresome, disdainful of nonintellectual involvements, and intrigued by high style, left Vassar in 1933 full of confidence ("judged by harsher standards than those of boarding school") and worldly wise, but essentially the same "bright wild girl from Seattle."

CHAPTER VI

HAROLD JOHNSRUD
(1933–1936)

T HE OPENING sentence of *The Group* announces the first marriage of the class of 1933 to take place after graduation. "It was June, 1933, one week after commencement, when Kay Leiland Strong, Vassar '33, the first of her class to run around the table at the Class Day dinner, was married to Harold Peterson, Reed '27, in the chapel of St. George's Church, P.E., Karl F. Reiland, Rector." The account of Kay and Harald's wedding service, and the breakfast that follows, is actually a description of McCarthy and Johnsrud's. In June 1933, one week after graduation and on the day of her twenty-first birthday, Mary McCarthy married Harold Johnsrud in the chapel of Saint George's Episcopal Church, on Stuyvesant Square in New York City. A dozen people attended the short service, though her good friends Frani Blough, who was at the Conservatoire Americain, and Elizabeth Bishop, "chiefly from lack of funds," were absent.

"It was all very exciting," Mary Johnsrud wrote to "Dearest Frani" in Fontainebleau. "Ten of us had breakfast at the Hotel Lafayette, with a swell punch with an applejack base, and there were a few more people at the church. My powerful bass voice (last heard in 'The Winter's Tale') changed to a faint, trembling soprano, which could not be heard, I learned, beyond the first pew. My knees shook so that I could barely stand." The bridegroom, despite his usual worldly manner, appeared tense. That night they went up to the Briarcliff Lodge, but because Johnsrud had to be at the theater, they were back in New York early the next morning. Already McCarthy regretted the wedding: "I knew, too late, that I had *done the wrong thing.* To marry a man without loving him, which was what I had just done, not really perceiving it, was a wicked action." She marveled that the wedding had taken place at all, wondered "why he decided finally to marry me," and why she had acquiesced. A short while later, however, she wrote Frani Blough that she and her husband were happy. "John's character has undergone a remarkable transformation, indeed, a metamorphosis. He is so goddamned nice that he puts me to shame. I am so glad we stopped being sensible and got married." Apparently the dissensions that had occurred so frequently the preceding summer had stopped.

On July 3 the couple moved into a summer sublet at 399 East Fifty-second Street. In the fall they rented an apartment on Beekman Place and hired a part-time maid to clean and cook dinner. Johnsrud was directing a Corey Ford–Russell Crouse musical called *Americana,* noteworthy only for its song "Brother, Can You Spare a Dime?" Even in the best of economic times, making a living in the theater is precarious; Johnsrud struggled to do so during a depression. Not surprisingly, paid work during the three years of his marriage to McCarthy was sporadic and diversified: he worked as an assistant to the abrasive and eccentric producer-director Jed Harris, wrote skits for musicals, directed for the Shuberts, was commissioned to put "clever dirt" into a salacious French farce, played supporting roles in several plays (*The Sailors of Cataro,* about a mutiny in the Austrian fleet; *Black Pit,* a "Marxian tragedy" about coal miners; *Panic,* one of Archibald MacLeish's lesser-known plays; and *Winterset* by Maxwell Anderson), and wrote witty plays that almost made it to the stage. One, *Anti-Climax,* was optioned by producer Frank Merlin early in 1934. Johnsrud wrote Frani Blough:

> The immediate reaction of Mary-John to this event: Dinner (Mary squab, me venison) at the Lafayette, with a quart of Piper Heidsick 1923.
> The proceeds from such a contract: $500 advanced against royalties, the play to be done before December 12 next.
> The present relations with Albert A. Ashforth, landlord: superb.
> The present status of Saks-Fifth Avenue, Bonwit-Teller and other bills: paid in full.
> . . . Attitude toward immediate and more distant future: hopeful and optimistic. (NO MORE LADIES, no better a comedy than mine, if as good, and doing only 8000 or 9000 weekly, which size gross both Merlin and I are sanguine of making, just sold to the pictures for 50,000, of which the author collected half.)

But *Anti-Climax* was never produced. Frank Merlin had optioned Clifford Odets's *Awake and Sing* at the same time, but having lost his backing, he was forced to let both options lapse. Johnsrud put *Anti-Climax* back on the market, plus another play he had just finished, a play his wife called "grand" but "strange." Neither sold. "We have had so much bad luck," McCarthy wrote Frani Blough, "that I can't believe in anything any more and I live in a state of constant apprehension, which is very bad for poor John's psychology. . . . The only thing you can do in these circumstances is to be as senselessly cheerful as possible."

A month later, at the end of October 1934, she had an emergency appendectomy and was forced to ask the Prestons for money. From the McCarthys she had been receiving Capitol Elevator dividends, but the depression had affected the grain business too, so that since graduation, almost eighteen months earlier, she had received only twelve hundred dollars. For Christmas she and Johnsrud "limited each other to five dollars apiece for presents for each other, and out of that he managed to produce four excellent presents, and I three. My family [the Prestons] contributed handsomely with a wine-colored dressing gown for John, and a black tunic dress for me as the chief articles of display."

In the new year they wrote a movie together, a humorous story about racketeers who, deprived of a profitable trade after Prohibition ends, go into the art business. Despite some initial enthusiasm at Columbia Pictures, there was no sale. "We have been doing a dozen things with an eye to financial gain," McCarthy wrote Frani Blough, among them the submission of short stories to popular magazines. Although at the time McCarthy had a low opinion of her own creative abilities and focused instead on her husband's talents, she had submitted a story to *Harper's* and another to *The New Yorker*. She was not surprised when both were rejected. She had, after all, been told by college teachers that she would make a better critic than fiction writer. And, in fact, her book reviews always found publication.

Her first published review was for *The New Republic*. Malcolm Cowley, who had promised her a book or two to review when she had gone to see him in the spring of her senior year at Vassar, sent her Glenway Westcott's *A Calendar of Saints for Unbelievers* in August 1933 and Lauren Gilfillan's *I Went to Pit College* in May 1934. Both reviews were published, but she was not sent another book for six years; the third review was her last assignment for *The New Republic*.

Apparently *The Nation* was more congenial, for she published three dozen pieces there during her "Johnsrud years." Numerous writers— mostly novelists, but sometimes biographers, poets, and short-story writers—were subjected to her incisive gaze. She wrote that Hilaire Belloc's *Charles the First, King of England* was a "tightly reasoned biography," in "a vigorous prose"; Nicolai Gubsky's *Bitter Bread* was "a novel of distinction"; Robert Graves's *I, Claudius* was "amazingly accurate and well-informed and at the same time full of color and imagination"; Vincent Sheehan's *Personal History* was a "first-class literary work"; Louis Zara's *Blessed Is the Man* was "as exciting and as promising a first novel as one will find"; and Anatoli Vinogradov in *The Black Consul* had created "out of the very confusion of the novel, its disordered time sequence, its unmotivated characters, . . . a powerful sense of life, of the mystery of human character, of the tumult of human events, of time passing, not time past."

Obviously, the young Vassar graduate could respond to a wide range of books with enthusiasm, yet she soon acquired a reputation at *The Nation* for astringency, because when she did not like a book, she said why in no uncertain terms. John Steinbeck's *In Dubious Battle* was "wooden and inert"; Kay Boyle's *My Next Bride* was "peephole, wish-fulfillment literature"; James Hilton in *Lost Horizon* was a poor imitator of the masters; Robert Graves in *Claudius the God* was "unable to understand his characters"; Alvah Bessie's *Dwell in Wilderness* was "a rambling family history, spirited but pointless"; Arnold Gingrich, *"Esquire's* live-wire editor," had done "a cheap, slick, machine-made job" in *Cast Down the Laurel*; George Cronyn in *Fortune and Men's Eyes* had written a "mechanical story"; Josephine Johnson's short stories were "repetitious"; Erik Linklater was "a pompous young pedant"; Stark Young in *So Red the Rose* was "not interested in truth but in romance"; Edith Olivier's *Alexander the Corrector* was like "a college paper done by a hard-working, unoriginal student." And of Whit Burnett's collection of short stories, she wrote, "It would be kinder to think that he had discovered the majority of them in an old trunk" than that he had written them.

It is not surprising that when Charles Angoff, one of *The Nation's* editors, decided to mount a large-scale attack on critics and book reviewers, principally those of the New York *Herald Tribune, The New York Times,* and the *Saturday Review,* he picked Mary McCarthy as the appropriate assailant. She was delighted by the "chance to star," but because she was only twenty-two, Angoff chose Margaret Marshall, *The Nation's* assistant literary editor, to collaborate with her. They were to write five articles, but Margaret Marshall fell ill, so Mary McCarthy did four of the five by herself as well as most of the fifth. The series, entitled "Our Critics, Right or Wrong," created a sensation, and despite Margaret Marshall's nominal coauthorship (her byline appeared on all five articles), commendation and censure, censure predominating, fell on Mary McCarthy alone.

The first article considered the careers of Thornton Wilder and Louis Bromfield, "whose meager, undistinguished novels turned the greater part of the critical press into as silly a set of sycophants as ever followed a Roman noble's litter." When critics ballyhoo the second-rate and ignore good work, they cheat the public, McCarthy contended. William Lyon Phelps, Burton Rascoe, Henry Seidel Canby, Arnold Bennett, William Rose Benét, John Farrar, Lee Wilson Dodd, and Isabel Paterson, all celebrated critics, consistently inflated second-rate talent for a gullible public, she claimed. A few critics kept their heads amidst all the hype, notably Henry Hazlitt in *The Nation,* but she concluded, "Criticism in America during the past ten years on the whole worked for . . . the debasement of taste."

In the second article, "The Anti-Intellectuals," Mary McCarthy assailed the *Herald Tribune* book reviewers, in particular Burton Rascoe, Hershell Brickell, and Isabel Paterson. They consistently displayed their anti-intellectualism, she said, by ignoring or putting down important works of literature while praising the second-rate; yet as rulers of the *Herald Tribune* book section they were "comfortable, established, and widely recognized" and seemed "to furnish their sizeable publics with demonstrable proof that it's smart to be stupid." Rascoe, for example, declared that *The Divine Comedy* was " 'no more worthy of admiration than a carved replica of the Battleship Maine assembled inside a bottle,' " yet he found *Lo!* by Charles Fort " 'one of the great books of the world' " and *One More Spring* by Robert Nathan such " 'a masterpiece' " and so " 'heartbreakingly beautiful' " that he was tempted to get a megaphone for Pennsylvania and Grand Central stations to " 'shout at people that *One More Spring* will save their lives.' " Isabel Paterson dismissed Hemingway's *The Sun Also Rises* with the curt " 'No story,' " said " 'I cannot read Joyce and who cares,' " and declared that Fitzgerald's *The Great Gatsby* " 'cannot very well go on living' " beyond the season. But she extravagantly praised *The Constant Nymph* by Margaret Kennedy and *Indeed This Flesh* by Grace Flandrau. Hershel Brickell insisted that Dos Passos's *Manhattan Transfer* " 'is unlikely to reach a very large audience,' " as opposed to Kathleen Norris's autobiography, *Noon.*

In the third article, McCarthy called the *Saturday Review* and *New York Times Book Review* critics "the great levelers." Unable to differentiate between good and bad writing, "they have been occupied in reducing the mountainous land of literature to a smooth, horizontal surface." In the fourth article, she attacked the reviewers of the *New Masses,* a literary adjunct of *Communist,* the official organ of the American Communist Party from 1927 to 1944. Shackled by political dogmatism, the *New Masses* writer must "applaud any proletarian novel, no matter how inept, on political grounds, and berate the bourgeois." In the last article, "Literary Salesmen," she exonerated reviewers of the daily papers for their critical inanities, since none had had literary training. Lewis Gannett of the *Herald Tribune* had been a specialist in foreign affairs, Harry Hansen of *The World* a managing editor, and William Soskin of the *Evening Post* a war correspondent before undertaking daily book reviews.

Times man John Chamberlain, she wrote, "so far outshines his fellow book columnists that we tend to overestimate his talents" precisely because his background was literary. In any case, McCarthy moaned, whatever a reviewer's training had been was wholly irrelevant to his purpose. His job was to sell books. Since his column, at the very least, had to pay for itself in publishers' advertisements, the inevitable conclusion was that criticism is most honest where it is furthest removed from advertising. In her final words on contemporary reviewing, she halfheartedly praised critics like Edmund Wilson, Joseph Wood Krutch, Rebecca West, Frances Newman, Louis Kronenberger, Clifton Fadiman, and Robert Morss Lovett, who "have seemed in varying degrees perspicacious, but their faint catcalls have been drowned out by the bravos of the publishers' claque. Moreover, none of these critics, with the exception of Mr. Wilson, has made any extended effort to relate what is valuable in modern literature to the body of the literature of the past."

The "Saint Valentine's massacre of reviewers and critics," as *Time* magazine described the series, made enemies, of course, but it gave Mary McCarthy an instant "name." It also established her reputation as a brutally honest critic bent on exposing literary ineptitude. *The Nation*'s editors were apparently pleased, as they commissioned another series from her, a review of contemporary drama critics. In "Our Actors and the Critics," she took theatrical reviewers to task for their inability to say anything concrete and helpful about acting. (Not long after the series ran, she produced her own example of a particularized critique of acting. In "Versions of Shakespeare," she described John Gielgud's style of playing Hamlet as "so decorated, so crammed with minutiae of gesture, pause, and movement that its general outline was imperceptible to an audience.")

In addition to the two series and several book reviews, *The Nation*'s editors asked McCarthy to assess the state of detective fiction over the last decade. In "Murder and Karl Marx," she claimed that the detective story in the years 1926–1936 had become "increasingly social-minded." Before the middle 1920s "the interest was focused on the puzzle" of discovering how a murder was committed and by whom, but when the "possibilities of the puzzle" were exhausted, mystery writers turned their attention to politics and social problems to heighten interest in their novels. With the exception of Carter Dickson, she wrote, all of them "present a virtually united front against any form of social innovation." Carter Dickson, on the other hand, "counts a life-long adherence to socialism among his other eccentricities."

Reviews in *The Nation*, no matter how sensational, did not pay well.

Thus, while Johnsrud struggled with his scripts, Mary McCarthy resorted to typing and editing chores for Benjamin Stolberg, a curmudgeonly but witty journalist who supported himself by doing free-lance work. At the time McCarthy worked for him, he was covering labor news for *The Nation, The New Republic,* and the *Evening Post.* Unfortunately, Stolberg was subject to frequent writing blocks. McCarthy concluded, after a while, that his current block was more or less permanent, so she resumed free-lance work for Emmanuel J. Rousuck, whose sometimes unpaid employee she had been the summer before her graduation.

The Carleton Gallery, where she had typed letters soliciting clients, specialized in selling portraits of dogs painted by the Englishwoman Maud Earl. Caged dogs, "wild with hunger," were often shipped by Railway Express to the gallery, which then delivered them to Maud Earl's apartment for a sitting. Mary McCarthy, who was frightened of dogs, had found working for Rousuck in 1933 sometimes traumatic. (Apparently she did not like cats either. One of the Vassar classmates she roomed with the summer she worked at the gallery remembers McCarthy's reaction to a stray kitten that wandered into the basement of their brownstone. "When Mary saw it . . . she screeched and carried on as though it were a snake about to attack her. I gathered she was not an animal lover.") But in 1936, when she spent half days composing letters and brochures for Rousuck, it was in the more serene environment of the Ehrich Newhouse Galleries. Rousuck had advanced to selling eighteenth-century English paintings of sporting scenes, the best by George Stubbs and Ben Marshall. (Later he rose to a vice presidency of the prestigious Wildenstein and Company.)

The good-looking son of a Jewish tailor from Cleveland, Rousuck had made and lost a pharmaceutical fortune in Ohio before he was twenty-two. When he arrived in New York, he knew nothing about art, but had a passionate love of dogs, especially the Boston bull terrier. In fact, he made his art debut in commissioning portraits of dogs. To court rich clients, he mastered the role of gentleman. He started calling himself Jay instead of Mannie, bought well-made and conservative clothes, filled his closets with highly polished shoes, and rented an apartment on Park Avenue that he filled with valuable antiques and art. He cofounded the National Museum of Racing at Saratoga, judged bull terriers at the annual and very social Madison Square Garden Dog Show, became a director of Guaranty Trust, turned himself into a celebrated womanizer (whom women trusted), and did all that was expected of a bon vivant who appeared regularly in Cholly Knickerbocker's column. He also had important gangland and police connections, but even so, he once spent a short time in prison for unpaid alimony, and another time he narrowly escaped jail after being caught wiretapping a competitor.

Mary McCarthy always liked Rousuck, even if he was something of a rogue. Others close to her never understood the attraction. Johnsrud resented Rousuck's not having paid her regularly the summer of 1933. Kevin McCarthy saw in Rousuck "a rough gem who smoothed himself over with fine tailoring, fancy apartments, and expensive restaurants." (His sister always said she liked being taken to Voisin and the Colony.) Edmund Wilson said it was her "outlaw side" that was fascinated by Rousuck. Whatever it was, she remained friends with Rousuck until his death in 1970, and this despite an uncomplimentary portrayal of him as Mr. Sheer in "Rogue's Gallery," a short story that became the second chapter of *The Company She Keeps.*

Rousuck had known that she was writing about him, so he invited her to dinner at the New Weston Hotel, suggesting that she bring her manuscript. She left the manuscript with the bellboy, who had been bribed by Rousuck to "lose" it. Later he read the manuscript (he had filched it out of the checkroom) and was furious. He threatened to sue McCarthy if she did not make changes. Together they made modifications, inventing objects of art for Mr. Sheer to sell, such as the shabby collection of priests' robes and the crystal cuff links and brooches adorned with portraits of dogs. Rousuck wanted cats, but McCarthy insisted on keeping dogs. Their revisions, obviously, did not fully disguise Rousuck, but he forgave her anyway. McCarthy continued to write descriptions of paintings for him on a free-lance basis.

While the manner in which the Johnsruds supported themselves required considerable energy and provoked occasional worry, their life, at least at the beginning of their marriage, was gay and even, at times, happy. This was owing partly to McCarthy's natural optimism and partly to Johnsrud's conviviality. Despite his sizable ego and cool reserve, he could be fun and sometimes even sympathetic. Yet his nature had "a sardonic twist that inclined him to behave like a paradox," McCarthy wrote twenty years after their divorce, "to follow the mode and despise it, live in a Beekman Place apartment while lacking the money to buy groceries, play bridge with society couples and poker with the stage electricians, dress in the English style and carry a walking stick while wearing a red necktie. . . . I suppose there was something in him of both the victim and the leader. . . . Notions of the superman and the genius flickered across his thoughts. . . . It was only in plays," [however,] "that he entered 'at the head of the mob.' "

When Johnsrud was not working in a play, he and Mary often joined

Vassar classmate Julia Denison for picnic lunches on the roof of her cousin's penthouse apartment. "The Johnsruds came complete with type-writers, beer, and sandwiches," Denison later recalled, "Mary to work on her book reviewing, John struggling with a script he was writing." Their social life consisted of bridge games, of literary parties (Granville Hicks remembered one at which McCarthy looked "very chic and very formidable, acting . . . as if she felt it was her party"), of evenings and weekends with Margaret Miller and Elizabeth Bishop, Mary's *Con Spirito* cohorts, of cocktail parties in their own apartment, of nightclub hopping from Harlem to Greenwich Village, and of dances at Webster Hall, where they met left-wing activists.

It was at one of these Webster Hall dances, when Johnsrud was on the road (he had a part in *Winterset*), that Mary McCarthy met John Porter, an attractive young man suitable for a "Romantic Adventure," she confided to Frani Blough. The Maxwell Anderson play, which had had a long run in New York, toured all winter and spring of 1936, giving Mary McCarthy ample time to fall in love with Porter. Although unem-ployed at the time of their affair, Porter liked to take McCarthy dancing, wheedling the necessary money out of his domineering mother, who, with her weak husband, lived on income derived from their tenements in Harlem. They had lost most of their money during the depression, but because John was their only child, they spent lavishly on him, send-ing him in style to Williams College and then to Europe, where he landed a job on the Paris *Herald Tribune* and met James Joyce. Porter was lively and cheerful, and a good dancer. A tenderhearted beau, who was eager to please Mary McCarthy, he liked to quote the French critic and novelist Rémy de Gourmont. By the time the theater company returned to New York, Mary told Johnsrud she wanted a divorce in order to marry Porter. Her husband was "very cut up," despite the fact (which McCarthy was unaware of at the time) that he had not been faithful to her.

In a remarkable piece of satirical self-exposure, Mary McCarthy pre-sented a fictionalized account of the breakup with Johnsrud and the affair with Porter in her first published fiction. "Cruel and Barbarous Treat-ment" appeared in the *Southern Review* in the spring of 1939. In it she is the "Married Woman" who desires a public stage for her affair. "Private cohabitation, long continued, was, she concluded, a bore. . . . She was now ready, indeed hungry, to hear What People Would Say."

The Johnsruds separated early in the summer. Just before leaving for Reno, where she obtained the divorce, Mary McCarthy took a week's holiday with John Porter at his parents' summer house in Water Mill,

on Long Island. On the train out West, however, she forgot Porter all
too quickly. She met a man with whom she only meant to have a few
drinks, but to her surprise, she woke up the next morning in his berth.
She turned the incident into a comic and honest look at herself in her
short story "The Man in the Brooks Brothers Shirt." The six-week
residency in Reno passed quickly and pleasantly. She lived in a boarding
house on Mill Street run by a woman who cooked superbly, and met an
instructor from the University of Connecticut with whom she toured the
state. During her Nevada residency she discovered that she no longer
loved Porter. Startled by his "embarrassingly sentimental and slightly
mechanical letters," she perceived that he was weak and not very bright,
which in the first flush of romance had not been apparent to her.

Before returning to New York, she stopped in Seattle to visit her
grandparents. Back in the East by late August, she no longer wanted to
marry Porter but lacked the courage to tell him. Instead, she reneged
on a promise to accompany him to Mexico, yet assured him she would
write care of General Delivery, Laredo. Since he had gone south to write
a travel guide, and planned to be back in New York within a short time,
she worried about how she would finally break the news. Worry gave
way to alarm when she received no responses to her letters. Her only
communication from Mexico was a Christmas package, with no name or
message, that contained a peculiar-looking rug made of pony skin and
lined with cheap pale blue rayon—tacky merchandise altogether uncharacteristic of John Porter. Because he had always been good at selecting the perfect present, she could not believe the rug was from Porter,
so she wrote the sender. A wire came back: PACKAGE COMES FROM
JOHN PORTER MEXICO. A month later Porter's mother, who disliked
McCarthy, called to ask if she knew where John was. His parents had not
heard from him, either, in the six months since he had left New York.
Many months later they learned he was dead. "He had died in a guest
house of neglect, on that older woman's property," McCarthy wrote a
friend. "He had been her lover and she had tired of him and put him
in a shack. There he contracted some disease and now I can't remember
what. Diphtheria, I think, but it might have been typhoid or typhus.
Nobody did anything about it, and he died."

Johnsrud, too, died prematurely. Continuing to write plays that were
never produced, he perished in a fire (he went into his burning room
to save a manuscript) in New York's Hotel Brevoort during World
War II.

PART THREE

CHAPTER VII

THE *P.R.* BOYS
(1936–1937)

ONE LEGACY of Mary McCarthy's three-year marriage to Harold Johnsrud was her initiation into the political left. Johnsrud was not an ideologue, but he did harbor a lifelong resentment of capitalism, probably stemming from his father's adversities. When Harold was a boy, Iver Johnsrud had been the scapegoat in an academic scandal that cost him his job as principal of a northern Minnesota school and forced him to become a door-to-door salesman. Bitterness about his father's humiliations disposed Harold Johnsrud to be receptive to leftist circles of people both in the theater and in his wife's literary milieu. Because of these acquaintances, he and Mary took part in a demonstration supporting a waiters' strike at the Waldorf (they were dressed in evening clothes); attended fund-raising affairs for sharecroppers, the Theatre Union, and the *New Masses*; and went to left-wing parties where, she later remembered, "the atmosphere was horribly sordid, with cigarette burns on the tables, spilled drinks, ashes everywhere, people passed out on the bed with coats or necking."

The dogmatism and humorlessness of so many of the people they met at these parties forestalled a serious political commitment from the Johnsruds. Still, McCarthy surprised herself by a book review she composed in Reno for *The Nation*. "Book bites Mary," an amused literary editor responded to her glowing piece on Sylvia Townsend Warner's *Summer Will Show,* a novel set in Paris in 1848. Although the heroine sacrifices husband, money, family connections, and friends to the Paris Commune, she finally finds peace and joy in *The Communist Manifesto.* Next, McCarthy requested an assignment to cover a Seattle labor strike for *The Nation,* which resulted in "Circus Politics in Washington State." "While my grandparents took comfort from the fact that I seemed to be against Roosevelt, the Democrats, and the tsars of the A. F. of L.," she wrote many years later, "they did not quite grasp my explanation that I was criticizing from the left."

Many intellectuals moved to the political left in the 1930s. For some, socialism was too mild a remedy for society's ills. Not surprisingly, they looked on FDR's New Deal as totally inadequate. Despite all that Roosevelt had accomplished in his first months in office, the economy remained intractable. Dozens of intellectuals espoused Communism, including

John Dos Passos, Sherwood Anderson, Erskine Caldwell, Lincoln Steff-
ens, Granville Hicks, Upton Sinclair, and Edmund Wilson. Wilson
urged taking "Communism away from the Communists," and subsequently added that Russia was "the moral top of the world where the
light never really goes out." Even F. Scott Fitzgerald was reading Marx.
New Russia's Primer, praising Russia's order and criticizing America's
disorder, was a Book-of-the-Month Club choice, and Will Rogers said,
"Those rascals in Russia have got mighty good ideas. Just think of
everybody in a country going to work." Yet the Communist Party in
America, even at its crest, never had more than seventy-five thousand
members. (The perception of many living in Greenwich Village, where
Mary McCarthy settled after her divorce, was that the numbers were
much greater.)

After a short stay in September at the Lafayette Hotel, where she had
had her wedding reception, she found a tiny apartment on Gay Street.
Elizabeth Bishop lived nearby on Charles Street in a building owned by
the same landlord. Lonely at first, McCarthy ate alone at home or at
Shima's or the Jumble Shop, retreats for writers, painters, and theatrical
people. Occasionally she saw Johnsrud, who was also living in the Village. She managed to survive, thanks to checks from the Prestons, the
now somewhat meager dividends from Capitol Elevator stock, the work
she continued to do for Emmanuel Rousuck's gallery, an occasional
review for *The Nation,* and part-time manuscript reading at home for the
publishing house Covici-Friede, where by the end of the year she was
working full-time as an editorial assistant at twenty-five dollars a week.
Most employees at Covici-Friede were either Communists or fellow
travelers. In fact, when Pascal Covici had wanted to publish John Steinbeck's *In Dubious Battle,* a book that McCarthy reviewed for *The Nation,*
one of his senior editors objected because it did not endorse the official
Communist line on labor warfare—the subject of the book.

By October 1936 Mary McCarthy was meeting people and enjoying
an active social life. James T. Farrell, who had just published the final
book of his Studs Lonigan trilogy, and his wife, actress Hortense Alden,
started asking her to the Sunday open houses they frequently gave.
Farrell was charmed by McCarthy's eagerness and air of expectation;
"she was just waiting for the world" was the way he remembered her
at these Sunday gatherings. In November the Farrells took her to a
publisher's party honoring a former cartoonist for the old *Masses,* a
defunct leftist magazine that had been as much interested in radical art
as in politics. During the party Farrell circulated among the guests,
asking whomever he could nab what he or she thought about the Mos-

cow Trials. McCarthy recalled the scene in her essay "My Confession."

"Do you think Trotsky is entitled to a hearing?" he asked each in turn.

"Trotsky? What has Trotsky done?" McCarthy replied.

Stories of the Moscow Trials had been in the papers since August, but McCarthy, who had been in Reno and Seattle when they first appeared, was hazy about the details. Farrell patiently explained that Trotsky had been accused of conspiring with the Nazis to assassinate Stalin and other Soviet officials and of fostering a counterrevolutionary plot within the Soviet Union. Trotsky had been the second most influential man in Russia after the October Revolution, but when Lenin died, he lost power to Stalin, who eventually deported him. At this time he was seeking asylum in Mexico and publicly criticizing Stalin.

"What do you want me to say?" McCarthy asked. "I don't know anything about it."

"Trotsky denies the charges," Farrell answered. "He declares it's a GPU fabrication. Do you think he's entitled to a hearing?"

"Why, of course," she laughed. "Were there people who would say that Trotsky was *not* entitled to hearing?"

"She says Trotsky is entitled to his day in court," Farrell told the guests crowding around them. "One more thing, Mary," he continued; "do you believe that Trotsky should have the right of asylum?"

"Yes, Trotsky, in my opinion, is entitled to the right of asylum."

Four days later she received a letter from something called The American Committee for the Defense of Leon Trotsky and discovered her name on the committee's letterhead. Furious that her name had been used without her consent, she determined to write to Farrell, one of the committee's organizers, demanding that he remove it. Before she acted, however, she started getting late-night phone calls from Communist acquaintances she barely knew, advising her to get off the committee. Most of the other committee members were also called; all were told they were undermining faith in the only power in the world that was fighting fascism. In addition to being harassed by telephone, McCarthy and fellow committee members were addressed in an open letter published in the *New Masses,* a monthly magazine committed to Stalinism, urging them to resign immediately from the Committee for the Defense of Trotsky. Fifty writers, editors, and artists signed the letter, among them Heywood Broun, Theodore Dreiser, Lillian Hellman, Corliss Lamont, and Lillian Wald. Following this, several members of the Trotsky defense committee issued public statements deploring the use of their names.

To McCarthy, it was clear that the Communist Party was trying to stifle the committee with heavy-handed tactics, so—even though she knew nothing about it, or about the Moscow Trials, or about Trotsky, for that matter—she leapt to the committee's defense. That the Communists and "fellow-traveling liberals" were "infuriated at the idea of a free inquiry" made her think Trotsky was probably innocent. To find out, as well as to defend herself against the Stalinists among whom she worked at Covici-Friede and whom she frequently met at parties, she read everything available on the Moscow Trials. It appeared to her they were "monstrous" frame-ups. She discovered, for example, that "the defendant, Pyatakov, flew to Oslo to 'conspire' with Trotsky during a winter when, according to the authorities, no planes landed at the Oslo airport; the defendant, Holtzmann, met Trotsky's son, Sedov, in 1936, at the Hotel Bristol in Copenhagen, which had burned down in 1912; the witness, Romm, met Trotsky in Paris at a time when numerous depositions testified that he had been in Royan, among clouds of witnesses. . . . These were only the most glaring discrepancies. . . . Everywhere you touched the case something crumbled."

The American Committee for the Defense of Leon Trotsky, which had formed a commission of inquiry into the Soviet charges against Trotsky, joined similar English, French, and Czechoslovak committees on an international investigating commission to review the Moscow Trials. This provoked an outcry from the pro-Stalin left. Several prominent intellectuals, many of whom had signed the *New Masses* letter attacking the committee members, published a manifesto which declared that to impugn the Soviet Union by casting doubt about the fairness of the trials was to deal "a blow to the forces of progress."

The commission sat from April 10 to 17, 1937, in the red and blue villa of Diego Rivera in Coyoacan, Mexico. The group was chaired by the American philosopher and educator John Dewey, seventy-eight years old at the time. Benjamin Stolberg, Mary McCarthy's one-time employer, was a member and so was John Chamberlain, one of the critics censured in "Our Critics, Right or Wrong." The commission had invited representatives of the Soviet government, the American Communist Party, and the Mexican Communist Party, as well as Joseph Brodsky, a noted Communist lawyer, to be present at the hearings and to have full power to cross-examine Trotsky. None accepted. The commission's questioning, painstaking and thorough, lasted four days. Trotsky submitted published articles, private letters, dozens of affidavits (authenticating this point and that) from witnesses scattered throughout the world. He displayed a vigorous mind, albeit straitjacketed by Marxism, and proved

to the commission's satisfaction that he was innocent. (Two years later a Soviet agent drove an ax into Trotsky's skull, thereby eliminating Stalin's most outspoken critic.)

The Moscow Trials split the American intelligentsia into Stalinists and anti-Stalinists. The Stalinists, of course, went along with the Soviet Union; and the anti-Stalinists, because of the difficulties they encountered in their fight against the Moscow Trials, learned to understand the modern Communist state and movement long before any other Americans. From this time forward, Mary McCarthy belonged solidly to the anti-Stalinists. As she explained later, "For my generation, Stalinism, which had to be opposed, produced the so-called non-Communist Left, not a movement, not even a sect, but a preference, a political taste shared by an age group resembling a veterans' organization."

Twenty years after Mary McCarthy's involvement in the Trotsky affair, she told James Farrell, "I knew you were complimenting me when you asked my opinion (for I really had no title to one) but I didn't think I was being asked for a signature. But I've never held that against you; it changed my life—for the better." At first, the change was evident only in small matters. At committee meetings, for example, she tried to act more seriously, like other members. (During one meeting she suddenly realized that she was the only person present who knew or cared that it was Valentine's Day.) She switched from the *Herald Tribune* to the *Times*. She gave up bridge, crossword puzzles, detective fiction, and popular novels. And she gave up her old Stalinist friends. Later the Moscow Trials provided a background for *The Company She Keeps*. Its heroine, Margaret Sargent, hotly defends Trotsky in "The Genial Host"; and in "Portrait of the Intellectual as a Yale Man," where the historical context is central to the story, she defends Trotsky among Stalinist editors who can fire her from the magazine job she needs.

What the Moscow Trials did, actually, was to turn Mary McCarthy into an intellectual in the French sense of that word—a literary person who is concerned with public affairs. Her interest was not with partisan politics but with larger issues, such as the nature of the Soviet Union; the prospects for socialism in the United States; and, later, the legitimacy of supporting the capitalist Western democracies in World War II; the plight of fellow intellectuals in totalitarian countries. Though the change in Mary McCarthy's life did not become clear to her until much later, it began with her involvement with the Trotsky committee. "Like Stendhal's hero, who took part in something confused and disarrayed and insignificant that he later learned was the Battle of Waterloo," she would remember, "I joined the anti-Communist movement without meaning to and only found out afterward, through others, the meaning or 'name' assigned to what I had done."

In late spring, after Trotsky's "counter-trial," Mary McCarthy began to see Philip Rahv. She had met him before at Farrell's parties and, knowing that he read Russian (as well as German, French, English, and Hebrew), had called on him for translations when Russian manuscripts arrived at Covici-Friede. At first, she thought he was "an intransigent . . . , pontificating young Marxist," but by summer they were living together, first in a friend's apartment on Beekman Place, then, in the fall of 1937, in their own apartment on East End Avenue. Rahv was born Ilya Greenberg in the Ukraine. Authoritarian and polemical, he insisted that literature began with Dostoyevsky and ended with Joyce and Eliot. He could be perverse, intimidating, and gruff. The sheer force of his personality was such that the young poet Delmore Schwartz called him "manic-impressive" and "Philip Slav." Schwartz wrote one page of a short story, called "The Complete Adventuress," about the McCarthy-Rahv affair. Although the lovers' identity is discernible without help, Schwartz removed any doubt by writing in the margin, "Mary and Philip (1937)."

Helena was a very handsome and very clever young woman. . . . When Helena met Stanislaus, a big and important radical politician, she felt for the first time that she was with one who pleased her whole being. She went to live with Stanislaus and she took a job which brought her into touch with radical politics. She soon found that there was a roughness about Stanislaus and a rudeness and a habit of being too serious in conversation which she did not like in the least. She tried to correct his rudeness and roughness, his habit of getting into taxis before she did, and his brusqueness in conversing with persons he did not estimate highly. And she tried to make him cultivate a lightness of tone in conversation, making him read the sophisticated metropolitan periodicals. Stanislaus was so pleased with Helena that he tried to improve himself, although lightness was foreign to his whole being. More and more, Helena felt an extraordinary admiration as well as affection for Stanislaus. He was superior to her and inferior to her in precisely the way that suited her profoundest need. To their friends who composed a curious circle in which those who were engaged in left-wing politics mixed with those from the theatre and the concert-hall, the infatuation Helena felt and expressed for Stanislaus was such as to make it difficult for one to keep a straight face, for Stanislaus might remark merely that the day had been a cold one for early October and Helena then felt compelled to declare that Stanislaus had a consciousness of the external world which disregarded nothing.

While living on Beekman Place with Rahv, Mary McCarthy had agreed to collaborate with Roger Craig, a *New York Times* writer, on a project for Modern Age Books. The well-known radio commentator H. V. Kaltenborn had sold a collection of his old CBS broadcasts to Modern Age. When the time arrived to turn this material into a book, the publisher discovered that much of it consisted of blurred and incomplete carbons. Thus Craig and McCarthy had to write the book almost from scratch, a task that they found most pleasant, though it took most of the summer of 1937. They worked in Kaltenborn's garden in Brooklyn Heights, frequently sipping spritzers with the great man himself— slightly egotistical and pompous, according to McCarthy, but nice—and his gentle German wife, who was charming.

Using Kaltenborn's chapter titles, the ghostwriters divided the topics between them. Thus, Mary McCarthy did the chapters on France, Spain, and the automobile-industry strikes. Despite a confusing amalgam of viewpoints—McCarthy wrote from an anti-Stalinist point of view; Craig was mildly conservative; Kaltenborn, some of whose material they felt bound to incorporate, was strongly conservative; and Kaltenborn's son tried to rewrite parts from his Stalinist perspective—*Kaltenborn Edits the News* received favorable reviews. The *Saturday Review*'s commentary was typical: "While necessarily confining himself to the 'high spots' of each country which he discusses, Mr. Kaltenborn shows excellent critical judgment both in the selection of facts and in comment thereon. Particularly is this true of his pages devoted to the Spanish Civil War." While it is true that McCarthy presented a balanced view of the fighting forces in Spain, what was more remarkable was the clarity of the presentation. Most contemporary versions of the Spanish Civil War were so garbled that a reader got lost in a maze of factions.

Besides the commission from Modern Age Books and her regular work at Covici-Friede, Mary McCarthy continued to write book reviews for *The Nation* (in the July 17 issue McCarthy and Rahv reviews ran side by side). Editorially, *The Nation* was pro-Communist, but Margaret Marshall, who edited the book section, frequently invited well-known anti-Stalinists to review important books. Rahv and McCarthy finally and dramatically dissolved any ties between themselves and the Stalinists in June, when they spoke in favor of Trotsky at the Second Writers' Con-

gress, supposedly a meeting of all antifascist writers but actually a congress of Stalinist sympathizers. Even so, they continued to publish in *The
Nation*. Also defending Trotsky at the congress were Dwight Macdonald, a former editor of Henry Luce's *Fortune*; Fred Dupee, until
recently the literary editor of the *New Masses*; and William Phillips, a
writer and speaker for the John Reed Clubs, organizations of aspiring
writers and artists sympathetic to Communism. Yet they, too, continued
to write for *The Nation*.

It was this very group of anti-Stalinists—Rahv, McCarthy, Macdonald,
Dupee, and Phillips—who revived the literary journal *Partisan Review*.
In fact, they were hard at work by summer. Rahv had already asked
Ignazio Silone, Harry Levin, Lionel Abel, and Meyer Schapiro to submit
articles for the new publication. Macdonald extracted a promise from
Edmund Wilson to do an article on Marxist criticism for the first issue.

"Fred and I have been looking for an office," Rahv wrote Macdonald
in August. "All kinds of things have been turned up and today Mary is
going down to see rooms in *The Nation* building. We ought to have one
by the end of the week and we are not going to pay more than $30."
They located in Union Square—an area of run-down buildings and
cheap shops—where radical demonstrations were frequently held. "The
whole region," McCarthy explained, "was Communist territory: 'they'
were everywhere—in the streets, in the cafeterias; nearly every derelict
building contained at least one of their front-groups or schools or publications. Later, when the magazine moved to the old Bible House on
Astor Place, the *New Masses* had offices on the same floor, and meeting
'them' in the elevator, riding down in silence, enduring their cold scru-
tiny, was a prospect often joked about but dreaded. The fact of being
surrounded physically, of running a gamut, was a concrete illustration of
their power in New York at that time, a power that spread uptown to
publishers' offices and to the Broadway theater and to various cultural
agencies of the government, like the W. P. A. Writers Project and the
Federal Theatre."

There was irony in their being "surrounded," since the new *Partisan
Review* had been "stolen," as McCarthy described it, from the Communists. The original *Partisan Review* had been a publication of the New
York John Reed Club. John Reed Clubs, named for the flamboyant
American journalist who had backed the triumphant Bolsheviks in the
Russian Revolution, had sprung up all over America during the early
1930s. Belligerently titled little magazines—*Left Front, Left Review, Left-
ward*, the *Cauldron, Blast, Dynamo, Anvil, Partisan*, and the *Hammer*—
were established by the various clubs to publish the proletarian poetry

and prose of their young and radical members. Philip Rahv and William Phillips had founded *Partisan Review* in 1934 as a New York John Reed publication. In 1935 the Communists jettisoned the John Reed Clubs, thereby giving *Partisan Review* its independence. From this point on, its relations with the Communist Party deteriorated until the end of 1936, when the magazine discontinued publication. Dismayed by the Moscow Trials, Rahv and Phillips severed all bonds with the Communist Party. A year elapsed between the suspension of *Partisan Review* and its revival. When the new *Partisan Review* appeared, in December 1937, its editorial board—besides Rahv and Phillips—included Mary McCarthy, Dwight Macdonald, Fred Dupee, and George L. K. Morris, who provided about three thousand dollars in operating funds a year. McCarthy felt that

> the magazine had accepted me, unwillingly, as an editor because I had a "minute" name and was the girl friend of one of the "boys," who had issued a ukase on my behalf. . . . I used to come down to the office on Saturdays . . . and listen to the men argue.
> And I remained, as the *Partisan Review* boys said, absolutely bourgeois throughout. They always said to me very sternly, "You're really a throwback. You're really a twenties figure." . . . I was wounded. I was a sort of gay, goodtime girl from their point of view. And they were men of the Thirties. Very serious. That's why my position was so . . . lowly. I had been married to an actor and was supposed to know something about the theatre so I began writing a theatre column for them. Once a month, late at night, after the dishes were done, I would write my "Theatre Chronicle," hoping not to sound too bourgeois and give the Communists ammunition. . . . At that time (or should I say still?) nobody connected with the stage had ever heard of *Partisan Review*.

She was certain that because she was an editor, her colleagues felt that she had to be given *something* to do, and since the other editors considered the theater to be of no consequence, if she made mistakes, who cared? "There is nothing of 'no consequence' that goes into the magazine," William Phillips said years later. "It was Mary's wit that prompted us to make her our drama critic."

Whatever the reason she was chosen, people liked her "Theatre Chronicle"; "it was something a little different," McCarthy later wrote. William Barrett, who became an editor of *Partisan Review* in 1945, believed that her theater reviews were not only the "most lively and sparkling writing" in the journal, but *her* best writing too. She was in her element, he wrote in a 1982 memoir, because she had a message—"the language of our current American drama had forsworn literature; as written, it could hardly be read." In a retrospective essay summing up her "Theatre Chronicle," McCarthy wrote on just this point.

> As a writer, I am troubled by the fact that most American plays are so badly written. This fact, if it is noticed at all, is usually justified in the name of "theatre," as though, for the stage, words did not matter and it was only the action that counted. But no theatre, except the American theatre, has ever been based on such a premise. The list of playwrights from Aeschylus through Shaw is a list of masters of language. Yet the American playwright is "excused" from this responsibility, like some wretched pupil bringing a note from his parent: "Please excuse Tennessee or Arthur or Clifford."

She continued reviewing for *Partisan Review* for two and a half decades, even though she was an editor only for the first three issues.

Later she was asked to write a theater column for *Esquire* and for *The New Republic* (she said no to both), and the director of Princeton's Christian Gauss Lectures invited her to speak on "Current Realism in the American Theatre." Still later she lectured on American theater during a State Department tour of Eastern Europe and the British Isles.

Farrar, Straus and Company published two collections of these reviews—*Sights and Spectacles: Theatre Chronicles, 1937–1956* and *Mary McCarthy's Theatre Chronicles, 1937–1962.* In the introduction to *Sights and Spectacles,* she deplored the "tone of cocksure, condescending cleverness" in the early pieces, but stood by her judgments.

From the beginning, *Partisan Review* boldly set out to do battle with the Stalinist zeitgeist, even though "the boys," as McCarthy called the principal editors, "were still committed to Marxism, and so were the other young men who figured on the masthead as editors, except one— the backer [George L. K. Morris]. The backer, a young abstract painter from a good old New York family, was so 'confused' politically that one day he went into the Workers' Bookshop (Stalinist) and asked for a copy of Trotsky's *The Revolution Betrayed;* he was wearing spats that day, too, and carrying a cane, and the thought of the figure he must have cut made the rest of us blanch. 'Did anyone recognize you? Do you think they knew who you were?' we all immediately demanded."

Their Marxism notwithstanding, "the boys" did not want any political ties. When Rahv and Phillips had founded *Partisan Review* the first time, its aims were to defend the Soviet Union, to combat fascism and war, and to promote a literature that would express the viewpoint of the working class. But in 1937 the separation of politics from literature became the cornerstone of the new *Partisan Review* 's editorial program.

The editors had determined to publish the best writers irrespective of their political bias. As William Phillips wrote, "T. S. Eliot's ideological conservatism automatically made him taboo in official leftist circles, but to the group around *Partisan Review* he was a major poet, and a revolutionary who—as Edmund Wilson put it in *Axel's Castle*—had accomplished in the area of sensibility a breakthrough analogous to Marxism in political thought." McCarthy expressed the same idea in a more earthy fashion: "We wanted to be wholly independent in artistic matters, and the daring of our attitude was summed up in the statement that we would print a poem by T. S. Eliot if we could get one (later we did)." The magazine's first editorial declared "unequivocal independence" and disclaimed "obligation to any organized political expression."

Not only did Stalinists on *The New Republic, The Nation,* and the *New Masses* attack this policy, but Trotsky himself deplored the editors' lack of ideological commitment, which he felt was essential for an effective struggle against Stalinism. After the first issue appeared, he wrote the editors:

> So far as your publication is concerned, it wishes, in the main instance, apparently to demonstrate its respectability. You defend yourselves from the Stalinists like well-behaved young ladies whom street rowdies insult. "Why are we attacked?" you complain; "we want only one thing; to live and let others live." Such a policy cannot gain success. It is my general impression that the editors of *Partisan Review* are capable, educated, and intelligent people *but they have nothing to say.* They seek themes which are incapable of hurting anyone but which likewise are incapable of giving anybody a thing. I have never seen or heard of a group with such a mood gaining success, i.e., winning influence and leaving some sort of trace in the history of thought.

Philip Rahv replied diplomatically:

> Given the narrow social and literary base from which we are operating—the isolation of the magazine from the main body of radical intellectuals, and the unprecedented character of our project in the sense that it is the first anti-Stalinist left literary journal in the world, encumbered with a Stalinist past, and subject to the tremendous pressure of the American environment towards disorientation and compromise—given all these adverse conditions it was inevitable that in the first few months of its existence the magazine should grope for direction, feel its way towards possible allies, incline to deal somewhat gingerly and experimentally with issues that ideally require a bold and positive approach,

and lastly—that in its recoil from the gross deceptions, the loud, arrogant proclamations and hooligan tactics of Stalinism, it should in some respects have leaned over backward to appear sane, balanced, and (alas!) respectable.

Privately, he wrote Dwight Macdonald:

> His letter is ridiculous, but he'll come around when he finds out that the burden of the world revolution is not on our shoulders, though we are eager to publish his writing on cultural subjects.

The political independence of *Partisan Review* was a strong factor in its evolution from a minor literary and political journal notable mainly for its repudiation of the Communist movement to its postwar eminence among intellectual periodicals. *Partisan Review* wielded a cultural influence, especially during the 1940s and 1950s, that no journal before or since has been able to equal. Yet, in the main, it was not the editors' determination to concern themselves with revolution in literature rather than in politics that ensured the magazine's success; it was, rather, their literary taste, discernment, and good sense. In the first issue, for example, they positioned the then-unknown Delmore Schwartz's "In Dreams Begin Responsibilities," one of the masterpieces of the short-story genre, as their lead piece, before contributions from established names like Edmund Wilson, Lionel Trilling, Sidney Hook, James T. Farrell, and even Picasso.

Delmore Schwartz often met Rahv and McCarthy for drinks at the Vanderbilt Hotel during the fall of 1937. In December she wrote a friend:

> Tonight I am having dinner with that young man who, I still insist, is a macabre personality, Delmore Schwartz. I am trying to get Covici to make him a good advance on a novel, and am being met, of course, with all the usual publisher's philistinism. Schwartz sent me the outline of his novel this morning. It's called, *The Conditions of Love, or Orpheus in Hell,* and it's about a modern man whose wife has gone insane and whom he must court back from a lunatic asylum. (I insist he's macabre.) In the course of the courtship, the author presents in caricatured, grotesque form all the stages of love. It sounds quite charming and pretty much indebted to Mann, but Mr. Covici doesn't "get it," he says, and I must carry to dinner (expense account) a whole catalogue of literal-minded objections.

After the dinner took place, she wrote:

> About Delmore Schwartz, Philip was right. He is just another precocious Bronx boy: I recognized that at dinner. At the same time I was right, for the boy is a monster, not in the way I thought, but still a monster. He is the most intellectual creature I have ever seen, so intellectual that he is inhuman. If D. H. Lawrence were to hear of him, I'm sure he'd come back from his grave to evangelize against him. He makes one feel that to admit in his cerebral presence any natural inclination or appetite—for food, company, love, gossip, comfort—would be to commit a most indecent solecism. The boy, it seems, has run through Spenglerianism by fifteen, neo-Thomism by seventeen, and Marxism by twenty. Now he has read all the books in the world, and has nothing left to shore up against old age. I brought him home after dinner, and he even struck a chill through Philip, who in some ways leans more to the Schwartz side than he does to mine, which is human-all-too-etcetera. . . . It must be wonderful to be non-frivolous.

Years later Mary McCarthy told Delmore Schwartz's biographer that she was fascinated by his "violet eyes"; he was "beautiful, a mischievous poetic child." Schwartz was dazzled by her, and over the years he devoted many manuscript pages to the vicissitudes of her love life and noted the most intimate gossip about her in his journal. He was intrigued not only because she was not at all prudish about sex, as he was, but chiefly because she represented an ideal of stability and strength that contrasted with his own emotional turmoil. Although he was habitually unhappy, he took solace from her genuine enjoyment of life.

CHAPTER VIII

EDMUND WILSON
(1937–1939)

ERHAPS because he had agreed to write a piece for the first issue of the revived *Partisan Review,* Edmund Wilson asked to meet the editors. When he came around to the office on a Saturday morning in October 1937, they took him to a nearby dive for a drink. McCarthy today remembers her odd choice of morning costume—a black couture dress with bands of fagoting, topped by a silver-fox fur—and that Wilson did not drink. Two or three weeks later Margaret Marshall phoned her. "You know, I've heard from Edmund Wilson," Marshall said, "and he wants to take you and me to dinner. I wonder why he's interested in me." McCarthy agreed to meet Marshall and Wilson at an Italian restaurant named Mary's, and then told the "boys" at *Partisan Review.* They were aghast, afraid that she would discredit them before they managed to get out one issue. "All my habits of mind were bourgeois, my fellow editors used to tell me," she subsequently explained. "They were always afraid that I was going to do something, in real life or print, that would 'disgrace *Partisan Review*'; this was a fear that worried me even more than it did them."

Their fearfulness and her respect for Wilson's reputation made her exceedingly nervous. He was already a distinguished man of letters. As managing editor of *Vanity Fair* and *The New Republic,* he had written about the cultural scene from Chaplin and the *Ziegfeld Follies* to the new literary generation of Hemingway and Fitzgerald. He passed judgment on innovators like Yeats, Joyce, Proust, Valéry, Eliot, and Gertrude Stein, subjects of his first important work, *Axel's Castle,* a ground-breaking introduction to literary modernism. At the onset of the depression he had traveled across America to report on its people and places, then collected the reports in *The American Jitters.* In the late 1920s he had even published a novel, *I Thought of Daisy.* In short, he was one of the best-known critic-journalists in the country.

Because McCarthy had concluded that Wilson was not a drinker, she got Fred Dupee to take her to a bar before the appointed dinner. He bought her several daiquiris, wished her well, and sped her on her way to the restaurant. In no time, she discovered that Wilson drank copiously. Before dinner he ordered several double Manhattans for himself and his two guests, wine with dinner, and B and Bs after. McCarthy progressed from tipsy to high to drunk in quick succession, but not before telling Wilson the story of her life. When she woke up the next morning in a room at the Chelsea Hotel and looked apprehensively at the figure in the bed, she was relieved to find Margaret Marshall. "Oh, I've disgraced *Partisan Review*," she cried to her startled roommate. Later she dragged herself home, where Philip Rahv had spent a sleepless night wondering where she was, and she collapsed. She stayed home from work for two days to recover from a monumental hangover.

No matter what she or the "boys" thought, apparently she had not disgraced herself in Wilson's mind, for she started seeing him—even though she continued to live with Rahv in New York, while Wilson lived in Stamford, Connecticut. By the end of November they were corresponding several times a week. On November 29 McCarthy wrote that "the happenings of the weekend have distracted me so that I can't concentrate," and the next day that

> I am still shaken up. It's pleasant but painful. I should like to come up some evening. I will need a little while to plan it. I am going to the theatre and having guests and dining with prospective Covici-Friede authors every night this week but Friday, and I think that's too soon, from a practical point of view.

And again, the following day she wrote:

> I am still *distraite.* My stomach bounces around and does odd, terrifying things, and my movements are jerky, my will relaxed, and I am full of odd, dreamy abstraction. . . . I know I do miss you. You have dislocated me, in a way. I should like to hear from you so as to get some new bearings. At the moment, I feel out of touch on all fronts, suspended. . . . This weekend I have to devote to writing my theatre column. By the way I intend to go to the Public Library and take out your book and read it—I mean the one with Daisy in the title. I feel I should learn so much, but that, I am afraid, is a delusion, for Philip has read it and he doesn't seem to have any arcane knowledge of you, or if he does he doesn't say.

The next day a curt and surprisingly noncommittal response arrived from Wilson, its objective apparently to make clear that "*I Thought of Daisy* is not autobiographical although it is told in the first person." Even so, she was back in Stamford four days later for dinner and most of the night, taking the milk train back to New York early the next morning.

The train was awful, in that dramatically musty way that milk trains have. The seats were upholstered in a dirty olive-green plush that you never see on normal trains, and half a carful of exhausted people were lying with their clothes disarranged in unlovely postures on the seats. I bummed a cigarette from the only person who was awake, a Jewish man from Springfield, who with his wife and a collection of relatives was on his way to New York to his sister's funeral. He had a little business in Springfield, he said, a haberdashery store where he'd been selling overalls for eighteen years. . . . He asked me if I worked in a "shop." He didn't pronounce the "h" and I didn't know what he meant, and he explained, "a factory." (Maybe you're right. Maybe my appearance is not or was not as soigné as it should be.) He was curious about where I'd been. I said dinner in Stamford, and he rolled his eyes and said "Youth!" reminiscently. . . . Was I going home to my family or . . . ? To my family, I said. Ah, he said, it's lucky it's not a husband; a mother always forgives. . . .

Just after the conversation took this rather sinister turn, I got off at 125th Street. But he was not the connoisseur of the human heart that he passes himself off as. I was surprisingly well received. The domestic situation is o.k. . . .

You are nice. I like you. I think about you pleasantly. I want very much to see you, but no more milk trains. I should have taken that earlier train. One really never wants more than one plans for, and emotional greediness is always unrewarding.

With or without sleep, Mary McCarthy managed to work all day at Covici-Friede, entertain prospective authors at night, volunteer her services to *Partisan Review* on weekends, attend Trotsky committee meetings, and continue to see Wilson weekly while letting no one, not even Rahv, know about their affair. Her next visit to Stamford took place on December 13. The next day she wrote Wilson:

Here is something funny. You remember my telling you in the taxi on the way out that I was supposed to be at the fight? Well, the taxi-driver, it seems, was a man of heart. As soon as I got in the cab at your house, he said without any preliminaries: "I suppose you'd like to hear more about the fight." Then he went on to give me a round-by-round description of it. I thanked him at the station, got out . . . , and didn't even need to buy a morning tabloid in the station to have a picturesque account of the fight at my finger-tips. . . . My dear, I miss you so much. I hope you will come to New York. I had a lovely time with you last night.

The next week they did meet in New York, as Wilson was on his way to spend Christmas with his mother in the house he had grown up in in

Red Bank, New Jersey. Wilson's stopover made her "very merry inside," she wrote him. She had to check herself from smiling openly in the subway and on the street. "I think you're wonderful. I miss you."

Her high spirits departed when she got word that her grandfather Preston had had a stroke on December 30. He died on January 1, 1938. "It was so damned unexpected," she wrote Wilson. "I was counting on his living for another ten or fifteen years. He had written me some rather touching Elizabethan letters on old age, but he was still very active in his law work, and I didn't take it very seriously. I thought of going out there, but it wouldn't have been any use, so I didn't. The whole thing has got me rather shaky: I can't hold a pen still."

In the middle of January she met her brothers Kevin and Preston for dinner. She wrote Wilson that "it will be trying because we have nothing real or natural to talk about, and the conversation inevitably falls into the question-and-answer formula." (She had seen little of her brothers since 1923, when her grandfather had taken her to Seattle. In 1929 she had stopped to see them in Minneapolis on her way to Vassar, and once, when Kevin was a student at Georgetown, she had met him in New York. Beyond a strong physical resemblance, she felt they had nothing in common. Later, however, she became close to Kevin, who stayed in New York to pursue a career in the theater.)

Two days after her reunion with her brothers, Mary wrote to tell Wilson that she "must be a little bit in love. . . . I think you're wonderful. I can't resist saying it, naively, like that." Two weeks later a small paragraph in a New York tabloid announced: "Edmund Wilson and Mary McCarthy are to be married in New Jersey Thursday and will make their home near Stamford, Connecticut. Miss McCarthy was at one time associated with Covici-Friede and is an editor of *Partisan Review,* to which Mr. Wilson contributes. She is best known as one of the authors of the 'Our Critics, Right or Wrong' series in *The Nation,* a few years ago, which concluded that the only living American critic of importance was Edmund Wilson." The wedding took place on Thursday, February 10, 1938, at City Hall in Red Bank, New Jersey. Mary McCarthy resigned from Covici-Friede and went to live with her new husband in a rented house on the Mianus River in Stamford.

The marriage astonished everyone. Philip Rahv had had no idea that Mary McCarthy had been seeing Wilson. ("He was terribly upset," Nancy Macdonald, Dwight Macdonald's first wife, remembered in 1982, "because he was very much in love with her, and she seemed so happy with him.") In fact, the elopement took the whole *Partisan Review* group by surprise." To Delmore Schwartz, however, the marriage was not so startling. He told everyone that Rahv had been so vehement in praising Wilson's critical acumen that the ambitious McCarthy was impelled to switch allegiance. It was true that Rahv frequently said, "Once we get him to contribute regularly, we have set the pace for others of his calibre." And, naturally, any twenty-five-year-old fledgling critic would have been enthralled by the attentions of a man of Wilson's stature. But why Mary McCarthy married Edmund Wilson is not entirely clear. She did not love him, she says today. In fact, when he asked her to marry him, she suggested they live together instead. That she did marry him was owing, probably, to her need for a more settled life. "Before we married," she later said, "he gave the appearance of a man of quiet habits with an interest in books, pictures, and music. He was well-known as a literary critic and I had admired his work even before I met him. During his courtship he held out great promise of a quiet settled life and the rearing of a large family."

The marriage was more understandable from Wilson's point of view. Judging from remarks he made in his journal that Mary McCarthy was "an amusing and provocative companion" of whom he was "extremely fond," and that he felt paternal toward her "child-like side," he certainly had not fallen in love either. But he craved the stability of marriage. His second wife had died in an accident. His first wife, the actress Mary Blair, whom he had divorced in the late 1920s, was now dying of tuberculosis. Wilson wanted to provide their fourteen-year-old daughter, Rosalind, with some sort of regular home life.

Edmund Wilson was an only child who descended from a long line of lawyers—at one time his father was attorney general of New Jersey—doctors, and clergymen. His mother's family traced its lineage to Cotton Mather. He grew up in New Jersey, attending school at Hill and Princeton, and spent summers at Talcottville in upstate New York, a rural spot settled by his ancestors in the 1700s. At the time of his marriage to McCarthy, he was a short, rotund, balding middle-aged man who dressed in rumpled suits. He was seventeen years her senior.

In matters both large and small, the two were very unlike. Wilson intimidated people, never engaging in small talk, but relentlessly quizzing those who happened to know something about a subject that interested him. McCarthy attracted people with her gregarious and optimistic nature. He was brusque and impatient in manner, incisive and abrupt in speech, and he delivered lectures—his chief means of communication—even to close friends. She was courteous and thoughtful, and an attentive listener. He was "a bourgeois family man" with "extremely strong notions of propriety," McCarthy told a friend; but she was too bohemian, Wilson thought, and for that reason he had no desire to associate with her *Partisan Review* friends, contemptuously referring to them as the "Partisanzy Review boys." He did not drive a car, but frequently hired taxis for one-hundred-mile excursions. She learned to drive during their marriage, much to her husband's dismay. He did not smoke, but after a long and arduous workday, he often consumed a bottle of whiskey. She was (and still is) a smoker. Despite their shared desire for stability, the marriage, his third and her second, was doomed from the start.

In a deposition at the time of their separation, McCarthy said:

> Directly after our marriage I discovered that he was addicted to drink and our life together became a series of violent episodes. After I became pregnant, he began beating me with his fists, he would kick me out of bed and again when I was on the floor. A short time before our son was born he knocked me down in the kitchen and kicked me in the stomach. At times he would hold me down on the bed and when I opened my mouth to scream he would hit me on the face and about the body. I was distraught and did not know what to do in my condition.

One thing she did about her condition was to begin psychoanalysis. During her seven-year marriage to Wilson, she was analyzed by three prominent psychoanalysts, Sándor Radó, Richard Frank, and Abraham Kardiner, one of the few Americans to have been analyzed by Sigmund Freud. McCarthy's analysis began in June 1938, only four months after her wedding.

The episode that precipitated the analysis occurred early in the month. The Wilsons had invited Allen Tate and his wife, Caroline Gordon, for dinner and the night. Mary, two months pregnant, went to bed after they had finished eating. Edmund and their guests lingered over drinks. Much later, after the Tates had gone to bed, Wilson stumbled into the bedroom, very drunk. Something infuriated him, because he tore the sheets off the bed with his wife in them, hurling her to the floor. McCarthy says it was because the sheets were blue, very unusual in 1938, that he became so angry. Whatever prompted the outburst, she got up and went back to bed without saying anything. In the morning, however, she flew at him with "How could you?" whereupon he punched her repeatedly in the breasts and slapped her again and again in the face. She started crying hysterically and then vomited, thinking all the while,

"What have I gotten myself into by marrying this madman?" Hattie, the Wilsons' maid, fearing Mary's frenzied state, called the doctor. By the time he arrived, Mary had calmed down.

Neither she nor Wilson disclosed the actual sequence of events. But because her face was swollen, one of her eyes was black, and her arms were badly bruised, and because she was about to superintend a move to another house, the doctor suggested that she go down to New York's Harkness Pavilion to rest while her husband and the maid packed up their belongings. She agreed, but insisted on New York Hospital, where she had had her appendix removed. The Wilsons ordered a taxi for the ninety-minute drive into Manhattan. When they reached the hospital's main entrance, on East Sixty-eighth Street, they let the taxi go, only to discover that no one in admissions had received advance word about McCarthy's arrival. Directed to another part of the hospital, she was admitted, without being told, to Payne Whitney, a mental health clinic attached to Cornell Medical Center. Wilson left for the night. What happened next was remarkably close, McCarthy says, to what befalls Kay in her novel *The Group.* As Kay recalls in chapter 13:

> Sitting there in the lobby, I was just beginning to wonder where the gift shop was and the florist and the circulating library when a tall doctor came out of an office to talk to me. He seemed awfully curious to know how I got the black eye. I laughed and said I'd run into a door, but he didn't get the joke. He kept on pressing me till finally I said, "I won't tell you." I didn't see why he should know what had happened between Harald and me. "We shall have to ask your husband then," he said. "Ask him!" I said, sassily, and I rather wondered what Harald would say. But by then of course Harald was gone. The doctor had the nurse take me upstairs into this depressing room, so drab, with no private bath, no telephone, no nothing. I decided, though, not to make a fuss then, but to go to bed and ask to have my room changed the next morning. While I was thinking that, the nurses got to work and searched me. I couldn't believe it. They went through my pocketbook too and took my matches away. If I wanted a cigarette, they said, I would have to get a light from a nurse. "But what if I want to smoke in bed?" Against the rules, they said; I could only smoke in the lounge or if a staff member was with me in my room. "I'd like a cigarette now," I said. But the nurse said no; I was to go to bed immediately. By this time, of course, I'd caught on to the fact that this couldn't be the regular hospital, but I kept getting these shocks. I was determined not to let them scare me but to act as naturally as I could. When the nurse left, I climbed into bed and was just starting to read the morning paper, which I'd never got

around to, when suddenly the light went out. I told myself it must be the bulb and I rang. Eventually the nurse opened the door. "My light's out," I told her. "Can you fix it, please?" but it seemed she'd turned it out herself, from the switch outside the door. I told her to turn it on again and she refused.

When the nurses removed her belt and the sash of her nightgown, tried to take her wedding ring, looked in her mouth for removable bridges, and kept peering at her through a Judas window, McCarthy realized she was in a mental hospital. That night, thinking about how a person could be put away for years by unfriendly relations, she had great difficulty getting to sleep. In the morning a psychiatrist appeared. When he asked how she had gotten the black eye, McCarthy told the truth. The psychiatrist explained that she was on the admissions floor of Payne Whitney. He predicted she would be moved to the fourth floor, where the relatively stable patients resided, provided her husband verified her story. But Wilson did not appear at the hospital until nine that night. As soon as he admitted that he had given his wife the black eye, she was transferred to the outpatient floor. Wilson persuaded her to say in the clinic at least until after he had completed the move. After all, he argued, she had Blue Cross coverage, thus a Payne Whitney sojourn would be cheaper than a three-week residency in a hotel. (Wilson himself had spent three weeks in a psychiatric unit in 1929.)

The self-imposed confinement was peaceful compared to life with Edmund Wilson. During her stay she participated in occupational therapy, played games, drank Ovaltine with the other patients; but most important, she started psychotherapy with Sándor Radó, a well-known Hungarian psychoanalyst. Meantime, Wilson encouraged his wife to get an abortion:

> About the pregnancy question, I have thought it all over again and I can't come to any other conclusion but that you mustn't go through with a child at this time. It's a disappointment because we'd counted on having one but, after all, we can always have one; and in the meantime it will land you in a situation that you are really unprepared for. You want it very much when you are feeling good about things; but you are still in a generally stirred-up condition and I think you are somewhat confused about this as about other things. You oughtn't to be let in for relationships and responsibilities which you're not ready for at the present time and which might ruin your relationship with me as well as interfere with your psychoanalysis.

Mary McCarthy did not follow her husband's advice, deciding to keep on with the pregnancy. She was discharged from Payne Whitney on June 29, exactly three weeks after admittance, with the diagnosis "Without psychosis; anxiety reaction." Edmund Wilson, who fetched her in a taxi, conveyed her to their new house, also in Stamford, on Shippan Point, a long slice of land that jutted into Long Island Sound. By coincidence, Sándor Radó had rented a summer house nearby. Once a week, in addition to discussing her dreams and childhood, she related her marital troubles, which had resumed almost at once, in hour-long sessions for which Radó charged five dollars.

The Wilsons' only child was born on Christmas. The day before, Mary had been in New York for Frani Blough's wedding and had then returned to Stamford. Less than eight hours later she was back in New York, having been sped there in a taxi for her son's birth.

Reuel Kimball Wilson was named for his father's forebears: Kimball was Wilson's mother's family name, and Reuel Kimball was one of Edmund Wilson's great-uncles. Despite his initial doubts about his wife's continued pregnancy, Wilson was extremely happy about Reuel's birth. He was fond of children, and while he never changed diapers or gave baths, he enjoyed amusing them. As soon as his son could sit up, he entertained him with "mouse antics" that he executed by manipulating his handkerchief. When Reuel got older, Wilson performed magic tricks, put on puppet shows, and took him to Walt Disney movies, which he himself loved. It was Mary, however, who read to Reuel, a practice she began early and kept up until he turned twelve.

Incompatibility was not the only difficulty the Wilsons faced in their marriage; with neither of them holding down a regular job, they never had enough money. Repeatedly Edmund interrupted work on a book-length project in order to turn out articles for a quick infusion of cash. Mary still received Capitol Elevator dividends, but during the first year of their marriage these amounted to only thirteen hundred dollars. Shortly before Reuel's birth, Wilson wrote Christian Gauss, his favorite Princeton professor, to inquire about part-time teaching at the university. "As my family gets larger, it gets to be more of a problem for me to make a living without a regular job," he noted. There was nothing for him at Princeton, but the University of Chicago offered him a teaching position for the summer of 1939 for a wage of twelve hundred dollars, which he gladly accepted. He taught two courses: one on Dickens and the other a criticism course on the "social interpretation of Taine and some of the Marxist stuff."

The Wilsons, with baby and nursemaid, left New York for Chicago on June 1, arriving by train during a prolonged steamy spell. They had sublet Professor Walter Blair's small five-room apartment in Hyde Park, the university section south of the Loop. Mrs. Blair was dismayed to discover four tenants when she had expected two, but the Wilsons convinced her that they would manage by setting up a cot in the dining room for the nurse.

Wilson liked the university. He wrote to Allen Tate that it was lively and interesting, and to John Dos Passos that

> the university is something fantastic—I can't do justice to it in a letter; but the faculty are much more lively and up-to-date and the students much more serious minded than they've seemed to me in general in the East. The professors at least have the feeling that education has new possibilities and that they're really trying to do something in their work. At Princeton, they're resigned to stagnation, and make a point of being old fogies. It's ironical that at a time when at Princeton, which has always had so much to say about humanistic studies, the study of Greek is totally dead, they should be teaching the language here to quite a large number of students, who start in as beginners in college and are reading the *Symposium* at the end of the first year. I have students in my courses of all races, religions, nationalities, and colors—including a German Catholic nun. Some of them are very bright.

The students, however, while in awe of Wilson's renown, were unimpressed by his teaching. Most said he was boring. One complained that Wilson did not seem to like intellectual give-and-take, a trademark of the Chicago method. In a typical Wilson class, a student would express a point of view and Wilson would nod and agree; then a second student might make another statement, diametrically opposed, yet Wilson would again nod and agree. Exasperated by the indulgent professor, several students dropped his courses. (When Mary McCarthy was in her last year at Vassar, she, too, had found Wilson boring. He had lectured on Flaubert, and she had found him "heavy, puffy, nervous, and a terrible speaker, the worst I have ever heard.")

The Wilsons socialized with faculty members, met Sherwood Anderson, enjoyed picnics at the shore of Lake Michigan and walks along the Midway—and quarreled as frequently and ferociously as they had in Connecticut. One night the police were called to quiet them. The fighting stopped when Mary took Reuel to Seattle for a visit with her grandmother. "How cute Reuel looked on his hands and knees in the upper berth, looking out with bright little eyes," Wilson noted in a letter to his wife. He wrote her frequently during their six-week separation, recounting his activities, which consisted mostly of entertaining his four-teen-year-old daughter, Rosalind, who had come to visit after Mary and Reuel had left. Wilson joined her in bicycling, riding, and swimming, and took her to the circus, the zoo, a Hedy Lamarr movie, an occasional dinner with various members of the English department; and once they went to Madison, Wisconsin, to call on a cousin.

But Wilson's initial enthusiasm for Chicago had by now vanished. Impatiently, he was waiting for summer school to be over, so that he could get to Cape Cod. He wrote his wife, "I've been getting bored with this place since you left, and from here the Cape looks like Heaven. Real live air and water, instead of the flatness of the lake and the oppressive inland climate." Two days later he reiterated his anguish: "I miss you and look forward with much yearning to a reunion in more propitious surroundings and in a more agreeable climate than this apartment which I have gotten to hate worse than any place where I think I have ever lived, and this weather, which has continued just as bad since you left." He had decided, he told her, to rent a house in Provincetown for the rest of 1939. His last letter to Seattle was short and curt. Annoyed that his wife wanted to buy a fur coat when he was down to his last dollar, he closed with "I'll be glad to write your grandmother when you drop a line to Rosalind."

Edmund Wilson arrived at the Cape ahead of his wife, who stayed in Seattle until after Labor Day. He rented a house in Truro Center, where they remained for the rest of 1939 and where their fighting continued unabated. In the last months of 1939, however, domestic problems were overshadowed by the news from Europe, where Hitler and Stalin had signed a nonaggression pact and proceeded to carve up the rest of the continent—a blow to the American Stalinists, who had continued to support the Soviet Union as the last line of resistance abroad to the Nazis.

The decade ended with the world at war for the second time in the century. The 1930s had been a formative period for Mary McCarthy, and she later remembered it vividly in *The Group:* minute details of dress, morals, manners, décor, food, drink, politics, social causes, economics, and the arts. She recreated its public and private disputes about Roose-velt and Freud, about Communism and fascism, about Trotskyism and Stalinism, and about the labor movement, the Spanish Civil War, the menace of Hitler, the depression, and the theater as a vehicle for social criticism. Personally, it had been a remarkable ten years for her too—Vassar, an affair with Philip Rahv, marriages to an actor and a leading critic, conversion to the non-Communist intellectual left, participation in the founding of one of America's most influential "little" magazines, and the establishment of Mary McCarthy as a critic in her own right—all this, and she was only twenty-seven years of age.

CHAPTER IX

WELLFLEET
(1940–1945)

CAPE COD makes an abrupt hook to the north at Chatham, forming what is called the Lower Cape or Outer Cape and including the towns of Wellfleet, located seventy-five miles out into the Atlantic; Truro, located next to it; and Provincetown, at the tip of the Cape. This part of the Cape, which attracts intellectuals, artists, and bohemians, became home to the Wilsons from the fall of 1939 until their separation, in 1945. But because the area was so isolated, they also rented something nearer New York City. Briefly, they returned to Trees, the house in Stamford they had occupied at the beginning of their marriage, because Wilson had accepted a job at *The New Republic.* Objecting, however, to the prowar stance of the publishers, he stayed only long enough to edit a special supplement honoring F. Scott Fitzgerald, who had died at the end of 1940. From 1942 to 1945 the Wilsons rented a succession of places in the city—on Stuyvesant Square, in the Little Hotel on Fifty-second Street, in the Gramercy Park Hotel, and on Henderson Place on the Upper East Side. At first only Mary, who was continuing psychoanalysis, came to New York with any regularity, but after 1943, when Edmund was made book editor of *The New Yorker,* both made the trip to the city frequently. Even so, the Cape was their real home and the place where they spent the most time.

They remained in Truro, where they had rented a house in the fall of 1939, until they moved to Wellfleet in the summer of 1940. Here they bought an early-nineteenth-century farmhouse just off the mid-Cape highway (now Route 6) with a five-thousand-dollar loan from Wilson's mother. This became Wilson's residence for the rest of his life. It was a spacious house with several downstairs rooms that looked out on rural views. Upstairs wooden doors, still carrying their original iron latches, led to bedrooms where floors and ceilings tilted noticeably. Cape Cod Bay sat one and a half miles behind the house, the ocean a short distance across the road in front of the house. Wellfleet, with its moors, marshes, inlets, and bald flats exposed at low tide, its dense pine and oak woods, and its tall sand dunes that edged the back shore, was ideal for the Wilsons, both for bringing up Reuel, who was now two and a half years old, and for writing with minimum interruption and distraction.

All day, every day, Wilson closeted himself in his study, and despite the storminess of his years with Mary McCarthy, he was able to publish several important books. *The Triple Thinkers* (1938) and *The Wound and the Bow* (1941) contain essays that range from analyses of authors like Hemingway, James, and Wharton to discussions of Freudian literary theory and the relationship of Marxism and historical interpretation to literature. *To the Finland Station* (1940) traces European revolutionary traditions from Michelet to Lenin to Trotsky. *The Boys in the Back Room* (1941), a title his wife thought of, discusses California novelists. *Notebooks of Night* (1942) is a collection of poems, essays, and a short story. *The Shock of Recognition* (1943), an anthology of American writers' critical views of one another, traces the development of literature in the United States from 1845 to 1938. And *Memoirs of Hecate County* (1946), a collection of six short stories that depict satirically the relations of an intellectual protagonist with his wealthy Westchester neighbors. During this period he interrupted his own work for six weeks to prepare F. Scott Fitzgerald's *The Last Tycoon* for publication, and then donated the money he earned to his friend's estate, saying, "I don't want to make money out of Scott." (The two had been classmates at Princeton.)

His wife, too, was productive during the difficult years of their marriage, publishing ten theater chronicles, four reviews, a memoir, five short stories, two articles, and a novel. This productivity was due partly to Wilson's strong encouragement of her writing. He insisted, despite having very little money, on hiring a nurse for Reuel so that McCarthy could devote part of each day to writing. When she wrote a review of John Dos Passos's *Adventures of a Young Man*—"The style with long, gobbled, average man's sentences running down at the end, its naive, You-know-me-Al habit of direct discourse, has become an iron corset that has constricted the voice-production of the author until he can only talk baby talk"—Wilson mailed his good friend and neighbor, Dos Passos, a cautionary note. Mary "has written about your book in *Partisan Review,* so that if you don't know how to write the next one, it won't be our fault."

Wilson was known for generously encouraging younger talent, and he could not help but be impressed by Mary McCarthy's. Very early in the marriage he told her she should try fiction. He actually confined her to a room, insisting she had a talent for writing short stories. She sat down and typed out "Cruel and Barbarous Treatment" "straight off, without blotting a line" in 1938. Robert Penn Warren published the story in the *Southern Review* in the spring of 1939.

Heartened by her success, she wrote six stories over the next three and a half years, all dealing with the same character. "About halfway through," she told an interviewer, "I began to think of them as a kind of unified story." The story became *The Company She Keeps.* Four of its six chapters were published in magazines before publication as a novel. "The Man in the Brooks Brothers Shirt" appeared in *Partisan Review* in the summer of 1941, but perhaps because the story's seduction scene was so controversial (later a reviewer of the novel characterized this story as "the performance of a highly gifted child who is deliberately and self-consciously trying to shock his elders"), *Partisan Review* rejected "The Genial Host." Indignant, Wilson fired off a letter to Fred Dupee: "I've thought there was something wrong in your shop ever since you passed up that short story of Mary's, which seemed to me the best thing she has written. You people owed her a chance to develop, since she was one of your original group." He also wrote Christian Gauss commending his wife's work: "Mary is well toward the end of a book that is something between a novel and a book of short stories—which I'm very much impressed by. I'm not sure she isn't the woman Stendhal." Clearly, Wilson's encouragement had spurred McCarthy on. (She herself admits, "I would never have written fiction if it hadn't been for him.") Apparently more receptive to "The Genial Host" than the *Partisan Review* editors, Robert Penn Warren published it in the *Southern Review* in the fall of 1941. "Ghostly Father, I Confess" came out in *Harper's Bazaar* in April of 1942. *The Company She Keeps* was published by Simon and Schuster in late spring of 1942.

Margaret Sargent, the protagonist of the novel, tries to find her true self by looking for reflections of it in others. She is a heroine with a background similar to McCarthy's own. The stories are autobiographical, and they include likenesses of several New Yorkers she knew, such as the rogue in "Rogue's Gallery," who is based on art dealer Emmanuel Rousuck, for whom McCarthy had worked, and the intellectual in "Portrait of the Intellectual as a Yale Man," who resembles John Chamberlain, the editor and critic she attacked in "Our Critics, Right or Wrong."

The heroine, unnamed in the first chapter, "Cruel and Barbarous Treatment," is described only as "She," a married "Woman With a Secret," delighting in an affair with a "Young Man," pitting husband against lover in a drama played partly for an audience but mostly for herself. "Actually she doubted whether she could ever have been an actress, acknowledging that she found it more amusing and more gratifying to play herself than to interpret any character conceived by a dramatist." When she grows tired of the affair, she tells her husband she wants a divorce to marry the young man. Then, when she decides she will not marry him after all, she begins to relish a new public role, that of "Young

Divorcee." The second chapter, "Rogue's Gallery," is an extract from memoirs begun by the heroine, and as such is the only chapter written in the first person. In it Margaret Sargent observes the business dealings of Mr. Sheer, who to her is an irresistible charlatan.

In the third chapter, Margaret Sargent worries that "her whole way of life had been assumed for purposes of ostentation," yet she appropriates another role, that of sophisticated New York intellectual, in order to impress "The Man in the Brooks Brothers Shirt," whom she meets on a westbound train. She gets her comeuppance the next morning when she wakes up in his berth, very hung over, and ponders the pathos and ludicrousness of her situation—the loss of her garter, her use of a safety pin to secure her underpants, her need to vomit when the stranger next to her tells her he loves her. When he pours a little whiskey—for medicinal purposes, he assures her—Margaret Sargent instinctively sees the comedy in a situation that minutes before she had described as the nadir. "There was an air of professional rowdyism about their drinking neat whisky early in the morning in a disheveled compartment, that took her fancy." The episode, in fact the entire story, is extravagantly funny, but critics complained, especially about the detail of the safety pin, which they called too "antiseptic" and "clinical." Years later Mary McCarthy told an interviewer that the safety pin was "a damaging detail about the heroine; it was a kind of detail that a worldly man would regard as sloppy and bohemian," and then compulsively disclosed the whole truth—"it was a detail against myself, really." Admitting that the story was autobiographical, she continued, "Nowadays people don't have buttons on underpants, but in those days they did have little buttons on the side that I hadn't bothered to sew on."

Meg is a dinner guest in the fourth chapter, "The Genial Host." Though annoyed that she has been solicited to "sing for her supper"—the host assembles acquaintances for their intellectual and political viewpoints—she performs as expected, hotly defending Trotsky before the Stalinist at the party, because she is too "poor, loveless, lonely" to be able to do without dinner invitations. In the fifth and longest chapter, "Portrait of the Intellectual as a Yale Man," Meg works for a Stalinist magazine from which she is fired for her outspoken Trotskyism.

In the last chapter, "Ghostly Father, I Confess," Meg finally settles down and marries a bullying architect. Her unhappy situation impels her to a psychiatrist's couch. As a matter of course her childhood, very much like Mary McCarthy's, is resurrected. While in analysis, Margaret Sargent loses her faith in psychiatry. She realizes that it is a false god whose price is the negation of personal responsibility. Psychoanalysis is a "ther-

apeutic lie," since its object is to perform a "perfectly simple little
operation," the putting to sleep of conscience—"you are not bad, you
are merely unhappy." The doctor must remove conscience, for it is the
source of her suffering. But Meg realizes that it is conscience which
enables her to see what is outside her own desires. Not to know when
one does wrong and not to care are to lose one's hold on reality and to
remain a child.

The book ends with Meg's determination to live with the pain of
knowing how flawed she is—"preserve me in disunity"—rather than to
lose her conscience. The confrontation with the psychiatrist resolves the
narrative, as well as the thematic structure of the six parts, because
Margaret Sargent, who had set out to find herself, learns that it is more
important to accept herself. *The Company She Keeps* is a kind of autobiography, and everyone in 1942 knew who her characters "really" were;
but now, when the gossip has died and the political-cultural background
has been forgotten, her art, in the end, is what endures. *The Company She
Keeps* is witty, entertaining, and alive with what Malcom Cowley called
(in a generally negative review) the "unusual quality of having been
lived."

Edmund Wilson thought the book marvelous. He recommended it to
Vladimir Nabokov, whose own work Wilson had championed when
Nabokov came to the United States. Nabokov read it and pronounced
it "a splendid thing, clever, poetic, and new—in fact, I'm flabbergasted."
The book reviewers, for the most part, were not as enthusiastic. *Time*
magazine's reviewer claimed it aroused "furious debate among the author's friends and victims"; Malcolm Cowley said it was "not a likeable
book, nor is it very well put together"; the *New York Times* reviewer
believed it was "full of contradictions" and "a fundamental immaturity";
and Clifton Fadiman wrote that "Miss McCarthy is no novelist" and
called the book nothing more than "back-fence gossip." Wilson was
disgusted that so few critics recognized what he saw as the debut of a
major new talent. Only Christopher Isherwood in *The Nation,* who
exclaimed about the "promise of fine things to come" and the reviewer
for *The Atlantic Monthly,* who called Mary McCarthy "a vivid original,"
were as enthusiastic. In any case, *The Company She Keeps* was recognized,
and it sold ten thousand copies, a very respectable sale for a first novel.

In August, only a few months after its publication, Edmund Wilson
met Arthur Schlesinger, Jr., at the time a history professor at Harvard,
on a Boston-to-New York train and got to talking about the book. "I
came down on the train yesterday with Schlesinger," he wrote his wife,
"and he told me very seriously that I oughtn't to let you 'go around

[Simon and Schuster] unchaperoned.' He said that they were so hard-boiled . . . that I or an agent ought to handle your business with them. I think that you probably ought at this point to put the whole thing in the hands of an agent. I am afraid that they gave you the run-around when you were in New York."

The reason the Wilsons were annoyed with Simon and Schuster was a dispute over the rights to the title of the book. RKO bought these rights on July 1, 1942, and used the title, *The Company She Keeps,* for a movie about a girls' reformatory. The contract between the author and the publisher called for a fifty-fifty split of movie revenue. Thus, Simon and Schuster insisted that they receive half of what McCarthy got from RKO. McCarthy said that since the sale was for the title alone, which had been completely her inspiration and to which the publisher contributed nothing, she should not have to share the proceeds of the sale. Simon and Schuster refused to budge from their position, and according to Maria Leiper, McCarthy's editor for *The Company She Keeps,* "that is what sent Mary McCarthy off to seek greener fields." It was owing to Maria Leiper that Mary McCarthy had come to Simon and Schuster in the first place. "It was she," McCarthy said recently, "who first wrote me apropos a story I'd written (perhaps 'Cruel and Barbarous Treatment') to ask if I had something larger that Simon and Schuster might look at."

Mary McCarthy chose Bernice Baumgarten at Brandt and Brandt to represent her. She remembers that Richard Simon, the Simon of Simon and Schuster, had once recommended Baumgarten, who was well known at the time in literary circles as the agent for S. N. Behrman, John Dos Passos, Ford Madox Ford, Edna St. Vincent Millay, and James Gould Cozzens (Baumgarten's husband), among many others. On October 28, 1942, Baumgarten sold the idea for a new McCarthy novel, tentatively titled *Better to Burn,* to Houghton Mifflin for $2,250. It was to be "not a realistic novel, but a work of analysis and abstraction," McCarthy wrote in an application for a fellowship to the John Simon Guggenheim Memorial Foundation. "Each episode will deal with some characteristic feature of married life as we know it: a quarrel, a lunch, a financial crisis, reconciliation, flight, a lie. So far as it is possible, the characters will be nameless, faceless; they will be seen in terms of relationship rather than in terms of themselves." Despite references from writers John Dos Passos, Allen Tate, Robert Penn Warren, and Christopher Isherwood, editors Robert Linscott and Ferris Greenslet, the Shakespearean scholar Theodore Spencer, and the librarian Bernhard Knollenberg, she was not awarded a fellowship. Nor did she write the novel, possibly because it too closely resembled *The Company She Keeps.*

She returned her Houghton Mifflin advance (only $750, which she had received on signing the contract) in 1949.

A professional association with Brandt and Brandt was not the only immediate consequence of *The Company She Keeps*. *New Yorker* editor William Maxwell read the book and liked it so well that he asked McCarthy to submit something to the magazine. "The Company Is Not Responsible" was the first of many short stories and memoirs she wrote for *The New Yorker*. (In the 1950s she entered into a "first reading agreement," which is still in force. In exchange for the first option on any fiction or memoir she writes, the magazine pays one quarter more than its usual fee for whatever it prints. A signed contract, for which McCarthy is paid, is renegotiated annually.) "The Company Is Not Responsible" describes a bus trip on Cape Cod during the World War II years, a serene period on the Cape, despite the appearance of a rubber boat from a Nazi submarine that came ashore one night on the beach near Provincetown, and despite the inconveniences of gas rationing, which forced everyone to hitchhike and to take buses that were always crowded and late. The camaraderie produced by these circumstances is the focus of "The Company Is Not Responsible." Crowded, the bus breaks down, yet the passengers, "together in amity," do not complain. "I leaned my head back on the white tidy of the dirty plush seat," McCarthy wrote, "reflecting on the good-naturedness of Americans, wondering whether it was the war or simply the new inconvenience of travel that made people so accessible to each other. Everything, I thought, is turned into a lark: the missed connections, the long lines of people waiting in the diner, the hotels that have no accommodations, the standing-room only on the trains."

Neither Mary McCarthy nor Edmund Wilson supported the war. Most of their friends, too, opposed America's involvement in World War II, at least at first. Their position was similar to that of World War I socialists who had refused to support either side on the grounds that the war was a struggle of rival imperialisms. So, while they deplored Hitler's Nazism, they objected to the capitalism of the other side. Many of them eventually recognized Nazi Germany as a far greater evil than the most hidebound capitalism, but "at the beginning of the war," McCarthy wrote of the *Partisan Review* editors, "we were all isolationists, the whole group. Then I think after the fall of France—certainly before Pearl Harbor—Philip Rahv wrote an article in which he said in a measured sentence, 'In a certain sense, this is our war.' The rest of us were deeply shocked by this, because we regarded it as a useless imperialist war."

Both Rahv and William Phillips supported the war after 1941, but Dwight Macdonald was adamant in his refusal to commit himself to the Allied cause. The fight among the *Partisan Review* editors over support or opposition to the war became the issue that shattered their alliance. In the struggle over editorial policy, Macdonald was aided by Clement Greenberg, the art critic he had brought onto the staff. When Greenberg joined the Air Force in 1943, Macdonald resigned and started his own publication, which he called *politics*. Mary McCarthy, who did not support the war either, continued to write her "Theatre Chronicles" for *Partisan Review*.

The war years brought Kevin McCarthy to Wellfleet several times. He had been drafted in 1942 and assigned to the military police. While he escorted German prisoners by train to war camps, his wife, the actress Augusta Dabney, went on tour with various plays, once doing summer stock on the Cape and once appearing in Boston. These performances occasioned several visits to the Wilson home, where Augusta Dabney learned to cook from her sister-in-law, for whom cooking had become a serious pursuit. Mary McCarthy had done little cooking during her Johnsrud years, and what she did—corned beef hash, salmon loaf with cucumber sauce (recipes that show up in *The Group*)—embarrasses her today. During the 1940s her taste grew more refined, even though food rationing made it difficult to get the natural ingredients she wanted. Even the decorations on her Christmas tree had to be natural (and edible)—cranberries, popcorn, and little homemade candies, which she strung in chains around the tree. Many of the foods she could not get in the stores she had to grow, and as a result, she became a serious gardener. Edmund Wilson described a typical picnic in one of his journals:

> For lunch we had had from the brown basket the classical boiled eggs, bean salad in glass jars, cucumber sandwiches, and sandwiches filled with some mixture of green chopped herbs and white cottage cheese (and there were bananas, tomatoes, and sliced sweetish green cucumber pickles which we didn't get around to eating); and had iced lemonade out of the thermos bottle and white California wine out of a glass jar that had been cooled in the refrigerator and that we tried to keep from getting tepid by standing it in the water.

Although Wilson was an inveterate journal-keeper, writing compulsively in his large-size ledgers all his life, he made few notes during his marriage to Mary McCarthy; the description of the picnic is one of the few. The reason for his unaccustomed reticence was the frequency and intensity of their quarrels. "Our life," wrote Wilson, "was sometimes nightmarish."

The marriage had been tempestuous from the beginning. According to Adelaide Walker, a neighbor and close friend of Mary and Edmund's, "the fault was mostly Wilson's. He was impervious, overbearing, and, at times, irrational in his relationship with her. He accused her of being a terrible mother when in truth she was devoted to Reuel, and it was he who was difficult." He expected her to give large parties often, a labor she thoroughly enjoyed, but he never helped with preparations or cleanup.

Insisting on complete control of every aspect of her life, Wilson would not let his wife have money. "When I inherited a little bit of money from the McCarthy family," McCarthy told an interviewer forty years later, "and I was earning a little bit of money from my writing—he made me put it in his bank account. And, of course, I couldn't have signature power on his bank account. I had to ask him for a nickel to make a telephone call. . . . Anyway, I fought. . . . I took a stand and Edmund gave in, and I had my own bank account, and that was the end of it." For a long time he forbade her to drive—she was too nervous, he said—even though it was difficult to live in the country (their house was located outside the town of Wellfleet) without a car. She and Reuel got around Wellfleet, Truro, and Provincetown by bicycle. Eventually, she managed to save money from her own earnings to purchase a second-hand Ford.

Edmund Wilson was possessive, jealous even of her female friends. The closest of these during the Wellfleet years was Adelaide Walker, whom McCarthy had met in New York when she was married to Johnsrud. (Adelaide Walker and her husband, Charles, had founded the Theatre Union in 1933, and Johnsrud had submitted a play to them and acted several times in their productions.) But it was not until McCarthy married Wilson that the two women got to be good friends. Charles Walker had been a friend of Wilson's since college days, but Wilson seemed less than gratified by their wives' friendship. Indeed, when the women saw each other four or five times a week, taking their children to the beach, sometimes shopping in Boston, Wilson became angry. According to Adelaide Walker, he resented the time Mary spent away from him because "he didn't like to feel that part of her was not completely turned to him." He was furious when she did not return from their outings exactly when he thought she should, and even before she got home, he would start checking up on where she had gone, whom she had seen, and what she had done. As Adelaide Walker later wrote to Wilson, she found his attitude toward Mary oppressive. (Despite her outspokenness, she remained close to Wilson for the rest of his life.)

> Over the years I had come to feel very uncomfortable with you in relation to anything about Mary because of your attitude towards our friendship. It was a perfectly simple friendship, really, founded in the first instance on the fact that she was your wife. As the years passed we found that we were very congenial. We always had a lot of "feminine" problems, children and house and cooking to talk about, but in addition we both were more interested in ideas and intellectual things than most women are. I was completely confused and dumbfounded by your disapproval and attitude towards our friendship, and—forgive me for speaking frankly— knowing it to be perfectly normal and in no way directed against you. On the contrary, as I say, you were really the root of it.

Wilson could also be cruel and unfeeling at times. When Mary was pregnant again, and Wilson was away, she and Adelaide Walker went to Provincetown for cocktails with Sándor Radó, McCarthy's first psychiatrist. Once there, she got sick. Rather than drive back to Wellfleet, she spent the night with Katy Dos Passos. The queasiness she had felt was caused by a miscarriage. Wilson accused Radó of inducing an abortion, a complete fabrication that only exacerbated his wife's depression at losing the baby.

The Wilsons' terrible quarrels were liable to erupt anywhere, anytime, before any person. There are faculty members at the University of Chicago who still remember their heated arguments. When art dealer John Myers told M. S. Pitzele, at the time an editor at *Business Week,* that Mary McCarthy and Edmund Wilson had moved next door to him on Henderson Place, Pitzele replied, "Don't I know!" It was Wilson's drinking that precipitated many of these outbursts. Adelaide Walker said later:

> Edmund certainly had an alcohol problem, which is no secret to anybody. But it's extraordinary in that he's the only person I've ever known who can drink so much and then turn out first-rate work. It's almost unbelievable. Everyone marvelled at it. He'd finish a piece of work and start drinking in a perfectly civilized way, and then he'd just go on and on. He'd drink everything in the house. This would last sometimes for several days. And he'd go to bed and be sick, and then wouldn't drink for a fairly long time. And he could also drink more or less normally at times. He didn't

always go on and drink himself into a stupor. But Mary had a very difficult time because he'd be very mean and satirical.

"A tyrant and paranoid" was how McCarthy characterized Wilson years later—"a rather pitiable man in a way, like a minotaur." Ten years after her separation from Wilson, at the time her novel *A Charmed Life* was published, McCarthy wrote Arthur Schlesinger, Jr., "Edmund is pathetic, probably because of the talent, which causes a kind of hopeless chasm between the man and the quill." There is a kind of pathos in Wilson's letter to her of July 13, 1944. "It may be that you and I are psychologically impossible for one another," he wrote. "I have never wanted things to be as bad as that because I have really loved you more than any other woman and have felt closer to you than to any other human being."

Wilson's recognition of their difficulties did not, however, make them easier for McCarthy to bear. McCarthy told Schlesinger "I've drawn on my own feelings quite directly [in *A Charmed Life*], in the chapter where Martha remembers her marriage." A passage in that chapter describes Martha's suffocating despair about her situation: "He casts a long shadow. I don't want to live in it. I feel depreciated by him, like a worm, like a white grub in the ground."

During the summer of 1944 she finally acted on her seven-year desire to free herself of Wilson. An incident after a dinner party precipitated her flight to New York.

> We had about eighteen people at the party. Everybody had gone home and I was washing dishes. I asked him if he would empty the garbage. He said, "Empty it yourself." I started carrying out two large cans of garbage. As I went through the screen door, he made an ironical bow, repeating, "Empty it yourself." I slapped him, not terribly hard, went out and emptied the cans, then went upstairs. He called me and I came down. He got up from the sofa and took a terrible swing and hit me in the face and all over. He said, "You think you're unhappy with me. Well, I'll give you something to be unhappy about." I ran out of the house and jumped into my car.

At the time of her escape she had already written "The Weeds," a story about a woman who leaves her husband and the flower garden she has cultivated so assiduously, but who returns home after a few days. Mary McCarthy also returned home, but not for long. In the fall of 1944 she and Edmund and Reuel moved to New York to a house on Henderson Place on the Upper East Side, a short dead-end street that resembled a London mews. Her sister-in-law, Augusta Dabney McCarthy, who lived on Fifty-sixth Street, occasionally took Reuel, who had already started first grade at Saint Bernard's, to Central Park. In January 1945 Mary McCarthy left Edmund Wilson for good. She left a note for him:

Dear Edmund,
This is the note in the pincushion. I'm afraid I don't see what else there is to do. Perhaps the fighting is mostly my fault, but that's not a reason for our staying together. . . . I'm sorry. This could probably all be managed with less éclat, but the only way I can ever break off anything is to run away.

Mary

She took Reuel and moved into the Stanhope Hotel. "The only husband I left for incompatibility was Edmund," she told her brother Kevin in 1979. "There was no other man in the picture when I left him. It was desperation."

PART FOUR

CHAPTER X

A DIVIDING LINE
(1945)

At the end of January 1945 Mary McCarthy and six-year-old Reuel moved from the Stanhope Hotel to Kevin McCarthy's midtown apartment, vacant because Kevin was still in the service and Augusta Dabney had gone on tour with a play. Edmund Wilson continued to occupy their house on Henderson Place. McCarthy consulted lawyers immediately about a divorce. In a deposition taken on February 23, 1945, she stated:

> Since the birth of our son I have tried to see this marriage through but from the time of its inception to the present time I have been compelled to suffer physical and mental humiliation at the hands of the defendant. This has occurred in the presence of strangers and in the presence of friends, before our servants, the defendant's daughter by a former marriage and even before our son who is now 6 years old. He has publicly accused me of infidelity. He has made this accusation before our son.

Wilson, whose deposition followed, objected:

> At no time did I ever attack her. I have found it necessary to protect myself against violent assaults by her in the course of which she would kick me, bite me, scratch me and maul me in any way she could. She has even gone so far as to break down a door to my study to get at me and she has on other occasions pushed paper under the door of my study to set fire to it.
>
> Plaintiff is the victim of hysterical delusions and has seemed for years to have a persecution complex as far as I am concerned. She seems to believe that I have attacked her and struck her on occasions when nothing of the sort has happened.

In his journals, Wilson admitted that he had behaved neurotically during the marriage, "as I usually do with women I live with . . . rebelling . . . as I used to do against my mother."

Both parties agreed to a separation on March 4, 1945. Wilson would pay sixty dollars a week in child support and give his wife custody of Reuel except for summers and half of Easter and Christmas vacations. McCarthy pressed forward for a divorce, which Wilson did not want.

Katy Dos Passos wrote her husband about a late-night phone call from Wilson shortly after he had signed the separation agreement: "He thought it was a crazy notion, but she was set upon it. . . . Antix [Anti-Christ, her nickname for Wilson] sounded depressed and gloomy."

At just this moment, *The New Yorker* agreed to let Wilson roam Western Europe as their correspondent. He left in mid-March. In June he wrote John Dos Passos that he would be home by the end of August, "though, as you probably know, Mary has made a shambles of the family and I'm faced with the prospect of doing something about the mess." Yet his subsequent actions made the "mess" worse, turning an unhappy situation into a bitter one. He claimed his wife had been locked up in the violent ward at Payne Whitney, that she was a hysteric of the classic type, given to wild and embarrassing scenes, that she was insane and getting worse, and that she was sinking into "alienation"—very sad, he added, because she had so many good qualities. He made so many other charges against his wife that Dwight Macdonald later said, "His insistence that she was insane was one of his pleasanter accusations."

Wilson had made the insanity charge in his reply to his wife's suit for separation. McCarthy's lawyers obtained a signed statement from Sándor Radó that he had treated Mrs. Wilson for psychoneurosis and that she exhibited no sign of insanity. Affidavits from Major Richard Frank and Dr. Abraham Kardiner corroborated Radó's statement. So, when Wilson and McCarthy got to court on October 10, 1945, Wilson backed down and agreed to settle. The lawyers retired to the judge's chambers, where the final terms—essentially the same as those already agreed to during the Wilsons' separation—were established. When the hearing was over, Nathalie Swan Rahv, Mary's Vassar classmate who had married Philip Rahv, and Adelaide Walker, who had come to testify for McCarthy, took her to Delmonico's in Wall Street for a celebratory lunch.

Adelaide Walker dreaded the return to Wellfleet, where she would have to face Edmund Wilson, who was furious that she had sided with Mary. Although she and her husband had empathized with McCarthy throughout the bitter divorce period, they were close to Wilson. Not wanting to meet him accidentally before explaining her position, she sent him a tactfully worded three-page, single-spaced letter, which said in part:

> I would, of course, have definitely preferred to make it all none of my business. I can't tell you how little anxious I was to be involved. But Mary

was very much alone, and in many ways much weaker than you, and it seemed cowardly just to run away entirely.

As for Reuel and taking him away from you, of course I would never have assisted in that. I questioned at once the fact that the suit was made for sole custody. Both Mary and the lawyer, and I'm sure Mary at least was sincere in this, assured me that when things had reached that state there was no other way—formally—to state the point, but that of course she never had any intention in the final arrangement of preventing you seeing Reuel whenever you like, having all vacations, weekends whenever you pleased, etc. I was entirely convinced—and still am—of Mary's sincerity on this. She has always been genuinely anxious, I think, for the relation between you and Reuel to be a good one and for Reuel to see and be with you. She has always said he was devoted to you and you to him and I felt sure she would do nothing to interfere with that. I did feel, however, that Mary was a good and devoted mother, and as a mother myself I sympathized with her feeling that Reuel must be with her during the school years for an unbroken stretch and that a six months and six months arrangement would be very bad for him. I also felt it was unwise and unfair to him for you to have too much specific control over decisions while he was with Mary. I think Reuel at that period was extremely dependent emotionally on Mary, children at that age, particularly an only child often is, and I felt any situation where he could become a bone of contention between you was the worst thing that could happen to him.

I always said—and to Mary—that I had no idea—in the sight of God, so to speak, who was right or wrong. It was only that, given an impossible situation, how was it to be liquidated without permanent harm to any of you?

Adelaide Walker and Edmund Wilson eventually resumed their close friendship after time had healed some of his rawest wounds, but for the present, he was in no state of mind to forgive. A letter from Katy Dos Passos to her husband described his mood:

I am in bed because of being worn out by a midnight visit from Antix who came unexpectedly to dinner and stayed all hours. He called a taxi twice and then sent it away and finally I took him . . . in the car long after twelve. I am just like Cinderella, you know. After twelve the Ball is over for me and I *haf* to go home. But could not as poor Antix talked all evening about his domestic sufferings which have indeed been frightful beyond belief. He told me his life with Mary from the beginning—it was hideous for years I guess and a good thing they have parted. Antix said she wanted to destroy him and his work. She had indeed undermined his work. (I thought so myself some time ago.) She kept telling him it was worthless and getting worse. Oh I felt sorry for both. Antix says all American women are Harpies. That is not true. "Perhaps you are not," he said, doubtfully. "Sometimes I think you are not like that. But you *are*—of course you are. They *all are.*" I said "Nonsense," but he said "Nonsense," too. "All of you."

I read him parts of your letters, and he said that was how he felt too. He said he was feeling miserable and wanted nothing but to get some kind of family going again. I guess he will marry as soon as possible. I wish I could pick out a wife for him. He will marry some Harpy I fear, or a young pretty gold-digger or nitwit. Oh dear. He had taken too much.

The resentment and anger that the divorce aroused in Wilson erupted in petty and petulant acts. When McCarthy gave her washing machine to Adelaide Walker, for example, Wilson demanded it back, insisting it was his.

"But Mary won it at the county fair," she said.

"True," admitted Wilson, "but it was my quarter that paid for the winning ticket." Dos Passos, acting as judge, affirmed McCarthy's ownership based on Wilson's having *given* her the quarter that purchased the lucky chance. In the end, Adelaide Walker reinstalled the machine in the Wilson house only because she found that Rosalind had been washing her father's laundry by hand.

Dwight Macdonald, who called Wilson a poor loser, remembered an occasion during the summer of 1945 when he dropped his son, who was a friend of Reuel's, at Wilson's Wellfleet house.

"Well, Dwight," sneered Edmund, "I see that you're driving my car this season."

"No. This was Mary's car. It was registered in her name, and she transferred it to me, and I paid her a dollar as a token payment. I never heard it was your car," Macdonald shot back. McCarthy had given her old Ford to Macdonald so that he could transport his family from their cottage to the beach. Later, when the two men met accidentally—and this occurred frequently, as they lived in the same neighborhood and their sons were friends—Wilson barely acknowledged Macdonald's presence.

Delmore Schwartz, inspired by another dramatic episode from McCarthy's private life, wrote an unfinished sketch about her and "her famous domineering husband." What was it that made this woman go from one marriage to another? the story's narrator asks. "Dinah," as she is called in the story, "wants to get married again so that she can once again have someone to whom to be unfaithful," one character remarks.

Conrad Aiken suggested a cartoon that would portray Wilson and McCarthy sitting opposite one another, with the caption to read, "The Shock of Recognition."

But all of this was ahead of McCarthy that early winter of 1945. Life was fairly peaceful, with Wilson in Europe; her only contacts with her estranged husband, at least until he returned to America at the end of August, were the checks *The New Yorker* mailed to her (the sixty dollars a week he had agreed to pay her was deducted from Wilson's paycheck) and the charming letters he sent to his six-year-old son. "The city is full of gloomy houses, and there is one street where every house is supposed to be haunted," he wrote from Edinburgh. "In one of the houses they say there is a ghost who helps you on with your coat when you leave. In this house where I am staying there is a large cat named Betty and a black cocker spaniel named Jean, and they sleep in a basket together. The old Scotch housekeeper calls them 'beasties.' " He told Reuel that in London he went to a musical about a yellow dwarf who carried off a beautiful girl to his house in the Weird Wood. In Rome he bought his son some marionettes, the kind "which have arms that move: a clown, a harlequin, a cavalier, and a funny man in a business suit." Throughout Italy there were no cats and dogs, he explained in another letter, because the people did not have anything to feed them.

While Wilson was abroad, President Roosevelt died; Hitler committed suicide; victory in Europe came; and, on August 6, 1945, an American plane dropped a single atomic bomb on the Japanese city of Hiroshima. The bomb destroyed two thirds of the city and killed many of its 343,000 citizens. No warning had been given. "I remember," Mary McCarthy subsequently wrote, "reading the news of Hiroshima in a little general store on Cape Cod . . . and saying to myself as I moved up to the counter, 'What am I doing buying a loaf of bread?' The coexistence of the great world and us, when contemplated, appears impossible." Another bomb was dropped, on Nagasaki, on August 9. By August 15 the war was over.

By the time of the Japanese surrender, Mary McCarthy, who had not supported the war theoretically or practically, now changed her mind.

Toward the end of the war, I began to realize there was something hypocritical about my position—that I was really supporting the war. I'd go to a movie—there was a marvelous documentary called *Desert Victory* about the British victory over Rommel's Africa Corps—and I'd find myself weeping madly when Montgomery's bagpipers went through to El Alamein. In other words, cheering the war, and on the other hand, being absolutely against Bundles for Britain, against Lend Lease, . . . against every practical thing. Years later, I realized I really thought Philip [Rahv] had been right, and that the rest of us had been wrong. Of course we didn't know about the concentration camps. . . . But once this news was in, it became clear—at least to me, and I still believe it—that the only way to have stopped it was in a military way.

Yet when she had wanted to donate blood, she felt obliged to discuss the prowar implications of such a gift with her antiwar friends.

The turmoil that brought devastation to Europe brought to America incalculable contributions from European refugees. Thousands of displaced persons poured into New York during the late 1930s and early 1940s. "America, I think, was greatly improved thanks to Hitler and Mussolini," Mary McCarthy told an interviewer in 1968. "The whole character of New York was changed by the appearance of these refugees who had a certain wisdom that was totally lacking in the crude society that was described in *The Group*." Thomas Mann and Bertolt Brecht were among the most gifted writers of their generation. Artist Max Ernst made surrealism accessible to a generation. The architects-in-exile of the Bauhaus School, led by Walter Gropius and Ludwig Mies van der Rohe, changed the appearance of the American city. Middle European physicists Albert Einstein, Hans Bethe, and Edward Teller ushered in the atomic era. Composers Paul Dessau and Arnold Schoenberg, painter Marc Chagall, philosophers Paul Tillich, Hannah Arendt, and Simone Weil—all made New York the most cosmopolitan city in the world, so full of talent and brains that no other city could hope to match it for excitement and promise.

One of these emigrés, a relatively unknown Italian antifascist journalist named Nicola Chiaromonte, became friends with Mary McCarthy during the summer of 1945. She had first met Chiaromonte the preceding summer when she was still living with Edmund Wilson. But it was during the summer of 1945, when she rented a house in Truro and Nicola and Miriam Chiaromonte occupied one nearby, that they began to see a good deal of each other. The friendship profoundly influenced her.

We talked about Tolstoy and about Dostoyevsky, and the *change* from someone like Edmund and his world was absolutely stunning. Nicola did not like Dostoyevsky and he had an absolute passion for Tolstoy. Anyway we would talk and it never occurred to me before to think of those writers as anything but two writers—as *Edmund* would have looked at them. One might have said that of course Tolstoy was a much better stylist and Dostoyevsky wrote bad Russian and so on. But that was a completely empty literary point of view by comparison. It really didn't involve thinking about what these people were saying! Talking with Nicola Chiaromonte was an absolute awakening, and I never got over it.

Wilson and the *Partisan Review* editors, too, she continued, had no moral core. "It never occurred to them that there should be a connection between what they read and wrote and their own lives, how they were living and what they believed in." McCarthy later conferred their restricted literary perspective on a female character in *The Oasis:* "She read Tolstoy, of course, but a certain virginal decorum preserved her from his ideas. 'I look on him primarily as a novelist,' she would demur when someone tried to wring from her at least an awareness of his message."

Nicola Chiaromonte was a dark and handsome man who looked like a monk, as his friends said. His manner was shy and modest, slow and grave, and there was nothing about him that glittered. He had been born in Rome in 1905 and grew up with two brothers—one of whom became a Jesuit; the other, a doctor—and a sister, who became a social worker. He graduated from the University of Rome with a law degree, then embarked upon a journalist's career. Immediately, he was silenced by the fascist government, so he emigrated to Paris, where he could write freely. In 1936 he joined André Malraux's squadron to fight for the Loyalists in the Spanish Civil War. (Malraux immortalized him as Scali in *Man's Hope.*) He broke with Malraux, finding him too servile to the Stalinists, and returned to France. When the Germans reached Paris, the parents of his Austrian-Jewish wife committed suicide, and she herself died of tuberculosis in Toulouse during their difficult exodus toward the south. Chiaromonte had to dig her grave, and then continue on to Algiers. Because it was Vichy-controlled, he proceeded to Oran and finally to Casablanca, where in 1940 he boarded a ship for America. He lived in America for the next nine years, writing for *Partisan Review, The New Republic, The Nation,* and *politics.* In 1942 he remarried. Nineteen forty-five was the second summer in Truro for the Chiaromontes.

For Mary McCarthy, the summer was idyllic. She had several houseguests, among them Clement Greenberg, who painted watercolors that summer; Hardwick Mosely, a Southerner who worked at Houghton Mifflin and with whom McCarthy was having "a transient love affair," as she described the relationship; Herbert Solow; Kevin and Augusta; and Eunice Clark Jessup and her husband, Jack, chief editorial writer for *Life* magazine, who arrived with their young boys and a large piece of

beef, a rare gift in wartime America. Also in Truro that summer were
Dwight and Nancy Macdonald, the Italian novelist Niccolò Tucci, Lionel Abel, James Farrell, Charles Jackson, who was visiting Robert Nathan, and the sculptor Tino Nivola. The core group—Mary McCarthy,
the Macdonalds, and the Chiaromontes—enjoyed many "wonderful
beach conversations," Mary McCarthy remembers, joined by whoever
was around. They read Shakespeare aloud in groups, feasted on picnics
in the moonlight, had talks at night by the fire, and went swimming in
the phosphorescent water. One morning McCarthy discovered Chiaromonte cleaning up around his cottage, a light blue apron tied around his
waist. Because she had never seen Edmund Wilson in an apron, she
never forgot the quiet domestic scene. Nor did she forget the conversations with Nicola Chiaromonte. Her intellectual outlook changed as she
saw that history could be interpreted in ways other than the ones to
which she had been accustomed.

Nicola Chiaromonte was a rarity among intellectuals of the time in
that he was a disciple of neither Marx nor Freud. He revered Plato,
believing that "in times of crisis the . . . Platonic form of reasoning
. . . appears as the only point from which we can glimpse . . . the light
of truth"; and he loved Proudhon, who, he said, "was a radical in
thought," questioning all accepted ideas and vested interests, "while
being quite often moderate in argument, because he did not believe in
the elimination of realities." Although a crusading socialist, Proudhon
held essentially libertarian views (he had a strong belief in individual
rights) that brought him in conflict with doctrinaire socialists like Marx.
Chiaromonte considered Marxism vague and illogical. "In the last analysis," he wrote for Dwight Macdonald's *politics,* "everything in the Marxist theory depends on the possibility of showing without equivocation
that the collective ownership of the means of production will necessarily
constitute a change for the *better,* and also on the possibility of rendering
reasonably clearly in what this *better* will actually consist."

The large number of psychoanalysts in Truro prompted discussions of
Freud, which provided Chiaromonte with the opportunity to question
whatever remained of Mary McCarthy's faith in psychoanalysis as a
doctrine. Her analysis had provided emotional relief during seven difficult years with Edmund Wilson, but slowly she had come to believe—as
did Martha Sargent in *The Company She Keeps*—that psychoanalysis was
based on a series of myths. And any lingering belief in analysis was being
undermined by her present happiness, now that she was free of Wilson.
"Analysts believe," she said later, "that you should stay in your situation.
I changed my situation and found that life was different." (Later she

made a group of psychiatrists the villains in one of her best short stories, "The Appalachian Revolution," which she wrote in 1954.) To find that Chiaromonte shared her views on psychoanalysis strengthened her own opinions.

Chiaromonte distanced himself not only from Marxism and Freudianism but from all doctrines. "His ideas did not fit into any established category," McCarthy wrote in a preface to a collection of Chiaromonte's essays. "He was neither on the left nor on the right. Nor did it follow that he was in the middle; he was alone." For him, the sickness of the twentieth century lay in the blindness induced by ideology. He rejected the notion that in order to understand anything a person must first believe in a larger theory which explains everything. The history of the Left had been shaped by the view that history has meaning and can be controlled; as a result it could be made to serve the ideals that the Left was trying to put in practice. But history, Chiaromonte wrote, "is not a concatenation of events or the outcome of decisions in high places but a mass of infinitesimal accidents and unexpected incidents."

McCarthy illustrates this idea in "My Confession," her 1953 memoir of becoming an anti-Stalinist, when she tells how Russia's and Trotsky's fate was determined by his decision one day to go duck hunting. He got wet during the hunt and caught the flu, which made him miss Lenin's funeral and the subsequent political struggle that changed the future of Russia. "One can foresee the consequences of a revolution or a war," wrote Trotsky with an existential shrug, "but it is impossible to foresee the consequences of an autumn shooting trip for wild ducks." Events have no rational (i.e., causal) relation to each other, Chiaromonte believed. "Rationality is present only when events are reduced to a web of concepts in an abstract construction designed to give them a single meaning. But to do this, one must completely disregard the specificity of the event whose 'true' meaning one claims to be seeking." Events never turn out the way they should; ideals have always been betrayed in an effort to convert them to reality. As a result, there has been a resurgence of the idea of fate in the minds of some intellectuals who once believed in progress.

Mary McCarthy discusses this underlying theme of Chiaromonte's *The Paradox of History* in an afterword to the American edition (also published in *The New York Review of Books*). "The faith in History, which was shattered by an historical event—the impact of the First World War—cannot in good faith be restored, since the confidence in Progress underpinning it, tacitly or explicitly, is no longer there. The collapse of that man-made structure can be dated—summer 1914—when a credo in a forward-directed History fell instant victim to history with a small h, history in a raw state, a 'senseless' accumulation of happenings." In other words, "the assassination of Franz Ferdinand at Sarajevo . . . triggered— for once the awful word seems suitable—a kind of rapid out-of-control automation in world events." And "that is a paradox, the irony, the joke, if you wish; it suddenly emerged with a painful shock that history un-processed, history in the raw, is what the ancients knew as Fate."

If fate is the unknown or that which is hidden, then it follows that there is a limit, a "boundary beyond which there stretch expanses of the unknown and unknowable." This is because we cannot really know the consequences of our actions. "If we could get to know the consequences of our actions," Chiaromonte said, "history would be nothing but an idyllic and constant harmony of free wills, or the infallible unfolding of a rational design. . . . But then we would not be free. We are free, however, and this means literally that we do not know what we are doing."

While Chiaromonte regarded the Marxist notion of class struggle as false, he warned that the greatest danger to individual freedom was the West's advanced regimentation of collective life. This, for him, was an inevitable consequence of the uncontrolled and uncontrollable authority bred by the egalitarianism peculiar to industrial society. The only practi-cal response to a collective society was withdrawal, not into self (the contemporary principle that the individual's sole purpose in life is to fulfill himself at any cost was the origin of twentieth-century violence, he said), but into groups. Decentralization was the only really revolu-tionary strategy. Like the Russian-born Italian writer Andrea Caffi (many of whose ideas Chiaromonte adopted), he wanted to see communities of politically concerned people who could, in the more human setting of smaller groups, develop alternative social aims and formations.

The idea that change, if it is to be brought about, will happen not through mass movements or war but through individuals in small com-munities was not new, but it seemed fresh and exciting to the small group that gathered around Nicola Chiaromonte that summer of 1945 in Truro. The notion that some resistance might be offered to the general mechanization in modern society took hold of everyone. In a way, this little company discussing the possibility of changing the world on a small scale was just the sort of embryo community that Caffi and Chiaromonte had in mind.

Chiaromonte introduced McCarthy to the writings of Simone Weil, a brilliant French mystic, who had died of tuberculosis and malnutrition two years before while still in her early thirties. Frequently, McCarthy could be spotted on the beach with her typewriter, pounding out a translation of Weil's essay "The Iliad, or the Poem of Force." Dwight Macdonald published the translation in *politics,* and years later said it was the best piece that had appeared in his journal.

At the center of the *Iliad,* Simone Weil said, was force; force was the epic's subject and hero. "Force," she wrote, "is as pitiless to the man who possesses it, or thinks he does, as it is to its victims; the second it crushes, the first it intoxicates. The truth is, nobody really possesses it." It changes hands so easily that it begins to seem independent, a blind automatic justice that kills those that kill.

> This retribution, which has a geometrical vigor, which operates automatically to penalize the abuse of force, was the main subject of Greek thought. It is the soul of the epic. . . . In Oriental countries which are steeped in Buddhism, it is perhaps this Greek idea that has lived on under the name of Kharma. The Occident, however, has lost it, and no longer even has a word to express it in any of its languages: conceptions of limit, measure, equilibrium, which ought to determine the conduct of life are, in the West, restricted to a servile function in the vocabulary of technics. We are only geometricians of matter; the Greeks were, first of all, geometricians in their apprenticeship to virtue.

What is implied in this quotation, Chiaromonte stressed, is that modern Western man not only admires force but thinks he can put it to good use. He refuses to face the inevitable fact that by accumulating force and ever greater power, he increases his capacity not only for good but for evil. In its perception of the reciprocal dehumanization of victors and vanquished, Simone Weil's essay was also an anguished response to the war with Hitler and the fall of France. (Interestingly, another Frenchwoman, Rachel Bespaloff—at the same time as Simone Weil but independently of her—wrote a series of essays called *On the Iliad,* which Mary McCarthy also translated.)

Nicola Chiaromonte's tutelage had a lifelong effect on McCarthy. Distrust of theory, anxiety about collectivization, and love of small communities would become predominant themes of her fiction. An abhorrence of lives lived according to abstractions was a peripheral theme in *The Groves of Academe* and *A Charmed Life* and a central theme of *The Group;* the idea of the unwanted and ubiquitous encroachments of mass society provided a nucleus for "The Appalachian Revolution," "The Hounds of Summer," and *Birds of America;* and the idea of small libertarian groups implanted in Mary McCarthy's brain in this summer of

1945 bore fruit in *The Oasis,* which was published in 1949. To her, the summer was "a watershed, a dividing line; everything was different after." More than twenty years later she wrote Chiaromonte a letter telling him what his influence had meant to her.

> Nicola, I've long wanted to tell you—and this seems a good occasion—that seeing you on the Cape in the summer of '45 was a crossroads in my life. In fact, *the* crossroads. I became a different person, though perhaps you didn't notice it, and I only saw it myself after a time, looking back. This has convinced me—of something you don't believe yourself—that change is possible for people. I mean inner change of course. All this sounds too redemptive, like Catholic literature for young people, but I haven't time tonight to put it better.

Chiaromonte, too, learned something from his friendship with Mary McCarthy. She showed him how attractive the light side of life could be, that a person could be too serious. (His widow, Miriam Chiaromonte, explains, "She creates a festive atmosphere wherever she goes and she is the best gift giver I've ever known. She gives lots of presents, and they are always right. I remember a cake of soap she gave me that summer. And there's a girlishness about her, a kind of innocence which is peculiar. She's sophisticated, but there's an ingenuousness that is touching. She never became cynical.") Chiaromonte also thought her zeal to do things well, whether keeping house or writing a book, most unusual. He marveled at her capacity for living and for writing. He thought the summer so memorable that almost twenty years later he wrote Dwight Macdonald, "My best summer vacations were the ones I spent in Truro in your company and Mary's. How far away those days now seem. We must thank the gods that our friendship has withstood the test of time."

As summer ended, Edmund Wilson returned from Europe to his house in Wellfleet. Reuel moved there, and his mother left for Nova Scotia to work on a novel. Charles Jackson, the author of *The Lost Weekend,* a best-selling novel that depicted a five-day alcoholic binge, had inspired her to write a similar story, but about the thirst for fame in the literary life—just as dangerous to self-respect as the thirst for alcohol, she believed. Mary McCarthy's treatment of the theme, unlike Jackson's, was to be satirical. By herself, she boarded a series of trains and a ferry to reach Yarmouth, where she wanted to work for a solid week without interruption. She had planned to stay in a picturesque inn or "fisherman's shingled cottage and take solitary walks along the beach to freshen [her] invention." Instead, she found a desolate town that consisted of banks, insurance companies, a movie house, and a hotel. She locked herself in a dingy room at that hotel, emerging only three times a day for meals, and pounded away at her typewriter—producing almost one hundred pages of a novel she called *The Caged Lion* before abandoning it forever. When she returned to the United States, no one believed that she had worked steadily and solitarily for a long week; they were certain she had gone off with a lover.

She and Reuel moved to a small town on the Hudson River, for she had accepted a teaching job at Bard College. "It is not my idea of heaven," she wrote Edmund Wilson, "but the pay, as college pay goes, is not too bad ($3,000 a year) and will be enough to support me without difficulty."

CHAPTER XI

ACADEME
(1945–1946)

MARY McCARTHY and six-year-old Reuel arrived at Bard College on September 15, 1945. They rented a rambling run-down house in Upper Red Hook, a tiny village consisting of a traffic circle, an abundance of elm trees, and a few houses. Upper Red Hook and Red Hook are the towns nearest Bard, which is located in Annandale-on-Hudson, not much more than a post office address. Like Vassar, only twenty-two miles to the south, Bard lies in the Hudson River Valley midway between the Catskills and the Berkshires. The campus, some of which borders the river, covers acres of rolling fields and streams. Founded in 1860, the school had been an Episcopalian college called Saint Stephen's, but when it was affiliated with Columbia University in the late 1920s, it became Bard College, named for one of its founders. When Mary McCarthy arrived in 1945, it was a small (eighty-eight students), coeducational, experimental liberal arts college independent of Columbia.

The director of admissions gave a welcoming party for her. The faculty were eager to meet their new colleague, but apprehensive about her becoming a member of their little community. "We had all read *The Company She Keeps* and knew how devastating she could be"; "It was something fearful to think of her coming here"; "She was known for her sharp tongue" were sentiments heard about the campus prior to the party. Fred Dupee, one of the founding editors of *Partisan Review,* who had taught at Bowdoin and Columbia and who had recently come to Bard to run the English department, was responsible for bringing Mary McCarthy to Bard. A dapper and dignified man with a puckish side, he had been telling everyone all week how friendly and sociable Mary McCarthy was and that they had nothing to fear from her. She came to the party in a white dress and dazzled everyone with her eagerness and curiosity. "I always remember the look of expectation in her eyes," said one delighted guest in later years. "Everyone she would meet was going to be wonderful and say something brilliant. She still has that look."

When Fred Dupee had asked her what she wanted to teach, she opted for a course in the Russian novel, "an intensive study of the three nineteenth-century masters, Tolstoy, Dostoyevsky, and Turgenev, with glances backward at Pushkin and Gogol, and forward at the short stories of Chekhov." After dozens of summer discussions with Nicola Chiaromonte, during which he had converted her to a preference for Tolstoy over Dostoyevsky, she was eager to reread and study the Russians. Primed by Fred Dupee to expect a beautiful and brainy New York author, the students were surprised and complimented by her nervousness. "It was my first experience as a teacher, and I was frightened," McCarthy would remember. "My students told me later that I looked so white the first morning of my course in the Russian novel that they thought they were going to have to carry me out bodily. No doubt I would have been scared anywhere, facing a body of students, but in a more conventional college students might not have been so perceptive." Because she was an enthusiastic teacher, often staying up half the night to prepare herself for the next day's questions, the students loved her. Frequently, she conducted class out of doors, until students complained about the cold that she, absorbed in class discussion, seemed oblivious to. At the end of the semester she gave a Russian-novel party at her house, bidding everyone to come dressed as a favorite character. She herself wore a paper train about her neck to suggest Anna Karenina.

In addition to teaching the Russian-novel course, Mary McCarthy met five students individually once a week to direct their reading in a particular author or period agreed upon in advance. Bard's system of one-on-one tutorials was difficult for the conscientious instructor, but it was often circumvented by steering several students to the same reading matter. Mary McCarthy, however, carefully selected topics suited to each of her five students. Before suggesting a subject, she talked with the students to get a sense of their interests and capabilities. During her two semesters at Bard she directed tutorials in Marcus Aurelius, Dante, Chaucer, Cinderella, Cocteau, Farrell, Richardson, and, for a brilliant sixteen-year-old male science prodigy who was dating a nineteen-year-old, the problem of the older woman in literature. There must be something of Mary McCarthy in Domna Rejnev, a character in *The Groves of Academe,* about whom she wrote:

> To be allowed, under the cover of duty, to pursue the world's history down to its recondite byways was, for Domna Rejnev, a pure nightly joy, a passion of legitimate conquest, and her students were quick to discover that they could not please Miss Rejnev better than by discovering a wish to study an author she had not read, preferably an old author, in some forgotten cranny of culture.

During the second semester she taught a course in the modern novel, beginning with Jane Austen and ending with Henry James. The word "modern" was deliberately, though somewhat fraudulently, chosen to describe reading that belonged mostly to the nineteenth century. "You had to call everything at Bard either modern or contemporary, or the students wouldn't register for it," she recalled in a 1961 interview. She had planned to teach a course on the critical theories of Aristotle, Horace, Sidney, Dr. Johnson, Coleridge, Arnold, Eliot, and I. A. Richards, but only three students registered for it. Had she called the course "Contemporary Criticism," she concluded, more students would have enrolled.

"She was wonderful for the bright students," a Bard colleague has said. "They got an example of sharpness of intellect. They were inspired by Mary." For some, the inspiration lasted a lifetime. One former student recently said, "All these many years later I am still reading in a sense for her," and another, that Mary McCarthy's "vigor and high expectations" stimulate her still.

McCarthy loved teaching at Bard. However, "it was all quite mad, crazy," she said in retrospect.

> I was staying up till two every night trying to keep a little behind my class. . . . Everything was reversed! The student was in a position to see whether the professor was cheating, or had done her homework. . . . But it was exciting; it was fun. . . . I liked teaching because I loved this business of studying. As for the students, some surely profited from the freedom of choice implicit in the Bard "way," which gave them a faculty perforce fresh and perennially inexperienced, that is, alive, though the cost was a great deal of midnight oil. So far as I know, Bard has seldom been boring, either to its students or its faculty, and boredom, highly contagious, is the great malady of education.

Much of Bard's pedagogical practice, which McCarthy referred to later as its "happy tradition of eccentricity," showed up in *The Groves of Academe,* a novel published in 1952. Henry Mulcahy, the "tall, soft-bellied, lisping man with a tense, mushroom-white face, rimless bifocals, and graying thin red hair," the book's protagonist and a consummate self-dramatizer, is based on a person who in 1945 was Bard's resident Aristotelian and Saint Thomas Aquinas scholar, a man Fred Dupee had hired to teach English and philosophy part-time. Despite the unpleasant picture of academia in *The Groves of Academe*—a picture based only partly on Bard—McCarthy liked the college, and also learned from it, as she explained when accepting an honorary degree from Bard thirty years later. "At Bard, in the midst of laughter and often breathless, I acquired a literary conscience," she said. "I was taught—or taught myself—the necessity of close reading, of repeated immersion in any given material, and this was a kind of awakening." Unfortunately, her teaching had left her no time to write; in her nine months at the college she had published only one short story, "The Unspoiled Reaction," a sketch for *The Atlantic Monthly* about children at a puppet show. Regretfully, therefore, she refused Dupee's invitation to stay another year.

Bowden Broadwater, a frequent weekend guest and an aspiring writer himself, was pleased by her decision not to return in the fall. A recent Harvard graduate who now worked for *The New Yorker,* Broadwater was twenty-five, eight years Mary McCarthy's junior and terribly impressed by her and her literary gifts. He had met her the preceding January, the same night she had left Edmund Wilson, when both had been dinner guests at Niccolò Tucci's apartment. They had run into each other off and on that winter, and during the summer McCarthy had invited him to Truro. But not until she went to Bard did she start seeing a lot of Bowden Broadwater.

Her friends were puzzled by her attraction to him. Unusually tall and slender, and always impeccably tailored in custom-made English suits, he cut an elegant and dandified figure that seemed at odds with her more casual and sometimes rumpled appearance. "He worked on her," one acquaintance has said, "and got her to stop wearing crooked stockings." To McCarthy, "there was something physically attractive about him, certainly, very pretty skin and gold hair but very, very nearsighted with very large spectacles that gave him a strange, tense look." He was effete (he even sucked his thumb occasionally); he talked with an affected English drawl which, with the omnipresent cigarette dangling from his lips, muffled his voice, so that listeners found it difficult to understand what he said; and he was snobbish, one of his friends said, like a character out of Waugh, laughing at the social ladder while climbing it.

The world-weary mien he assumed obscured his considerable assets for most people, not including McCarthy, who knew him as brilliant, witty, well-read, intuitive, and a fine, critical reader—"tremendously talented, much more talented than I," she has said. Moreover, he was generous and sophisticated, and responsible for a certain development in her taste in all areas—art, clothes, even life-style. At the time Bowden

Broadwater was visiting Mary McCarthy at Bard, she lived in a big tumbledown house and her clothes never seemed to be on straight, but after she started living with him, her apartment, her clothes, her very style of living became more elegant.

Nearly everyone had a theory about the alliance: her Broadwater period was the youth she had missed by getting involved after college with heavy, serious men; she liked Broadwater's style and taste; he represented a rest period, a necessity after seven sorry years with Edmund Wilson; she loved his sensitivity to literature and art; she had a great need to shock, and Broadwater seemed shocking to her friends; he was interesting enough to complement her. There was probably an element of truth in all these speculations, but no acknowledgment of captivation or fascination in any of them. McCarthy was enchanted by Broadwater's quality of otherworldliness. That he was also a gadfly amused her too, although in later years she found the trait tiresome. Reuel showed that he understood something of the attraction when he told baby-sitters that "Bowden makes Mummy laugh."

Bowden Broadwater came to Bard nearly every weekend. McCarthy got students to baby-sit while she and Bowden went out. The most frequent were Barbara Anderson, who later married Fred Dupee, Ellen Adler, the daughter of Stella Adler and stepdaughter of Harold Clurman, who at the time was directing Maxwell Anderson's *Truckline Café,* in which Kevin McCarthy had a part, and Eve Gassler, who later became McCarthy's literary executor. The girls were impressed by her courteousness and by the feeling she imparted that they were bestowing a gift with their baby-sitting. Although the students were eager to help Mary McCarthy, they felt uncomfortable with Broadwater, especially when he drove them back to campus at the end of an evening. Still, they could see that he and McCarthy had fun together. Mary and Bowden went to parties in the neighborhood and gave several themselves. Most were for the Bard faculty and students, but for one, a garden party, they invited their New York friends. McCarthy served cakes in which she had baked quotations from *The English Galaxy of Shorter Poems,* and tea sandwiches that she had made in her big stone basement-kitchen.

McCarthy managed her entertaining with very little money. But that never seemed to make any difference to her spirits. She owned few clothes and drove an old Ford, rattling back and forth over the bumpy back roads from Upper Red Hook to the campus and to New York. Even so, her monthly expenses consistently outran income:

Rent	$ 50.00
Coal	80.00
Man to stoke furnace	31.00
Cleaning woman	26.00
Laundry	27.00
Gas and electricity	18.00
Food	60.00
Woman for afternoons, Reuel	26.00
Total	$318.00

Her take-home pay of $207 a month plus Wilson's $60-a-week mainte-nance gave her a monthly income of $447. But in addition to the $318 in fixed expenses, she had clothes, doctors' bills, personal expenses, including the telephone, and Reuel's tutor. "His Saint Bernard's prepa-ration didn't really qualify him for the 2nd grade," she wrote Wilson. "I have been having him tutored at home, and during the last week he has suddenly made astonishing progress, and has been advanced out of the dummy group he was sitting with. He has an excellent teacher, who thinks he has a very high IQ."

Mary McCarthy and Edmund Wilson's relations were fairly tranquil during the fall and winter, until she suggested that Reuel spend half of his Easter vacation with her, since he had been with his father all of Thanksgiving and most of Christmas. Wilson exploded:

> I want to have Reuel through the whole week of the 21st. . . . You will remember that you took him away from the house in the middle of February a year ago without even letting me know where he was; that when I got back from Europe, he was with me for only a few days before you took him away to Red Hook, where it is impossible for me to see him except during vacations; and that, when his vacations came, there has always been some very good reason why you could not let him be with me. I have seen almost nothing of him for more than a year and his grandmother has hardly seen him at all. I know how much satisfaction this kind of thing gives you, that you are always able to find excellent reasons for the unpleasant things that you do, and I know that I must be prepared to settle down to a lifetime of unpleasantness with you whenever Reuel is concerned. But I want to remind you that I am also in a position to make things difficult and uncomfortable for you, and that is not a good thing for Reuel to be made the object of continued hostilities between us. . . . You have no right to keep him for half his Easter vacation.

Wilson certainly had a point, as he had seen little of his son during 1945, although the reason for that was his five-month absence in Europe. Being kept away from Reuel was precisely what he feared would happen as a result of the divorce, as Adelaide Walker's letter to him attests, but the divorce agreement, which he had signed, stipulated that "the husband shall have custody of the child for one-half of the Easter holiday vacation and one-half of the Christmas holiday vacation provided, however, that the wife shall have the child all Christmas day."

At the close of the school year in 1946, Reuel went to live with Wilson in Wellfleet while McCarthy prepared to make her first trip to Europe. Needing a journalist's card to travel abroad so soon after the war, she obtained one from *Town and Country,* for which she agreed to contribute a story about traveling conditions in postwar Europe. Typhoid and small-pox shots made her so sick that she missed the ship she had booked passage on, and she languished in New York over the long Fourth of July weekend in Mannie Rousuck's apartment. Again, a week later, all ready to leave by plane, she came down with a streptococcus infection that soon developed into viral pneumonia. When the pneumonia cleared up, she was still not well. Her doctors suspected mononucleosis. By this time, it looked as if she would never leave, even though Broadwater, with whom she had planned the trip, was waiting for her in Paris. When she had sufficiently recovered, there was no available transportation from New York. She wrote Reuel, "I haven't gone yet because the boat isn't ready. It is taking a load of flour to Europe, and the weather has been rainy, so that they didn't dare pack the flour for fear of getting it wet. (If it got wet, I suppose they would have a shipload of paste.)" Undaunted, she entrained for Montreal and Halifax. Somewhere be-tween the two cities she lost her footlocker, the footlocker in which she had stuffed "everything that Europe presumably had not":

> . . . a quire of typewriting paper, the peach-pit oil, sixteen-and-a-half dollars' worth of Schrafft's candy, an electric warming pad, coffee, three giant boxes of absorbent cotton, Kleenex, smoked turkey, toilet paper, a coffee jar with a loose top filled with Rinso, three boxes of bath soap, two lengths of woolen material, and ten cartons of Lucky Strikes.

In Halifax she boarded the *M. V. Georgic,* one of the lesser-known ships of the Cunard Line, where she was crammed into a cabin with eighteen other women for a grueling ten-day crossing. When she disem-barked at Liverpool, she was still plagued by a lingering cold, but pro-ceeded to Paris, where she finally joined Broadwater, who had been awaiting her arrival for several weeks. He was with Carmen Angleton, the sister of the legendary James Angleton, whose career in counterintelligence began with the OSS during the war and continued after the war in the CIA, where he served as chief of counterintelligence from 1954 until 1974. McCarthy thought Carmen Angleton was "quite wonderful, a smoky, still, feminist heroine, a romantic bluestocking." During their week together in Paris, McCarthy ran into Peggy Guggenheim, whom she had met several years before in Wellfleet, and persuaded Guggenheim to go with her and her friends to Venice. But on the overcrowded train McCarthy, who had still not completely recovered, worsened. Worried about her rising temperature, the foursome got off in Lausanne, even though they did not have the required Swiss visas. They went to a hotel and called a doctor, who prescribed a "mustard plaster, a fearful purgative, and *boissons alcoholiques*." Carmen Angleton, who had lived in Italy (with the exception of the war years) since she was twelve, now left Lausanne to meet her father in Milan. When McCarthy's temperature rose to 104 degrees, Peggy Guggenheim "suddenly remembered" she had had a baby in Lausanne, and so was able to find a better doctor. "He got us moved to a pension in Ouchy," according to McCarthy, "and Peggy stayed; she used to go to the beach with Bowden and take her neat little swimming bag. And then she departed and went off to Venice."

In 1946 Peggy Guggenheim was far better known than Mary McCarthy. Born into the fabulously wealthy Guggenheim and Seligman families, she had made a name for herself as one of the century's outstanding collectors of contemporary art. She moved to Paris in 1920 and opened her first gallery in 1938. Samuel Beckett had told her that she should be interested in contemporary art because it was a living thing, so she made that the specialty of her gallery. Marcel Duchamp taught her the difference between abstract and surrealist art. She acquired works by Picasso, Braque, Kandinsky, Mondrian, Léger, and Brancusi. Only when the Germans approached Paris did she return to New York. In 1942 she opened a galley, Art of This Century, on West Fifty-seventh Street. There she exhibited her collection of cubist, abstract, and surrealist art. Of opening night, she wrote in her memoirs, *Out of This Century,* "I wore one of my Tanguy earrings and one made by Calder, in order to show my impartiality between surrealist and abstract art." She exhibited the then-unknown Americans Robert Motherwell, Mark Rothko, and Jackson Pollock. She was married for a time to Max Ernst. Having decided to live again in Europe, she was traveling about the continent, trying to decide where to settle, when she met McCarthy in Paris. It was as a result of this trip that Guggenheim eventually decided to buy a palazzo on the Grand Canal in Venice, where she lived for the rest of her life.

When McCarthy was well enough to continue the trip, she and Broadwater, following Lord Byron's footsteps, left Lausanne for Milan and then Venice, where Peggy Guggenheim met them at the train station in a gondola. They introduced her to an Italian they had met on the train, and he tagged along with the three Americans. McCarthy later described Guggenheim's casual affair with him in "The Cicerone," a short story that was published in *Partisan Review* in 1948.

Polly Herkimer Grabbe, Peggy Guggenheim's fictional name, is "middlingly but authentically rich," a "flowerbulb heiress" who has had "many husbands." She is "an indefatigable Narcissa" who believes that sexual intercourse is a quick transaction with the beautiful.

> She proceeded to make love, whenever she traveled, as ingenuously as she trotted into a cathedral: men were a continental commodity of which one naturally took advantage, along with the wine and the olives, the bitter coffee and the crusty bread. Miss Grabbe, in spite of her boldness, was not an original woman, and her boldness, in fact, consisted in taking everything literally.

McCarthy illustrates this matter-of-factness in the way Polly Herkimer Grabbe describes, for her American visitors, one evening's lovemaking:

> For a moment, they saw him all shrunken and wizened. ("My dear, he is much older than you think," said Miss Grabbe confidentially), and another glimpse revealed him in an aspect still more intimate and terrible, tossing the scapular he wore about his neck, and which hung down and interfered with his love-making, back again and again, lightly, flippantly, recklessly, over his thin shoulder.

Peggy Guggenheim was not pleased by the likeness, but continued to see McCarthy anyway. The two women, an unlikely couple, got along well and remained friends until Guggenheim's death.

McCarthy, having spent more time convalescing than touring, left Venice and returned to New York in time for Reuel, who had been reenrolled at Saint Bernard's, to start school. She rented a room in a cheap hotel they hated, tried without success to find an apartment, though McCarthy admits she did not look as hard as she might have, and then moved in with Bowden Broadwater and his sister. The Broadwaters lived in a tiny apartment that Reuel called "the anthill," at the corner of Fifty-seventh Street and Third Avenue. It was in a tenement building that belonged to the Catholic Church, an ugly brown five-story box stuffed with tiny apartments that shook when the Third Avenue Elevated clattered by. "The Elevated concealed by the . . . ruffled gray and white draperies," Broadwater wrote in "Ciao," a story about the early weeks of their life together that appeared in *Paris Review* fifteen years later, "shook itself down Third Avenue; the bridge table wiggled; the French Premier fell." The apartment, which Broadwater described accurately in his sketch, was on the fourth floor. A covered bathtub in the kitchen did triple duty as a tub, kitchen table, and counter. The wiggly bridge table served as the dining room table. There was no refrigerator, but the ice man came every morning at six.

Edmund Wilson objected to these living arrangements. He wrote McCarthy in October, "I am enclosing a check for the two months last summer during which, at your suggestion, I did not pay you maintenance. I want you to try to get a more comfortable apartment than the one you are in. Reuel's room and the bedroom do not have any heat and his room is so located that Miss Broadwater will have to go back and forth through it. The combined kitchen and bathroom is another bad feature. I suggest that you buy some furniture. If you need more money than the regular maintenance, let me know. I do not see how the [four] of you can possibly live in that place through this winter. Even electric heaters won't help much." A week later Mary McCarthy answered his letter: "We haven't found any better place to live. So far as I can find out, none exists under $500 a month. As far as heat goes, however, it is very comfortable here—I found a modern electric heater for Reuel's room that almost overdoes it."

Although four persons living in such a tiny apartment must have caused some problems, McCarthy remembers it as a "great deal of fun." She was in no hurry to marry Broadwater until a friend wondered about the propriety of the household from Reuel's point of view. It was then she decided marriage was a good idea. She married Robert Bowden Broadwater of Oakland, Maryland, on December 18, 1946. A Lutheran minister officiated at the small ceremony. It was Broadwater's first marriage. Eunice Clark Jessup and her husband gave the reception at their East Eighty-third Street brownstone. The bride was thirty-four, the groom twenty-six.

CHAPTER XII
REALISTS AND
IDEALISTS
(1947–1949)

"THE MORNING of February 18, 1947, three months to the day after my marriage, found me stumbling through the Want-Ads in the *Times*. I had been reading them daily for some time in order to give the impression to a certain person that I still believed that someone might really hire me." Bowden Broadwater, who wrote these words for his story "Ciao," had actually been married two months on the morning of February 18, 1947. The "certain person" who believed that someone might hire him was "the dear wife," as he referred to Mary McCarthy, her pretty sparkling eyes "like green shampoo shaken well." Instead of looking for a job, he wanted to

> walk in the sun down Park Avenue and over to my hideaway, the quiet library of the Harvard Club, where I have cautiously managed to preserve a membership, acquired in the prosperous war years when my 4–F status had induced several employers to breach their form of never hiring, for just such occasions as this. There, smoking a light cigar while the clock advanced the hour without comment, I could stretch out in a comfortable armchair with the ease of the deliberately unemployed, perhaps reading more of the novel I had begun the week before or even dozing.

While Bowden Broadwater did not much enjoy being a statistic on the New York unemployment rolls, he was not eager for 9 to 5 employment. He hoped, rather, to become a fiction writer. Although he wrote well, as these excerpts indicate, he was tortured by writing blocks. What little he did produce he could not sell. He kept trying, nonetheless, during the first half of his marriage. Finally, he took assignments reviewing books for newspapers.

It is to his credit that he took a passionate interest in his wife's career, performing chores and discharging obligations that would normally have descended upon her. He helped with household chores, willing to vacuum, polish, and dust, though he left cooking to his wife. (Once, when she was out of town, he "reverted to a hermit's diet of raw fruit and milk and greeted [Mary] like a starved cat, pointing speechlessly toward the stove when [she] came in the door.") He always protected her from intrusion, insisting that she get a long, uninterrupted period in her study each day. Bowden Broadwater was a good husband for Mary McCarthy, which she understood and appreciated. The good care he took of her was at least partly responsible for her prolific output during their fifteen-year marriage.

In the late spring of 1947 Bowden Broadwater took a salaried job with a magazine. "Bowden has at last got a job," Dwight Macdonald wrote Nicola Chiaromonte, "helping edit something called *Medical Digest,* which is the *Reader's Digest* of the medical field, and crusades against socialized medicine. The offices are in New Jersey, so the poor fellow has a long trip each way every day. But the pay is good and he'll stick it out for a while. They'll probably be in town all summer because of it." In fact, the job did not last for long, and the Broadwaters spent the summer of 1947 in Pawlet, a small town in southwestern Vermont. They rented a house called Derby Hill, which dated from the American Revolution. The house was in an isolated spot, "with deer, snakes, nice wild strawberries, raspberries, and blueberries," McCarthy wrote Dwight Macdonald; it was a glorious place perched above mountains that, in the mauve-blue distance, looked like a cavalcade of animals hurrying toward the vanishing point on the horizon.

Reuel spent the summer in Wellfleet with his father, though he did visit Pawlet. Always protective of his wife's quiet time, Broadwater explored the area, swam and fished with Reuel, and generally whiled away part of each day with him so that his mother could write for a few scheduled hours. Although Broadwater was not particularly fond of children, he was good with Reuel, and reasonably strict as well. Reuel liked him and was happy in the new household. He was equally at home in Wellfleet, even though Elena Wilson, his stepmother (Wilson had remarried in 1946), gave birth to a daughter early in 1948, thereby displacing him from his privileged position as only child. (Rosalind, Wilson's oldest child, was living in Boston and working for the *Boston Globe.*) Of course Reuel, who had lived on the Cape since he was a baby, had friends there, as well as a dog and a cat, and he knew and loved every inch of the terrain. (Reuel Wilson still visits Wellfleet every summer.) But like many an alert child, he tried to get his own way by "managing" his parents. Because his mother and stepfather often referred to Wilson as "the monster," it was all too tempting to complain about what he hoped they would interpret as his father's "monstrous" qualities. "Dear Mummy," one such reproach began,

> Papa dear is being as *HORRIBLE* as ever and Elena isn't being so nice either. They wouldn't let me go to Charlie's today to see the kittens

because it rained last night. The dogs are better but it seems someone
down beat them and beat reckie in the cheek. I got the new monopoly and
books. My father wasn't nice to me last night at diner nag, nag. When you
don't nag me I act better.

At the same time that he groused about his father in letters to his
mother, he told his stepmother "that entirely different things were expected of him in the two households." Understandably, Wilson decided
"that it is perhaps not a good thing for Reuel to go back and forth
between us at this age too much. It is hard enough for him as it is." In
another letter he observed, "I'm afraid he has been resorting to the
technique of playing one parent off against the other. This seems to be
inevitable in these situations, but ought to be discouraged." Reuel, of
course, continued on as before, living with his mother during the school
year and with his father during the summer, and dividing Christmas and
Easter vacations between them.

In the fall Broadwater went to work again, this time at *Partisan Review*
as an editorial assistant. His duties included reading unsolicited manuscripts and copyediting, which was practically nonexistent at *Partisan
Review,* since its writers allowed no changes to be made in their work.
Dwight Macdonald, for example, was piqued when a printer capitalized
God in a paper he had written for a symposium on religion. He needed
the lowercase *g* to make his point, he said, so the galleys were changed
to conform to his original manuscript. The little copyediting that was
required, however, Broadwater did. He had wanted to redesign the
cover and layout, but Nathalie Rahv made all design decisions. So, when
his salary was cut during a period of retrenchment, he quit. This was his
last "regular" employment until he accepted a teaching position at Saint
Bernard's eight years later.

McCarthy, however, accepted a teaching job at Sarah Lawrence, at
two hundred dollars a month, during the 1948 spring semester. Sarah
Lawrence, a school she did not like because "the students were so poor,"
was established in 1928 by businessman William Lawrence, who transformed his Bronxville estate into a liberal arts college for women and
named it after his wife. Bronxville, only fifteen miles north of New
York, was an easy commute by train. McCarthy later used parts of
Harold Taylor, the president at the time of her tenure, as a character in
The Groves of Academe. But it was another novel by a Sarah Lawrence
faculty member that gained fame for its satirical portrait of this academic
community. The novel was *Pictures from an Institution;* its author, Randall
Jarrell, was primarily a poet, but as he told Robert Lowell in a letter, he

could not resist making such a gallery of caricatures.

Gertrude Johnson, simultaneously heroine and villainess, was partly based on Mary McCarthy, though Jarrell denied it. When McCarthy asked him if Gertrude was based on her, he replied, "No, it's me. You know—like Flaubert." Privately, he told Philip Rahv that it seemed "funny to have [Gertrude] confused with Mary McCarthy whom I know slightly and don't know too much about, but she *is* the same general type as Mary McCarthy, her books are like, and I got five or six happenings or pictures from Mary McCarthy." Not surprisingly, many readers believed that Gertrude was a portrait of McCarthy. In *Pictures from an Institution,* "Gertrude Johnson was, of course, the novelist. . . . Gertrude had, as her enemies put it, a hard heart and a sharp tongue." She was at Benton, Jarrell's fictitious name for Sarah Lawrence, "collecting for the Book. . . . She was a continuously witty and occasionally humorous woman. She loved to make people laugh, just as she loved to shock them. . . . Her books were a systematic, detailed, and conclusive condemnation of mankind for being stupid and bad." Her "grammar, syntax, and punctuation were perfectly orthodox," and "her style made everything sound as if it had been dictated by the spirit of Geometry." McCarthy was not bothered by the portrait. Gertrude Johnson did not resemble her physically, nor was her fictional husband much like Broadwater. "The only points in common that I was able to find," she said much later, "were that Gertrude had a satirical way of writing and used local materials, so to speak."

The postwar years were extremely happy for Mary McCarthy. Not only was her marriage a source of contentment, but the times themselves buoyed her spirits.

> After the war was the very best period, politically, that I've been through. At that time it seemed to me there was a lot of hope around. The war was over. . . . The bomb had been dropped on Hiroshima, and there was a kind of general repentance of this fact. This was before the hydrogen bomb; and we never ever dreamed that the Russians were going to get the atomic bomb. . . . It seemed possible still, utopian but possible, to change the world on a small scale.

Mary McCarthy, Dwight Macdonald, and Nicola Chiaromonte decided, therefore, that the time was ripe for making connections with nonaligned intellectuals of the Left in Europe. Believing that the major political parties and large organizations merely preserved the status quo, they determined to form a small group that would interact with similar groups in Europe. Thus, what came to be called Europe-America Groups was started in the spring of 1948 by thirty New York intellectuals. Besides Mary McCarthy, the guiding spirit—the "spark plug," as Macdonald called her—the group included Dwight Macdonald, Nicola Chiaromonte, Paolo Milano, Nicholas Nabokov, Isaac Rosenfeld, Dorothy Thompson, Bertram Wolfe, Alfred Kazin, Elizabeth Hardwick, Delmore Schwartz, Saul Steinberg, Niccolò Tucci, *Partisan Review* editors William Phillips, Philip Rahv, and William Barrett, and philosopher Sidney Hook. Their aim was to give material help to European intellectuals, to promote public discussions here and abroad on cultural and political matters, and to establish regular channels of communication between American and European intellectuals. They wrote and signed a manifesto which began:

> We are a group of people from various intellectual professions in America who have gotten together to provide some center of solidarity with and support for intellectuals in Europe on the basis of certain ideas which we would like to make explicit. Like ourselves, these intellectuals are isolated, not only from the great power blocs that divide the world, but also to a large extent from each other. Many have unwillingly resigned themselves to passivity in the face of the extreme polarity of Soviet and American power.

The signers contributed money, except the *Partisan Review* people, who "rather grudgingly . . . joined (they didn't like the notion of 'non-aligned intellectuals of the left') . . . and gave their names," Mary McCarthy remembered thirty-four years later, "but not even five dollars' worth of help." She made the first, and largest, donation of five hundred dollars, having just inherited twenty-three thousand dollars from the sale of her Capitol Elevator stock. The signers also raised money by sponsoring an art auction, which netted them one thousand dollars; a party, to which they charged admission; debates, one of which was a heated argument between Sidney Hook and Mark Van Doren on Henry Wallace's presidential candidacy; and lectures, such as Nicholas Nabokov's "The Soviet Attack on Culture," which was followed by a panel discussion by Meyer Schapiro, Mary McCarthy, Lionel Trilling, and Dwight Macdonald.

Three quarters of the money raised was to be given to Nicola Chiaromonte, to use as he saw fit in Europe. The remaining money would go to Walter Goldwater, the treasurer, to buy and ship books to European intellectuals. Just before this disbursement, a special meeting was held in the late spring at Philip and Nathalie Rahv's, ostensibly to suspend fund-raising for the summer, since most members would leave New York until the fall. Some time before the meeting, McCarthy learned that a faction led by Sidney Hook wanted to use the group's funds, at this time more than two thousand dollars, for another purpose. "They planned to be in the majority," McCarthy recalled, "and vote to transfer our treasury to some other entity. I became very busy calling friends who had contributed but would normally never have come to a meeting, not being 'political,'" like her brother Kevin and his friend Montgomery Clift. Mary McCarthy has long remembered "the faces of Hook and company when they looked around Rahv's living room and realized they were not in the majority." The money from the treasury was disbursed as originally intended.

The group disbanded until the fall of 1948, and Nicola Chiaromonte left for Europe with the promised three-quarters of the treasury. When he wrote Mary McCarthy in July to report on disbursements, she and Broadwater were in a rented house in Cornwall, Connecticut, a lovely town, with a covered bridge, in the western part of the state very near the Berkshire Mountains. ("We are having a luxuriant summer with vegetable gardens and fresh eggs and milk and chickens and cheap heavy cream and all the scenery thrown in," she wrote Dwight Macdonald.) According to Chiaromonte, Albert Camus, who had been most helpful in introducing him to useful people, suggested that the Americans re-work their manifesto. Its vagueness made European intellectuals nervous. (In the fall, members did draw up a "compromise" manifesto, which was equally "unexceptionable" and "on the dull side," according to Dwight Macdonald, because of the need to accommodate *Partisan Review*'s "get-Russia-at-all-costs attitude.") Chiaromonte concluded his letter with "dear Mary, I feel extremely thankful for everything you did to bring E/A groups into real existence."

She responded immediately, but to Dwight Macdonald rather than to Nicola Chiaromonte. "My preliminary impression is one of almost shame at the seriousness of the European response to our very trivial and muddling efforts. I feel as if I had gotten somebody with child in the course of an innocent flirtation. It makes both of us [herself and Bowden] think very strongly that something better must be done with Europe-America Groups. . . . I am absolutely sick of the way I am living, the lack of accomplishment and seriousness, and one year succeeding another with nothing's being changed." She suggested, in six typed pages, issuing "Europe-America Bulletins," broadening the membership, and living communally with a small, congenial group—"Some attempt at a communal program of living still appears to me to be the most obvious solution."

Although Macdonald concurred, the continued existence of Europe-America Groups was in jeopardy. He outlined the reasons for this in a letter to Nicola Chiaromonte. From the beginning, a split between "Hook and the PR boys, the right opposition," and McCarthy and himself had "stymied action." Moreover, "E/A objectives are too vague and its members too variegated (and with too little personal connection.) This might not be bad in a big well-heeled outfit. But EAG has to survive as a 'band of brothers,' or not at all. And there is not much brotherhood about it now. I'm afraid Mary was right—as against you and me—in her idea of splitting EAG and sloughing off the PR-Hook crowd." Finally, wrote Macdonald, "no one wants to carry the ball," for "no one has appeared to do the work except Mary" and she was "only halfhearted" owing to the tension created by ideological differences. EAG's last gasp for life was an appeal, consisting of a redrafted statement of purpose, that was mailed out to one hundred intellectuals. Lack of response to the mailing—sent out exactly one year after Hook and his allies tried to divert EAG money to another group—ended EAG. It was officially dissolved at a meeting in the spring of 1949, when the last two hundred dollars in the treasury was disbursed.

Mary McCarthy transmuted her frustration and disappointment over the bitter factionalism surrounding Europe-America Groups—which had been, after all, a completely harmless organization—into the gentle satire of *The Oasis*. She wrote this short novel for a contest sponsored by the English journal *Horizon*, considered, like *Partisan Review*, its country's leading literary magazine. *Horizon* devoted its entire February 1949 issue to *The Oasis;* Random House published it as a book in August. McCarthy had started work on *The Oasis* in the spring of 1948, while she was at Sarah Lawrence, and continued all summer in Cornwall. She worked each day from nine to two in a little shed on the property she and Broadwater had rented, readying the manuscript for the competition's closing date of October 1. Her writing did not prevent her from entertaining weekend guests, however. The Macdonalds and Margaret and Fritz Shafer, friends from Bard, were among the weekenders.

The title for McCarthy's new book, she told an interviewer, came from Arthur Koestler, who at the time was writing about the possibility of establishing small libertarian groups, or oases, that would try to change the world on a small scale. This idea was of course exactly what

Nicola Chiaromonte, Dwight Macdonald, and Mary McCarthy had been discussing since the summer they were together in Truro. "For years I used to have a dream," she told another interviewer, "of living in some sort of anarchist utopia which would have maximum freedom which implies of course maximum self-discipline. Anarchist utopia means that there would be no established central criteria." McCarthy created an imaginary version of such a community in *The Oasis*. But the failure of Europe-America Groups had undermined her confidence that such an endeavor could succeed.

The Oasis is a fable about a group of New York intellectuals—clearly based on her own circle—and one businessman, who together form a utopian colony in an antiquated, abandoned hotel in the Taconic Mountains, in the vicinity of Pawlet, Vermont (where the Broadwaters had summered in 1947). Founded in accordance with the precepts of an Italian anarchist, Monteverdi (obviously Nicola Chiaromonte), who never appears in the book, the colony is supposed to set an example for "a network of autonomous, cooperative communities with unlimited freedom for the individual." Moreover, the group hopes to sponsor an "Operation Peace," which would bring over Europeans with a desire to join their libertarian venture. But dissension splits the group in two from the beginning. The purists want to put into practice Monteverdi's notions of justice and freedom. Their leader, whose conception of politics is too demanding, too pure, to be workable, is Macdougal Macdermott, the fictional version of Dwight Macdonald. Mac Macdermott "ten years before . . . had made the leap into faith and sacrificed $20,000 a year and a secure career as a paid journalist," just as Macdonald had left a lucrative and secure job with Henry Luce's *Fortune*. Macdermott "had moved downtown into Bohemia," just as had Macdonald and his wife, Nancy, who lived on Tenth Street on the fringes of the Village. Macdermott "dropped the use of capital letters, and became the editor of a libertarian magazine"; Macdonald's publication, which he founded in 1944, was called *politics* with a lowercase *p*.

The realists come to Utopia to shuck off the pressures of everyday life, and on the outside chance that the purists will succeed. They do not believe, as the purists do, that anyone "could resist history, environment, class structure, psychic conditioning" and find unlimited freedom. Will Taub, who is based on Philip Rahv, is their leader.

> Facts of any kind, oddities, lore, local history, intoxicated the mind of this realist, whose own experience had been strangely narrow—a half-forgotten childhood in the Carpathian mountains, immigration, city streets, the

Movement, Bohemian women, the anti-Movement, downtown bars, argument, discussion, subways, newsstands, the office. This was all he knew of
the world; the rest was hearsay, upon which his materialist imagination
was continually at play, building on straws of report vast structures of
conjecture and speculation. . . . Concealment was second nature to him
(though he had nothing to hide); he liked confidences, closed rooms, low
voices; his eyelids were normally drooped and his gaze darted out between them, following events narrowly, like a watcher behind shutters.

Trouble begins for the Utopians even before they leave New York.
First, they discuss what is appropriate to bring to the oasis. "Agreeing
in principle, that the machine was to be distrusted, they had nevertheless
voted to use in their experiment the bicycle, the carpet-sweeper, and the
sewing machine, any machine, in fact, to which a man contributed his
own proportionate share of exertion and which tried him like the plough
and the hoe." Then they hotly debate whether to admit businessman Joe
Lockman, a go-getting nonintellectual, to their group. Joe, determined
to get more spiritual profit out of the oasis than anyone else, is finally
accepted, since "ostracism . . . would indeed have been an ugly beginning for a community devoted to brotherhood." Then, after the dispute
about Joe Lockman's eligibility for Utopian membership, they debate
"was it to follow . . . that *anyone* could be admitted to Utopia—a thief,
a blackmailer, a murderer?" Why not, ask the purists; impossible, say the
realists. Finally, they leave New York in a "cavalcade of cars, well-
stocked with whiskey, cans, and contraceptives," but the debates continue.

As soon as they arrive in "paradise," Joe Lockman precipitates two
crises, putting an ancient stove out of commission and frightening Will
Taub with a prod from his shotgun. Taub, in retaliation, tries to get
Lockman expelled from the settlement, which gives rise to more discussion and argument. The major crisis, however, occurs when interlopers
pick the colonists' strawberries. The ensuing and interminable analysis
about "What To Do" parodied the typical EAG meeting. The members
question whether they are justified in excluding anyone and whether it
matters that they want their own strawberries for a picnic dessert rather
than to sustain life. They argue about whether to use threats or force to
evict the intruders. They are, in short, talkers and not doers.

In the end, two Utopians chase the trespassers away with Joe Lockman's gun. The colonists, however, do not appreciate the irony in their
having protected their property while simultaneously subscribing to
Proudhon's maxim, "Property is theft." Only one of their company

understands the meaning of their failure. Katy Norell, something of a stand-in for the author—a person with "a strong will and weak character" and an awkward compulsion to tell the truth—realizes that to try to embody virtue on the communal level is absurd until it is accomplished on the individual level. That the Utopians fail to make a genuine community is unfortunate, but their attempt should not be held against them. They try because they *are* intellectuals. All Utopian colonies have failed, McCarthy implies, but society outside is a greater failure.

Although Mary McCarthy has said that she is not conscious of much satire in her books, she remarked once that "the only one that aimed at the moral reform of its targets, if that is the word, was *The Oasis*. I really think I hoped to show them (the realist faction: Macdougal Macdermott is incorrigible) how they looked and sounded exposed on a mountaintop." Unable to refrain from intellectual wrangling, both the realist and purist factions sound ridiculous.

The reviews of *The Oasis* were, on the whole, unenthusiastic. Brendan Gill in *The New Yorker* did characterize the novel as "an absolutely unmitigated triumph of wit and writing skill." But more typical reviewers' reactions included "mild entertainment," "small rewards for reading so many words," "a philosophical disquisition with fictional trimmings." "[The Utopians'] sins are intellectual," wrote Henry Rago in *Commonweal*, "and so their torture is in kind; they simply have Mary McCarthy watching them."

Ironically, most critics complained that she was too gentle. Gorham Munson, for example, wrote in the *Saturday Review* that "Miss McCarthy is more amused than critical because she was too close to her material, too much identified with it herself." Even Brendan Gill, in his otherwise positive review, wrote that it was too bad she ended the tale on a note "of cheerful assent to the malevolent conditions of life." T. J. Ross in *The New Republic* contended that "the 'satire' contains one of the friendliest and most sympathetic portrayals of intellectual people that I know of; in fact, as a story *The Oasis* is not a success because of the imbalance between the affectionate and winning presentation of the characters and the presentation of the satirized situation in which they're involved." Paul Goodman, no exception to the Mary-is-too-kind grievance, blamed the satire's "toothlessness" on "Mrs. Broadwater's habitual sunny friendliness," and then proceeded to parody the book in a review in *Furioso*, Carleton College's literary magazine. Edmund Wilson, who habitually championed his former wife's work, complained in a letter, which the magazine published, that a book by Mary McCarthy deserved "more serious consideration."

Philip Rahv was flabbergasted by the reviews. How, he wondered, did the critics detect cheerfulness, sunniness, gentleness, amusement, friendliness, sympathy, and affection in *The Oasis* when he perceived nothing but malice? He was furious about his portrayal, and threatened to sue McCarthy (so, too, did a stranger with the same name as the businessman). Rahv went to a lawyer, but Dwight Macdonald persuaded him not to bring suit. "You realize, Phil, in order to win this lawsuit, you have to prove that you are Will Taub," Macdonald said. "Are you prepared to make that kind of jackass out of yourself?" Rahv got the point, abruptly halting all talk of legal action. He was, however, "wounded to the quick." "I thought it was cruel to Philip," Elizabeth Hardwick says, "because he was very vulnerable." Rahv's fellow *Partisan Review* editor, William Barrett, recorded how the shock of reading *The Oasis* temporarily healed a rift between Rahv and his colleague William Phillips, a rift that had begun when Phillips complained to Rahv that he "had talked too freely against the other [editors] behind their backs." Barrett remembered:

> For a while [Rahv] went into virtual seclusion. For a whole week he did not come to the office, and that was a rupture in his habits so violent that it could be produced only by something on the order of a catastrophe. He needed that daily walk to the office, the satisfaction of curiosity in ferreting out the mail (not always his own), and above all the escape it provided from staring at the typewriter in the pangs of authorship. He saw only his wife and . . . yes, William Phillips. For it was only the latter from whom he could draw consolation at a moment like this. William assured him that he was not discredited, that nobody around town took the caricature as accurate, and, finally, that Rahv wasn't really like that at all. . . . What was amazing was that there was no real break in his friendship with Miss McCarthy. For his part he could come to regard her act of writing as the play of a very brilliant child who does not quite know what she is doing. And for her part she probably had not thought her victim would be wounded, for it was all in such fun.

In one way, William Barrett was right that "it was all in such fun." The Broadwaters had a wonderful time during the creation of *The Oasis.* ("That book," says Elizabeth Hardwick, "came about through the influence of Bowden. He thought all those people were a scream.") Walter Goldwater, the treasurer of Europe-America Groups and a fleeting character in *The Oasis* ("I'm the man who looked like a nailfile," he cheerfully recalled), found the book amusing and accurate. "I don't think Mary was vicious, she just described."

But Harold Kaplan and Saul Bellow, both contributors to *Partisan Review,* were outraged by *The Oasis.* Kaplan wrote to Rahv that

> Bellow and I . . . spent half the night talking about Mary McCarthy's alleged story. Perhaps there is something of an outraged masculine reaction involved (as I believe there was in much of the critical reaction to her first book) but we believe this thing is so vile, so perfect an example of everything that is nasty in New York and everything that is sterile in recent American writing, that we came to the conclusion that something should be done about it. The worst of it is not her stupid caricature of you but the utter cadaverous deadness of the whole thing: no life, no talent, no movement; the jokes are gruesomely flat, the story has no point, there is no literary (and hence—this is our great grief—no moral) justification for the whole thing, except a bewildered and rather pathological vengefulness. What has happened to this woman? Bellow and I are toying with the idea of writing a joint letter, or a dialogue, to point up some of the meanings of this foul piece—but now that a few days have gone by I question whether it is worth bothering about. People here who do not know the PR crowd find it utterly impossible to read this so-called story— so why waste our brightness on a document which should never have got beyond the file of a competent psychiatrist?

Rahv sent a copy of the letter to Dwight Macdonald with the postscript "It might be a good thing to show this to Mary. Perhaps it will wake her up from the miasmic dreams in which she has been moving of late."

Macdonald himself, although he was the most comical character in the fable, reacted to it quite mildly. As he wrote Nicola Chiaromonte:

> Have you read "The Oasis" yet? Almost no one likes it around here except me. And I didn't like it the second time I read it anywhere near as much as when I heard Mary read it originally. Do you think it is vicious, malicious, and nasty?

And instead of forwarding Kaplan's letter to Mary McCarthy, Macdonald included it with his letter to Chiaromonte, commenting that it was "true to some extent, but just as bitterly inhuman as Mary's story, really, and even more exaggerated; maybe I'm a centrist; I know the intensity of the feuds and polemics now running about repels and frightens me."

Chiaromonte answered:

> Mary's story has caused quite a stir over here (you must keep in mind that Paris has by now become to a great extent an American city, with the Saint-Germain section literally occupied . . .) the aforementioned stir being on the whole quite negative, I am sorry to say. I myself should have liked to be enthusiastic about the story, but alas I am unable to do so. Mary is certainly a brilliant girl, but why she should be so hopelessly literal, I can't understand.

Macdonald agreed.

> Mary's story: yes, too literal; also too much on the surface; yet I think the reaction against it is excessive; some very witty and penetrating remarks; most serious criticism I've heard is that the people caricatured cannot learn anything about themselves and their weaknesses from it; as one, I have to agree; you of course are the Holy Ghost, hovering over the scene but exempt, by virtue of your sacred character from either criticism or (alas) specific description.

Part of everyone's pique was that Mary McCarthy had published her caricatures of the *Partisan Review* crowd in *Horizon*, "the English magazine which was rather the opposite number to *Partisan Review,*" William Barrett wrote in *The Truants,* "and this was as if she had gone across the street to tell her bad news in a rival home." Margaret Marshall, the literary editor of *The Nation,* whose name appeared with McCarthy's as coauthor of "Our Critics, Right or Wrong," thought publishing abroad was clever and malicious, and added that McCarthy "has no qualms about using her best friends and closest associates as material for her fiction."

Despite their annoyance with Mary McCarthy, several of her "victims" joined ranks with her the weekend of March 25–27, 1949, to infiltrate the Cultural and Scientific Conference for World Peace, the last major effort of American Stalinism to reestablish itself as a cultural force in this country. The aim of the conference, held at the Waldorf-Astoria Hotel, was to promote a conciliatory attitude toward the Soviet Union by having American fellow travelers meet with their opposite numbers from Eastern and Western Europe. The conference was to consist largely of talks by pro-Soviet Americans and Eastern-bloc Communists. Among its sponsors were Lillian Hellman, Dashiell Hammett, Leonard Bernstein, and Aaron Copland. McCarthy and her fellow anti-Stalinists planned to go to the meeting to make anti-Communist speeches from the floor. McCarthy, Dwight Macdonald, Robert Lowell, and Elizabeth Hardwick had registered as delegates in February. They were told they would get admission tickets in time to attend. McCarthy informed Sidney Hook. "He just laughed on the phone," she recalled recently, "and said, 'That just shows how naive you are. You won't get tickets.' " Because Hook had tried unsuccessfully to secure a place on the program as a speaker, he thought it unlikely that the Stalinists would welcome any anti-Stalinists to their conference. He was wrong, and he was annoyed, said McCarthy, that she and friends would get into the conference's meetings and he would not. So, at the last minute, Hook organized a diverse group of anti-Stalinist intellectuals who agreed only that pro-Soviet propaganda had to be answered. The group was called Americans for Intellectual Freedom. With little money and several volunteers, the group rented a suite at the Waldorf for the purpose of preparing anti-Stalinist press statements, of planning a rival meeting the last day of the conference, and of coaching those who had the three-dollar tickets of admission on what they should say from the floor.

While right-wing anti-Communists picketed outside the Waldorf, Hook and his friends insisted that the left-wing anti-Communists inside write speeches for the next day. One of Hook's group was so sure they would not be permitted to speak, McCarthy remembered, he suggested that they tie themselves to their chairs, and when they got tossed out of the meeting, that they give their prepared speeches—mainly embarrassing questions about what had happened to missing Russian writers—to the press. "I don't think this will happen," McCarthy objected. "They gave us tickets." Macdonald, Lowell, and Hardwick agreed with her. "You goddamned intellectuals," McCarthy remembered Hook's deputy saying; "give me those Catholic workers." (He was referring to the picketers outside the hotel.) Finally, the Hook group convinced McCarthy and friends to go home and write speeches, which they did. The next day they arrived at the conference "with umbrellas and a truculent state of mind," as McCarthy recalled.

As it turned out, Louis Untermeyer, the chairman, was perfectly willing to let McCarthy's contingent have the floor, although only for two minutes per person. Even so, they banged on the floor with their umbrellas to get recognition. Mary McCarthy asked Harvard scholar F. O. Matthiessen, who had called Emerson a predecessor of the Communist

Party, if he thought Emerson would be able to live and work in Russia today. No, Matthiessen conceded; on the other hand, he countered, Lenin would not be able to live in the United States. Macdonald challenged A. A. Fadayev, head of the Soviet delegation, to reveal the truth about missing Russian writers. Fadayev denied there were any missing.

Most of the speeches were pro-Soviet. A retired bishop from Utah spoke about the glories of Russia, and the Russian composer Dmitri Shostakovich praised Stalinist criticism of his music. Frederick Schuman, a professor of government at Williams College, tried to give the conference a less partisan cast by asserting that there were elements in both Russia and the United States favoring war. When Fadayev said that no one in Russia wanted war, Schuman backed down and claimed that only Americans wanted war. Toward the end of the conference, the young novelist Norman Mailer, who, as an official participant of the conference, was expected to deliver another pro-Soviet speech, horrified the Stalinists by denouncing Russia as well as the United States.

From the standpoint of its organizers, the conference was a shambles. Howard Fast, a member of the American delegation, asked McCarthy and her group to go for a drink at an East Side hotel. Feeling sorry for the American Stalinists and also curious about their reactions, McCarthy, Macdonald, Lowell, and Hardwick went to their cash-bar "reception."

In retrospect, Mary McCarthy found the events of the Waldorf conference amusing. She started a short story about the conference but never finished it, maybe because the disparity between the near-hysteria of some of the Americans for Intellectual Freedom and the impotence of the Stalinists seemed too implausible for fiction.

PART FIVE

CHAPTER XIII

PORTSMOUTH
(1949–1952)

ARY McCARTHY was discouraged by the negative reactions of the *Partisan Review* crowd to *The Oasis* and dismayed by the reviewers' failure to distinguish what she saw as a *conte philosophique* from a conventional novel—a failure that led them to censure it for the wrong reasons. "I am tempted by the criticisms," she wrote Arthur Schlesinger, Jr., "to mimeograph an exegesis of *The Oasis*." So, when Hannah Arendt, who at the time had written a few political essays that McCarthy thought highly of, wrote her that "*The Oasis* is a gem," McCarthy was elated. In fact, Hannah Arendt's comment marked the beginning of a long and intimate friendship.

The two women had first met in 1944. Hannah Arendt had read *The Company She Keeps* and liked it. But when she next saw McCarthy, at a party at Philip Rahv's apartment in the early spring of 1945, she was not so admiring. Amazed that Hitler was so uncomprehending as to have longed for the Parisians' love during the German occupation of their city, McCarthy said she felt sorry for him. "How can you say such a thing to me, a victim of Hitler and a person who has been in a concentration camp?" Arendt exploded. And she marched straight to Philip Rahv, demanding, "How can you have this kind of conversation in your home and you a Jew?"

Not until Dwight Macdonald included both women in a small group that met several times early in 1949 to discuss the future of *politics* did they get the opportunity to speak to each other again. After one of the meetings, when they were alone on a subway platform, Arendt observed that they always seemed to agree about whatever was being discussed. "We two think alike," she said. Emboldened by Arendt's friendliness, McCarthy apologized for her Hitler remark, and Arendt confessed she had not been in a concentration camp. The note praising *The Oasis* was written shortly after this reconciliation.

It is not surprising they became good friends. Both women possessed penetrating minds that set them apart from most people; both responded ardently to art, music, and books; and both paid respectful attention to the details of everyday living.

Many years later, after Arendt's death, McCarthy wrote about what drew her to this formidable woman.

She was a beautiful woman, alluring, seductive, most speakingly the eyes, which were brilliant, sparkling, as though rays of intelligence leaped out of them, but also dark pools of inwardness. There was something unfathomable in Hannah that seemed to lie in the reflective depths of those eyes. When she talked, it was like seeing the motions of the mind exteriorized in action and gestures as she would flex her lips, frown, pensively cup her chin. Hannah is the only person I have seen *think*. I will tell you how she did it. . . . She lay without moving on a sofa or day bed, her arms folded behind her head, eyes shut but occasionally opening to stare upwards. This lasted—I don't know—for ten minutes, probably, to half an hour. I would tiptoe past her if I had to enter the room.

Like many other people, Arendt was attracted by what she saw as the child in Mary McCarthy, that singular combination of innocence and worldliness which she described in a 1959 letter of recommendation to the John Simon Guggenheim Memorial Foundation.

What distinguishes her from other writers . . . is that she reports her findings from the viewpoint and with the amazement of the child who discovered that the Emperor had no clothes. The point is that her impetus springs from the fact that she, like a child and unlike anybody else in society, always begins by believing quite literally what everybody says and thus prepares herself for the finest, most wonderful clothes. Whereupon the Emperor enters—stark naked. This inner tension between expectation and reality, I think, runs like a thread through most of her work since *The Company She Keeps.* It gives her novels and stories a rare dramatic quality which, oddly enough, is often independent of the plot.

Hannah Arendt started including Mary and Bowden Broadwater in the circle of European emigrés she often invited to dinner at her modest apartment on the West Side of Manhattan. By the middle 1950s the women had begun a correspondence in which they not only discussed politics, literature, and philosophy but also shared confidences. Arendt, for example, told no one but McCarthy when her angina was first discovered, in 1971. In like manner, McCarthy used Arendt as a mail drop when, in 1956, she was having an affair with an English critic. Over the years they visited and telephoned regularly, took trips together, read each other's work, and dedicated books to one another—Arendt's *On Violence* to McCarthy in 1969 and McCarthy's *Birds of America,* her favorite among her novels, to Arendt in 1971. In addition, McCarthy made editorial suggestions when Arendt asked her to "English" her manuscripts, and she was always present whenever Arendt delivered a major lecture—the Christian Gauss Lectures at Princeton University and the Gifford Lectures at Aberdeen University, for example—or received an award—the Danish government's Sonning Prize, in Copenhagen, among others. McCarthy capped two and a half decades of devotion to Arendt by becoming the literary executrix of her estate in 1975.

Hannah Arendt, six years older than McCarthy, had been born in Hanover, Germany in 1906. She studied philosophy under Martin Heidegger at Marburg University and Karl Jaspers at Heidelberg University, earning a doctorate at twenty-two. Like Nicola Chiaromonte, she had been shaped intellectually by the Greeks, especially Plato, and had also voiced distaste for Marxist and Freudian ideologies. She was thrust into politics by what she later termed an "outbreak of history": the rise of Adolph Hitler. Because she was Jewish, she had to leave Germany, and in 1933 she escaped with her first husband, Günther Stern, to Paris, where they divorced and where she married Heinrich Blücher, a self-educated former Communist seven years her senior. The Blüchers and Hannah Arendt's mother managed to get to America in 1940. Hannah Arendt became an American citizen in 1951.

At the time Mary McCarthy and Hannah Arendt met, Arendt was unknown outside a small group of emigrés in New York. She had written a few political essays in which she explained how stateless people had been reduced to superfluousness. Whatever merit the notion of the rights of man against the state may once have had, she argued, it had become clear that in a world of nation-states, to be stateless was to have no rights whatsoever. The first right of man was to belong to a political society. Without state membership, one was unwanted, displaced, expendable. When she published her first and most widely read book, *The Origins of Totalitarianism,* in 1951, she became famous. In it she analyzed the two major forms of twentieth-century totalitarianism, Nazism and Communism, linking them to the anti-Semitism and imperialism of the nineteenth century. Although the term *totalitarianism* had been loosely applied to any and every form of political intimidation, for Hannah Arendt it was an entirely new phenomenon. Crimes on such a scale as those committed by Stalin and Hitler, she said, broke down all standards hitherto known.

During the next twenty-four years, until her death in 1975, Hannah Arendt achieved international eminence with many essays and books. Because she objected to "schools of thought," thereby confounding attempts to pigeonhole her ideas in any ideological sense, she managed to inspire or infuriate almost all sectors of the political spectrum. Mary McCarthy sprang to her defense more than once during those years. At first, though, it was Arendt who encouraged McCarthy by praising *The Oasis.*

In June of 1949 the Broadwaters moved to Portsmouth, Rhode Island, a ten-minute drive from Newport, on Narragansett Bay. They had been looking for a place to buy outside of New York ever since Mary had received her share of the proceeds from the Capitol Elevator sale a year before. The house they bought had been built in 1850 as a "frugal, foursquare farmhouse with a graveyard in a grove, a copper beech, a weeping elm, a pond at the edge of which are masses of high-bush blueberries, watercress, and forget-me-nots, and fifteen acres now leased by a Portuguese dairy farmer." The property, which sat on Union Street, was enclosed by a stone fence. "Everything is incomparably beautiful and serene here," McCarthy wrote Elizabeth Hardwick, "the light, the trees, the streets, the blue water." They moved right after Reuel had finished the school year at Saint Bernard's. (Edmund Wilson was pleased. He had complained often about Reuel's living arrangements in the cramped conditions of the Broadwaters' Fifty-seventh Street apartment. "You *must* find a decent place to live," he wrote. "You cannot keep him there another year.")

On June 21, her thirty-seventh birthday, McCarthy wrote Kevin that they were "camping out, cooking on an electric plate in the denuded parlor, surrounded by cartons, . . . washing the dishes with cold water in the bathtub." To save money, they did some of the renovation themselves. Even so, there were "painters and plumbers and paperhangers everywhere." Like everyone who gets involved in fixing up an old house, they ran into more problems than they had anticipated, including a leaky roof and damage done by workmen. As McCarthy reported to Elizabeth Hardwick:

> The first day the movers drove in and took a branch off the tree; the plumber followed, made an estimate of $270 to put in hot water, and backing out, ran into Bowden's car (much laughter), wrecking the rear fender and the tail-light. . . . Yesterday a tattooed youth who was laying the linoleum in the kitchen managed to fall through two windows, on opposite sides of the room, so today the glazier is here. . . .
>
> Despite the havoc, I am very happy; Bowden too. New sources of energy have sprung up in him; he is scything or mowing the lawn or putting up towel racks at every instant, and I have suddenly found myself in the position of the grasshopper; it is quite astonishing. The kitchen has just been finished and is the only habitable room; it is royal blue with white wainscoting and woodwork, dark blue linoleum floor, and a wonderful

new gas stove (found by Bowden in Consumer's Research) and a huge white General Electric icebox. These appliances, though I've only had them a day, have quite changed my outlook on technology; they do make life easier and pleasanter, more appreciably then I would have thought possible; I am filled with pride and joy in these possessions. The red table is in the kitchen and we have eaten our first regular meal, looking out on Mr. Lacerda's cows and the pond turned pink in the sunset. We have found flowers in the garden, two white climbing roses, and the ruin of a formal plan, one blooming peony and myrtle. The vegetable garden has been ploughed by Mr. Lacerda and I am raking it, but there is a drought so one can't plant yet.

After nine weeks of scything, raking, planting, painting, scrubbing, stripping, sanding, sewing, polishing, bleaching, and laundering—from eight in the morning until eight at night—they had finished, in addition to the kitchen: the sitting room, "a dream-yellow with green furniture and little red table and white woodwork . . . , very gay and farmhousey and not like a decorator's illustration, and fine thin white Irish linen curtains," which McCarthy made herself; the dining room; the library; the parlor, with pomegranate wallpaper; the hall; their bedroom, "all white and gold with a white floor"; and Reuel's bedroom, with "a sturdy grey" floor. But the Broadwaters had very little with which to furnish their newly refurbished rooms. Fortunately, Dwight Macdonald's wife, Nancy, had just inherited a large number of antiques, and she pressed McCarthy to take two desks, a spool bed, several barrels of china, and assorted lamps, mirrors, and knickknacks.

McCarthy, so busy with the house, had scarcely noticed how infrequently Reuel, who was spending his usual summer with his father, had written. She sent him a postcard with a gentle reminder:

Dearest Reuel:

Do write. Dwight tells me you and Mike are very friendly—what else is new? Have you learned any more swimming strokes? Can you dive? We have been working so hard that we haven't had time to go in the water for weeks—Bowden has learned to be a first class painter, like a professional. . . . There are millions of butterflies here. Is your net still in one piece? We miss you and talk about you a lot. Do ask your father if he knows where you can get a puppy.

Love, xxxxxx,
Mummy

She and Broadwater continued to work long days, distracted only by the "myriads of birds, butterflies, and soft breezes, cattle grazing everywhere and the smell of hay and clover," as well as by "a fine beach to swim at, not as dramatic as Cape Cod, but rather municipal and shipshape," for which they paid "ten dollars a season to the town for the upkeep." By fall their work on the house was finished. The only break they had taken was a trek to Boston for the wedding of Elizabeth Hardwick and Robert Lowell, two friends they would see a great deal of in the coming years.

Reuel arrived in Portsmouth in September, in time to start seventh grade at Saint Michael's, a local Episcopal school. His mother and stepfather now had time to explore their surroundings, which they had already taken quite a fancy to. Mary wrote Dwight Macdonald that there was no bohemian life whatever, but that even so,

> B. and I are both fascinated. This neighborhood, or perhaps its money, has in some way promoted the real proliferation of character. Everyone is strange, but not impotently so; these creatures have *realized* themselves in a positively tropical fashion. Middle-class suburbs in Westport, Westchester, Vermont, in Red Hook, don't prepare one at all for the startling fact that one isn't bored outside of the *Partisan Review* circle. One feels on the edge of some exhilarating discovery, probably an illusion.

She described many of these characters in letters to friends. There was the "weird" Catholic convert, an army widow who lived nearby, "a kind of circuit-rider of the refined convent set, traveling from the Ursulines to the English Benedictines, as from one army post to the next, always on bivouac, no simulation of piety, but an immense authoritativeness." There was another Catholic convert, a Miss Fortune, a religious artist who designed church interiors; a young Episcopalian from Newport named Nicholas King, who became a lifelong friend of both Broadwaters; and a go-getting professor of political philosophy from Berkeley, who taught a course for captains and admirals at Newport's Naval War College in which they studied ethics, metaphysics, and aesthetics, including whether counterclockwise is esthetically more beautiful than clockwise, or vice versa, "all part of the U.S. campaign against Communism," McCarthy wrote Elizabeth Hardwick.

The most extraordinary person in the neighborhood was Miss Alice Brayton, a seventy-two-year-old waspish New England spinster, who possessed a beautiful home and a great deal of money. She had become a local institution both for her eccentricities and for her famous topiary garden. Her property, which sloped down to Narragansett Bay, was ideal for a garden, since its proximity to the ocean made for mild winters. Her green animals, as she called her topiary collection, were elevated on a grassy platform behind her large white frame house. A giraffe, a camel, an ostrich, an elephant, a horse and rider, a swan, a pair of peacocks, a unicorn, a bear, a boar, a cock, and a she-wolf were larger than life-size.

The first day they moved into their house, Miss Brayton called on the Broadwaters with a bouquet of sweet peas. A month later Mary had decided she was a "strange woman." When she told Miss Brayton that a friend had just married Robert Lowell, the acid-tongued lady replied (wrote McCarthy to Elizabeth Hardwick) that she recognized "no Lowell since James Russell." Her conversation was "a series of traps and mines" and fascinating stories about her life, most of which were not true, McCarthy reported. But she had written two books, *George Berkeley in Apulia* and *George Berkeley in Newport,* both privately printed, which McCarthy admired enough to call to the attention of her editor at Random House. She thought the books were "quite commercial," she told Robert Linscott, "but you can look for yourself and meet their compiler." Apparently Linscott did not agree, for Random House never published them.

The Broadwaters liked Miss Brayton, and she liked them, entertaining them frequently. Her annual Christmas party so captivated Mary that she adapted certain features of it for her own holiday celebration. On Christmas morning Miss Brayton stood outside her back door next to a tall spruce tree, which was hung with prettily wrapped presents, and welcomed relatives and neighbors. Everyone took a gift from the tree as he or she entered the house, then unwrapped it and placed it on the dining room table, which had been converted to a present-exchange for the occasion. When everything had been unwrapped, guests chose the particular gifts that suited them. From Miss Brayton, McCarthy also got the idea of using a strip of tan canvas for the front steps of her Union Street house. Even today, there is a tan duck runner (new) on the front and back steps of her Castine, Maine, house.

Miss Brayton introduced the Broadwaters to Newportians—"One weekend Miss Brayton took us to lunch at Bailey's Beach, introduced us to everyone as some persons who had bought a farm (a real *farm*) in Portsmouth, and considers us now launched." Social Newport, as distinguished from historic Newport, a colonial town with narrow cobbled streets, and from navy Newport, at that time one of two main fleet bases on the Atlantic, begins at the top of the hill with Bellevue Avenue. Here, moving out past Ochre Point toward Bailey's Beach and the famous "Ten Mile" or Ocean Drive, is strung an unbroken line of bizarre palaces, called "cottages," most of them the offspring of a strange architectural crossbreeding of incompatible styles. The Newport social scene both amused and intrigued the Broadwaters. Mary Meigs, a painter who sometimes visited friends of theirs, wrote:

> The Newportians behaved like rich people, a fact which seemed to fascinate Mary and Bowden, not displease them as it displeased me. For Mary and Bowden, the Newportians were not threatening, but rather, subjects of literary interest and analysis. . . . I was disgusted by the superficial chitchat of the Newportians and was unable to answer the kind of questions they put to me. I even had the feeling that, had it not been for the protective presence of Mary and Bowden, these people would have torn my awkward and serious self to pieces.

The Broadwaters were more interested in their own friends than in Newport socialites. Even before the house was completed, they had welcomed Eve Gassler and Al Stwertka, who would be married there in 1950; Paul De Man, later a professor at Yale; Robert Linscott, McCarthy's editor for *The Oasis;* the art critic Harold Rosenberg and his wife, with whom the Broadwaters visited Touro Synagogue in Newport ("more pungently medieval than any cathedral I've ever seen," McCarthy said); the Lowells; and the Schlesingers. The Macdonalds were expected for Thanksgiving 1949, but because McCarthy had a miscarriage, they did not come.

"This letter is just a premonition," she wrote on November 20, 1949. "I'm writing it from Newport Hospital, where I've been since yesterday morning—a miscarriage, alas, rather long-drawn-out. I *think* I'll be out Monday and consequently should be well enough to have you for Thanksgiving, but in case it shouldn't turn out that way, I thought I'd better warn you. . . . I do want to see you and would find it very cheering, so I'm taking a hopeful attitude. But there may be complications. The classic fall on the stairs . . . brought about this dismal result." She did not get out of the hospital in time to have the Macdonalds for the holiday. In mid-December, still feeling bad, she wrote Elizabeth Hardwick that "we are a little depressed around here for obvious reasons."

They were also "very strapped" financially, "thanks to doctors' and hospital bills," as McCarthy wrote Edmund Wilson. Reuel, too, had been sick off and on with sore throats and colds. His mother thought he would probably have to have his tonsils removed. But more pressing than "the drain of these colds dragging on through every winter" was "the school question." Reuel was not doing as well academically as he should have been. McCarthy blamed "the uninspired character of the teaching" at Saint Michael's. She wanted him to change schools at the end of the school year. Reuel, who was popular with his schoolmates, did not want to leave Saint Michael's "for fear of having to be a 'new boy' all over," his mother told Wilson. Dwight Macdonald, who had seen a lot of Reuel over the summer in Wellfleet, found the boy to be highly intelligent, so there was no question of his ability. Macdonald wrote McCarthy:

> Reuel and Mike [Macdonald's son] have been getting thicker and thicker. Nancy and I are delighted, as, I think, the Wilsons are. Both are much brighter and more intellectual than the other kids around. . . . Mike can beat Reuel at pingpong and of course is much more scholarly about sports; Reuel knows more about literature, and, I gather, is more inventive and enterprising in leading expeditions, most of a punitive kind, to spy on and harass various older persons. So they are really well matched. Of course, there may be a rupture; they're both quite "temperamental."

In the end, Reuel did change schools; he entered Saint George's, another local Episcopal school, for his eighth grade.

Just as in New York, Bowden Broadwater encouraged and prodded his wife to write, acting, in a way, like her manager. Although he was still writing stories, including one about Newport called "The Last Resort" that was never published, and reviews for the Providence *Journal* and the *New York Post,* he continued to help with domestic chores. Thanks in part to his help, McCarthy was quite prolific during their almost three and a half years in Portsmouth.

Early in 1950 she wrote a ten-part series on night life in Greenwich Village that appeared in the *New York Post.* In case anyone had missed McCarthy's well-known story "The Man in the Brooks Brothers Shirt," the *Post* ran the complete story in a special Sunday supplement shortly before printing the series, which McCarthy wryly dubbed "The Lesbian in the Brooks Brothers Shirt." Her ten articles, entitled "Greenwich Village at Night," appeared consecutively from February 20 to March 3. In preparation, she had moved into a Village hotel with "an awning outside with quiet lettering," which "intimates that the management has certain 'residential' pretensions, which the lobby, with its single light hanging over the desk, its weary lounging clerk, its cigarette-vending

machine, and its grimy tiled floor, as in a public lavatory, instantly dispel.
. . . All that is necessary is to jettison one's hygienic scruples," for "the
place is so dirty . . . the idea of drawing the line anywhere becomes
ludicrous." For more than a week she explored the all-night restaurants,
espresso bars, and lesbian and homosexual hangouts, starting at dusk and
returning to her hotel at dawn or after. Her escorts for her nightly
excursions varied: Eve Gassler and Al Stwertka; John Myers, a *View*
editor and future director of the Tibor de Nagy Gallery; Nancy and
Dwight Macdonald; and Bowden Broadwater, who came down from
Portsmouth for a weekend. Her reports of what she encountered were
remarkably frank for 1950. About one lesbian bar she wrote:

> The other two continue to dance, not well, but with more feeling; the tall
> one bends over the other, pressing her lips to her cheek, her ear, her hair
> more and more persuasively and yet clumsily. The music stops and they
> fall apart; . . . every few minutes, a different pair of girls go, hands enlaced,
> into the ladies room behind the orchestra, outside which, against the wall,
> stands a Negro maid in a red dress, like a proctor on guard. They emerge
> in a short time and immediately separate, with a matter-of-fact air of
> depletion. Fifteen minutes later they are back, with another partner; . . .
> a Negro prostitute in a flame dress, soul-kissing with a white-haired old
> daddy from uptown; his short fleshy tongue arches masterfully and
> strikes at hers, but for some reason the deal is not consummated—the girl
> drifts off alone.

The whole scene—from the show where male homosexuals dressed in
women's clothes and the female homosexuals in men's; to the gay bars,
which ranged from quiet and genteel to very rough; to the lesbian
hangouts, where she learned that most of the habitués were runaway
high school girls without jobs or money who slept all day in cheap rooms
far uptown and spent all night drinking, dancing, and mugging drunks
for rent and food money—was squalid rather than wicked. Her conclusion after ten nights of observation: "Each individual life, in this show-
case of oddities, is idiosyncratic and inviolate, like the glass-flowers at the
Peabody Museum in Cambridge. This is the only house-rule of the
Village after dark, and it is plainly not one that will build cities or
cathedrals; on the other hand neither will it destroy them, and this, in
the present era, is a thought fraught with pleasure."

This foray into newspaper journalism dismayed her intellectual
friends—Dwight Macdonald wrote Nicola Chiaromonte that the series
was "VERY bad"—and titillated her Newport-Portsmouth acquaint-

ances. Nicholas King remembered that before the series appeared, his neighbors, "who couldn't make much of *The Oasis*," dismissed McCarthy as an avant-garde writer. But afterward, she was seen as glamorous for daring to cavort with homosexuals, drug pushers, and the down-and-out homeless of Greenwich Village. From early 1950, when the *Post* articles appeared, until she moved away from Portsmouth, in December 1952, Newport acquaintances kept abreast of all she wrote, which was quite a lot. Besides the *Post* series, she published a piece on Sartre for *politics*, a two-part essay on women's magazines, an article on Simone de Beauvoir for *The Reporter*, an article deploring the intimate connection between American professors and the worlds of publishing and government for *The Listener*, a critique of Eugene O'Neill's *Moon for the Misbegotten* for *The New York Times*, two short stories and two memoirs for *The New Yorker*, a long piece on Vassar for *Holiday*, and two books.

Cast a Cold Eye, a collection of short stories and memoirs that had already appeared separately, was published in September 1950 by Harcourt, Brace and Company, the publishing house that would bring out most of McCarthy's subsequent books. Dissatisfaction with Random House had prompted her move to Harcourt, Brace. When Random House had sent her a prepublication copy of *The Oasis*, she had written Robert Linscott, her editor, with two complaints:

> It looks really very nice, except that the red is too uncertain of itself, flirting with publishers' maroon, and that the reproduction of the photograph is simply vile. I've written a letter to Ralph Ellison advising him to protest or withdraw his name—how did they contrive to ruin the original, of which I have copies here in proof of the difference? What is your own opinion of this monstrosity?
>
> Another grievance, and I have done. On page 21, the phrase "while they themselves played trustees to the law of cause and effect" appears. The word is *Trusties*—I corrected it back to that in the proof, after a first emendation by your editor. I mean *trusty*, see Webster: *a convict considered trustworthy and allowed special privileges*, and I really object quite strongly to having quite a funny joke excised by someone who, on correction, still thinks he or she knows how to spell, but not apparently how to read with wit or awareness. If another edition is ever printed, I should like to make sure that this is changed, partly from a fondness for the original and partly on principle: nobody editing a manuscript is entitled to re-correct an author's correction without a query or, as clearly in this case, without even an inner doubt. *I know how to spell "trustees" when I want to spell it*, and anyone who thinks otherwise is not sensitive to words and the capabilities of those who use them.

A week later, in a letter giving directions to Linscott on how to get to Portsmouth (he visited the Broadwaters in August 1949), she asked, "Why doesn't Random House take an ad for *The Oasis* in *Partisan Review?* The ads cost only about twelve dollars and that's where my public is." Despite her friendship with Linscott, Random House did not do enough to promote the book, she thought, so Bernice Baumgarten, her agent at Brandt and Brandt, found another publisher for *Cast a Cold Eye.* She called Robert Giroux, at the time editor-in-chief at Harcourt, Brace, to ask what he thought of Mary McCarthy's work.

"I love it," Giroux responded. "Isn't she happy at Random House?" When Baumgarten replied negatively, Giroux offered to publish *Cast a Cold Eye.* But when he mentioned his acquisition of McCarthy's book to Jean Stafford, whose commercially successful novels—*Boston Adventure* and *The Mountain Lion*—he had edited, she announced, "You're not going to be *my* editor, if you're *her* editor!" (Giroux has no idea why Stafford felt this way about McCarthy, but he speculates that she might have felt threatened by a literary competitor.) Stafford's antagonism might have had something to do with the fact that her former husband, Robert Lowell, was now married to McCarthy's good friend Elizabeth Hardwick. In any case, Giroux enlisted Denver Lindley, an erudite and cosmopolitan editor he had just hired, to edit *Cast a Cold Eye.* Lindley remained McCarthy's editor until he left Harcourt, Brace in the early 1960s, at which time William Jovanovich took over McCarthy's editing.

Of the seven pieces collected in *Cast a Cold Eye,* four had appeared in *The New Yorker*—"The Weeds" in 1944, "The Blackguard" in 1946, "Yonder Peasant, Who Is He?" in 1948, and "The Old Men" in 1950; one in *Mademoiselle*—"C.Y.E." in 1944; one in *Town and Country*—"The Friend of the Family" in 1947; and one in *Partisan Review*—"The Cicerone" in 1948. Although *Cast a Cold Eye* contained some of McCarthy's best writing to date—namely, the memoirs of her Catholic grandmother and Protestant grandfather that later became part of *Memories of a Catholic Girlhood*—it was the title of the book, drawn from the short story "The Old Men," that attracted critics' attention.

"Cast a cold eye on life, on death" is the epitaph on William Butler Yeats's tombstone. In "The Old Men," a young man, uncertain of his identity, decides that the self is merely a point of departure for impersonations, and that reality is to be avoided. Thus, why not live selfishly, he reasons, and takes Yeats's epitaph as his motto for living. McCarthy came to regret using the epitaph for the title of this collection of three memoirs and four short stories. As Robert Lowell had predicted, unfriendly critics permanently affixed the handy epithet "cold eye" to her.

Right away, the reviewer for *The New York Times* declared that "Miss McCarthy's eye is cold indeed and almost surgically sharp; and while the object of its merciless contemplation may be a fictional Francis Cleary ["The Friend of the Family"] or an actual grandmother remembered ["Yonder Peasant, Who Is He?"], the reader has a feeling of being watched, and just as coldly, himself."

Dwight Macdonald happened to be in Portsmouth—having stopped at the Broadwaters' en route from the Cape to New York—when the reviews of *Cast a Cold Eye* appeared. He wrote Nicola Chiaromonte about them, adding that no matter how astringent the criticism of her work, McCarthy still seemed to make enough money to support the household. She got $800 for her *Post* series, $1,000 for her article on Vassar for *Holiday,* and $3,000 for her *New Yorker* stories, he reported. "Bowden doesn't do much of anything so far as I can make out—maybe he writes—but no one will take his stuff apparently." He went on to say that McCarthy was beginning to find life in the country boring. "She wants to revive *politics* with me [it had folded in 1949] so as to Get in Touch again—she and Bowden would put it through a cheap local press there, Bowden would raise the dough, Mary and I would edit it—don't know, rather prefer to do it all myself if it is to be done—very fond of Mary but nervous about a certain frivolity, lack of responsibility, eccentricity there, especially with Bowden around." After that unfavorable assessment, he conceded that she worked hard and was at this time "working on a novel about college life."

The novel, *The Groves of Academe,* was published in February 1952. McCarthy had been working on it since moving to Portsmouth; she finished it in September 1951. She wrote Elizabeth Hardwick that she felt "a little dazed, for I have worked terrifically all summer to finish it, eight or nine hours a day." She called it "a *real novel,* at any rate full length, and with the usual mixture of narrative and dramatic treatment. I'm awfully anxious for you to see it; to me, it appears more conventional than my previous works, but others say that isn't so. I feel as though I'd turned some sort of corner in my life and made a permanent commitment, which is nice but also strange."

Because she had recently taught at Bard and Sarah Lawrence, it is not surprising there is something of both places in this novel of college life. From Bard she used several faculty members including one former colleague as the protagonist, spouses, bits and pieces of the college president, and even a few students, in the book's cast of characters, as well as a poetry weekend she attended there in 1948; and from Sarah Lawrence she used certain traits of its president in one of her characters.

But the fictional Jocelyn College was taken from neither school. "I really wanted to make a weird imaginary college of my own," McCarthy told an interviewer in 1960. "I even took a trip to the Mennonite country in Pennsylvania to try to find a perfect location for it which I found . . . near Lititz, Pennsylvania, the home of the pretzel. There's a very charming old-fashioned sort of academy, a girls' college, there. . . . It had the perfect setting, I thought, for this imaginary college of mine."

The two and a half years she spent writing the novel coincided with the "witchhunting" period brought on by Joseph McCarthy, a United States senator from Wisconsin, whose anti-Communist campaign created an atmosphere of fear in the country. He charged, usually with little evidence, that Communists had infiltrated the United States Department of State and other areas of government. His accusations and subsequent investigations affected thousands of people. College professors, entertainers, journalists, clergymen, and government workers came under suspicion. McCarthyism, as this red-hunting state of mind came to be called, is the axis on which *The Groves of Academe* turns. The plot is based on the recognition that while in the outside world it was dangerous to have once been a Communist, in the academic world, a former Communist had to be defended. Thus, when the protagonist, the incompetent, irresponsible, self-pitying, but brilliant Henry Mulcahy, an instructor at the progressive Jocelyn College, is informed that his contract will not be renewed, he pretends to have been a Communist so that he can claim to be the victim of a witch-hunt. Mulcahy knows that to have been an ex-Communist will make him the automatic beneficiary of the code of academic freedom. He also knows that no self-respecting college president would dare fire even the most incompetent former Communist, for fear of losing caste as a liberal. But when the president and a faculty committee question an old anarchist acquaintance of Mulcahy's, who is at Jocelyn for a poetry conference, they discover that Mulcahy has never been a member of the party. The ever-inventive Mulcahy, who has been told about the interrogation, improvises a new course; he confronts the president and, using the secret investigation as evidence that the president has betrayed his liberal principles, forces *him* to resign.

The Groves of Academe is a satire not only of "kneejerk" liberalism but of progressive educational systems and the craven behavior of the academic community that nourishes Professor Mulcahy. Reviewers, for a change, praised McCarthy for satirizing avant-garde intellectual orthodoxies, for "a rare talent for corrosive satire," for "a stunning, narrowly aimed accuracy," and for her affinity with Molière and Congreve. Ironically, Mary McCarthy had written in her application for a Guggenheim

Fellowship (which she was awarded in 1949), "my intention is not satirical; . . . in fact, I am trying to curb an overly satirical and self-recriminatory tendency in my work." In an eight page description of her plans for *The Groves of Academe,* she outlined a far more complicated plot than the one she actually used, and then summarized her plans in a brief but provocative paragraph:

> I cannot say what its contribution to knowledge or art will be; the milieu is relatively unexplored by fiction. . . . My ultimate purpose as an artist I do not know either. It seems to me that if one knows this, one is not an artist; the execution of a work is an act of discovery and a career can only be planned in detail by a careerist. One's purpose in sitting down to any project is to find how much of specific knowledge or general truth this material will yield, what, so to speak, there is *in* it, and one's purpose as an artist more generally is to continue to do this again and again to different areas of experience.

When McCarthy set to work on *The Groves of Academe,* she found herself struggling with the problems of point of view and voice. There would have been no reason to imitate her own voice in *The Company She Keeps* or in *The Oasis,* since, as she herself wrote in her Guggenheim application, her first two novels "had something of the character of a personal history," but in *The Groves of Academe,* she began experimenting. "The whole question of the point of view tortures everybody," McCarthy told an interviewer in 1961. "It's the problem that everybody's been up against since Joyce, if not before. Of course James really began it, and Flaubert even. You find it as early as *Madame Bovary.* The problem of the point of view, and the voice; *style indirect libre*—the author's voice, by a kind of ventriloquism, disappearing in and completely limited by the voices of his characters. What it has meant is the complete banishment of the author. . . . Because you find that if you obey this Jamesian injunction of 'Dramatize, dramatize,' and especially if you deal with comic characters, . . . there is so much you can't say because you're limited by these mentalities." *The Groves of Academe* is a ventriloquial act. Because she writes in an assumed voice, impersonating that of Henry Mulcahy, she almost creates a dramatic monologue. In her essay "Characters in Fiction," McCarthy later wrote about the difficulties and dangers in adopting this style.

> Now the normal way of telling [Mulcahy's] story would be from the outside or from the point of view of one of the professor's sympathizers.

But I found no interest in telling it that way; to me, the interest lay in trying to see it from the professor's point of view and mouthing it in the clichés and the hissing jargon of his vocabulary. That is, I wanted to know just how it felt to be raging inside the skin of a Henry Mulcahy and to learn how, among other things, he arrived at a sense of self-justification and triumphant injury that allowed him, as though he had been issued a license, to use any means to promote his personal cause, how he manipulated and combined an awareness of his own undesirability with the modern myth of the superior man hated and envied by mediocrity. To do this, naturally, I had to use every bit of Mulcahy there was in me, and there was not very much: I am not a paranoid, nor a liar, nor consumed with hatred, nor a man, for that matter. But this very fact was the stimulus.

In every novel from *The Groves of Academe* on, McCarthy has written not in her own voice, but from the point of view of others. Mary Meigs, the real-life model for the artist, Dolly Lamb, in McCarthy's *A Charmed Life,* was hurt by McCarthy's fictional portrait because she did not understand that *A Charmed Life,* like *The Groves of Academe,* was another impersonation, another ventriloquial act. In the novel, Dolly, a painter, befriends Sandy Gray, who calls her work sick, cramped with preciosity and mannerisms. "Mary seemed to want to quench my faith in myself," Mary Meigs wrote in a recent autobiography. "She activated the dormant seeds of doubt that made me so ready to hate myself and my work. And the turn of the screw was that it is not Mary McCarthy . . . who judges Dolly's work, but her spokesman, Sandy Gray, who has the virtue of honesty." But Sandy Gray is not Mary McCarthy's spokesman nor is he honest, though he calls himself honest. In fact, Sandy Gray's despicable behavior toward his ex-wife and his hatred of protagonists Martha and John Sinnott, who are clearly sympathetic characters, make him the villain of the novel.

Again, when *The Group* appeared, many readers, including critics, showed they had misunderstood McCarthy's approach to voice and point of view when, in calling attention to the many clichés that fill the novel, they criticized her for banality of style. The clichés were the point, however, for *The Group* was conceived in the various voices of the main characters. So, too, was *Cannibals and Missionaries,* McCarthy's last novel, which is told from eight points of view.

That authors feel an obligation to dramatize or mediate "probably has something to do with the spread of democratic notions, no one wanting to claim omniscience," McCarthy has written. This means a contemporary novelist does not tell; he or she only shows. But in the nineteenth century, the golden age of the novel, the great novelists told anything and everything; in fact, the intellectual and expository component of these novels is immense. And the reader quickly recognizes the character who represents the author, one "with full powers to comment on what is happening and draw the necessary conclusions," like the omniscient narrator who speaks for Tolstoy in *War and Peace.* But today, owing partly to Henry James's influence, there is no factual exposition. The present-day novelist is deprived of the right of authorial intervention.

McCarthy has wondered if this seeming incapacity to write straightforwardly is owing to "a lack of necessary conviction of centrality," or if it is just a matter of being influenced by the current fashion, "imposed on any artist by the evolution of the medium: poets *cannot* write classical sonnets any more and novelists *cannot* use the omniscient auctorial manner. If we try it today, it sounds like an affectation. . . . In other words, we would be writing a self-conscious 'period' piece."

Mary McCarthy's serious and continuing concern with the nature and function of authorial presence in a work of imaginative literature began with *The Groves of Academe.* When she has narrowed her focus to the perceptions of a single consciousness, Henry Mulcahy in this novel, or to the perceptions of multiple consciousnesses, as in *The Group* and *Cannibals and Missionaries,* she has limited herself in many ways. What is lost, McCarthy has admitted, is that "the common world that lies between the contemporary reader and the contemporary author remains unexplored, almost undescribed, just as queer and empty a place as Dickens' world would be if he had spent eight years recording the impressions of Fagin or the sensory data received by Uriah Heep."

What McCarthy has lost through her ventriloquial approach is something of her own intelligent and witty voice. Even so, a distinctive sense of the author is still palpable in her work, just as it is in the work of other writers who, like herself, pursue a strict policy of noninterference. Just as a playgoer gets a sense of the person Shakespeare behind his plays, so, too, a reader learns something about the person Mary McCarthy from reading her novels. And that is why Nicola Chiaromonte, who did not like *The Groves of Academe,* finding it "very clever and confused," could say, "However, I like Mary's mind very much. There is something really generous and passionate about it, for all her smartness." What Chiaromonte "hears" in any McCarthy fiction is the strong, unsentimental, moral voice that speaks for a just and ordered world. Doris Grumbach, a novelist and critic who wrote a biography of McCarthy in 1967, also recognizes McCarthy behind the ventriloquism, but she hears a different voice than that heard by Chiaromonte. "McCarthy's fiction suffers from that insistent voice, which sounds everywhere in her work. It is always elitist." To John Aldridge, "her characteristic tone of voice . . . is that of a self-righteous little girl lecturing her elders on matters that they have grown too morally soggy and mentally fatty to comprehend." Mary McCarthy herself acknowledges the insistence of her voice in a work of fiction when she says, "If one means by style the voice, the irreducible and always recognizable and alive thing, then of course style is really everything."

Dwight Macdonald was among those who disliked *The Groves of Academe.* He found two principal flaws. There was too much discussion, he thought, the "usual static quality, even worse than in *Oasis*—acres of intellectual arguments, back and forth, like a tennis match." Several critics shared this complaint. One wrote that "through their constant self-analysis her characters come near to reducing her novels to groves of thought." "Motives are unearthed under motives unearthed under other motives. . . . Scrupulousness becomes obsessive. . . . She wants justice done, and to be seen to be done; and it is a little fatiguing to watch justice being done at such length."

Macdonald also complained about what he saw as the unlikable characters in *The Groves of Academe.*

> Why does she have to be so goddamned snooty, is she god or something? You begin to feel sorry for her poor characters, who are always so absurd or rascally or just inferior and damned—she's always telling them their slip's showing. She doesn't *love* them, that's the trouble, in the sense of not feeling a human solidarity and sympathy with them—can't create real characters without love, or hate which is also a human feeling; she has just contempt and her poor puppets just wither on the page. Is she really like that? Or is she just kidding *me* along too, and making all sorts of snooty little footnotes in her head as we talk? The trouble is she is so damned SUPERIOR to her characters, sneers at most of them and patronizes the rest.

The reviewers of *The Groves of Academe* were split on this issue, some sensing a real sympathy for the characters, others agreeing with Macdonald. The reviewer for *The Atlantic Monthly,* for example, wrote that "she appears to revel in making every character contemptible or ludicrous," and John Chamberlain wrote that "no professional enemy of the egghead could be more severe on a group of double domes than is Mary McCarthy in her collective portrait of the Jocelyn faculty." But Louis Auchincloss, Isaac Rosenfeld, and Robert Halsband disagreed. Auchincloss saw "more sympathy on her part than appears at a first reading for the poor souls"; Rosenfeld thought "the characters come off rather well"; and Halsband felt that "her compassion for them is implicit."

What Dwight Macdonald did not know was that McCarthy's lengthy examination of motives in *The Groves of Academe* was deliberate. In her Guggenheim application, she wrote that "the study of a scruple has perhaps never . . . been carried so far." This dogged persistence in analyzing her characters' motives and actions, sometimes with the "exhaustiveness of Proust," is characteristic of all her novels. Sometimes she even pokes fun at this tendency. When she puts a description of Racine's style in the mouth of a character in *A Charmed Life*, for example, she might be speaking of her own: "Racine is a scientific observer of human behavior; he takes a single action and enlarges it, under his microscope, the way you might study a plant or the organs of an animal." And while McCarthy's later fiction shows an ability to love her characters, her purpose in her third novel, as suggested by the epigraph—"And search for truth amid the groves of academe"—is to demonstrate how the human defects of her characters impede the search.

During the summer of 1952, the Broadwaters' last in Portsmouth, McCarthy went to Seattle to visit her grandmother, who had broken her hip. Although she did not know it at the time, this would be the last time she ever saw her. (Augusta Preston died in February 1954). When McCarthy returned from Seattle, Broadwater suggested they sell their house. The land across the street had been sold to a developer who planned to subdivide it into building lots for little row houses. And although they enjoyed their neighbors' eccentricities, they were not amused by their prejudices. "I cannot account for it: the most terrible passions seem to be sweeping the population," McCarthy wrote Dwight Macdonald, "from the boarding-house keeper to the mother of an old school friend . . . to the mesdames at Bailey's Beach." She told Elizabeth Hardwick that "Miss Brayton's views on the Portuguese are in no way unique, being held with fierce passion by everyone who is not Portuguese on the island. . . . This xenophobia has curious consequences. The painter told Bowden that most of the people on our road were refugees; Bowden was rather astonished at this, until he found out that in the painter's mind *refugee* and *Portugee* were synonomous."

They decided to look for a new house on the Cape, but first they had to get Reuel ready for boarding school. He entered Brooks School, in North Andover, in September. By the end of October they had found a house to buy; it was located on Pamet Point Road in Wellfleet, not far from Edmund Wilson's house. They spent Thanksgiving in Portsmouth so that Reuel, home for vacation, could see his local friends before moving. After Reuel returned to school, his mother and stepfather vacated the Portsmouth house, followed the moving van to their new one, supervised the movers and some workmen, and departed for New York (their new house having no heat). There they settled temporarily in the Chelsea Hotel.

I N MARCH of 1952, one month after the publication of *The Groves of Academe,* Mary McCarthy attended another Waldorf conference, the purpose of which was to discuss the defense of free culture. During 1949 Eastern European and Soviet Communists had organized a peace congress in Poland; then, in early 1950, a meeting for intellectuals in East Berlin. These conferences were powerful instruments of Soviet propaganda in Europe, and they worried left-wing, anti-Stalinist intellectuals, who countered with a plan for a big congress in West Berlin; its slogan of cultural freedom would offset the Communist rallying cry of peace. When one hundred Western writers, artists, and scientists met in West Berlin in June, they formed the Congress for Cultural Freedom. Their five-day meeting culminated in a manifesto that Arthur Koestler read to the twelve thousand people who attended the concluding session. "Intellectual freedom," he solemnly stated, "is one of the inalienable rights of man."

The Congress for Cultural Freedom sponsored at least a dozen magazines, the best of which were *Tempo Presente* in Italy (Nicola Chiaromonte was one of its editors), *Der Monat* in Germany, *Encounter* in England (Dwight Macdonald became one of its editors for a short time), and *Preuves* in France. Mary McCarthy, though she was never a member of the Congress for Cultural Freedom, published articles in its magazines and even spoke at two of its conferences.

The Americans who had attended the first conference (former Atomic Energy Commission chairman David Lilienthal, Harvard historian Arthur Schlesinger, Jr., actor Robert Montgomery, novelist James T. Farrell, playwright Tennessee Williams, and authors James Burnham and Sidney Hook) spearheaded the formation of an affiliate at home. The American Committee for Cultural Freedom—a successor to Americans for Intellectual Freedom, founded three years earlier by anti-Stalinists of divergent views to offset the Stalinists' "Cultural and Scientific Conference for World Peace," held at the Waldorf—sponsored a Waldorf conference of their own on the last weekend in March 1952. Once again, the American anti-Stalinists demonstrated how ununited they were. Six hundred writers, artists, scientists, and other intellectuals disagreed about whether the greatest danger came from Communism or, as *The*

New York Times put it, from "ill-aimed anti-Communism that struck against intellectual freedom as well as subversion." This was a reference to Senator Joseph McCarthy's "witchhunting."

Mary McCarthy was one of the featured speakers at the conference. Taking the position that McCarthyism was the major threat to free culture, she clashed with Sidney Hook and Max Eastman, who held that the real danger was from the worldwide Communist conspiracy. McCarthy opened her speech by defining cultural freedom:

> The term "cultural freedom" is on everybody's tongue today. It is contended that we in America have it and the Russians don't, that we in America don't have it, that we are losing it; a committee exists to defend it, yet even within that committee there appears to be disagreement as to what cultural freedom is and hence whether it is imperiled, say by Senator McCarthy, or by the activities of Communist schoolteachers or by both or neither. . . . So much must certainly be granted by any rational person: cultural freedom, in the old-fashioned sense of the freedom of works of art and ideas to circulate, is still more or less intact in the United States.

Even so, she told delegates,

> the idea of a society, stern, resolute, dedicated, hard, has made tremendous headway with certain intellectuals and demi-intellectuals, particularly of the ex-fellow-traveler and ex-party member type. . . . For these people, cultural freedom, in the sense of the genuine freedom of individuals, must be deferred until some future date when everybody will be in total agreement; on that date, it can be afforded.

These are the people, she concluded, that "threaten cultural freedom as they make common cause with the enemy from without," like Senator McCarthy.

Mary McCarthy was amazed, she wrote Elizabeth Hardwick, that "on the fringes of the PR group, there is now an affinity for Senator McCarthy. . . . Dick Rovere, at the *New Yorker* party, had just come in from a session of the Committee for Intellectual Freedom, where a majority . . . had declined to issue even a mild criticism of Senator McCarthy, who is now regarded as a Necessary Evil. I'd heard something from Hannah that was similar and thought she was exaggerating. She says Rahv, who is too intelligent . . . for this sort of thing, is becoming increasingly isolated from the other PR patriots."

Mary McCarthy was so distressed by what was developing into Senator McCarthy hysteria that she hatched the idea of enrolling in Harvard

Law School in order to be able "to argue civil liberties questions." She felt "that the legal position in America was being weakened, that the old jurists were extremely good, but the younger ones who were replacing them were not of the same quality at all and that the country needed a very strong legal system to protect itself against such things as Senator McCarthy." Although she was serious, a friend convinced her that forty was too old to start law school.

Instead, she decided to start a magazine. Having determined that there was a national need for "a decent magazine in the field of politics," she persuaded Arthur Schlesinger, Jr., Hannah Arendt, Dwight Macdonald (whose own *politics* had folded in 1949), and Richard Rovere, a former editor of the *New Masses* and *The Nation* and currently the author of *The New Yorker*'s "Washington Letter," to join her in devising such a publication. *The Nation* and *The New Republic* no longer occupied central positions in American intellectual life, and although *Commentary* and *The Reporter* were respectable, they had never achieved an equivalent importance. Mary McCarthy believed that the liberal magazines were "just so dead, so weak and timid," in their reaction to Joseph McCarthy, that a strong independent journal would be welcome. Moreover, these old liberal magazines ignored the phenomena of ordinary American life, "the sort of thing that novelists and short story writers used to do," McCarthy wrote. "Just as portrait-painting has ceased to be practiced by any but fourth-rate artists, so the face of current reality in its ranch-type houses . . . and new multiple-dwelling projects has been left by writers in a sort of Moslem seclusion." What she envisioned for the magazine was the kind of work done by George Orwell in *Down and Out in Paris and London, Shooting an Elephant,* and *Homage to Catalonia* and by Walker Evans and James Agee in *Let Us Now Praise Famous Men.* And in keeping with her recent impulse to become a lawyer, she planned to have a legal-aid column dealing with constitutional and civil-rights questions. Finally, the liberal magazines already in existence mimicked each other. "The truth, at its simplest," she wrote in *The Listener,* "is that people, not just liberal intellectuals but ordinary liberal people, teachers, doctors, lawyers, and so on, are made restless at seeing their own opinions mirrored week after week in the journals that are written for them. What they object to is not lack of agreement with their own political conclusions but the sense of mechanical repetition that drones from these familiar pages."

Senator McCarthy was a case in point, she continued. Although he had been making headlines for four years, no one had tried to examine him seriously as a man or as a phenomenon. Instead, "the liberal magazines, old and new, prefer to treat him as a nightmare and thereby heighten the helpless terror of their readers, who have already been conditioned to pure masochism as a substitute for thought in politics." Her prospectus, written to attract financial backers, emphasized this tedious mimicry, blaming it on an alarming growth of conformity in America. "We do not believe that conformity is the *necessary* by-product of the idea of equality between men," she wrote, and concluded with an assurance that, unlike the "fretful style" of the current liberal magazines, this prospective publication would not advise public officials or endorse candidates for office. "Its main function is to observe, describe and analyze the trends it sees in mass-society, to take notice, in a word, of what is going on."

Early in 1953 McCarthy, as managing editor, set up a meeting with her cofounders at the Chelsea Hotel. The board of editors had already received a letter from her outlining ideas for possible articles. The proposed magazine, she had written,

> would fix its attention on totalitarian elements present in America, as well as abroad, and by this I mean mass-culture, Henry Luce, radio, television, Nixon, Whittaker Chambers, the *Freeman,* the *Mercury,* the Catholic hierarchy, psychoanalysis, . . . James Burnham, the demoralization of the middle class, foundations, . . . municipalized bathing-beaches, the psychology of the expense account, social work. The list of these hateful phenomena is monotonous; we all talk about them incessantly in private conversation, but they're either ignored in print or treated in terms of banalities. . . . What about life in Levittown or Stuyvesant Town? The only thing we hear about these strange new places is that they won't let Negroes into them. . . . I'd like to know what's taught in the big Catholic universities, like Fordham (a big change, I suspect, is taking place there, perhaps an improvement in many ways), and why doesn't somebody make a study of Bishop Sheen. . . . And what about a good article on Senator Taft, not Taft as a symbol, but what is he?

Agreeing on aims, the founders grappled with practical matters. The new magazine, they decided, would be called *Critic.* It would be a thirty-two-page monthly with a format resembling the London *Economist*'s; the cover would consist of the title, the table of contents, and the first paragraphs of editorial comment—short, lively miscellaneous paragraphs on the events of the month, to be written by Dwight Macdonald. Thirty-five thousand dollars would be needed to cover the anticipated deficit for the first year.

Because Mary McCarthy presumed that "to raise the money would be very easy," she undertook fund-raising chores. Arthur Schlesinger, Jr., at the time a professor at Harvard, solicited patrons from Cambridge, but important canvassing had to take place in New York. Accordingly, McCarthy called on or wrote individuals such as Thornton Wilder, Joseph Alsop, New York's Senator Herbert Lehman, and Hodding Carter; publishers such as The Viking Press, Simon and Schuster, Harcourt, Brace, and Farrar, Straus; *The New Yorker;* and the Ford Foundation. In many cases, she was not seeking money so much as ideas on where to get money. A month later, she admitted, "no money yet"—except a small, two-hundred-pound remittance from an Englishwoman that was to be set aside to pay her compatriots for contributions. Undaunted, McCarthy wrote Texas and California millionaires who had backed other liberal New York enterprises, as well as prominent or wealthy individuals closer to home, such as George Shuster, Edgar Kaufman of the Pittsburgh department store family, and Claiborne Pell. Finally, she secured a patron, Jack Kaplan, the president of Welch Grape Juice, although "he would come in if someone else [would]," which meant she had to raise matching funds to actually get his money. She announced this semigood news with weary resignation: "I must say I detest all this." On the advice of a friend, she rewrote the prospectus and, with the help of an accountant, drew up a more professional-looking budget. Then she resumed fund-raising, talking to Daniel Bell, Louis Harris, Oren Lehman, Mrs. Douglas Auchincloss, and Lauren Bacall.

Frequently, she met someone for lunch or dinner to make her presentation. "I'm drowning in floods of Béarnaise sauce," she wrote Arthur Schlesinger, Jr. By the end of October 1953, after ten months of effort, Mary McCarthy gave up. Although she had originally estimated $35,000 as sufficient to launch *Critic,* "that was not the view" of her potential backers, she says today. They "could think of nothing smaller than $100,000. We never could find a backer who didn't 'think big.' " She had secured pledges of $50,000, but these were contingent on her raising the full $100,000. "About the magazine," she wrote Schlesinger, "I really can't go on with it. We're in a state of monumental brokeness. I didn't do any writing—nothing I didn't throw away—from January to June, the fund-raising period. Since January I've earned a total of $300— lecture fees. The things I wrote during the summer are taking forever to sell. . . . Moreover, the heart has rather gone out of me; there seems to be some sort of 'lesson' in all this. Perhaps some people can combine fund-raising with writing; I evidently can't. So perhaps I couldn't combine editing either."

The lecture to which she alluded was delivered at the Breadloaf School of English at Middlebury, Vermont. "Settling the Colonel's

Hash," as the published version of the lecture was called, was provoked
by the response to an autobiographical story entitled "Artists in Uniform" that had been published in *Harper's* in March 1953. The story is
an account of her encounter with an anti-Semitic Air Force colonel she
met on a train to Saint Louis. (She had been on her way to give a lecture
in Missouri.) The piece opens as she meets the colonel in the club car.
When he makes one anti-Semitic remark after another, she goes back to
her own car, where she sits opposite two nuns. But when the train
reaches Saint Louis, and they both get off, he convinces her to eat lunch
with him. He orders hash; she has a sandwich. They continue to argue
about anti-Semitism. When she reveals her married name, he errone-
ously assumes that Broadwater is Jewish and thus thinks he understands
why she has been defending Jews.

The story depicts an incident that actually took place, yet it gave rise
to all sorts of misinterpretations. Many people assumed it was fictional,
probably because McCarthy created an unflattering self-portrait—the
woman in the club car and the station restaurant is patronizing and
moralizing. In fact, McCarthy frequently pictured herself unflatteringly
in her books, a habit Bowden Broadwater disliked. A man from Mexico
wrote to criticize McCarthy's choice of menu; salads would have been
more appropriate to the hot weather described in the story, he said. An
instructor of freshman English, who had assigned the story to her class
for critical analysis, asked McCarthy to "label" the symbols—the two
nuns, the greens and pinks of the author's costume, what she and the
colonel ate—since most of the class had decided that the story had
symbolic undertones. These responses led McCarthy to draw a distinction between natural and literary symbolism, and this became the subject
of her lecture.

"There were no symbols in this story," she wrote in "Settling the
Colonel's Hash." "There was no deeper level. The nuns were in the
story because they were on the train; the contrasting greens were the
dress I happened to be wearing; the colonel had hash because he had
hash." The colonel's hash and the author's sandwich are natural symbols,
she continued, illustrating differences in food taste, temperament, and
background between McCarthy and the colonel. She selected a conven-
tionally feminine dish, while the colonel ordered a typically masculine
repast. In this sense, "all human actions are symbolic because they represent the person who does them."

Had the colonel ordered a fruit salad with whipped cream, this choice
would have indicated a complexity in his character that his actual selection did not. Likewise, the contrasting shades of green in the author's

outfit were—she discovered after the colonel had guessed that she was some kind of artist—a too representative symbol of her taste in clothes and hence of herself as a person. She had no wish to parade as an artist, but in choosing that particular combination of skirt and blouse and accessories, she had become a symbol of an artist. At the same time, she had picked them because she liked the outfit.

The English instructor and her students who wanted "labeled" symbols were looking for something else. "They supposed that I was engaging in a literary or artificial symbolism which would lead the reader out of the confines of reality into the vast fairy tale of myth, in which the color green would have an emblematic meaning." The essay concludes with general observations about the process of her writing, which is a process of discovering natural symbolism. Every story is an "act of discovery," she says.

> A cluster of details presents itself to my scrutiny, like a mystery that I will understand in the course of writing or sometimes not fully until afterward, when, if I have been honest and listened to these details carefully, I will find that they are connected and that there is a coherent pattern. This pattern is *in* experience itself; you do not impose it from the outside and if you try to, you will find that the story is taking the wrong tack, dribbling away from you into artificiality or inconsequence.

What little writing Mary McCarthy produced in 1953 was turned out during a summer vacation in New England. The holiday did not take place in Wellfleet, however, for she had agreed to stay away during the period Reuel was with his father. A friend had offered the Broadwaters a month's use of a house in East Montpelier, Vermont, where they spent part of June and July. The "secluded corner . . . with its spruce forests and mountain panoramas and round red cow barns and abandoned quarries and bears and wildcats and beavers" was the setting for one of Mary McCarthy's best short stories, "The Appalachian Revolution," which was published in *The New Yorker* in 1954. In the story, an idyllic vacation retreat is invaded by unwanted tourists. Specifically, a group of unattractive psychiatrists and their wives sunbathe and swim in the lake, which belongs by rights of usage to the "old" summer people of Minster, McCarthy's fictional name for East Calais. The newcomers' presence endangers the warmth and cohesiveness of the summer community. ("The Hounds of Summer," about a similar situation in Italy, appeared ten years later.) The story raises the question, Can any beautiful place long resist the encroachments of mass society? In the second half of the twentieth century, the answer must be no. "Minster was feeling the effects of a technological revolution that was just as unsettling as a geological upheaval like the Appalachian Revolution which had metamorphosed the mountain ranges."

Late in the summer of 1953 the Broadwaters went to Wellfleet. Their return caused social complications for Elena Wilson, Edmund's current wife, who refused to accept invitations to events where she was apt to confront Mary McCarthy, which drastically curtailed her social life in the tiny village. The Broadwaters' red house, not far from her own, was high up a hill and surrounded by locusts, oaks, and pines, wild roses and blueberries. The preceding fall Broadwater had painted the rooms of the 1790 structure in pale pinks and yellows, with white for the paneling. The house did not look nearly so bright and cheerful now, owing to a careless tenant. Montgomery Clift, wanting to be near his close friends Kevin and Augusta Dabney McCarthy, who had rented a cottage in Truro, occupied the Broadwater house as soon as he had finished filming *From Here to Eternity* in May. At this period in his life, he was consuming vast quantities of liquor and pills, which accounted for the mess that greeted the returning owners. There were cigarette burns on windowsills, under the bathroom cabinet, in drawers; the white rug in the living room was badly spotted (one evening Clift had broiled a steak in the fireplace, and as he attempted to place it on a platter, it sailed onto the white rug. Laughing wildly, he proceeded to carve the meat on the rug before serving it to his horrified guests); and Mary McCarthy's herb garden was torn up (Clift had driven through it one night on his way to the garbage dump).

Augusta and Kevin McCarthy did their best to put the house in order before the Broadwaters arrived, but most of the refurbishing was left for Bowden. The condition of the house was recalled in the opening of a short story, entitled "A Charmed Life," that appeared in *The New Yorker* a year later.

> John Sinnott cut his hand trying to raise a stuck window in the downstairs bathroom. They had been established in their new-bought house a month, and John was still doing minor repairs. The summer tenant had left a row of cigarette burns on the upstairs-bathroom mantel, a big grease spot on the rug in the dining room (where he had spilled a platter of steak). . . . The tenant was a bachelor lawyer from New York, with a theatrical clientele.

The story eventually became the first chapter of the novel with the same title.

Halfway down the hill, some two hundred feet from the Broadwaters' house, was a smaller, yellow dwelling purchased by their friend Mary Meigs, whom they had met in Newport. Meigs had had no idea of buying a house in Wellfleet when she accompanied the Broadwaters there on a house-hunting trip the preceding fall. But when she and the Broadwaters looked at two houses on Pamet Point Road, she "fell in love . . . at first sight" and bought the smaller one, even though both were "irresistible, perfumed by the smell of box." Many years later she wrote in her autobiography that it had puzzled her why "Mary McCarthy and her husband, Bowden Broadwater, . . . had chosen to live in the same village as Mary's ex-husband, Edmund Wilson—a choice . . . which . . . provoked endless gossip among the Wellfleetians. Had they made this choice because a beautiful old house was for sale there? Or was Mary looking for the subject matter for a new novel? In any case, she acquired both."

In *A Charmed Life,* a large part of which McCarthy wrote in the Pamet Point house, she gave her own musings on the subject. Martha, the protagonist, "was in a delicate situation," like McCarthy's own. "She ought never to have come back here," and she and her new husband, John, knew it. Still . . .

> She and John would not have to see the old crowd or go to parties. . . . Lots of the wives and husbands, too, came back with new spouses, . . . and nobody thought a thing of it. . . . Their conventional friends said, "Aren't you very courageous?" . . . John and Martha had laughed and shrugged. They liked to be brave; dauntlessness was their medium. The fact that Martha trembled gave a shimmer to their exploits. They had bought the house because, as Martha explained to sundry perplexed listeners, they were afraid of being afraid to buy it. They rose to the challenge.

For the Broadwaters, the challenge was to be short-lived. Because their house had no heat, they stayed only until late October, when they closed the house for the winter and went to New York. In January 1954 they left for Europe.

This was Mary McCarthy's second European trip and, because Reuel was in boarding school, would last five months, considerably longer than her first, eight years earlier. Portugal was their destination because it was cheap. They stayed there for a little more than three months, principally in the small community of Paria da Rocha (Rock Beach). "There are a number of hotels and *pensaos* where you can get a room and three meals, with wine, for two dollars and forty-five cents a day," McCarthy wrote in a "Letter from Portugal" for *The New Yorker.* Any product or service that had human labor as its chief component was cheap, she wrote Dwight Macdonald; anything imported was dear. Although in Portugal the police, the newspapers, and the youth were all mobilized into an organized, disciplined unit and all opposition was illegal, there was no evident political intimidation. "Mister Rodriguez of Lisbon," an entertaining account of a day spent in the company of a government bureaucrat, who took Mary McCarthy on a tour of housing projects in Lisbon and to his house for high tea, describes this anomaly. *The New Yorker* had cut this report from her "Letter from Portugal"; *Harper's* published it as a separate entity.

During their Portuguese residence McCarthy's grandmother died. Augusta Preston had been senile for some time. She had been lucid for only part of McCarthy's last visit, a little over a year before. Her death, then, was not the shock to McCarthy that her grandfather's had been. Reckoning she could be of little assistance to anyone in Seattle, she remained abroad. Her aunt Isabel Preston wrote informing McCarthy that she would inherit her grandmother's diamond wristwatch and out-of-date silver-fox fur coat, and that Augusta's securities would be divided among her four grandchildren.

In April the Broadwaters went to England. They stayed with Malcolm Muggeridge, at this time editor of *Punch,* and his wife. During their stay, Mary delivered a talk at Broadcasting House on anti-Americanism in England. The talk was published shortly after, as "Thoughts of an American in England," in *The Listener.* Both talk and article noted ironically that the Englishman's anti-Americanism coincided with the typical American's pro-British feeling. The Broadwaters returned to the United States, arriving in New York on May 20, 1954. They went immediately to Wellfleet. Before Reuel had started boarding school, McCarthy had agreed to stay away from Wellfleet when Reuel was visiting his father. But now that she and Wilson were dividing his school vacations, she felt free to return.

McCarthy worked all summer and fall on *A Charmed Life,* "writing," Mary Meigs recalled, "in the little front room where itinerant clergymen used to sleep, with the circular bookcase turning on its stem like a Lazy Susan." At the same time, Arthur Schlesinger, Jr., hard at work on the first volume of his history *The Age of Roosevelt,* used the Broadwaters' barn as a hideaway for writing. At the end of the summer McCarthy volunteered to read his completed manuscript. By the time she mailed an assessment—a candid, devastating letter in which she told him his book sounded too much like the speeches he had been writing for Adlai Stevenson—the manuscript had gone to the publisher. Realizing that she was right, and grateful that she cared enough to write a detailed critique, he recalled and rewrote the original manuscript. *The Age of Roosevelt, Volume I: The Crises of the Old Order, 1919–1933,* published by Houghton Mifflin in 1957, became a Book-of-the-Month Club selection.

When the weather turned cold, the Broadwaters left Wellfleet. They rented a house, called Paradise Farm, in Newport, where McCarthy continued to work on *A Charmed Life.* "I love it here," she wrote Hannah Arendt, "with fires burning or ready to burn in seven fireplaces and views of snow-covered fields and pale-blue ocean out the windows." As always, she invited lots of guests.

In February 1955 the Broadwaters sailed again for Europe. Louis Lorillard, a Newport friend, had offered his Capri villa as a perfect place for McCarthy to finish her novel. "Capri is operatically lovely," she wrote Dwight Macdonald, "volcanic cliffs and blue and turquoise sea. It's full of flowers and oranges and lemons at present, a riot (actually) of wisteria and orange and peach blossoms." A Yugoslav cook produced wonderful meals. "Latest, a spinach gnocchi," she wrote Arthur Schlesinger, Jr., "with tiny cut-up crepes . . .; also stuffed escarole with raisins, olives, and anchovies." Capri with its horde of bohemians reminded her of Provincetown. "In fact," she wrote Macdonald, "the whole world, I think, will soon be like Provincetown. Lesbians dominate here, instead of homosexuals, but the inevitable Bennington-type girls come and marry fishermen or boat-guides. The police are very active, throwing people off the island. A contessa with ninety-six dogs has been the most recent evacuee. . . . There is a terrific quota of alcoholics and as many crutches and casts among the expatriates as there are at Lourdes. Naturally, there's an active branch of AA. Communism does not seem to be a problem."

A Charmed Life was finished in April, freeing the Broadwaters to travel. They went to Pompeii, "which was horrible," McCarthy reported, "dust and stones and guides eagerly showing you crypts full of bones." Next they visited Naples, spent a day in Positano, and went thence to Rome, where they met Carmen Angleton. Then the three friends set out for Greece in a jeep, arriving there in May.

"I am pregnant," she wrote Hannah Arendt. "I came to Greece only half-aware of this fact, disbelieving it, rather like St. Elizabeth when she got the news." She knew for certain when she started bleeding on the island of Mykonos. In Athens a doctor severely restricted her activity, ordering her to stop traveling, to find a place to live with an elevator, to stay off her feet as much as possible, and to forgo wine. Although the "alarms and incertainties" were wearing, she was extremely pleased about the prospect of having a baby, but she was to be disappointed. She had a miscarriage in Paris in early June. When she felt better, the Broadwaters flew to London to join Reuel. After a few days the three of them returned to France, where they "did a good deal of conscientious touring, with dogged reference to the guidebook," McCarthy wrote Katharine White. "We rented a car and did the George Sand country, the Dordogne, the Lower Pyrenees and Côte Vermeil, as well as the Riviera and quite a lot of Burgundy. Reuel loved Paris and St. Tropez—in short, the glitter and the gold."

In the middle of August, Reuel and Broadwater returned to America. Reuel had to get back to school; Broadwater left because he and his wife were barely speaking to each other. McCarthy says the first really serious altercation between them occurred at Capri, but the precise cause of it, she later contended, was "a mystery to me." They continued to be "on very poor terms," so McCarthy decided to stay in Europe for a few months alone.

Many people wondered why they had married in the first place. Since they both could be so caustic, no one imagined the Broadwater marriage as a love match. During the Broadwater marriage, "Mary's tongue was preternaturally sharp," Mary Meigs wrote, "and her green eyes glinted dangerously, when the swift flicker of her smile would make you wonder whether or not she were friendly or ferocious." "Mary's smile is very famous," Dwight Macdonald told an interviewer. "It's not what it seems at all. It's a rather sharkish smile. When most pretty girls smile at you, you feel terrific. When Mary smiles at you, you look to see if your fly is open." She could be abrasive, a friend recalled recently—"She would say devastating things to people, and because she was totally honest and never pulled any punches, people were terrified of her. People are afraid of extreme cleverness and a sharp tongue and pen." In Broadwater's case, the malicious comments he frequently made put people on edge. As one friend has put it, "He has a very waspish tongue." According to another friend, "Bowden was invited everywhere, yet everyone was terrified of him." Actually, both Broadwaters scared a lot of people. McCarthy's friends have said that she became Bowden-like during the marriage, and Broadwater's friends noted that after their divorce he did not seem "so bitchy" anymore. "Bowden might have exacerbated that side of her," a friend said recently, "but it was very much a part of her."

Up to this point, the Broadwater marriage appears to have been satisfactory to both parties. Broadwater was brilliant, possessed style and taste, and was as socially gregarious and full of curiosity as his wife. They had a good time together. Moreover, Broadwater was a cultivated person, remarkably knowledgeable about architecture, art, and literature; a should-have-been editor who responded sensitively to her writing; a conscientious stepfather; a social and intellectual gadfly who enjoyed being Mary McCarthy's husband; and, most important, a tough manager who always protected her from intrusions. McCarthy herself later acknowledged how crucial this kind of support is for a writer. "Being an artist or a serious craftsman of any kind takes a lot of time and practice and can rarely be tucked into the housewife's spare moments, between vacuuming the carpets and warming the baby's bottle."

Although she had been grateful for Broadwater's assistance, she told Dwight Macdonald that she was beginning to feel suffocated by the marriage. Even so, she had no thought of divorce at this time. In fact, Broadwater was in New York looking for an apartment for them and for a job, which would be his first since 1947. McCarthy was still in Europe when *A Charmed Life* was published in November. All the while she was working on the book, Broadwater kept saying that it would be impossible to go back to their house after its publication. Their friends and neighbors, he insisted, were bound to be angry at McCarthy's portraits of them and their village, and indeed they were. So, the Broadwaters sold their home to Mary Meigs, who was relieved to see them go.

A Charmed Life is set in the imaginary New England town of New Leeds, a run-down bohemian village that closely resembles Wellfleet. Martha Sinnott, a writer, moves back to New Leeds with her second husband, John, after having left her first, Miles Murphy, from this very town several years before. Miles and his new wife live nearby. The Sinnotts return, they claim, to test their own strength by maintaining order and achieving personal goals (Martha will write a play) while among the New Leedsians, who live unproductive lives—drinking too much, living on a combination of dividends and borrowing, preferring talk to work, and strenuously avoiding conventionality. Having defined themselves in terms of their revolt from middle-class American life, especially its work ethic, the New Leedsians aspire to be critics and artists without discipline; they live in a condition of directionless drift and lassitude. Because nothing much matters to them, they cannot be hurt; in short, they lead charmed lives.

"Daunted and somewhat abashed by their resemblance to the other New Leedsians," John and Martha Sinnott are driven to prove they are different; they, unlike the other townspeople, must show they have no self-destructive bent. So, too, Mary McCarthy worried at first about how easily she found herself fitting in in Wellfleet. But in the end, she concluded she was safe. "I really think there is such a thing as catharsis in writing," she wrote Arthur Schlesinger, Jr., after finishing the novel. "That is, I'm now utterly dauntless before the prospect of becoming a New Leedsian, which seems to me, now that I've faced it, a child's bugaboo." In facing the prospect fictionally, she also laughed at it and herself.

> "You always were a rebel," said Dolly. "You'd be the same if you lived in Scarsdale." "No," said Martha. "If I lived in Scarsdale, I wouldn't care what the neighbors thought. And I wouldn't want to reform them." "You want to reform these people?" asked Dolly, with a quizzical smile. Martha nodded. "Of course. I'm trying to set an example. It's not only vanity; there's also a corrective impulse. 'Let your light so shine before all men.' That's the very height of my folly. John and I are making ourselves ludicrous with our high-toned ways. I know it but I won't desist. It becomes a form of fanaticism. They can kill me, I say to myself, grandly, but they can't make me be like *them.*"

Martha's New Leedsian friends do their best to make her like them. They see to it that she and Miles meet at a reading of a Racine play in French, after which Miles makes love to Martha on her sofa, as John is out of town. Later Martha learns that she is pregnant, and not knowing whether John or Miles is the father, she decides, after much soul-searching, to get an abortion. Driving home after having secured the money to pay for it, she is killed.

Once again, Mary McCarthy used real-life models extensively in her novel. But she adapted and changed them for her artistic purposes. Miles Murphy, adept at "the history of ideas" and at "amassing information," thus suggesting Edmund Wilson, was not merely a portrait of McCarthy's second husband. As she wrote Arthur Schlesinger, Jr.:

> He's not really meant to be Edmund, but a modern type of "compleat" man who is always a four-flusher like a piece of imitation Renaissance architecture. To the extent that Edmund is a boor and a four-flusher . . . , Miles is a kind of joke extrapolation of him—minus the talent, minus the pathos . . . ; I've used certain episodes, altered from my married life with E., as the raw material to create him, and I've drawn on my own feelings quite directly, in the chapter where Martha remembers her marriage. But it's all changed around—not for purposes of disguise, but to

make a new whole, as for example, the fire, the dead stepchild, Martha's flight in her nightgown, which are not versions of anything that happened in reality, but new inventions called into being by these new people. . . . Edmund has in common with Miles a capacity for behaving *incredibly*. But I'm not under the illusion that he would buy a portrait of me by Warren Coe or by Titian; or that he would bluster into my house and make a pass at me. Nothing could be farther from his character, which is that of a bourgeois family man; he has extremely strong notions of propriety.

Because of the obvious connection between the situation and setting of *A Charmed Life* and McCarthy's own life, critics latched on to the novel as a roman à clef. McCarthy has always objected to such literal-minded readings of her books. Those who regard her novels as guessing games or treasure hunts for the real-life models of her characters are missing the point. "What I really do is take real plums and put them in an imaginary cake," she has said. "If you're interested in cake, you get rather annoyed with people saying what species the real plum was."

She is well aware that the writer who wishes to write about what she knows will find her own life the best source material, or, as McCarthy has put it, "The relation between life and literature . . . is one of mutual plagiarism." But once taken into a work of fiction, a character or situation from life is inevitably transformed. McCarthy commented on this when she described how Flaubert evaded questions about real-life models. He "was no doubt sick of the gossip and somewhat remorseful, like most authors, for what he had started. . . . At the same time, as an author, he must have resented the cheapening efforts of real life to claim for itself material he had transmuted with such pain in his study." Even the real-life name of Madame Bovary's model, Delphine Delamare, "sounds like a hack's alias for Emma Bovary."

McCarthy was often amused by other people's reactions to her work. In an imaginative and entertaining essay on Natalie Sarraute, included in *The Writing on the Wall* (1970), she talked about a widespread perception of how authors use their experience. "The others fear [an author] as a spy concealed among them, pretending to be minding his own business while covertly taking notes. . . . Knowledge, they think, is power, and in their view, this note-taking is a power play: he has got them where he wants them, in a book, appropriated them for his own purposes." McCarthy realized that no amount of adaptation or transformation could prevent people, particularly those people who *are* the models for fictional characters, from seeing her sort of fiction as portraiture, or caricature. The same was true for Flaubert, she wrote. *Madame*

Bovary "was fraught with embarrassment for its author who foresaw, while still writing it, the offense he was going to give his neighbors by the heavy dosage of Norman local color he had put in. And as often happens, whatever he did to change, combine, disguise, invent, probably made matters worse, purely fictive episodes being taken as the literal truth."

Her Wellfleet neighbors, in any case, thought McCarthy had used life a little too baldly in *A Charmed Life.* Phyllis Given, a neighbor and friend of McCarthy's from the days of her marriage to Edmund Wilson, said in a letter to John Dos Passos just after the novel's publication:

> I had a long call from Bowden Broadwater two nights ago. . . . We had a fine chat in which I said I thought the book was outrageous, and why didn't Mary try fiction. (I think I wrote you that they have sold their house. Bowden seemed sad about it. They are an extremely odd pair.)

Mary Meigs recalled the effect that *A Charmed Life* had on her and others who appeared in it.

> It was as though all of Mary's victims had been struck down with a wasting disease. I saw them, pale and shaken, unsure of themselves, unsure of everybody else (for this awful image of themselves might now be accepted as the true one), and I dragged myself about in a state of doubt and self-loathing for a long time.

Even McCarthy admitted that in the summer after *A Charmed Life* appeared, the women did not dare appear barefoot in the supermarket in Wellfleet, and the original of Warren Coe—in the novel an unknown artist who, at fifty, has sold canvases only to his father-in-law—was unable to ask his usual questions or say things like "Pardon my French," "Excuse me for living," or "I could eat that rug," leaving him without conversation.

Warren Coe and his wife, Jane, are both comic characters whose life-style fits in perfectly in run-down New Leeds. Jane loves to entertain, for example, but when she does, something is always amiss.

> Either there was no ice or else there was no soda water, . . . or she had forgotten to get salt, for the dinner, or sugar, or there were mouse-droppings in the flour. These things did not matter, Warren assured her, but Jane had felt a little bit embarrassed, a few nights before, when they had had Miss Lamb to dinner, and they had found they were out of paper

napkins and paper towels and Kleenex, so that they had had to give her toilet paper, folded neatly by Warren, for a napkin. They used to have linen, Warren told Miss Lamb, with a tender glance, like a hug, at his rosy spouse, but Jane had given it all away, except for the sheets and pillow slips, which did not have to be ironed. . . . Labor-saving schemes of one kind or another played a large part in Jane's thoughts.

In reading McCarthy's description of the real-life models for the Coes, it is clear that their household was quite recognizably depicted in *A Charmed Life.* Visiting them in 1951, she wrote Dwight Macdonald, "Icebox out of order; out of Kleenex, paper napkins, paper towels, toilet paper, oranges, lemons, mustard, among other items I heard asked for." But they were "planning to remedy this situation by buying the super-colossal size of everything, including, doubtless, oranges." The husband simply told his wife, "But, dear, you're so nice and relaxed." Another time, McCarthy wrote her sister-in-law, Augusta McCarthy, that she and Broadwater "were offered a martini made with cold water; the cream was sour. . . . By the end of the visit I should have appreciated the archaic sight of a saucer under a cup. But there was a great deal of brilliant sun and serious conversation." It is obvious that Mary McCarthy had a genuine affection for the real-life Coes, just as the fictional Coes "were the best-liked couple in New Leeds," but it is just as obvious the Coes would not have relished being described in this manner in a book. Some of her real-life sources—Peggy Guggenheim, Dwight Macdonald, Emmanuel Rousuck—tolerated McCarthy's appropriation of them for her purposes. Others resented the way she wielded her pen.

She herself is aware that her portrayals can hurt, but it is not in her nature to write any other way. In a 1968 interview she said, "I can't stop myself. I go and do it, and hope they won't suffer too much and will find some way of regarding it as palatable, that in the end they will forgive me." In 1982, after she had read Mary Meigs's autobiography, she wrote an uncharacteristic apology to her former neighbor for turning her into Dolly Lamb in *A Charmed Life.*

It pains me awfully to think of your suffering all those years over these passages. Misread by you or not, they are still my doing, by the invention of Dolly. I grossly invaded your privacy, and that I am sorry for, even though I don't know how to rectify and never did. I *cannot* stop using real people in my fiction. Hannah, as so often, had the explanation: "You are a critic, and so you must quote." As you see, it's a kindly explanation.

And apropos of it, dear Mary, there was no intention in me to give you pain.

"Mary picks up on the ridiculous side of people," says Angélique Levi, her French translator and good friend. "It's her inspiration, the core of her humor, and her vision of things." Such a vision will inevitably result in pain for all but the most secure of her real-life models. Miriam Chiaromonte calls this vision "a naughtiness, but she is naughty to herself as well." McCarthy does frequently turn a satiric gaze on herself. Martha Sinnott, for example, is "a strange, poetical-looking being, with . . . straight hair done in a little knot," who "only spoke the literal truth . . . that was her peculiarity." This is precisely Mary McCarthy's idiosyncrasy: an urgency to tell the whole truth, as she sees it, about herself and others, no matter what the consequences.

But perhaps, in the end, McCarthy felt that *A Charmed Life* had too much real life in it to work properly as the novel she had envisioned. A half-dozen years after finishing it, she questioned her success in bringing it to life.

> There may be something wrong with the novel, I don't know. But it was always supposed to have a fairy tale element in it. New Leeds is *haunted!* Therefore, nobody should be surprised if something unexpected happens, or something catastrophic, for the place is also pregnant with catastrophe. But it may be that the treatment . . . was too realistic, so that the reader was led to expect a realistic continuation of everything going on in a rather moderate way. It was, to some extent, a symbolic story. The novel is supposed to be about doubt. All the characters in different ways represent doubt.

That *A Charmed Life* is about doubt was not perceived by a single reviewer in 1955. Even now, her intended meaning is not apparent. In the late 1960s, in a letter to Nicola Chiaromonte, she characterized *A Charmed Life* as "a book I don't much like at this distance in time."

CHAPTER XV

VENICE OBSERVED
(1955–1956)

M ARY McCARTHY was still in Europe when *A Charmed Life* was published. She had planned to sail home with Bowden Broadwater and Reuel in mid-August on the *Ryndaam,* but three days before she was to leave, she was offered an opportunity to stay abroad. Georges and Rosamond Bernier, who had just started the art journal *L'Oeil,* wanted also to publish a series of books on cities famous for their art collections, to be written by professional writers rather than by art historians. Knowing that McCarthy was in Europe, they asked her, through a mutual friend, if she would be willing to write a profile of Venice. ("We figured," Rosamond Bernier Russell recalls, "that with Mary's keen brain and intellectual curiosity, she could write a good profile.") McCarthy had never heard of the Berniers, yet they would become well known in a very short time for producing what was generally considered one of the finest art journals in the world. Mrs. Bernier's friendship with artists like Picasso, Matisse, and Miró was one reason for its rapid preeminence. McCarthy was hesitant about accepting an offer from people she knew little about, but because of her increasing friction with Bowden, she agreed to write the profile. She saw Reuel and Bowden off to America, and she went to Lausanne to meet the Berniers.

"Mr. Bernier seems to expect a compendium of every phase of Venetian life from the ancients to the present day," she wrote Carmen Angleton, "touching on art, music, sport, theatre, manners and customs, plus the dates of all the Doges." Appalled by her ignorance of all things Venetian, especially of its art ("I'd never heard before that there was more than one Tiepolo, or more than one Tintoretto, that there was a son. I vaguely knew Bellini, but didn't have any idea that there were three Bellinis"), she tried to maneuver the conversation so as not to alarm her patrons. Despite such daunting revelations, she enjoyed the trip because she liked the Berniers, especially Rosamond, who was "a very straight, sweet, hard-working, lively American girl; Mr. Bernier is rather like a film director, with dark glasses and insomnia and a lot of technical know-how in art."

The Berniers liked Mary McCarthy too, and were surprised and touched to discover, during nine days together in Venice at the Hotel Bauer Grunwald, that in spite of her reputation as a formidable, self-sufficient, intimidating, and intransigent personage, she was actually shy and vulnerable. Like the typical American in a Jamesian situation, she seemed unsure of herself among contessas, worrying about what to wear for luncheon and dinner parties. Moreover, the Berniers understood all too well how little she knew about the city. They therefore provided tours and secured a card for her at the Correr Library.

She rented an apartment in a big, somber house, filled with heavily gilded furniture, that was located in the old Cathedral Quarter of Venice, called the Castello District, on the east side of the city. Her four large rooms—"all quite charming in bourgeois Venetian rococo, blue and white stripes and painted seashells and Tiepolos on every cabinet," as she wrote Carmen Angleton—overlooked the garden of a palazzo. The entrance hall and bathtub were to be shared with the landlady and her children—but only, McCarthy recalled in her profile of Venice, " 'when you are out,' the agent hastily stipulated. You do not have to worry; they do not take many baths." He also insisted that, for tax purposes, the Signora's husband lived elsewhere—an outright fabrication, Mary McCarthy would discover. "The specialty of this little man . . . seemed to be renting apartments that were already occupied. He had begun by trying to rent me his own apartment, with himself in it."

Despite the odd arrangement, she signed a lease. Her landlady, apparently regretting the transaction, gradually repossessed McCarthy's four rooms. The repossession began with the feeding of the Signora's cat, which she had put out to live on the roof during the time the apartment was rented. " 'Permesso,' says the Signora, bursting into my sitting-room with a paper full of garbage. She opens the window and thrusts the paper out" for the cat. Before long, hairpins, a hair dryer, nylon underwear hung to dry, mascara and brush, powder and comb—all belonging to the landlady—appeared in McCarthy's bathroom. One day, the bathtub was filled with the Signora's soaking laundry, which, when her tenant did not complain, became a permanent fixture. Next, the landlady and her family started "borrowing": McCarthy's soap, powder, cleaning fluid, and perfume disappeared. When Carmen Angleton came for a visit, "the Signora takes her aside to ask her, *per piacere,* where she buys her toothpaste. 'Mario *loves* it!' she declares, alluding to her son." Another time she informed her tenant, "Your glasses exactly fit my eyesight." Later the family's vegetables and dairy products appeared in McCarthy's icebox, their ironing board was set up in the kitchen, until finally "the entire family except . . . the Signora, is established around the kitchen table . . . watching me cook and commenting curiously, to each other."

The landlady's encroachments amused Mary McCarthy, who was

away from the apartment all day anyway. Drama critic Stark Young, who was in Venice at the time, and Peggy Guggenheim lent her books on Venice, which she could read at home, but most of her research had to be done at the Correr Library. Besides reading, she explored the museums and churches. "I've seen a tremendous quantity of art. . . . Best of all, I think, I like the Carpaccios in S. Giorgio degli Schiavoni . . . and the Tintorettos in the Accademia, especially the Crucifixion."

Bowden Broadwater wrote to say that he and Reuel had arrived home safely. Reuel had proceeded to North Andover for his last year at Brooks. Broadwater took up temporary residence at the Hotel Schuyler on West Forty-fifth Street, which he described as a fleabag, while he looked for an affordable apartment and a teaching job. His efforts were halfhearted, however, because, he told his wife, New York was hot, dirty, and depressing. Mary McCarthy, at least for the moment, was not any more cheerful. She wrote Carmen Angleton, "I've been having a perfectly wretched time in Venice; I can't stand the conspicuous solitude I feel myself to be in. . . . It would be bad enough anywhere, but Italy (and Venice!) seem a subtly contrived torture for the solitary individual; everybody stares and accosts and pities and condemns. I hardly eat because of the waiters' pity when I ask for a table for *una persona*."

As it happened, she was rarely alone. The Berniers were with her until the end of August. Then Arthur Schlesinger, Jr., arrived, followed by Hannah Arendt, who came for a week. In addition Peggy Guggenheim, who, according to McCarthy, was "still indignant about 'The Cicerone' but has been nice in the intervals of forgetting what it is she has against me," entertained her compatriot. McCarthy enjoyed a very social hiatus at the Hotel Continentale in Milan, where she saw dozens of old friends who were attending a Congress for Cultural Freedom conference. Isaiah Berlin's wife, who was also at the conference, gave McCarthy a letter of introduction to Countess Anna Maria Cicogna. Right away, Countess Cicogna invited McCarthy to a luncheon for Bernard Berenson, the renowned authority on Renaissance painting, who had come to Venice for a Giorgione exhibition. She was invited to join Berenson at the Hotel Europa, from which Countess Cicogna's gondola would take them to her palazzo. When McCarthy appeared on the landing stage of the Europa, Berenson, at ninety a little figure all wrapped up in shawls, put his hand on her arm and said, "Tell me—did you bring your pessary?" (The year before, McCarthy had caused a stir with a *Partisan Review* story called "Dottie Makes an Honest Woman of Herself," about a young woman's visit to a doctor's office to get fitted for this contraceptive device.) Never having met the great man before, McCarthy was embarrassed by his question. But thinking quickly, she recalled the name of a small town known as the home of "Pala di Pesaro" by Giovanni Bellini. "No. I've never been to Pesaro," she responded.

Berenson had become famous as an advisor to millionaire art collectors and, most conspicuously, to Lord Duveen's rich customers. Late in life he remarked, quite accurately, that most of the Italian paintings that had come to the United States had his visa on their passport. His knowledge and memory were prodigious, and his villa, I Tatti, outside of Florence, was a magnet for European and American intellectuals and celebrities. Berenson was a wraithlike figure whose frailty was belied by the strong lines of his bearded face and the ready flow of his talk. He and McCarthy got on well, as he was vitally interested in her work and made other allusions to it during the luncheon. Cross-examination was his forte; it was one way he stayed youthful and aware of everything that was going on in the world.

After their initial meeting, Berenson twice invited McCarthy for dinner in his suite at the Europa. Both times he sent his companion away, so he could talk to McCarthy alone, all the while running his aged hands up and down her bare arms. He was "a regular old Volpone of ninety summers," she wrote Hannah Arendt, "with a glistening gold smile, more like a puma, really, than a fox." Berenson had told his secretary, after meeting McCarthy the first time, that if he had been younger, he would have propositioned her "straightaway." He also claimed that she was the only person he had ever written a fan letter to, he so admired her writing. McCarthy, a stern judge as always, did not admire his. She wrote Carmen Angleton:

> I've been reading Burckhardt's The Cicerone. Do you know it? Very good, I think; most of Berenson is cribbed out of it, in my opinion. Berenson's Venetian Painters is terrible; so is his book on Lotto. The whole feel of the man is flabby and unpleasant. As a literary critic, he would be simply derisory.

Early in November, at which time he was back in Florence, Berenson invited McCarthy to I Tatti. She did not accept, because she was booked to return to the United States on November 24.

Berenson's secretary, William Mostyn-Owen, a recent graduate in art history from Cambridge University, had stayed in Venice for a while after Berenson left. He took McCarthy to Treviso, Mantua, Modena, and Bologna. Mostyn-Owen and McCarthy saw each other twice again that fall, and they remained friends for life.

McCarthy also made friends in Venice with another Englishman, Francis Haskell, a research student who was also working on a book. Mutual diligence led to their getting acquainted. The first to arrive when the Correr opened and the last to leave when it closed at six, they could not help but notice each other. In the beginning they merely nodded and exchanged pleasantries about the weather. Later they occasionally stopped at a bar for a drink before returning home. But not until they met unexpectedly at a formal luncheon did they learn each other's names. Haskell, who had read *The Oasis* and *The Groves of Academe,* was surprised that the very pleasant individual he saw every day at the Correr was none other than the sardonic American author.

From this time on, the two researchers enjoyed many evenings together, mostly at McCarthy's apartment, as she thrived on cooking dinner for friends. Carmen Angleton, who shared the apartment with McCarthy for several weeks, set a linguistic example for her two friends, who wanted to improve their Italian. Angleton was already fluent, having lived in Italy off and on since 1933, when her father had taken over the National Cash Register Company franchise there. Wrapped in heavy overcoats and blankets owing to the Signora's stinginess with heat, the three native English speakers read aloud from the works of Carlo Goldoni, the eighteenth-century Venetian dramatist. During these evenings they also talked about art and Hannah Arendt; laughed about the landlady, who entertained herself by trying on Carmen Angleton's clothes; and discussed at length the ideas of Roberto Longhi, a twentieth-century art historian, whose brilliant and novel interpretation of Venetian art impressed Mary McCarthy. Despite her doing Longhi's difficult *Cinque Secoli di Pittura Veneziana* with Carmen Angleton and her attempts to communicate with her landlady in pidgin Italian, McCarthy was not fluent enough at this time (she later became fluent) to do much reading in the language. Fortunately, she was able to do quite a lot of her research in English. John Ruskin, Augustus Hare, William Dean Howells, and Bernard Berenson had all written about Venice in English; the memoirs of Giovanni Casanova, a native Venetian, had been translated into French, in which McCarthy was fluent; and Jacob Burckhardt had been translated into English.

When McCarthy finished her research, she sailed for New York, arriving in December 1955. She started writing the book aboard the *Liberté* and finished it in three months. Broadwater had still not found an apartment by the time she arrived. By early 1956, however, they were settled in "a rather nice apartment, though too small, with a terrace and a gardenia plant and geraniums, on East 94th Street," and Broadwater had secured a teaching job at Saint Bernard's, the private boys' school on the Upper East Side that Reuel had attended.

McCarthy's long essay on Venice, entitled "The Revel of the Earth," appeared first as a two-part series in *The New Yorker* in July 1956. The Berniers brought it out as a large coffee-table book in time for Christmas gift-giving. *Venice Observed,* as the essay was now called, was the best-selling art book of 1956. Bernard Berenson told McCarthy that he did not like it. She replied that she was proud of it.

> It seems to me original; I don't know of anything like it. What its quality is, if one can be objective about one's own work, is a certain intensity of *thought,* a revolving of Venice in the mind, as though to hold it up and ask, "What is it?" . . . The facts, of course, are familiar, but the discovery of a pattern in them is, so far as I know, completely new. No other writer I could find had ever even *tried* to look into the facts for a pattern or a symmetry, though Venice, unique among cities, seems to solicit just such an act of recognition. I was *forced* to think about Venice for myself, finding no precedent.

Indeed, she had turned out a brilliant generalization about Venice, finding unexpected patterns in a mass of detail.

Venice Observed is a synthesis of the city's people, its art, its position as a once-mighty Renaissance city now become tourist magnet, as well as a compendium of what other writers down through the centuries have said about the city. Its history, from the beginnings of the Republic (as a refuge from Attila) in the fifth century through the days of Venice's glory as a maritime power to the fall of the Republic at the end of the eighteenth century; its artists and their work, from Paolo Veneziano to Francesco Guardi; its government, including the complex method of "electing" the doge; and the past and present doings in Torcello, Burano, and Chioggia—all illustrate, according to McCarthy, a central fact about Venetians: that they were *"a commercial people who lived solely for gain."* Thus, the Venetians invented the income tax, statistical science, the floating of government stock, and the gambling casino; and after commercially developing the glass mirror, they jealously guarded a monopoly on its manufacture and distribution for over a century by bribing and threatening those who understood the art.

Even the city's fairy-tale loveliness can be attributed to its orientation to trade. Images of beauty in fairy tales are images of money—caskets of gold and silver; a miller's daughter spinning gold; the cave of Ali

Baba, filled with gold and silver; Aladdin's underground garden, in which jewels grow on trees—and these are the elements of Venetian art and architecture. The Venetians' fascination with gold led them to look on everything as a surface to which gold could be applied, and nearly all the buildings display highly decorated facades. Painters, too, were attracted by brilliant color. The Venetian merchants' easy familiarity with brocades, silks, and damask is reflected in Venetian painting, "from the beginning to the end a riot of dress goods." Small wonder Venetians did not take pleasure in the unworldly saints like Saint Francis, Saint Aloysius, and Saint Anthony, but preferred soldier saints like San Marziale, Saint Martin of Tours, and San Liberale with their magnificent uniforms, or the early bishops of the church arrayed in glittering robes. Although most Renaissance artists were in love with death, McCarthy observes, the skull rarely appears in a Venetian painting. "The absence of fanaticism in Venetian life, the prevalence of mundane motives in politics are reflected in the concreteness, the burnished order and sanctity of Venetian painting."

The artists themselves, who came in pairs or trios like painting firms— three Bellinis, three Vivarinis, two Tintorettos, four (at least) Bassanos, two Longhis, two Tiepolos, two Riccis, two Guardis, three Caliaris, four Vecellis—proclaimed the businesslike character of Venetian civilization. And so did everything about Venice. The ideal citizen of this ideal republic was "reasonable, peaceful, avid only for consumption." Even the Crusades were for Venetians merely an opportunity to make money; the city acted as shipping agent for the Crusaders.

In the present day, Mary McCarthy's landlady, who lives apart from her husband for tax purposes, is a true daughter of Venice. Not only does she repossess the apartment she has rented to an American, but she "frisks among my possessions, touching, testing, sniffing." She brings vendors around. Her goldfish, which are pale from lack of food, get no nourishment other than the chemicals given off by the coins at the bottom of their bowl. The fish become "an allegory of Venice, a society which lived in a bowl and drew its sustenance from the filth of lucre."

Venice Observed is a tightly organized and highly original essay, but the reader comes away from it with the distinct feeling that McCarthy is more amused than inspired by Venice. From the opening sentence— "The rationalist mind has always had its doubts about Venice"—to the last—"There was a petrol shortage, and the Allied command, having made secret contact with the gondoliers' co-operative, officially 'captured' Venice with a fleet of gondolas; even war in Venice evokes a disbelieving smile"—one understands why. It would be temperamen-

tally difficult for such a truth-seeker to derive inspiration from a trompe-
l'oeil city like Venice. Its architecture is stage architecture. Venetian
architects decorated the fronts of buildings, "which captivate the eye by
tricks and blandishments," but left the backs looking like warehouses.
Even the Palladian churches, especially San Giorgio Maggiore, "are
disappointing when examined closely; they require mist or night illumi-
nation—tricks of stage make-up—to work their illusion, which is that of
a mirage or iridescent bubble seen across the water." And this most
romantic of all cities has no legendary lovers, no Paolo and Francesca,
no Petrarch and Laura, McCarthy complains. Venetians, she concludes,
are characterized by their love of show, and their city is a "frail shell,"
"a city of fantasy."

Despite McCarthy's criticisms of their city, Venetians liked the book.
Countess Cicogna thought it "a charming book, full of intelligent remarks." She said she would not recommend it as a guidebook, however,
because "it is too personal." When it appeared in *The New Yorker,*
McCarthy wrote the new editor, William Shawn, that "both numbers
have passed from hand to hand down the bathing cabanas on the Lido.
It is a success here; the leading local authorities have pronounced favorably."

Most critics liked the book. Sacheverell Sitwell, who reviewed it
for *The New York Times Book Review,* was an exception. He allowed
McCarthy "some amusing and true comments on Venice and the Venetians," but the book was "written with the overbright smartness that
reads best between the glossy covers of a magazine. . . . What is wrong
with Mary McCarthy! . . . There is something annoying and worth
reading on nearly every page. Perhaps no other writer could irritate so
much or write this book so well."

Sitwell's criticism was similar to Berenson's. Even so, McCarthy was
proud of her essay. She did not, however, like the appearance of *Venice
Observed* and suggested that the way the Berniers had put the book
together might have been the reason Berenson did not like it.

> The presentation is a different matter. I now feel rather sorry that I lent
> myself to what seems mainly a fashion enterprise. I ought to have foreseen
> this, but I didn't. The text is simply buried in chic and folderols; it would
> take a Diogenes to find any honesty in a volume that looks like this. Alas,
> I took you for such a Diogenes. I don't blame anyone though, for having
> their back put up by all that fancy dress. The book looks cynical; that's the
> only way I can describe it. My hope is that some time, when this market
> has been exploited to the limit by the publishers, the text can be reprinted

in a plain small volume with perhaps a few black and white illustrations in the back. (It would be nice if the reader could look at *some* of the pictures I talk about: a consideration that played almost no part in the present volume.)

The book was a glossy, expensive volume. Its sixty pages of color illustrations and its seventy-odd black and white photographs were the work of three photographers. André Chastel, professor of art at the Sorbonne, contributed comments on Venetian civilization as well as notes on the plates. McCarthy was affronted by the Berniers' engagement of another writer, particularly because she first learned of him from an advertisement. This had been done, no doubt, because the Berniers were themselves alarmed by what she had produced. "We really didn't want her to write about art," Rosamond Bernier Russell recently recalled. "We did not ask Mary McCarthy for a book on Venetian painting, but a book on Venice. The part on painting was not the strongest part of the book, but she is the kind of independent, strong-minded writer who would say, 'Take it or leave it'; and if we hadn't taken it, there would have been no book. Bernier was most distressed by this and although he really thought it was not up to his standards, he took it."

Francis Haskell, now a professor of art history at Trinity College, Oxford, and a leading art historian, agrees that experts on Venetian painting do not like the Venice book, yet he adds that McCarthy's insights are original. Her real gift, he adds, is that she writes about painting in a way that enables the reader who has never seen a certain picture to see it in his mind's eye, an ability professional art historians rarely possess. McCarthy's comments on Giorgione's painting "The Tempest" illustrate the vividness and immediacy of her response to painting.

> The stoppage of time in Giorgione has a partly idyllic character. But the idyll is charged with presentiment. . . . The presentiment is in "La Tempesta," which used to be called "The Soldier and the Gypsy"—in the lurid light and dangerous stillness of the moment in the center of a storm when the elements seem to pause as if to gather their forces. A jagged streak of lightning darts across the greenish sky, yet in the foreground a kind of false sunlight illuminates a peaceful scene. The red-jacketed, lissom soldier, posed at attention like a herald, the naked gypsy woman, the nursing baby, the green water in the river under the wooden bridge are all absolutely still, as if unaware of the forces that are about to be unleashed on them.
>
> Something frightening is about to happen—this is the suggestion of the

painting, which glues the spectator to the spot, just as the curious group is rooted to the landscape. Yet this is the oddest part; they are not rooted but seem to have been put there by hazard. "Who are they?" "What are they doing there?" The current school of art criticism discourages such questions; you are expected to look at this startling scene simply from a chromatic point of view. But a Giorgione always *disturbs*. The man and the woman are a queerly assorted pair, and a great distance separates them. Is he her betrayer or has he been sent to guard her? Against what? His handsome profile betrays nothing; he is an attitude, a stance. But the woman's eyes are on you, unmoving, like an arraignment; her swollen belly and the suckling child strike a somber note of reality in the phantasmagoric setting. There is an asp-bite to the picture. "This is your handiwork," the woman's body and unflinching eyes seem to say. To the onlooker? To the gallant soldier? The presentiment detaches itself from the storm poised overhead and by a mysterious inversion attaches itself to the past: something frightening has happened and is fixed forever—that is the painting's second suggestion.

An infinite duration, yet not even a moment has passed, only the fraction of time that it takes a bolt of lightning to flash across the sky.

Art became a consuming interest for McCarthy as a result of her work on *Venice Observed.* When she started the project, she realized that her knowledge of art was fragmentary. But she had a wonderful time exploring the city and searching through its archives. ("Maybe I should have been an historian" was her first reaction to the research.) By the time she had finished *Venice Observed,* she understood that "everything in Venice, in Italy for that matter, really points to Florence, everything in the Renaissance anyway, like signposts on a road. Whenever you're near discovery, you're near Florence." During the next three years she worked on a book on Florence. Off and on over a period of years, up to the present day, she has also been working on a book on Gothic art, and she constructed the plot of her 1979 novel, *Cannibals and Missionaries,* around questions of the value of art. Obviously the Berniers' unexpected invitation to Venice generated much more than a profile of a city.

CHAPTER XVI
FLORENCE
AND A VILLA
(1956–1959)

MARY MCCARTHY, accompanied by a large black Chevrolet sedan, left New York for Naples on May 2, 1956, aboard the *Cristoforo Colombo.* She had been so eager to get back to Italy that she did not wait for Broadwater, who had to remain in New York for the remainder of the school year. Before he joined her at the end of June, she had visited Bernard Berenson at I Tatti and had started an affair in Rome.

Carmen Angleton met the ship and together they drove to I Tatti, just outside Florence. The drive was somewhat perilous, Carmen Angleton remembers, not only because of the oversize American car on an undersize Italian highway, but chiefly because of her friend's limited driving experience. Mary McCarthy concurs: "I had an accident, hit a child, but fortunately I was only going five miles an hour. It unnerved me, and I wasn't a good driver anyway." Nevertheless, they got to I Tatti safely.

Villa I Tatti, a squarish Tuscan farmhouse expanded by Berenson to include two wings and a courtyard flanked by formal Italian gardens, was named for the Zati family who owned the villa in the sixteenth century. Its thick walls of Tuscan stone plastered over with a pale yellow stucco, the villa rose three stories to a sloping red-tiled roof. At each story, there was a row of seven French windows flanked by green shutters. The house commanded a sweeping view across a valley. By the time of Mary McCarthy's visit, the estate included seventy acres, thanks to Berenson's frequent purchases of adjoining fields and olive groves. Inside, in addition to his collection of Renaissance art, including Domenico Veneziano's "The Madonna and Child" and Cima's "San Sebastian," was one of the great private libraries in the world. But what most impressed Mary McCarthy was the serenity of I Tatti. This was due in part to its sheltered position on a Tuscan hillside, but mostly to the careful orchestration of Nicky Mariano, Berenson's companion and secretary of forty years, and her sister Alda Anrep; together they saw to it that everything ran smoothly. "It seems to me," McCarthy told Berenson some time later, "that of all the places I've been, I Tatti is the one where there is the most time; one bathes in pools of time. This extraordinary faculty you have for arranging time in spaced intervals must be connected, somehow, with your long life. Perhaps you can explain it."

In Rome, where Carmen Angleton had booked a room for her at the Hotel d' Inghilterra, she met John Davenport, an English critic—for a while the fiction reviewer for the *Observer,* and a onetime heavyweight boxer. Although in London he had a reputation as a heavy drinker who became obstreperous when inebriated, in Rome it was his dazzling vocabulary and sensitivity to language, as well as his forceful personality, that struck Mary McCarthy. They began an affair almost immediately. When Davenport left Rome, they wrote each other frequently. On June 6 she told him that she had "read you on Mr. Weeks while walking . . . with my friend Carmen; we laughed aloud in applause"; on June 10, that she was sorry to leave the Inghilterra "and my tile-and-chimney pot vista"; on June 20 from Milan, that "I hear you have something on Compton Mackenzie in *The Observer,* which I'm going to read in the English library this afternoon. I used to love his spy stories when I was in school: *Extremes Meet* and *The Last Courier,* where secret agents were named Keats and Milton and Shelley"; on June 24, that she had spent a day "viewing all the Bramante and paleo-Christian (I love that word) churches in Milan"; on June 26, still from Milan, that "I've wanted all day to answer by letter, but it's been an *awful* day, proofs and other things, so this monk [on the front of the postcard] will have to speak for me in his dejected way, looking forever out his window, forever hangdog, the outsider. . . . Or is the monk more like you?" Bowden Broadwater arrived in Europe at the end of June. He and Mary and Carmen Angleton set out at once on a tour of Italy, including a visit to Vallombrosa, where Berenson had a mountain retreat.

Because of the affair with Davenport, relations between the Broadwaters were strained, which must have made Carmen Angleton uncomfortable. In any case, she left them in Milan, and they continued touring until July 6, when they stopped in Venice. They stayed there for the rest of the summer.

All the time, McCarthy continued writing Davenport. On July 3 from Torri del Benaco she wrote, "This is a pretty, rustic place on Lake Garda, with wonderful icy swimming, but my inner agitation gives me the keenest sensation of imprisonment." On July 12 she told him that Venice was "madly cultural; last night I saw Montherlant's *Port Royal* at the Fenice; very fine. The night before, *Bérénice* in the outdoor theatre on S. Giorgio"; and on July 18, that she and Broadwater were "moving to Peggy G.'s this morning"—a temporary arrangement while they looked for an apartment.

They found an enormous apartment, an entire floor of a palazzo, with

four balconies overlooking the Grand Canal. Fortunately, the apartment was equipped with "plenty of very nice linen and a good supply of silver and dishes," for the Broadwaters' social life in Venice was extremely active. They entertained frequently, not only for old friends like the Macdonalds and Tuccis but for various acquaintances who kept turning up in Venice all summer. And they were invited everywhere. Venice was very lively at this moment, McCarthy wrote Berenson. "Present: Schiaparelli, . . . Elsa Maxwell, Clare Luce, Stravinsky, the Duke and Duchess of Windsor. The latter I haven't seen. Stravinsky I liked very much—an amiable, seasoned fox. Elsa Maxwell seemed much like any other fat, fussed hostess of her age; such are the kindnesses of time. Clare Luce, on the other hand, seemed a little pathetic; her white legs and arms thin as sticks. Bowden found her pretty. Anna Maria has been giving lots of dazzling parties with wonderful food. I like her more and more, find her complex, abrupt, and puzzling." They were having such a good time that she wrote Carmen Angleton begging her "to come and share the apartment and fun." As an added inducement, she wrote that "our domestic life is more peaceful than when you last witnessed it, though J. D. is still a thorn. But I have a feeling that this is going to resolve itself; if not, I shall have to resolve it . . . somehow; I don't quite know how."

Reuel, who had graduated from Brooks in June and had just finished a summer course for foreigners at the Sorbonne, came to Venice with a friend. By mid-September, Broadwater had left for London to see some plays before heading back to New York and the start of another Saint Bernard's school year, and Reuel had departed for America and his freshman year at Harvard. After such a madly social summer, McCarthy appreciated the "solitude, walking, reading, climbing the stairs to the library. It's a repetition of last year, except that now I welcome this lone state in which everything seems poignant and transfixing." She was alone in Venice until the end of September. Tony Bower, the friend who had been the intermediary between her and the Berniers the year before, had promised to meet her in Venice to drive her and the big Chevrolet to Paris, but he wired her at the last minute that he would meet her in Padua instead. Peggy Guggenheim, who gave a dinner the night before her departure, was furious at Bower, knowing McCarthy was a fearful driver. When Guggenheim remembered the protagonist's fatal automobile accident at the end of *A Charmed Life,* she took it upon herself to drive McCarthy to Padua. After reaching Paris, McCarthy went to Amsterdam to meet Hannah Arendt for a Rembrandt show. Following that, there were a few days in London, where she saw John Davenport. On

October 18 she sailed first-class to New York on the *Queen Elizabeth.* No sooner had she arrived than she and Broadwater drove to Cambridge to see Reuel; they stayed with the Schlesingers.

From the time she returned to New York in the fall of 1956 until she left again for Europe in the spring of 1957, she worked on and finished her autobiographical book *Memories of a Catholic Girlhood.* During the preceding thirteen years she had written and published eight memoirs—"C.Y.E." in *Mademoiselle* (1944), "Yellowstone Park" in *Harper's Bazaar* (1955), and "The Blackguard" (1946), "Yonder Peasant, Who Is He?" (1948), "A Tin Butterfly" (1951), *"C'est le Premier Pas Qui Coûte"* (1952), "The Figures in the Clock" (1953), and "Ask Me No Questions" (1957) in *The New Yorker. Memories of a Catholic Girlhood* is a collection of these autobiographical sketches.

The book opens with an essay addressed to the reader. "This record lays a claim to being historical—that is, much of it can be checked. If there is more fiction in it than I know, I should like to be set right; in some instances, which I shall call attention to later, my memory has already been corrected." Accordingly, she appended essays to seven of the eight memoirs, explaining that she was forced to make a few compromises with regard to the names of actual people; that in the interest of telling a good story she invented dialogue that nevertheless was close to the spirit of conversations that she remembered in substance if not in detail; and, finally, noting certain minor points in the memoir that either seemed dubious or had been corrected by her uncle Harry. "How typical this is of Mary's mind," a close friend has said; "she's always trying to make clear what is factual and what is fiction."

Despite McCarthy's careful attempt to distinguish fact from fiction, several reviewers doubted her sincerity. Some of the complaints were mild—"And it is also obvious that on occasion the *memoiriste* has succumbed to the impish blandishments of the fictionalist." Others were venomous—"Mary McCarthy wanted quite simply to lie about her experience, then makes things all right by confessing the lie, while at the same time capitalizing on the fact that the reader would come upon the lie first, accept it as truth, and be impressed by it before he would come upon the notes informing him that he had been duped."

In fact, there are surprisingly few changes in the "notes"—surprising because, aside from her brother Kevin, a year and a half her junior, she had no one to consult. Most people, even those with living parents, harbor manifold incorrect impressions of what occurred during their childhood, but they have other people who can set them straight. In the beginning of *Memories of a Catholic Girlhood,* McCarthy herself writes about correcting her own child's erroneous recollection that during World War II Mussolini was thrown off a bus on Cape Cod.

> This memory goes back to one morning in 1943 when, as a young child, he was waiting with his father and me beside the road in Wellfleet to put a departing guest on the bus to Hyannis. The bus came through, and the bus driver leaned down to shout the latest piece of news: "They've thrown Mussolini out." Today, Reuel knows that Mussolini was never ejected from a Massachusetts bus, and he also knows how he got that impression. But if his father and I had died the following year, he would have been left with a clear recollection of something that everyone would have assured him was an historic impossibility and with no way of reconciling his stubborn memory to the stubborn facts on record.

Mary McCarthy did commit a few errors of fact in *Memories of a Catholic Girlhood.* She was mistaken about her McCarthy ancestors being "wreckers"; Simon Manly Preston did not attend West Point, but a school founded by a former superintendent of West Point; Roy McCarthy was not a graduate of the University of Minnesota, although he had been an undergraduate there, and he was not attending law school when he met Tess Preston, but entered after Mary was born; Florence McCarthy, the husband of Roy's sister, Esther, was not Protestant; Mary's grades at Garfield High School were better than she remembered; and, finally, her mother's family's name is misspelled in the book (curiously, no one corrected this). For the most part, however, McCarthy's memories were quite accurate.

More important, *Memories of a Catholic Girlhood* contains Mary McCarthy's best writing and is one of the most amusing and moving chronicles of growing up in English. As the reviewer in the New York *Herald Tribune Book Review* put it, "Miss McCarthy, who writes better than most people, here writes better than herself." It is not only the high quality of the prose but also the depth of understanding for its superb gallery of characters, including herself, that sets this book apart from her others. The re-creations of her Jewish and Catholic grandmothers and of her Protestant grandfather, recalled unforgettably by their gestures, mannerisms, speech, and even silences, are rich portraits. Even the minor characters are extraordinarily lifelike. Who can forget austere Miss Gowrie, in whose Latin classes Mary McCarthy learned to love classical literature?

A cough and a tobacco stain on the second finger of her right hand told us that she was a heavy smoker, but we learned from the riding master's wife that Miss Gowrie steadily refused to take a cigarette anywhere near the Seminary and blinked with disapproval when she heard that other teachers did it. This watchfulness of conscience brooded likewise over her favorites; that is, her better students, for she knew no other measure. You could tell you were in Miss Gowrie's good graces by the bad-conduct marks she set firmly opposite your name in the school record book. In fact, in all her ways she was a stoic of the Roman mold, recalling that matron cited in Pliny, the terrible Arria, who, to encourage her husband to commit suicide, plunged a dagger into her own breast, drew it out, saying, "It doesn't hurt, Paetus," and handed it to him.

Just as memorable are the Sacred Heart nuns, whom she sees as startlingly aristocratic and intellectual as compared with the parochial school nuns she had known at Saint Stephen's.

Like all truly intellectual women, these were in spirit romantic desperadoes. They despised organizational heretics of the stamp of Luther and Calvin, but the great atheists and sinners were the heroes of the costume picture they taught as a subject called history. Marlowe, Baudelaire—above all, Byron—glowed like terrible stars above their literature courses. Little girls often were reciting "The Prisoner of Chillon" and hearing stories of Claire Clairmont, Caroline Lamb, the Segatti, and the swim across the Hellespont. Even M. Voltaire enjoyed a left-handed popularity. The nuns spoke of him with horror and admiration mingled: "A great mind, an unconquerable spirit—and what fearful use they were put to." In Rousseau, an unbuttoned, middle-class figure, they had no interest whatever.

Finally, the Bent sisters, whom McCarthy, as a high school student, visited in Medicine Springs—a town in the middle of Montana that was so small "it did not even figure on the railroad map on our timetable"—fascinated McCarthy because of

some quality—levelheadedness, I suppose—that reassured older people. They never got into trouble, no matter what they did, while I was either in high favor or on the verge of being expelled. Unlike me, they did not seek to make a point; they merely did what they wanted, in a bald, impersonal way, like two natural forces—a sultry dark-browed wind and light playful breeze.

Mary's grandmother Augusta Preston, with her son Harold, Mary's uncle, around 1914.

Mary's grandfather Harold Preston.

The McCarthy families out for a drive, 1907. J. H. McCarthy's family is in the center car (J. H. is hatless; Roy is in the front passenger seat).

Roy McCarthy (in front) with graduating classmates from the University of Washington, May 1915.

(Courtesy, Vassar College Library)

Mary's mother Tess McCarthy, holding Kevin, with Lizzie and J. H. McCarthy at right, May 1915.

Mary, age two, with her grandfather J. H. McCarthy, Seattle, 1914.

Therese (Tess) Preston McCarthy
with her children, fall 1918.
Left to right: Kevin, Mary,
Sheridan, Preston.

Mary, eight years old, dressed for
her First Communion, at St.
Stephen's Church, Minneapolis.

Mary McCarthy (center) on her seventh birthday, with her McCarthy cousins and brothers Preston and Kevin (back row, third and second from right).

*Mary McCarthy on the
way to a Vassar College
dance, 1933.*
(Mrs. Richard Goss)

*McCarthy with her first husband, Harold Johnsrud, on their wedding day (her
twenty-first birthday)—June 21, 1933.*

*Philip Rahv in
1971.*

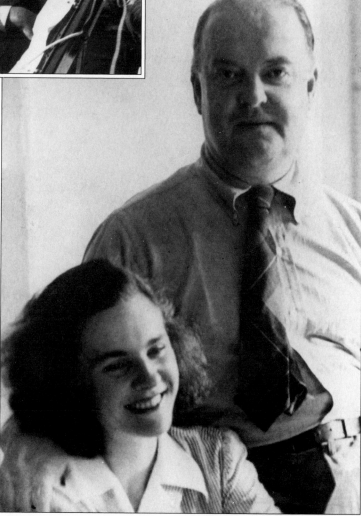

McCarthy with Edmund Wilson, Wellfleet, early 1940s. (Sylvia Salmi)

Mary McCarthy and Bowden Broadwater with friends at their East 57th Street apartment, 1949. Rear, left to right: Bowden Broadwater, Lionel Abel, Elizabeth Hardwick, Miriam Chiaromonte, Nicola Chiaromonte, McCarthy, and John Berryman. Front: Dwight Macdonald and Kevin McCarthy. (Kevin McCarthy)

Mary and Bowden, Portsmouth, 1951. (Kevin McCarthy)

Bowden Broadwater, Portsmouth, early 1950s.

(Kevin McCarthy)

Mary with her brother Kevin, 1956.   (Inge Morath, Magnum)

McCarthy with friends, 1966. Rear, left to right: Heinrich Blücher, Hannah Arendt, Dwight Macdonald, Gloria Macdonald. Front: Nicola Chiaromonte, McCarthy, Robert Lowell.

James West, Poland, 1961.

McCarthy with Reuel Wilson, in Orgeval, outside Paris, 1961.

The Wests' house in Castine, Maine, in the early 1970s.

Mary McCarthy visiting North Vietnam, 1968.

McCarthy with William Jovanovich, Castine, late 1960s.

Mary McCarthy in her garden at Castine, early 1980s.

But it is her own self-portrait that is best. Admitting that "it was the idea of being noticed that consumed all my attention," she depicts herself, as usual, in an unflattering, yet humorous, light.

> Though I often stood first in my studies, the coveted pink ribbon for good conduct never came my way. I suppose this was because of my meanness, in particular the spiteful taunts I directed at a supercilious fat girl, the petted daughter of a rich meat packer, with heavy rings on her fingers and a real fur coat, who was my principal rival for honors in the classroom. . . . Was it my fault if she blubbered when I applied, perfectly accurately, a term I had heard mothers whisper—*nouveau riche?* Wasn't it *true,* I argued, when I was rebuked by Madame Barclay, our mistress of studies, and wasn't fat Beryl always boasting of her money and curling her baby lip at girls whose mothers had to work? It wasn't kind of me, replied Madame Barclay, but I did not think it kind of her when she passed me over for Beryl in casting the class play. Everyone could see that I was much the better actress, and the leading role of haughty Lady Spindle was precisely suited to my style. . . . Up to the last moment, I could not think they would really do this to me; I knew the part by heart and practiced the lines privately against the time when they would recognize their error and send for me to rescue them. But, incredibly, the play went on without me, and my only satisfaction, as I sat in the audience, was to watch Pork Barrel forget her lines; I supplied them, to my neighbors, in a vindictive whisper, till somebody told me to hush.

Dwight Macdonald, who liked *Memories of a Catholic Girlhood* better than anything else she wrote, told Nicola Chiaromonte it "was unlike her usual stuff. Why doesn't she write like that? Why does she feel such an absurd need to be ultrasmart?" He liked the memoirs, he said, because they were "*felt* for once, and direct and simple and moving. Maybe she can only love herself as a fictional character!"

When *Memories of a Catholic Girlhood* was published, in May 1957, McCarthy was back in Europe. She was headed for Italy, as usual, but first stopped in London to see John Davenport. She did not see him, however. In a letter to Hannah Arendt, she told the dismal story of what happened.

When she could not reach Davenport by phone—it had been disconnected for nonpayment of the bill—she called a man he had identified as his cousin to arrange a rendezvous. The man was not Davenport's cousin. "Did he tell you that?" he asked. "I think I'd better tell you that John is a pathological liar." The story the "cousin" told McCarthy was not pretty. Davenport was known for stealing small objects from friends' homes and books from the *Observer* office and then selling them; he spent an inordinate amount of time in pubs; he was frequently drunk and violent; and he ran about London telling anyone who would listen that his wife was mad. (He had had several wives and children.) Furthermore, he had lied to McCarthy about his ancestry, and he had bragged all over London about his affair with the famous American writer. These revelations shocked McCarthy, for she had only seen his good side—his wit, his generosity, the elegance of his intellect, and the scope of his scholarship. She met the "cousin" once more and decided not to see Davenport.

"What was the point?" she asked Hannah Arendt. "We couldn't make love, thanks to the publicity John had given the affair, and if we talked simply, I wouldn't be able to dissemble the knowledge I now had. The truth is, I still care about him, just as much as ever. Oh Hannah, isn't it awful? I still would do anything for him, . . . but what *can* I do? Bowden knows all of the above except my feelings. Naturally he is feeling vindicated and delighted that I did not see John. And loyalty to him (Bowden) under the circumstances was a motive that sustained me in not seeing John." Although the revelations about Davenport had upset her terribly, she did not leave London for almost a week because she could not change her reservations at the Albergo della Signoria, where she was booked to stay in Florence. Fortunately, Dwight Macdonald was living in London, having taken a position for a year as an editor at *Encounter,* one of the Congress for Cultural Freedom magazines. Even so, as McCarthy went about London with old friends, she was torn, she told Hannah Arendt, between longing to see Davenport and terror of meeting him accidentally.

When she finally arrived in Florence, she had bronchial pneumonia. The Albergo della Signoria had no restaurant, she told Macdonald, "but the *padrona* comes up twice a day to my room to discuss the invalid viands she is going to have served to me and to arrange the flowers. Oh what broths and scraped apple flavored with lemon peel and chicken breasts and slivers of white sole, and delicately sliced oranges; I feel like a baby." When she was well, at the end of the month, she went to I Tatti for a few days, feeling almost as frail and feeble as Berenson. Laurence Olivier, on his way to Venice and Yugoslavia with *Titus Andronicus,* came for lunch while she was there, bringing with him a much needed "supply of fresh energy."

After a long weekend with Berenson, she moved into an apartment on the Via Romana owned by a Count Alberti, a lineal descendent of the Renaissance architect Leon Battista Alberti. She would describe the ubiquitous traffic and noise of the Via Romana—"truly infernal, demonic"—in the opening of her next book, *The Stones of Florence.* She complained by letter to Macdonald and Berenson that she was living a life of "forbidding solitude." Her only consolation was that "last year, under similar circumstances, I lost ten pounds here, because I only ate one meal a day, not being able to pocket my pride and eat two meals alone in public, sequitur. At least one comes out of it thin." But, as in Venice, her seclusion lasted only a few days. She attended parties at Elizabeth Borghese's, at the Villa Ombrellino, at Countess Rucellai's, and at the home of Luisina Milani, a friend of Nicky Mariano; and she also had dinner with Joseph Alsop and his mother and young niece—all within a few days of leaving I Tatti. A week later she told Berenson that she had been busy seeing "lots of new people—too many to list—and taking Italian lessons." She reported all this in a letter that included choice morsels of local gossip served up for his enjoyment. "Oh dear," she concluded, "don't repeat any of this. I've just been reading how the best people in Florence, including the Brownings, didn't want to receive Mrs. Trollope on account of her sharp tongue."

Bowden Broadwater arrived in mid-June; Reuel, who was spending his third consecutive summer in Europe, came nearly every weekend in July, riding his Vespa from Perugia, where he was attending the university's school for foreign students. Except for occasional trips about northern Italy, the Broadwaters stayed in Florence for the entire summer. By the time Broadwater left in September for the start of the school year, they had many Florentine friends.

One of them, Countess Cristina Rucellai, lived in a well-preserved Renaissance palace designed by Leon Battista Alberti and built by Bernardo Rossellino in the mid-fifteenth century. A full-page photograph of the windows of the Palazzo Rucellai appears in *The Stones of Florence.* The Rucellai family was a distinguished one, with a long line of poets, philosophers, and public figures. Countess Rucellai saw the Broadwaters often.

Harold Acton, another new Florentine acquaintance, was an amusing, elegant man and an accomplished writer. He entertained the Broadwaters at his magnificent villa on the Via Bolognese—the fourteenth-century Villa La Pietra, approached by a long double avenue of cypresses. Originally a typical early-Renaissance country house, it had been altered over the centuries: the central open courtyard with its marble fountain had been roofed over with a skylight; a circular staircase had been installed in lieu of a narrow Gothic one; handsome lodges had been built at the outer gate; the central portion of the northwest facade had been raised to accommodate a spacious ballroom; and—because the garden of an Italian villa is considered an architectural extension of the house—a series of broad terraces, each like a separate garden, had been leveled from the slope descending behind the house. Besides priceless treasures inside the villa, the gardens contained more than one hundred statues collected by Acton's father. Sir Harold, like Countess Rucellai, admired Bowden Broadwater's wit and intelligence but marveled at Mary McCarthy's vivid eyes, which took everything in.

Another new friend, Roberto Papi, was a highly cultured, charming, good-looking Florentine who loved his city and conveyed this love during many excursions with the American author. (Several Florentines suspect he fell in love with her as well.) Papi was a writer and poet, though his style tended to be labored. (A long essay about Berenson had left the great man puzzled as to what Papi thought about him.) Fortunately for Mary McCarthy, Papi was a better talker than writer, for he charmed her with his eagerness to expound on Florence. Her Florentine friends think that what she got right about the city she got from Papi. She dedicated *The Stones of Florence* to him.

During the summer of 1957, however, she was not planning a book on Florence, but rather a long essay comparing her impressions of Florence with those of Bologna and Mantua. When Broadwater returned to New York in September, she remained behind to work at the German Institute, the oldest institution in Florence devoted to research in Italian art, "trying to understand Renaissance theories of perspective and the vanishing point." It was not until after she herself had returned to New York, having sailed on the *Liberté* in October, that she decided to concentrate on Florence. Georges Bernier had written to ask her to do such a study, but she promised it to Harcourt, Brace instead, because she was unhappy with the treatment she had received from Georges Bernier.

Relations with the Berniers are rather strained now. I gather they say I am "temperamental." The only person who has given me a straight story about anything connected with the book has been Reynal (the publisher in New York), and he has been left out in the dark too, except about the American edition—perforce. I've also been annoyed to find out, second-hand, that my name was omitted from the cover of the French edition. . . . I like the Berniers despite all this, but I think that Georges' character is incorrigibly *rusé* and full of double talk. . . . If one is going to have business dealings with him, one must simply accept this, with resignation, which is the attitude I'm trying to adopt. On the positive side is their enthusiasm and energy.

Rosamond Bernier Russell later admitted that McCarthy had good reason to be annoyed with Georges. At the time, nonetheless, the Berniers felt somewhat betrayed: as the owners of a fledgling business, they had taken quite a gamble in publishing *Venice Observed.* She remembered that when they tried to sell the book to American publishers, no one would buy it. " 'What was it,' they asked, 'an art book? a history?' So we published it at our own expense." McCarthy, on her part, has said she was "never sorry for having done" the Venice book for the Berniers. As it turned out, *Venice Observed* initiated a genre of glossy "city" books, written by distinguished writers and published by various publishing houses.

In New York during the winter of 1958, McCarthy worked "very hard, too hard," on the Florence book, she wrote Berenson, "so that I was put to bed for a week by a doctor for what they call 'a complete rest.' . . . Why did I ever tackle this Florence book? I think it will be better than the *Venice,* but it has been much, much harder to do, and the average reader, I'm afraid, is going to find it boring—too serious." She even sacrificed a spring trip to Sicily with Broadwater in order to continue working.

Her only respites came during a short trip to Boston in January to see Laurence Olivier in *The Entertainer,* about which she had promised to write for *Harper's Bazaar* (in her review she said she liked John Osborne, whom she viewed as a ranker, weedier Shaw); a lecture for Colgate students in March; and a round of parties—one of them a cocktail party at her Ninety-fourth Street apartment—for Anna Maria Cicogna, who had entertained so often for her in Venice. "She has made New York seem like Venice at the height of the season," McCarthy reported to Berenson.

"I'm giving a cocktail party for her tomorrow—a typical New York party with thirty people, all of whom have a little 'name' and all of whom will probably frighten Anna Maria to death, particularly when crowded into my sitting room and yelling at each other. She will have to treat it as if she were a tourist, watching a national pastime, like a bull fight. . . . I am all a-tremble, and the apartment is reeking with furniture polish, and a colored man is in the next room plying the floor-waxer, and I have washed two dozen new glasses, and my art-dealer friend . . . is lending me his maid and is sending me a shipment of smoked salmon and sturgeon that I don't want and I am about to rush downtown and buy some caviar and foie gras to mitigate this, and my brother is coming tomorrow to mix the drinks. I haven't given a big party for years and feel appalled and certain I shall forget something essential."

By May 1958 McCarthy was back in Florence, this time with Evelyn Hofer, the photographer that Harcourt, Brace had picked to illustrate *The Stones of Florence.* Cecil Beaton had wanted to do the pictures, but Harcourt, Brace declined, fearing that he would want to do a "Beaton book," that McCarthy would want to do *her* book, and that the two would never settle on what it would look like. Evelyn Hofer was not as well known as Beaton. Although she had begun her professional career in Mexico in the early 1940s, she did not arrive in New York until after World War II. With her classic eye for form, she was the perfect choice for *The Stones of Florence,* and as it turned out, architectural photography was her forte. After the publication of McCarthy's book, Hofer was commissioned to do the photographs for V. S. Pritchett's three city books—on London, New York, and Dublin—and for James Morris's book on Spain.

When McCarthy and Hofer arrived in Florence, it rained for days on end. After they finally began work, nothing seemed to go right. "In fact," McCarthy wrote William Shawn in mid-June, "the photographic situation here has been grinding me into little pieces. The girl-photographer who came with me is charming and talented but not at all equipped to meet the inherent, implacable difficulties: furious friars running out of churches, yelling 'photographing forbidden'; endless permissions to be wheedled out of authorities and private people; the language; the light; the problem of finding a car and driver (she doesn't drive); the problem of finding a reliable boy to carry the equipment, including a fifty-pound tripod; of finding a dark room, an icebox to keep film, an enlarger." Broadwater, summoned by cable, came to the rescue on June 13. He managed to get Hofer to various sites with a minimum of fuss.

Evelyn Hofer used old-fashioned equipment: a big camera with old lenses, shutter, and tripod; a black hood under which she ducked her head. She owned a Rolleiflex and a Leica for "taking photographic notes," but insisted on the big camera for the actual pictures she would use for the book, since she required long exposures. Her proudest achievement, a photograph of the interior marbled wall of the Bapistry, required a two-hour open shutter. The cumbersome camera discouraged speed and superficiality, allowing her to concentrate on essences. Unlike most photographers, intent on capturing the moment, what is eye-catching and unintentionally candid, Hofer looked for images of inner identity, trying to understand a building's or a statue's or a painting's fundamental character. As a result of the logistical difficulties, and her painstaking method, after five weeks in Florence she had produced only a small number of photographs.

In the end, her methods succeeded; her photographs were stunning. Florentines called them sensitive. Ulrich Middeldorf, the head of the German Institute, said they were exquisite—"What lovely things! Some of them are quite astounding, beautiful, most telling, and often they are better than any others I have ever seen of the same objects." When *The Stones of Florence* was published, reviewers, even those who did not like the text, unanimously praised Hofer's photographic illustrations. "Some of the best architectural photographs that have been taken of this city," wrote one; "superb in their technical qualities," wrote another, "with caressing velvety blacks and creamy whites and sharp focusing on details of tombs, torch holders, crypts, church facades, palaces, and garbage cans." McCarthy, too, liked the photographs.

Hofer had finished her work by the end of July. The Broadwaters went to Maratea, a luxurious retreat on the wild Calabrian coast, two hundred and fifty kilometers below Naples, for three weeks with Carmen Angleton. During August they stayed in Rome for two weeks, in Paris for a few days to meet Reuel, who had been working there, and, finally, in London for two weeks before sailing home on the *Flandre*. Despite the stormy weather, the week on the *Flandre* was relaxing. They read a good deal; Mary, *Doctor Zhivago,* which she thought "a beautiful, magical book and very sad."

Back home, the Broadwaters worked on the layout of photographs with editors from Harcourt, Brace, who had never done a book of this kind. Both Broadwaters were perfectionists, taking infinite pains about how the book would look. McCarthy wrote Berenson that, having just finished John Pope-Hennessy's book on Italian Gothic sculpture, she was certain she knew how not to organize pictures. The way Phaidon had arranged the figures and plates of Pope-Hennessy's book, "it would take an octopus to handle the volume." Bowden Broadwater also had definite ideas about the design of *The Stones of Florence,* having had valuable experience with layout at *Partisan Review.* McCarthy remembers "what fun it was then to come in on Saturday morning and work on assembling the Florence book, spreading out text pages and photographs on the floor, and nobody there" except the Broadwaters, a layout editor, and William Jovanovich, who, even though he was only thirty-eight, had been president of Harcourt, Brace for three years. "And the result was that beautiful book, which I doubt that we could have made if we hadn't been alone in those unmanned offices." Another consequence of these Saturday meetings was that Mary McCarthy and William Jovanovich got to be good friends.

Unfortunately, photographs of several important paintings, statues, and buildings that had been commissioned from Florentine photographers to supplement Evelyn Hofer's work had not arrived in New York. McCarthy had to ask Ulrich Middeldorf, the head of the German Institute, where she had done research, to intervene. Middeldorf, a German-born Renaissance art expert, had taught at the University of Chicago from 1935 to 1953. Mary McCarthy first met him during the summer of 1939, when she and Edmund Wilson lived in Chicago.

Dozens of letters and cables flew back and forth across the Atlantic, generally in response to the frantic request "Could someone from the Institute possibly call up and find out what happened?" Middeldorf was accommodating, tracking down recalcitrant photographers, getting photographic replacements, arranging for new pictures to be taken, and cajoling permissions from reluctant curators and churchmen. Even so, mishaps kept occurring: one photographer photographed the wrong objects; another fractured his left foot, disabling him for a necessary ninety-foot ascent on a scaffolding; and the Swiss firm that would print the book suddenly announced that all photographs had to be in their hands by the end of March or there would be no fall delivery. Almost forced into a 1960 publication date, Harcourt, Brace persuaded the printer to grant an extension.

Small wonder that Mary McCarthy told William Shawn, "I shall never, never write another book of this kind or take on so much responsibility." The refrain "If I ever get this book done" gave way over the months and months she worked on it to "Wasn't it of *Romola* that George Eliot said: 'I began it a young woman; I finished it an old woman'?" Indeed, before the book appeared, in October of 1959, several statements in the manuscript had to be updated for *The New Yorker,* which published her work as "A City of Stone" (in three parts). Even so, she told Katharine White that she loved the city of Florence, "but it is tremendously difficult and complex—a far cry from Venice, the difference between a dream and a complicated discourse."

As a lover of Florence, she paid tribute in her essay to all the things that had personally moved her in the city, through her encomiums giving expression to her own outlook on life and thought. "I felt that through the medium of writing about this city, its history, its architects and painters—it was possible for me to say what I believed in."

Florence for her is the tough, virile city of the fifteenth century, when Brunelleschi, Donatello, Masaccio, and Uccello were imposing their vision of space on the world. She especially admired Brunelleschi, whose architecture "is a species of wisdom, like Socratic and Platonic philosophy, in which forms are realized in their absolute integrity and essence: the squareness of square, the slenderness of slender, the roundness of round. . . . Brunelleschi's dome compels a kind of slow, surprised recognition; it is the way a dome 'ought to be.' " McCarthy revels in the substance, solidity, and monumentality of the century's architecture, the spare, economical character of its sculpture, and the daring originality of its painting. In particular, she admires the art produced during the quattrocentro and the Republic, characterized as it is by simplicity, restraint, economy, and a wise division of space. Keen on discipline and moral standards, she sees fifteenth-century Florence as embodying these virtues. In the same way that she venerates Caesar and the rule of law, she admires the stern Republican truthfulness. She thereby links her own vision of the world to the greatest achievement of Florentine art. And she makes it clear that she thinks the great era of Florentine culture came to an end with the Republic. She dislikes the cinquecento because much of its art—at least the art of the second half of the century—is, she feels, manneristic and pretentious. She views the seventeenth and eighteenth centuries as periods of decay and decline.

Always the synthesizer, McCarthy aims to make her reader see Florence—like Venice—as a coherent personality. "Florence is a manly town," which

> makes no concession to the pleasure principle. . . . Against the green Arno, the ochre-and-dun file of hotels and palazzi has the spruce, spare look of a regiment drawn up in drill order. The deep shades of melon and tangerine that you see in Rome, the pinks of Venice, the rose of Siena, the red of Bologna have been ruled out of Florence as if by municipal decree. The eye turns from the mustard, buff, ecru, pale yellow, cream to the severe black-and-white marbles of the Baptistry and of Santa Maria Novella's facade or the dark-green and white flashing gold of San Miniato. On the Duomo and Giotto's bell tower and the Victorian facade of Santa Croce, there are touches of pink, which give these buildings a curious festive air, as though they alone were dressed up for a party. The general severity is even echoed by the Florentine bird, which is black and white—the swallow, a bachelor, as the Florentines say, wearing a tail coat.
>
> The great sculptors and architects who stamped the outward city with its permanent image or style—Brunelleschi, Donatello, Michelangelo—

were all bachelors. Monks, soldier-saints, prophets, hermits were the city's heroes. . . . Except for the Madonna and her boy-baby, women saints count for little in the Florentine iconography.

Moreover, Florentine painters were known for their "strange ascetic habits." The palaces, pleasant enough on the inside, present fortresslike facades on their outside. "This is a city of endurance, a city of stone," McCarthy wrote.

Bernard Berenson died before her book was published, but she had read parts of the manuscript to him. Once again, he was critical of her work. He deprecated the notion of assigning sexual identity to a city, telling McCarthy it was "sentimental twaddle" to call Florence masculine, and he deplored what he called the "*New Yorker* touch" in the first chapter, which describes contemporary Florence as an overnoisy, crowded city with a severe traffic problem. It was a good description journalistically, Berenson conceded, but exaggerated, he thought. Always autocratic and dictatorial, even toward his friends, he could be ruthless and unkind when he did not like something. Mary McCarthy was hurt by his remarks. Sir Harold Acton and Countess Rucellai, who saw her the same evening he delivered them, would remember her as tearful and upset at his reaction. They also recalled her own admission of Berenson's initial reaction to news that she would write about his adopted city: "But, my dear, what do you *know* about Florence?" Nevertheless, Berenson admired McCarthy's facility of verbal expression. Few people he knew could discourse lucidly on art by transposing pictorial values into words, but Mary McCarthy had this gift, and he wrote about it in his diary.

Took Mary McCarthy to Gricigliano back by the Sieci and along the Arno. Tuscany at its most enchanting moment, a wonder and joy for my eye. But Mary scarcely opened her eyes to all this beauty. Yet she will write about it, and be evocative and give readers the longing to come and experience for themselves, as I never, never could. Such is the power of a gift for words, and the technique for using them. The accomplished writer need not feel, nor muse, nor think as much as I do, but he will make his reader do so, as I cannot.

Harold Acton agrees, adding that her descriptions of Pontormo's frescoes are the best he has ever read, especially valuable to those who have never seen them. Her description of Pontormo's "Deposition" in the church of Santa Felicita is a good example. (Curiously, it elicited a great deal of negative comment from the reviewers of *The Stones of Florence.*)

> Because of the darkness of the chapel he uses pale boudoir shades reminiscent of ribbon and silken coverlets; the pale soft lifeless body of Christ, carried by attendant nacreous figures, might almost be the center of a chiffony Bacchanale. There is no sign of the Cross or of any solid object. A drift of pale-green chiffon is lying on the ground in the front of the picture, and the mourners are dressed in peppermint pink, orchid, gold-apricot, sky-blue, scarlet, pale peach, mauve-pink, pomegranate, iridescent salmon (orange-persimmon-yellow), and olive-green. All the figures are ethereally feminine, except for a tiny bearded old man whose head is seen in one corner. The two bearers of Christ's drooping, supine cadaver are wide-eyed girlish pages with pearly, satin-smooth arms, silky short gold curls and white shapely legs; one of them is wearing a bright blue scarf or ribbon. An utter detachment from what has happened characterizes this bizarre epicene ensemble; about to shoulder their burden, the bearers turn their curly heads, as it were, to pose for the picture, and the one on the left, with Cupid's bow lips parting, has assumed an expression of pathetic, pretty surprise. The choreographic grouping of harmonious candy tints, flowing gestures, and glistening white tempting flesh makes an eerie morbid impression, as though Cecil Beaton had done the costumes for a requiem ballet on Golgotha.

The ballet-on-Golgotha image disturbed several reviewers. According to *The New York Times Book Review,* "The artists of Florence . . . never dreamed that their hard labors and steady passion were destined to provide material for a display of cleverness." Yet it is just such an arresting comparison that enables a reader to *see* the "Deposition." In fact, it illustrates one of McCarthy's shrewdest criticisms of cinquecento art: "the faculty of eliciting inappropriate comparisons is always a mark of strain in art, and the early Florentine Mannerists possess this faculty to the highest degree. The detachment of their tapering figures from the action they are supposed to be performing . . . prompts the onlooker to associate this dissociated work with the realm of common things. . . . The banished real world returns in an unpleasant way, forcing itself in where it does not belong."

Berenson would at least have liked the way *The Stones of Florence* looked; it was printed in blacks and whites, with only a few color plates. He had urged her not to do it in color. "It could be very elegant, certainly, all in black and white and greys," he had said, "like courses of Tuscan marbles—something more refined than the present taste in art books, something more chaste, like Brunelleschi in Santo Spirito or the Pazzi Chapel. Luca della Robbia. Or Santi Apostoli. Or the Laurentian Library." She accepted his advice and acknowledged in the text that "white, black, grey, dun, and bronze are the colors of Florence—the colors of stone and metal, the primitive elements of Nature out of which the first civilizations were hammered—the Stone Age, the Bronze Age, the Iron Age. The hammer and the chisel strike the somber music of Florentine art and architecture, of the Florentine character."

McCarthy's Florentine acquaintances did not like the book. Sir Harold Acton regretted her depreciation of everything after the Republic; Countess Rucellai claimed McCarthy saw the city from the outside, thus she did not "catch" the mentality of Florentines; and Professor Middeldorf declared she had the wrong slant because she was stubborn and did not listen to him. Her New York friends were more enthusiastic. Hannah Arendt called it superb; William Jovanovich was pleased by the way her prose conveyed "factual, historical information while at the same time coloring it with the tones of the past." But Dwight Macdonald, not so approving, found "far too much insider snobbishness, far too many facts and far too little feeling." Chiaromonte, who wrote a positive critique for *Partisan Review,* privately told Macdonald that he admired her research and readability but saw "many questionable ideas or cracks, as usual. . . . But that is Mary, an overly intelligent woman, with a streak of foolishness."

In the early part of the decade, long before the Florence book appeared, Mary McCarthy had started work on a novel. "It has eight heroines," she wrote Berenson, "starts in the 1930s and describes twenty years of progressive notions in sex, architecture, interior decoration, child-rearing, as refracted through the eight dizzy little prisms." By the time *The Group,* as she finally titled it, was published, in 1963, she had been working on it intermittently for eleven years. Despite having an apartment to herself all day, with her husband at Saint Bernard's and her son at Harvard, she found it increasingly difficult to work in New York. Writers, intellectuals, and their European friends always seemed to be turning up. During the late fall of 1958 and early winter of 1959, she and Broadwater attended parties for the Philip Toynbees, the Kenneth Tynans, Elizabeth Bowen, Baroness Blixen (Isak Dinesen), Kingsley Amis, John Wain, Cecil Beaton, Christopher Isherwood, and Stephen Spender. Local friends like Niccolò Tucci came to tea frequently. She managed, anyway, to write a review of Harold Rosenberg's *The Tradition of the New* for *Partisan Review* and a remarkably clear précis of Hannah Arendt's dense *The Human Condition* for *The New Yorker,* to execute a successful application for a Guggenheim Fellowship, and to deliver a lecture at Northwestern University. In addition, she frequented the theater, opera, ballet, and concert hall, and attended readings at the Ninety-second Street Y Poetry Center, where she herself read the first chapter of *The Group,* "which brought a lot of laughter from the audience."

Seeking to get away from the distractions of New York, Mary McCarthy looked for a country house for the summer of 1959. She found one in Vermont, returning to Derby Hill, the setting for *The Oasis,* where she and Broadwater had summered in 1947. "We have a vast sweep of view," she wrote Nicky Mariano, "of three distant mountain chains and nearer by, farm land with cows and fodder crops across the valley. . . . I love the changing light and fickle mountain weather, with thunderstorms and hailstorms pouring down pieces of hail exactly like ice cubes from the Frigidaire all over the lawn. We have a big cleared table of a lawn with tall trees and stone walls against the mountain view." What she loved about Vermont, she had decided long ago, was that it reminded her a little of the western United States with its vistas, broad valleys, and chain of distant mountains, its "abandoned mines, No-towns (so named), caves, and deposits of gold, silver, garnets, and diamonds, besides iron and marble." The Broadwaters lived in almost total solitude, a "strict isolation ward watched over by Bowden," as Macdonald put it, so that she could make progress on her novel. Evelyn Hofer came for a short visit; the galleys of *The Stones of Florence* appeared, requiring immediate attention; and Reuel stopped by after a summer of touring Yugoslavia and Italy on a Lambretta. Otherwise, McCarthy worked without interruption during an unusually productive summer.

Dreading the return to her hectic New York life, she wrote her Venetian friend Anna Maria Cicogna, asking if she could rent one of her apartments late in the fall. Late fall is cold and damp in Venice, Countess Cicogna wrote back. "If it's not for writing about Venice, come to my villa in Tripoli where the weather will be mild." Already in New York when she received the invitation to Libya, she accepted at once. On October 23 she left for a seven-week visit to the Arab city.

Countess Cicogna's father had been governor of Libya until 1925. His wife, who loved Tripoli, purchased a villa there in 1929. The villa was built of Carrara marble in the Arab style. The living quarters, with their divans and heaps of cushions and richly colored rugs, surrounded a columned patio with a majolica-tiled fountain, beyond which were palm trees, beds of red, pink, orange, and yellow flowers, a pond of water lilies, and "a big Kodachrome-blue Hollywood swimming pool." Although all this luxury was hidden behind white walls in a suburban street, the sprawling enclosure contained two courtyards and a large guest wing. "It is a brilliant oasis," McCarthy wrote William Jovanovich, "in a desert of oil wells, sand, American and British armed forces living in 'cute' multiple-housing ranch-type shacks with names like 'The Hole in the Wall.' "

Life within the oasis was "a great basin of leisure," Mary McCarthy wrote the Lowells. "Of course it's really a commodity produced by industrious servants weaving an implacable spider-web of idleness around one. . . . Every garment you wear is washed or simply ironed the minute you step out of it, and there's a continual game with the maid to keep her from washing a slip you've worn for two hours and have taken off to go swimming. At luncheon and dinner, a constant changing of plates, six changes at lunch, ash trays and glasses are whisked away in the salotto or the salottino or the patio or the 'harem' the minute you've used them."

The villa was always full of guests, who occupied themselves with hunting gazelles or partridges, with shopping in the souks for gaudy striped silks or leather jackets, and with sight-seeing trips to the two excavated Roman cities, Sobrata and Leptis Magna. The massive seaside theater at Sobrata had been so carefully restored after thirteen centuries of burial in the sand that it could be used again. The Leptis Magna ruins were more extensive. The forum, baths, theater, and well-preserved basilica of Septimus Severus were all eloquent reminders of Roman enterprise. The trips to the ruins were "extremely organized," McCarthy wrote the Lowells, "with two servants going along with hampers of food, hot and cold, every kind of drink, chairs, tables, an awning; a snack is provided for 12:00 when you are still in the ruins." When guests tired of sight-seeing, shopping, or hunting, they busied themselves with calisthenics (the hostess had imported a masseuse who taught gymnastics) and games. During the weeks Mary McCarthy was present, one group of guests "antiqued" a mirror and later another group painted a glass plate about the size of an ordinary room. "These are all extremely elaborate processes, requiring innumerable trips into town, purchases of Scotch tape, paint brushes, toothbrushes, turpentine, paint, absorbent cotton, gold leaf, silver nail polish, silver foil, and countless experiments *in piccola.*"

Mary McCarthy participated in little of the activity in the compound. As she wrote the Lowells, "Everyone here but me and the leaping train of Venetian servants does absolutely nothing." She was the only guest

who used the pool, usually taking a swim around 5 P.M. Taking advantage of the ideal conditions for work, she wrote two chapters in a little over three weeks, typing nonstop for eight to ten hours a day. Even with that schedule, she studied Italian grammar during her breakfast in bed and read Manzoni for half an hour while "resting" before dinner, as well as Veblen's *The Theory of the Leisure Class* ("uncannily apropos"). Dinners provided a stimulating end to her productive days. The guests and her hostess were "charming, kind, civilized, . . . intelligent, well-dressed; they were all without exception ardent anti-Fascists. Most of them have read quite a lot and about what they haven't they're very well informed."

Before coming to Tripoli, Mary McCarthy had accepted an invitation from the State Department to deliver a series of talks in Eastern Europe and the British Isles that would begin early in 1960. Rather than return to America for two weeks, she arranged to meet Broadwater and Reuel in Vienna on December 19, stopping off in Rome for a few days beforehand. The three of them were together in Austria, Czechoslovakia, and Poland until mid-January, when the men returned to New York. Although neither spouse knew it at the time, the McCarthy-Broadwater marriage was over.

PART SIX

CHAPTER XVII

COUP DE FOUDRE
(1960–1962)

*T*HE GROUP, which Mary McCarthy had been trying so hard to finish in Vermont and Libya, would not be published for more than three years. This was the result of her meeting and falling in love with the man who became her fourth husband. James West, the Public Affairs officer for the American Embassy in Warsaw, directed the embassy's branch of the United States Information Agency, which was sponsoring McCarthy's tour. Both Broadwaters and Reuel met West when he took them to dinner at the Diplomats Club the night they arrived. West arranged McCarthy's itinerary during her four weeks in Poland (December 28, 1959, to January 22, 1960). After that came three weeks in Yugoslavia (January 23 to February 13), where she alternated three prepared talks in five cities—Belgrade, Novi Sad, Ljubljana, Zagreb, and Sarajevo; and two weeks in the British Isles (February 15 to March 3), where she addressed audiences in seven cities—London, Leicester, Oxford, Manchester, Leeds, Nottingham, and Edinburgh. During the Poland tour Broadwater and Reuel had to return to the United States, Reuel to Harvard for his last semester and Broadwater to Saint Bernard's.

McCarthy and West saw as much of each other as possible. Both felt their first meeting "was a *coup de foudre*," McCarthy wrote her uncle Frank Preston. They decided to get married as soon as possible. As both were already married, this would not be easy. Making matters worse, West was the father of three small children—aged seven, six, and four. The difficulties McCarthy encountered in trying to restructure her life brought about a dizzying mobility during the next three years. Before the marriage, she spent time in Rome, Warsaw, Vienna, Copenhagen, New York, Alabama, Berlin, and on the Ligurian coast; and after the marriage, in Switzerland, Poland, the Ligurian coast again, Connecticut, Seattle, San Francisco, New York, and Washington, D.C. Not until the late spring of 1962 did she finally settle in Paris, and even then, she did not move into her own apartment until the end of the year. As a result, *The Group* was not completed until 1963.

James Raymond West was a handsome, distinguished man of forty-six, whose looks, McCarthy often said, compared favorably with those of her other three husbands. "None of my other husbands was good-looking," she told Doris Grumbach some years later. "Of course I've had affairs with good-looking men, but I've never married one—until now." West came from Old Town, Maine. Like McCarthy, he had been brought up by grandparents, his parents having divorced when he was two. Unlike her, he was an only child. After Bowdoin College, he had worked for *Babson's Reports* in Washington and for *Aviation* Magazine, and at twenty-seven he had managed the Wharf Theater in Provincetown. During the war he was a navigator in the Air Force, teaching celestial navigation to cadets as well as flying transports out of Italy. Two years after the war, he left the service as a major. Starting his government career as assistant director of the Foreign Operations Administration in Paris, in 1954 he was transferred to the United States Information Agency in Washington. After some training in Polish, he was sent to the American Embassy in Warsaw. When he and Mary McCarthy met, he was unhappily married to a much younger woman, his second wife. Although he was not Irish, he reminded Mary of the McCarthy men, "not only one of them, but all of them," she wrote Edmund Wilson; "that is, with a certain wild solitary streak combined with an engaging air, combined with a kind of solidity. But maybe it's only that like my father and my grandfather and Uncle Harry he has prematurely grey hair." She also characterized him as "a direct actionist, very honest, very intense, likes danger, very strong-willed," and "a very nice man, very masculine, very responsible."

Had not Arthur Schlesinger, Jr.—who, with Alfred Kazin, Ted Weeks, and Paddy Chayefsky, had been among the first American writers' delegation to Eastern Europe—suggested her name to the State Department for its second delegation of American writers, McCarthy would never have met James West. The State Department's program foresaw a series of speeches, but in reality these became impromptu talks, to audiences that sometimes consisted of university students, at other times of children, senior citizens, or intellectuals, or a combination of several groups. "You didn't know what kind of audience you were going to get, so it was useless to prepare," McCarthy recalled a few years later of the time in Yugoslavia. "Sometimes you'd find old people in adult education, sometimes school children, and you'd just have to improvise to the situation. You know, tell the story of your life, or *anything*." McCarthy usually talked about the problems of writing novels in the second half of the twentieth century (out of which came two of her major essays in literary citicism, "The Fact in Fiction" and "Characters in Fiction") or about contemporary theater in America (out of which came "The American Realist Playwrights").

McCarthy loved Poland. ("One catches faint nuances of Darling, they're playing our country" is the way English journalist Katharine

Whitehorn described this attachment.) But she was not as enthusiastic about Yugoslavia, because the intellectuals reminded her of American Stalinists of the 1930s. Sarajevo—a poor, shabby town with a cobble-stoned medieval marketplace and a handsome Turkish-built mosque, the finest in the Balkans—was famous as the hometown of Gavril Princip, who had assassinated Archduke Francis Ferdinand, heir to the Austro-Hungarian empire, and, in so doing, had set off World War I. Officials from Sarajevo's Writer's Union, bundled up and waiting in the snow, welcomed McCarthy at the train station with a large bouquet of red roses. She was taken to the same hotel that Archduke Francis Ferdinand and his wife, Sophie, had occupied on June 28, 1914, the day Princip fired his infamous shot. Her lecture on the novel was attended mostly by elderly "doctrinaire functionaries, reactionaries in the sense of being still unreconstructed from the Stalinist period," and two young transla-tors, probably the only English-speakers in the town. Choosing examples from Russian and classical French fiction to illustrate her points, assum-ing that these were the works the audience would know, McCarthy was surprised by the response of one annoyed listener who demanded to know why she had ignored that great American writer Jack London. When she admitted to knowing very little about London, she angered the Union members. The translators, though, were delighted with her and asked her to join them and their friends at a café after the lecture.

The young group, antagonistic toward the literary bureaucracy of the Writer's Union, commandeered its old, beat-up car and took their American visitor to a mountain lodge, where they rode the ski lift back and forth over the tops of the fir trees. Though McCarthy acknowledged a fear of heights, she relished their protest gesture. She also enjoyed their discussions of the pre-Socratic Greek philosophers, Nietzsche, and Si-mone Weil. Committed to Marxism, these young Yugoslavs hoped, nonetheless, to find a way to blend it with more libertarian philosophies.

In Ljubljana she was forced to jettison her usual lecture when, instead of facing a "normal" audience, she found herself in front of schoolchil-dren and old people. Remembering Philip Rahv's division of American writers into two polar types—"paleface" writers like Henry James, with his "drawing-room fictions," and "redskin" writers like Walt Whitman, with his "open-air poems"—she tried to classify writers along these lines. Today, she laughingly tells how much she managed to confuse at least some of her listeners. At the end of her lecture, a little girl approached her to ask for the address of an Indian reservation.

In England she gave six lectures in ten days, including one-night stands in Manchester, Leicester, Nottingham, and Leeds. From Edinburgh, where she spent two days, she wrote Nicky Mariano that she felt like one of the "barnstorming actors of the old days." After her last lecture, on March 3, 1960, McCarthy raced to Paris to meet James West.

The State Department had booked a hotel room for her until March 13, but in her official itinerary she wrote across the name of the hotel "Cancel; staying with friends." "Friends," of course, meant James West. She had not "gone underground" completely, however, for Bowden Broadwater had her Paris telephone number. When he phoned and West answered, he wanted to know what was going on. McCarthy told him she had fallen in love with a man she had met on the tour, and that she wanted a divorce. In spite of the quarrels and infidelities of recent years, Broadwater was totally unprepared for the news. As McCarthy told a friend later, "Bowden has taken this very hard, partly from shock, and I have not enjoyed that part, needless to say." She would not tell Broadwater who the man was; when he found out, he was surprised it was none other than the Warsaw embassy's Public Affairs officer whom he had found so personable.

McCarthy tried to keep West's identity a secret, resulting, she wrote Nicky Mariano, in "all sorts of funny rumors as to who this man can be (Malcolm Muggeridge, Chiaromonte?)." As she explained, "I am trying not to tell, for certain positive knowledge will make his divorce more difficult; his wife can be persuaded more readily on the grounds of total incompatibility than if she is sure he wants to marry me."

By April 1, 1960, McCarthy was back in New York, fetching her books, clothes, papers, photographs, as well as her grandmother's silver, and leaving everything else—once more exercising "her habit of leaving . . . possessions behind whenever she got a divorce," as she wrote of Rosamund in *Birds of America,* her sixth novel. After dispatching a trunk to Rome, where she had arranged to occupy Carmen Angleton's empty apartment, she flew back to Europe.

McCarthy moved into the apartment—"a veritable dust bowl, not having been lived in for sixteen months"—to wait until she and West could get divorces, "not as easy as one had imagined in the first flush of certainty," she soon realized.

Margaret West told her husband she would not be able to grant a divorce right away, explaining that her parents planned to visit her in Poland during the summer. The parents came and at first tried to effect a reconciliation. When they saw that that was impossible, they sought to obtain the best possible settlement on behalf of their daughter. Discussions of the terms of the settlement consumed the summer and continued on into the fall, but by December, West had secured a promise that his wife would give him a divorce "early in the year."

Bowden Broadwater, meantime, "still very unhappy and sad, but better," Hannah Arendt wrote McCarthy, focused his attention on what he would do with his life. By mid-May, Arendt could write, "He never was so nice before, never. As though something has happened to wake him up. I told him rather bluntly he had lived so far in a kind of fairy-tale land, and he replied: are you sure I am fit to live in any other kind of land? Which of course is the precise truth of the matter. . . . By and large I think this is a catastrophe for him, and it is still better than no catastrophe ever." However, by September, "under the impression that he is being treated as a *quantité négligeable*," Bowden decided he would not agree to a divorce until after West had gotten his. "The sad truth of the matter is that he loves you," Arendt wrote, "and that he has discovered this in a sense only *après coup*, after you have left him." When McCarthy complained about all the delays, Hannah Arendt shot back, "You write that it was just 'too ridiculous' for the two of you (Jim West and you) to be 'the passive foils of other people.' If you want to look at the matter in these terms at all, then it seems to me rather obvious that you both are the victims of your own, self-chosen past. This may be inconvenient but it is not ridiculous, unless you wish to say your whole past was not only a mistake, but a ridiculous one." In November, Broadwater wrote his wife agreeing to a divorce, though, as Hannah Arendt observed, "his life is in ruins."

Meanwhile, McCarthy remained in Rome, "waiting and trying to write and be stable and orderly," but living in "harrowing suspense and meeting [West] every other weekend at some midway point: Vienna, Geneva, Copenhagen, though that isn't exactly midway for me. . . . This is a nineteenth-century situation with mid-twentieth-century stage accessories (airplanes and telephones) and the far-off promise of a twenty-four-hour Mexican divorce." Despite the suspense and distractions, she did work, mainly on turning her State Department talks into essays. *Partisan Review* published "The Fact in Fiction" in the summer of 1960 and "Characters in Fiction" in March-April 1961; the theater talks became an essay that changed titles depending on where it appeared: "Realism in American Theatre" for *Harper's* (July 1961), "Americans, Realists, Playwrights" for *Encounter* (July 1961), and "The American Realist Playwrights" in *On the Contrary,* a collection of McCarthy essays originally published between 1946 and 1961 that Farrar, Straus and Cudahy brought out in 1962. Of course, McCarthy had to keep writing in order to live. By April 1960 she had received royalty checks for *The Stones of Florence,* amounting to a little more than $10,000, and money for signing a contract with Harcourt, Brace for a reissue of *The Company She Keeps.*

In June 1960 she went to Berlin for a Congress for Cultural Freedom meeting, principally to see old friends, and then to Poland for three weeks. When West got a vacation, he and McCarthy drove to France for three weeks. The trip was difficult—McCarthy later wrote Hannah Arendt that their car "broke apart part by part all the way across Czechoslovakia, Germany, Alsace, Vosges, Brittany, Normandy, Ile de France, and then back again. It was in nineteen garages, with its own complaints plus the language problems." But after forty-seven consecutive days together, McCarthy could say she had "never been so happy or so totally, entirely in love."

James West returned to Warsaw to face his wife's parents and to resume work, and McCarthy went to Bocca di Magra, a tiny fishing village on the Ligurian coast of Italy. She had been invited there by Miriam and Nicola Chiaromonte, who lived in Rome not far from the apartment McCarthy had been occupying. The Chiaromontes arranged for McCarthy to share a white stucco house with Mario and Angélique Levi, a couple she had met in Paris during her first trip to Europe, in 1946. (In later years Angélique Levi would translate several McCarthy books into French. Mario Levi, an Italian, was a good friend of Nicola Chiaromonte's.) McCarthy's second-story, three-room apartment had a balcony that looked across the narrow Magra River to the marble-streaked mountains of Carrara, where, she had written in *The Stones of Florence,* "Michelangelo, like some strange Ibsen hero, spent years . . . quarrying marble for his statuary."

Bocca di Magra was located at the mouth (*bocca*) of the Magra River, which empties into the Ligurian Sea. On days when the sea was calm, the Chiaromontes and the Levis, with all their children and friends, including Mary McCarthy—a group numbering about thirty—took a late-morning boat to a cove near a great spur of marble called Punta Bianca. Mary McCarthy described the beach there in "The Hounds of Summer," a short story about Bocca di Magra, which became the fictional Porto Quaglia.

> The White Rock was the chief lure and secret beauty of Porto Quaglia. Parties of bathers were taken there every morning by the fishermen in little yawls with inboard motors; informal excursions ran several times before noon from the pier in front of the inn, and regular passengers were

picked up at the rickety little wooden landings along the river, off the single main street. . . .

The White Rock was really a mass of rocks and cliffs of pure milk-white marble that formed a towering point jutting into the sea. Above it, on a steep mountain flank, grew ilex and pine and wild olive trees. The water around it was a pale green and exceptionally clear. If you swam out beyond your depth you could still look down to the white marble shelving that extended along the sea floor like a vast bath for sea horses or Tritons. Along the shore it formed deep caves.

Bocca di Magra was just the kind of place Mary McCarthy loved. "Not at all a deluxe life—quite the opposite," she would recall. "We looked at stars at night, and that's the kind of life I deeply enjoy." During this particular summer, her first of many in Bocca di Magra, she wrote Carmen Angleton that "twice, the children and the waiters have come running to tell us to hurry and see the American satellite or 'spallone' in the sky; there on the waterfront it's rather like watching fireworks on a childhood Fourth of July. Some people are learning a little astronomy." And a few years later, she remarked that she was "really most happy in a community, such as that of Bocca di Magra, or Cape Cod in the summer of '45. Such slightly Utopian communities are, I suppose, secular monastic societies." This humble, unchic fishing village was a kind of intellectual commune frequented year after year by the same French and Italian (with a sprinkling of English, Irish, and American) writers, journalists, and editors, who played chess, read, discussed books, and took walks. Besides these regulars, their friends and relatives kept turning up—the Bruzzichellis, Florentine friends; Madame Levi's father; and Carmen Angleton. There was so much community life that McCarthy got only a little writing done—mostly in the early mornings, before joining the group for swimming and the Levis for splendid midday meals. "Twelve sit down to table every day in the garden," she wrote Angleton. "It is a very Renoirish atmosphere, with children of all ages, and makes me think that Renoir was really the great celebrant of the joys and rites of middle age." The café in front of the inn, Sans Facons, "with thirteen rooms, running water, and a bath for general use," as the first sentence of "The Hounds of Summer" described it, was the social center of this community where everyone met for "Campari and soda before dinner, and something called Kina-caldo or Italian cognac after." Some of the men played chess while the others sat and talked in large groups until eleven or eleven-thirty. Every other night, everyone waited with Mary McCarthy for Jim West's call from Warsaw; there were only two phones in the village, one at the inn and another at Doctor Biso's.

Mary McCarthy did not see James West again until the middle of September 1960, when she left Bocca di Magra to meet him for a ten-day sojourn in Rome, followed by six weeks in Warsaw. West had talked her into coming to Poland incognito, since his divorce was by no means assured, so she moved into a hotel room with Communist Party emblems on the bedspreads and curtains. Other than a visit to Reuel, who, having graduated from Harvard in June, was now in Cracow on a fellowship to study Polish literature, she hardly left the room; and under these conditions, she started working once again on *The Group*. "We've passed a very strange period, six weeks, together, in almost complete isolation," she wrote Carmen Angleton, "except for ten days with Reuel in Cracow and southern Poland. This state of ostracism, partly self-imposed, in the midst of a totalitarian regime, was like a weird glimpse of the Hereafter, in that one was stripped of everything related to one's social identity, one's material pleasures, comforts, habits, etc. To me, it's been a revelation of [Jim's] nature, of sheer goodness, strength, straightness, sweetness, gayety, simplicity. . . . I feel very happy and pleased with my luck."

Nevertheless, the uncertainty of the situation was trying, she wrote Hannah Arendt. "Love apart, there is the impossibility of making plans ahead, the lack of a stable place to live, the prospect of being separated again from one's books and papers and living in hotels." In the middle of November the embassy asked West to "keep up appearances"— namely, to attend official functions with his wife—until their affairs were settled. At this point, West went to Ambassador Jake Beam and told him of his predicament: that his wife "would not leave Poland, and that he himself was ready to resign from the foreign service or ask for a transfer—whatever was necessary to detach her from himself." The ambassador gave the Wests an ultimatum: she must leave or West would be transferred. Margaret West agreed to go, though she managed to delay her departure for another six months. Neither Mary McCarthy nor Jim West was ever sure why, exactly, she was so reluctant to move.

Because James West's wife had rented a Paris apartment that she had left vacant, Mary McCarthy occupied it after she left Warsaw. This being the first time she had lived in Paris, she felt "quite timorous about the mechanics of it—laundry, groceries," she told Carmen Angleton, but luckily the Levis, whom she saw often, were nearby. West came to Paris for a week before Christmas; Reuel and a girlfriend for the holiday. After Christmas, Reuel went to London while his mother stayed on in Paris waiting for news about West's divorce.

Reuel came back to Paris on his way to Cracow. Later his mother wrote Edmund Wilson about Reuel's activities:

> He likes his life in Cracow, . . . has taken up his Russian studies again, and has decided to stay until September. He is very much in with the younger Bohemians of Cracow, where he is celebrated for his "anti-Communism." . . . He had a young Norwegian neutralist friend, with whom he was always arguing, on a theoretical plane, and the Poles were charmed by these arguments. The only one I heard wasn't about politics but about *Hiroshima, Mon Amour,* which Reuel sailed into like an old *Partisan Review* contributor. Though I'd not seen the film, I nearly kissed him and told him he was a true son of his parents.

Reuel was a highly intelligent, personable, and gentle young man about whom his mother was always getting glowing reports from her friends, whom he frequently visited on his travels around Europe. While in Cracow, he saw James West often, for he went up to Warsaw every two or three weeks to stay with him and to shop at the PX. "Reuel seems to be extremely attracted by Jim," McCarthy wrote Hannah Arendt. "I think he feels the lack of a virile and straightforward man in his family. Bowden is a child, and Edmund is an old woman."

Suddenly, at the end of January 1961, James West got his divorce. McCarthy promptly left for Alabama, which grants the quickest divorce in the United States. Afterward, she stopped for a visit with her brother Kevin, who had just gotten a good part in *Advise and Consent,* and sister-in-law Augusta in their new house in Dobbs Ferry, New York. Now that McCarthy and West were free to marry, they turned their attention to furnishing the Warsaw house they would occupy. Because there was practically nothing to buy in Poland, they met in Copenhagen, where they spent a week picking out furniture. "We didn't fight once about furniture, whatever that may mean," she wrote her brother and sister-in-law. "Bowden and I, even in our most loving days, were always at each other's throats when we started to furnish a room. And Edmund and I. . . ." When West went back to Warsaw, McCarthy headed for Paris, staying only long enough to give her lecture on the American realist playwrights; then she went to Rome to get her belongings from storage and mail them to Poland, and also to visit Miriam and Nicola Chiaromonte and Carmen Angleton. She wrote Kevin from Rome that "the streets were full of women selling armfuls of narcissi and daffodils and the markets were full of spring peas, red, white, and green salads, young artichokes, and tiny field asparagus."

Her obvious joy amused Nicola Chiaromonte, who told Dwight Macdonald that

> Mary acted all through the period of her "engagement" as if this was her first love, and was going to be her first marriage—sweet, but slightly false, nevertheless more than false, unreal and unconvincing, like some of the psychological cracks in her novels. But maybe Jim is going to have a "humanizing" effect on M. Although, I doubt it. She is going to be the Queen again—and he the Prince Consort. Will she be able to take the life of a diplomat's wife? That's another question—with her marvelous girlishness, Mary really thought that back in Warsaw she was going to be free to make all the cracks she wanted about the U.S., the State Department and so forth. We realized that talking to her here in Rome. Anyway, she is a lovable woman and a wonderful friend.

Nicola Chiaromonte was not the only person who commented on this soon-to-be-forty-nine-year-old woman acting like a young girl in love for the first time. But in fact, despite three previous marriages and many affairs, this was the first time McCarthy had ever truly been in love. As she told a Florentine friend, she was "more deeply in love than I have ever been; indeed, the whole thing has been a kind of revelation, as though I had never known that creature called Man before."

Since McCarthy was already living in Paris, she and West decided to get married there, even though she had to satisfy a thirty-day residency requirement. And since they planned to be married on April 15 in the Town Hall of the 8th Arrondissement, the neighborhood where her apartment was located, she had just enough time if she went back to Paris right away. While waiting for April 15, she kept busy "fighting through the French red tape to get permission to be married—you have to have sworn documents from the embassy, from the Consulate, from a lawyer practicing in Paris, which then have to be presented to the Ministry of Foreign Affairs, to the Mairie, and the Préfecture, together with chest x-rays and blood tests; each of these offices has different hours and you arrive, after a long Métro trip, to find them closed or you wait in line and learn when your turn comes that you are waiting in the wrong place." In addition, she had to get a new passport, new passport photos, and apply for a Polish visa. Then on March 27, two weeks before the wedding, she had to move out of her apartment—a disappointment, as she had wanted to hold a reception there. To complicate matters further, she had to continue living in the same arrondissement to fulfill her residency requirement, so she needed a place in the immediate vicinity. Fortunately, she found a nice room at the Hotel Chambiges, around the corner from her apartment on rue Clément Marot, but the move necessitated another shipment to Poland. Somehow she remained relatively unruffled, and calmly wrote Carmen Angleton:

> I've wished so often that you were here this last week while doing my wedding shopping. I'm still undecided between an olive-green suede belt and a tree-green velvet ribbon; so I bought both. And a green chiffon (in two tones—pale and olive) bonnet from Elizabeth Arden that . . . looks rather like the boudoir caps my mother used to wear in the nursery. (Many doubts about this item.) And some pale pink shoes from Perugia. . . . On your advice I tried Dior, but their shoes don't fit me at all. At the Dior branch of Delman's they offered to make me a pair of pink shoes. . . . The pocketbook (pale pink???) remains to be bought. I fear I'm going to end by looking like something in a high school pageant.

Carmen Angleton arrived in Paris two days before the wedding to give a dinner party for the bridal couple and their friends. The next night the Berniers entertained at a big dinner in their Paris apartment; McCarthy was on good terms with them again. The morning ceremony took place in the 8th Arrondissement Town Hall, the most elaborate in Paris, with its crystal chandeliers and its amplitude of red plush and gilt. The guests—Reuel; Carmen Angleton; *New Yorker* writer Janet Flanner; Peter Harnden, the best man, and his Russian wife; Dwight Macdonald and his second wife, Gloria; A. S. Frere of the English publishing house William Heinemann and his wife; the Berniers; the Levis; the novelist James Jones and his wife, Gloria; Kot Jelenski, a Polish friend from the Paris office of the Congress of Cultural Freedom; and Evelyn Hofer— were seated on two rows of chairs. (The Chiaromontes could not come because Nicola was convalescing from a recent heart attack.) The French-speaking guests found it amusing that the mayor, apparently ignoring the bride's full-grown son and the groom's white hair, delivered his standard speech: "And you, madame, will find life very different now." Yet the irony lay not in the mayor's ignorance—he did not know that this was the bride's fourth marriage and the groom's third—but in the fact that he was right. Life for Mary McCarthy would be very different after this marriage.

* * *

Marriage to an American diplomat, neither an intellectual nor a New York, effected a decisive and welcome break with her past. As she told an interviewer twenty years later, "I really did develop a kind of horror of the sort of tinniness of New York intellectual and literary life." And it also changed her. As she confided in Hannah Arendt, "My love for Jim is increasing till I am quite dizzy. I find myself changing or perhaps that is not the right word, coming to life in a new way, like somebody who has been partly paralyzed. And I've become conscious in myself of certain shrunken or withered character-traits that I never reckoned with before. Quite unpleasant they are too. You remember my telling you once that my marriage to Bowden was just two people playing, like congenial children? Well, I slowly realize that all my love affairs and marriages have been little games like that—and snug, sheltered games."

McCarthy's friends and acquaintances noticed a change in her too. As Rosamond Bernier Russell puts it, "I think Jim West made a tremendous difference in her life. First she married her father with Edmund Wilson, and her son with Bowden Broadwater, and then she married the right man with Jim. Jim is a most sweet and quiet and sensitive man, and I think it's the first time Mary had real emotional stability. This was a loving, kind, extremely indulgent man. With Jim West came this gentler side of Mary, and I saw her tremendous kindness and understanding to Jim West and his children." McCarthy's English publisher, Lord George Weidenfeld, agrees, adding that West's calm reassurance, tender affection, and strength have made her more self-assured. And several American friends have observed that McCarthy is no longer so quick with the caustic remarks that made the Broadwaters notorious.

Dwight Macdonald told McCarthy that after thirty years of experiment, she had found Mr. Right, and told Nicola Chiaromonte that James West was "a gentle, sweet, responsible family-man type, who may be able to give Mary just the combination of lover and father she needs." A journalist who wrote about their early life together speculated that "the impulses that cause a father of three to leave a pretty housewife in her thirties for a fiftyish authoress are not standard, nor is he. As amusing to talk to as she is, he has a Past—a cultural past, a theatre-managing past; and the force that swept Mary McCarthy off her feet was clearly the explosion of that stored charge. 'He kept saying you remind me of the thirties,' she said; and the reawakening was symbolized for her by his books: 'His shelves were covered with books on international finance, politics, things like that; then one day they were all gone: he'd brought

up his old books from the cellar and the shelves were filled with philosophy and Henry James."

Another change was that Mary McCarthy would be faithful to this husband, as she had not been to the others. But the most profound change, she told Hannah Arendt, was that the "honesty" of this love ("everything is offered; nothing is held back") made her "aware of how prudent (in spite of being romantic) I've always been myself, how many precautions I take against being wounded."

After the ceremony, there was a luncheon in Orgeval, a suburb of Paris, at the best man's house. Although it rained intermittently, the party was "grand," Dwight Macdonald informed Nicola Chiaromonte, a "'fête champêtre' typical of Mary." There were "five tables, waiters in white gloves, champagne, fish mayonnaise, roast duck, strawberries and cream—all transported to the house of a friend an hour out of Paris." "I had no doubt that Mary's wedding would be 'grand,' " Chiaromonte responded. "That's her style—a fairy-tale style, I should say—occasions are to Mary challenges to the imagination, which is one of her most charming traits, probably the most charming, since her wonderful generosity is part of it."

The Wests set off for a wedding trip to Zurich, Bern, and Interlaken. What should have been an idyllic week in Switzerland was marred by learning that West's former wife had moved back into his Warsaw flat the day before his marriage to Mary McCarthy. Margaret West stayed in West's apartment for several weeks, pleading a series of circumstances (the lack of a passport for her maid; having to be quarantined when her daughter came down with chicken pox) that she said made it difficult for her to move out.

The Wests' domestic situation made the U.S. embassy in Warsaw uncomfortable. That West's former wife was occupying government housing assigned to a foreign service officer and traveling on a diplomatic passport when no longer married to a government official, and that his present wife was on her way to Warsaw, also to occupy government housing and also traveling on a diplomatic passport, created, in the ambassador's mind, an impossible duplication. Moreover, it was a diplomatic nightmare, especially in a country where the secret police were eager to make use of such a situation. At this time, the U.S. foreign service was an old-fashioned, conservative organization; quite naturally, therefore, a titillating tale of a famous writer married to one of its own officers, whose previous wife was still living in his apartment, filtered throughout the service. Everyone followed the developing story with excitement. All of this would have been funny, McCarthy wrote Angleton, except for "thinking about those [West] children's future."

At first, West refused to return to Warsaw until his ex-wife vacated his apartment. He had left behind a great deal of unfinished work, however, and he decided he would better understand what was happening by being on the scene rather than by calling Warsaw every day— "providing he didn't see or talk to Margaret," McCarthy wrote a friend. "Which . . . was the ambassador's view too." So the Wests headed for Poland. McCarthy decided to stay in Cracow with Reuel until everything was settled, but when Reuel could not be found, "we turned back from the Czech border and spent Friday night in Regensburg (a beautiful town on the Danube with an exquisite rococo church) and he put me on the train at 5:30 A.M. for Vienna and drove off alone to Poland, with dishes and linen and coffee and cheese, and as it turns out, all my handbags and my umbrella." When West reached Warsaw, he was forced to camp out in a new house, sleeping between a pair of blankets.

West had arranged for the embassy people in the Information Service to meet McCarthy's train in Vienna. When she arrived there, embarrassed by her sudden and unexplained separation from her husband, McCarthy told a story about her visa, "not wanting to spread the scandal, . . . which the ambassador is trying to contain, apparently, in Poland," she wrote Carmen Angleton. "But Jim's goose, we both think, is probably cooked anyway, as a result of [Margaret West's] return. If so, he will be transferred in August, if not (and I fear this privately) sooner." No sooner had she mailed this letter to Rome than she suffered a slipped disc at the top of her spine. After two and a half weeks of excruciating pain in a Vienna clinic, she arrived in Poland in a wheelchair. By the end of June she was "faintly ambulant in a surgical collar, like a pillory, and not permitted to write"; she told William Jovanovich, "The nerves of my right arm down to the fingers were caught between the vertebrae. I couldn't even read much, partly because of the heavy drugs, to lessen the pain, and partly because with my immobilized neck I couldn't hold anything heavier than a magazine before my eyes. All of this, I suspect, is the price of a year and a half of tension and uncertainty." She knew Jovanovich would be disappointed, since her physical ailments meant further delay on *The Group;* hence, she hesitated in informing him of West's imminent transfer, August 1, and his required two-month home leave. (All foreign service personnel who serve abroad have to return to the United States for a minimum of two months every three years.) She did tell him, briefly, but her letter was principally praise for her new husband. "He has been sweeter and more resourceful than I thought anyone could be under such circumstances. And rather worn out himself because *I* couldn't sleep, even with sleeping pills and pain-killers; he'd make herbal teas at four in the morning or light cigarettes and talk."

Although both Mary and Jim West would have liked another tour of duty in Poland, they did not get it. They suspected that this was because of the domestic upheavals of the preceding spring. The furniture, books, and silver that had been expressed from New York, Rome, Copenhagen, and Paris had to be packed once again, but their destination the Wests would not know for nearly three quarters of a year. For the present, they drove to Bocca di Magra, where they stayed until they left for America. The Chiaromontes, Levis, and Bruzzichellis, and Reuel, traveling with Renata Adler, were already in Bocca di Magra when the Wests arrived. Shortly after, West's three children came.

Life in this village on the Ligurian Sea was, everyone agreed, paradisiacal. To ensure its remaining this way, "an organization has been started for the defense of Bocca di Magra, with Einaudi as president; I am vice presidentessa," McCarthy reported to Carmen Angleton. "It is all very ridiculous, the backbone of the group consisting of some reformed fellow-travelers who are against the wicked capitalists of the Monte dei Paschi of Siena, which owns great tracts of the mountainside and wants to sell them for house lots. The fellow-travelers themselves are for the 'development' of Bocca di Magra but along modern, 'planned' lines, with green belts, etc. Nicola says he's not sure which will be worse. But he is a Defender of Bocca di Magra too and on the council; we meet with the various mayors and discuss planning, garbage disposal, traffic regulations. . . . This Sunday it's the mayor of La Spezia—at a 'cocktail' at the house of the lung doctor from Carrara." A plaque commemorating the group—Società degli Amici di Bocca di Magra, 20 Agosto 1961—hangs today in the hilltop house of Luigi Biso, the local doctor. It boasts thirty-nine signatures, including those of Giulio Einaudi, Valentino Bompiani, Mary McCarthy, Jean Bloch-Michel, Italo Calvino, and Dwight Macdonald. The Wests left Bocca di Magra on September 8. West's children, Daniel, Alison, and Jonathan, returned to their mother, who was now living in Paris; their father and stepmother went to America.

They rented a house in Stonington, Connecticut, for James West's home leave. At John Myers's suggestion, McCarthy had written James Merrill, a Stonington resident whom she had not seen since the 1948 poetry weekend at Bard College that she had described in *The Groves of Academe*. Merrill secured a house for their stay. Stonington, a small seaport town that has become primarily a summer resort, lies in the extreme southeast corner of Connecticut. It is the only port in the state that feels the effect of the open sea. It faces a gap left by Fishers Island and the eastern tips of Long Island, through which the Atlantic rolls in toward the coastline until it breaks on a chain of reefs.

The village of Stonington is a tonguelike piece of land of only 275 acres that marks the separation of Stonington Harbor from Little Narragansett Bay. It juts out on a long point to a lighthouse; the town is so narrow that the sea is on both sides of it. For several hundred years the village had made its living from whaling and sealing enterprises. By the time the Wests arrived, the fishing fleet was down to ten boats, moored at decrepit wooden piers. The house the Wests rented was in the Portuguese section of town. (Whaling ships in need of crews had, from the 1840s on, often picked up Portuguese men in the Azores and Cape Verde; by now, nearly half of Stonington's population was Portuguese.) "Jim watched the cormorants outside our house on piles," McCarthy wrote Carmen Angleton, "and we walked in bird sanctuaries where they have Great Horned Owls." The house and the bird sanctuary later made an appearance in the first chapter of *Birds of America*.

> That was when he and his mother had first come to Rocky Port, in the fall, out of season; she had rented a home near the water, in the "wrong" section of the village, where the Portuguese lived. From his bedroom window, he used to watch three cormorants that stood on pilings in the cove and he had been counting on seeing them again on his return.

The pretty part of town, where the summer people lived and where the restored classic-revival houses were located, boasted a well-preserved customs house, markets, and a bank, all with pillars and porticoes. In this section, "most of the houses had sprouted little historical notices, bordered in yellow, also hand-lettered and with ampersands and wavy dashes, telling when they had been built and who had lived there or kept a school or a tavern or a marble yard there." This interest in preservation amused McCarthy, who wrote a friend that "when you go to a cocktail party you are handed a martini-on-the-rocks in a highball glass; saves the work of refills. All this is particularly ironical in a self-consciously clapboarded village, in which each house has a sign in quaint lettering giving its eighteenth-century date and the fact that it was built by Ebenezer Somebody, a ropemaker."

Throughout the rest of 1961 the Wests used Stonington as a departure point for various trips. Mary took over a class for Hannah Arendt's seminar in Machiavelli at Wesleyan University after Heinrich Blücher had a stroke; she delivered the Harcourt, Brace lectures in literature at Columbia University; she visited her uncle Frank Preston, who was mourning his wife's death, in Seattle; and she stayed with Reuel, who was a graduate student in Slavic studies at Berkeley. Although he was convalescing from a broken jaw, "he was in good spirits," she wrote Edmund Wilson, "and enthusiastic about his Slavic studies, especially about Old Church Slavonic; he talked with great brio about this, comparing it to Russian primitive painting. . . . His character and mind are splendid, and he is as praiseworthy as people say he is. An adorable boy. Very *fine*. And he grows more elegant—in his gestures and in his thought." West, who had made several trips to Washington during the fall, joined his wife on the West Coast trip, primarily to see his father. They got back to Stonington in time to relinquish their house to its owner, and to move to an apartment in the center of town belonging to James Merrill—"a single, large room, formerly the ballroom of the Elks Hall, now divided with blue and white room-dividers and decorated with posters of Gustave Moreau." By year's end they were still without fixed abode or destination.

Early in the new year Sonia Orwell came to New York. Orwell, who had married George Orwell a short time before his premature death, had first met McCarthy in the early 1950s during her first trip to New York. She had known about McCarthy since 1949, when Cyril Connolly, for whom she worked at *Horizon,* had devoted a full issue to *The Oasis.* The Wests (and the Kevin McCarthys) gave a party, which people still talk about, to welcome her to town and to say goodbye to all their friends—not that they had any idea where they were going. Seventy-five guests—among them Zero Mostel, E. G. Marshall, Philip Rahv, William Phillips, Blair Clark, Dwight Macdonald, W. H. Auden, Robert Lowell, Elizabeth Hardwick, Robert Silvers, Arthur Miller, Richard Rovere, Niccolò Tucci, the Dupees, the Shafers, Hannah Arendt, Emmanuel Rousuck, James Merrill, David Jackson, Caroline Freud, Reuel Wilson, Renata Adler, and Inge Morath—arrived at Kevin and Augusta's Dobbs Ferry house for dinner and recitations. Before and after dinner, a cassoulet that had taken three days to prepare, they put on scenes from plays by Harold Pinter, J. P. Donleavy, and Robert Lowell; Mary McCarthy read a poem by Yeats; and Zero Mostel acted out a monologue, "Cultured Bombs," written by Tucci.

In February 1962 the Wests temporarily moved to Washington. "Life has got more and more dizzying," McCarthy wrote Carmen Angleton. "I feel as if I were being spun in a General Electric dryer. At present,

I'm in Washington, playing nursemaid or housemother to the Schlesinger children while Arthur and Marian are traveling around the world on a Food for Peace tour. Meanwhile Jim is in Paris, seeing the Secretary General of the O.E.C.D. about a job as director of an information program. . . . Meanwhile we dangle. . . . My life has been so perturbed and overturned that I've not written anything for months—not even a literary word." Since the previous August, they had been roosting or perching in other people's houses, guest rooms, and apartments, or in a series of hotel rooms. She wrote Hannah Arendt that this was her first taste of bureaucratic experience, which consisted of an exceedingly uncomfortable sensation of powerlessness. Arendt replied that it was time she learned how the other half lives.

James West returned to Washington with good news. He would go to Paris, on loan from the State Department, as the first director of information of the recently formed Organization for Economic Cooperation and Development. The OECD, which grew out of the Organization for European Economic Cooperation—established in 1948 to allocate Marshall Plan money and to coordinate work on European economic recovery—was born at the end of 1960, when eighteen European countries, the United States, and Canada signed an agreement to set up a similar operation in mid-1961. A major function of the organization is to issue economic data. Governments, banks, industrial concerns, and multinational companies buy these data—published in both French and English—since the OECD has access to information that enables it to make detailed economic analyses and accurate short-term forecasts. As director of information, West would have three divisions under him—publications, press, and sales.

The Wests left for Paris on March 20. It was especially nice for James West to be back in Paris, where he had lived before and where his children now resided. They were enrolled at the highly respected École Alsacienne. The Wests stayed in a hotel until they could move into a rented apartment. Then, early in May, they bought a fifth-floor, eight-room apartment, where they still live, in a mid-Victorian building on the rue de Rennes, a wide commercial street on the Left Bank. The front of the apartment faced the street, but from the back, the Wests looked straight into a garden of a convent whose bells calling the nuns to vespers sounded every afternoon. The apartment needed such extensive renovation that they would not move in until the end of the year.

They had the usual difficulties with workmen. "I discovered last Saturday," McCarthy wrote Carmen Angleton, "that the workers had burned the shelves of an eighteenth-century bookcase Jim had given me for my birthday—to keep warm while putting in the plumbing." In August they went to Bocca di Magra for a month with Jim's children. In addition to the usual summer regulars and their guests, Niccolò Tucci, Isaiah Berlin, and José Ferrer turned up during the time the Wests were in residence. Because the International Writers' Conference in Edinburgh was under Sonia Orwell's direction that year, Mary McCarthy sacrificed a week of Bocca di Magra to attend. In the fall the Wests made weekend trips to Deauville, where Mary played roulette for the first time in her life, to Fécamp, and to see a beautiful but ruined Benedictine monastery, Saint Wandrille, which made a brief appearance in *Birds of America* ("some Catholic convert told [Peter] the monks took pilgrims for the night"); engaged in an active social life necessitated by Jim's job; saw a good deal of friends—the Levis, the Geists, Janet Flanner, Ernest Hauser, John Ashbery, at the time a young *Herald Tribune* art critic, and Larry Rivers, who did a McCarthy portrait. But mostly they worked. "Jim . . . doesn't get home from the office often until eight or even nine at night," McCarthy wrote William Jovanovich. "It's a much tougher job than running the culture and public affairs program in Poland." She produced a short story and three long literary essays.

The story, "The Hounds of Summer," was about Bocca di Magra. Another tale of encroachment like "The Appalachian Revolution," it had been inspired by the commercialization that was slowly taking place in the little Italian village. "New eyesores were apparent all along the road," McCarthy wrote Carmen Angleton; "a gasoline pump on the water, a pizzeria with a hideous flagged terrace where there used to be a weeping willow and a seat" were further blots on the landscape.

Her essays about Vladimir Nabokov's *Pale Fire,* Shakespeare's *Macbeth,* and J. D. Salinger were published in 1962. "A Bolt from the Blue," a six-thousand-word review of *Pale Fire,* characterizes the novel as "one of the very great works of art of this century, the modern novel that everyone thought was dead and that was only playing possum." Her review is like a map, tracing patterns and spotting allusions and quotations, to help the reader find his way through the maze of Nabokov's novel.

"General Macbeth" offers a fresh look at Shakespeare's tragic hero.

> He is a general and has just won a battle; he enters the scene making a remark about the weather. 'So foul and fair a day I have not seen.' On this flat note Macbeth's character tone is set. 'Terrible weather we're having.' 'The sun can't seem to make up its mind.' 'Is it hot/cold/wet enough for you?' A commonplace man who talks in commonplaces, a golfer, one

might guess, on the Scottish fairways, Macbeth is the only Shakespeare hero who corresponds to a bourgeois type: a murderous Babbitt, let us say.

This picture of a conformist addicted to banalities, with neither the pluck nor the imagination of his wife, appealed to Hannah Arendt—"I fell greatly and enthusiastically in love with the Macbeth article"—who was at the time writing her own novel interpretation of a murderous Babbitt figure, Adolf Eichmann, whom she would characterize as banal.

The Observer had asked McCarthy to do an essay on Salinger. She hesitated before accepting, figuring that *The New Yorker* people who admired Salinger would be upset—"I like Shawn, the editor, and I realized this was going to be a pain to Shawn and I was not crazy about that idea, but you can't let yourself be inhibited by all these relationships you are in." She thought it more important, however, "to say what appears . . . to be the truth about Salinger." What she demonstrates in "J. D. Salinger's Closed Circuit" is that his characters are members of an exclusive club of superior beings who live on a closed circuit to which everyone else has no access. "Salinger's world contains nothing but Salinger, his teachers, and his tolerantly cherished audience—humanity. Outside are the phonies vainly signaling to be let in." Salinger, she says, is just like Hemingway, who also "sees the world in terms of allies and enemies," and for both Hemingway and Salinger, whoever is not a club member—and membership is determined by how a person talks, how he smiles, how he drinks, and other stylistic signs of superiority—is not just an outsider but a phony.

Much as William Jovanovich liked McCarthy's essays and stories (he was especially upset when she revealed that "The Hounds of Summer" was written to pay for the work being done on the Paris apartment, immediately offering to increase the advance on *The Group* and to pay a separate advance for a book about Jerusalem he wanted her to do), he tried to convince her that "your best course is to first finish *The Group*— and to do this with a minimum of interruption." A month earlier he had assured her "the book is extraordinary, truly, and I've been thinking it might be one of the few important books that is about women without being actually *for* women. For the love of literature, *do* keep going!" He kept importuning: "Is there any way you can give me a hint of a shadow of a suggestion of when *The Group* will be ready?" At the end of November 1962 McCarthy wrote that she would be finished by the next April. A jubilant Jovanovich wrote back, "I had a fancy luncheon for critics and reviewers and witnessed their intense interest in *The Group*. The advance publicity should be tremendous. I am certain no other book of yours was launched as this one will be."

It had been an exhausting three years, beginning in Warsaw and ending in Paris, with dozens of moves in between. All this movement, and the fatigue it produced, made intellectual work difficult and, combined with the pressure of deadlines, generated depression—an unusual state for Mary McCarthy. In fact, she wrote Carmen Angleton, she felt as if she had "migrated, like a soul, into the body of another person, a rather inert body." With more characteristic optimism, she ended the letter with the hope that "a new life is going to begin as soon as we have moved in [the apartment]—a tranquil, airy life."

CHAPTER XVIII

BESTSELLER
(1963)

THE TRANQUIL life Mary McCarthy envisioned at the end of 1962 did not come to pass. By coincidence, both she and Hannah Arendt were catapulted to celebrity status—Arendt by the publication of her book *Eichmann in Jerusalem* and McCarthy by *The Group*. Because of her closeness to Arendt, McCarthy was drawn into the controversy surrounding her friend's book before her own came out. *Eichmann in Jerusalem,* which was published in the spring of 1963, appeared earlier in the year as a five-part series in *The New Yorker*.

The book was Hannah Arendt's report of the trial in Israel of Adolph Eichmann, for having directed the deportation of Jews to concentration camps. She characterized Eichmann as an average, undistinguished man of middle-class upbringing, whose behavior was correct, even polite; a man without identifiable criminal tendencies or even a sadistic streak; a man not even very high up in the Nazi hierarchy, who got his instructions and obeyed them and, in later years, seemed surprised that anyone would fail to see the necessity for him to have acted as he did. Arendt's final assessment of Eichmann's personality was that he was "banal." Jews were astounded that she saw Eichmann not as the moral monster the Israeli prosecutor had called him but as a tiresome, boring, trivial man, a cog in the machine of death that had so effectively shipped Jews to the gas chambers. (In a letter to William Phillips, Mary McCarthy expressed her opinion that "Hannah has got hold of something very important and not yet fully understood in this question of ordinariness or banality.") But the outcry over banality was as nothing compared with the controversy touched off by Arendt's charge that Jews had collaborated in their own destruction. She claimed that more Jews would have escaped death if their leaders had not cooperated with the Nazis. "There was no possibility of resistance," Arendt conceded, "but there existed the possibility of *doing nothing*." Without the cooperation of the Jewish Councils, fewer Jews would have perished.

Discussion of these Jewish Councils filled ten pages out of some three hundred, but no one missed it. *The New York Times Book Review* asked Judge M. A. Musmanno to review *Eichmann in Jerusalem*. As a judge at Nuremberg and at the Einsatgruppen Trial (the Einsatgruppen had murdered over half a million Russian Jews in the first three months following

Hitler's invasion of the Soviet Union), he was eminently qualified. According to his reading of the book, Arendt had defended the Gestapo, Himmler, and Eichmann, but had slandered Jewish victims. A headline in a Jewish paper charged "Self-Hating Jewess Writes Pro-Eichmann Series." Siegfried Moses, on behalf of the Council of Jews from Germany, made what he called a "declaration of war" on Arendt's book. (Even before the book's publication, the Anti-Defamation League of B'nai B'rith sent out a memorandum to all its regional offices, national commissions, and national committees informing them of the *New Yorker* series and alerting them to Arendt's defamatory conception of "Jewish participation in the Nazi holocaust.") Nahum Goldmann, president of the World Zionist Organization, insisted that Arendt had accused European Jews of letting themselves be slaughtered by the Nazis and of displaying cowardice and lack of will to resist.

The most depressing attack, at least from Arendt's point of view, came in *Partisan Review* from Lionel Abel, who charged that Eichmann came off better in Arendt's book than did his victims. She was angry because she considered *Partisan Review,* where she had published several essays, to be friendly. She told editor William Phillips that publication of Abel's review, in which Abel had even intimated that she had been dishonest in *Eichmann in Jerusalem,* showed "a lack of respect for me as a person and as a serious writer." She was pleased that two friends, at least, rose to her defense. Dwight Macdonald lodged a strong protest with Phillips, and Mary McCarthy shot off letters to Philip Rahv and Phillips, demanding, *"What made you do it?"*

Phillips, in his memoirs, *A Partisan View,* says that Abel had asked to do a review of *Eichmann in Jerusalem* and that when "it turned out to be an essay, not a review, and an assault, not a puff," he worried over whether or not to publish the piece. He showed it to Arendt and Macdonald, and both felt it should not appear in *Partisan Review.* Then, he reports, Rahv insisted that a commissioned piece had to be printed (though this seems at odds with his statement that Abel had volunteered to do the review). Abel, in his memoirs, *The Intellectual Follies,* insists that the *Partisan Review* editors asked him to review the book. Furthermore, they must have expected him to be critical, he thinks, because he had treated a previous book of Arendt's, a collection of essays entitled *Between Past and Future,* very harshly.

"My first reaction," McCarthy wrote to Arendt, "was that in your place I wouldn't reply. But I believe this is feminine, like refusing to answer someone who has offended you, pretending not to hear him. Secondly, this strikes me that this is the reaction of a novelist. You cannot

defend your own novels, normally, for this amounts to your saying you
are good, and that is not your right, only the right of your reader. But
I do think you can and even have to defend your ideas."

Arendt refused at first to answer her critics. "As I see it," she told
McCarthy, "there are no ideas in this report, there are only facts with
a few conclusions, and these conclusions usually appear at the end of each
chapter. The only exception to this is the epilogue which is a discussion
of the legal aspects of the case. In other words my point would be that
what the whole furor is about are facts and neither theories nor ideas.
The hostility against me is a hostility against someone who tells the truth
on a factual level, and not against someone who has ideas which are in
conflict with those commonly held." (Dwight Macdonald disagreed with
Arendt on this point: "Her book is NOT just 'a factual report' but is also
a polemic, a sermon, and an essay in moral evaluation," he said.) Arendt
did, however, supply McCarthy with a densely argued letter on the
issues, which McCarthy used in preparing her twelve-page reply to Lionel Abel's review. Later, Arendt made her own formal reply to her
critics, in *The New York Review of Books.*

McCarthy's "The Hue and Cry" appeared in *Partisan Review* in early
1964. In the essay, McCarthy wrote about her discovery that, in general,
reviews of *Eichmann in Jerusalem* by Jews were unfavorable and those by
Gentiles favorable. Moreover, the division of reactions to *Eichmann in
Jerusalem* along Jewish and non-Jewish lines was even more pronounced
in private conversation, she reported. (William Phillips thought that her
"division of the antagonists into Jewish and Gentile only fueled the
polarization.") Then she answered Abel's points, one by one. Jews who
condemned Arendt for describing Eichmann as banal, McCarthy wrote,
wanted "to make the *criminal* fit the crime." Moreover, Arendt's
charge—that without the cooperation of the Jewish Councils so many
millions of Jews would not have died—was self-evident, McCarthy felt.

> Had the Nazis been obliged to use their own manpower to select Jews for
> the extermination camps, number them, assemble them, ticket their prop-
> erty, and so on, they would not only have rounded up fewer Jews, but they
> would have felt the drain in their military effort; had Hitler persisted in
> the Final Solution, at the cost of diverting troops to carry it out, the war
> might have ended somewhat sooner. It is clear that refusal to cooperate
> would have met with terrible reprisals, but these reprisals in turn might
> have demoralized the army and the civilian population both in Germany
> and the occupied countries, and chaos, the nightmare of generals, might
> have been the result. The Final Solution was preferred by the Nazis to

mass massacres by shooting because it could be carried out smoothly and efficiently—almost peacefully. And this allowed not only the Germans and the people of occupied countries but the Jews themselves for a long time to remain ignorant of the true destination of the cattle cars moving east, on schedule.

She concluded her defense of Arendt with a characteristic synthesis:

> But I took the book mainly as a parable for the Gentiles, a lesson in what was possible for the average man, the neighbor, who is not obliged to stay at home with the doors closed when the police cars come for the "Jews" next door—Jews figuratively speaking, since it might happen again, might be happening now, and the Jews of the past may not be the "Jews" of the present or the future.

Although McCarthy predicted "this is going to make a lot of new enemies (not including, I hope, Hannah)," Arendt was delighted with the piece.

When the first part of *Eichmann in Jerusalem* had appeared in *The New Yorker,* Mary McCarthy was hard at work trying to finish *The Group* for the April 1963 deadline. "I've lost all perspective and have no idea whether what I'm doing is good, bad, or indifferent," she told Hannah Arendt. "It is just drudgery, animal drudgery; I remind myself of a beast—an ant or a mole or an ox. The main thing is to push on and deposit the burden. On Jovanovich's lap."

While she worked in Paris on the last three chapters, Harcourt, Brace & World was already preparing the completed chapters for printing. "We are proceeding to set *The Group*," William Jovanovich wrote McCarthy early in February. A few days later he wrote again to discuss first serialization rights. Since Bernice Baumgarten had retired from Brandt and Brandt, McCarthy no longer had an agent. She handled her own rights. (Baumgarten did, however, come out of retirement to handle the movie sale of *The Group.*) "Dottie Makes an Honest Woman of Herself"—which, with slight revision, became chapter 3 of *The Group*—had appeared in *Partisan Review* in 1954. Because Jovanovich felt "strongly that it is seriously important for *The Group* to come out at the end of August and get a jump on the flood of Fall books," there would be little lead time for magazines to place material in their forthcoming issues. As a result, only one magazine, *The New Yorker,* published excerpts. "Polly Andrews, Class of '33"—which, with revision, became chapters 11 and 12 of *The Group*—appeared in *The New Yorker* at the end of June 1963.

At this time also, German and English publishers were clamoring for rights to *The Group*. (The novel became a best-seller in both countries.) Eventually, through her English representative, A. M. Heath and Company, she sold foreign rights to *The Group* to Danish, Dutch, Finnish, German, Hebrew, Hungarian, Icelandic, Italian, Japanese, Norwegian, Polish, Portuguese, Serbo-Croatian, Slovak, Slovene, Spanish, and Swedish publishers. It was also sold in English-speaking countries throughout the world.

McCarthy finished writing chapter 15, the last, on April 1. By May 20—much sooner than normal in book publishing—she had page proofs. Harcourt, Brace was rushing the book into print in the certainty that it would be a big seller. Even McCarthy thought so—"I'm very much excited by all the excitement about the book." In July she wrote Jovanovich, "I'm beginning to get cables and letters about movie rights for *The Group*. . . . It's exciting, all this, and rather stupefying, especially since my life hasn't changed to go with this improbable money. In fact I'm doing my own housework and riding the Metro and not answering letters as usual. I *have* bought a gold-and-diamond Cartier bracelet to go with my grandmother's ancient diamond watch, but at the moment I'm just washing dishes with it hanging from my wrist." When *Newsweek* announced its intention of putting McCarthy on its cover and sent a reporter to follow her around Bocca di Magra, where she and West and his children had gone for the month of August, Jovanovich was jubilant. Although, it turned out, McCarthy did not make it to the cover (she was preempted by the Civil Rights March on Washington), she did get a four-page story inside.

The Group was published on August 28, 1963, and immediately became a best-seller. Jovanovich wrote McCarthy that "the book has gotten off to a flying start. It was reviewed, as you know, on the front page of *The New York Times Book Review* a week ahead of publication. You got the cover story in the *Saturday Review;* there are 58,000 copies of *The Group* in the bookstores presently; and it appears on *The New York Times* bestseller list this weekend, which means that it made the list in the shortest possible span of time." McCarthy answered happily, "The sales are stupefying. . . . It is all wonderful and nutty." At the end of September, Jovanovich cabled her: THE GROUP NUMBER ONE ON TIMES BEST-SELLER LIST SUNDAY. . . . 95,000 COPIES IN PRINT.

Although Harcourt, Brace's promotion and publicity people had pushed the book long before publication, they had to work without much cooperation from McCarthy. She had very definite ideas about the propriety of an author's selling his or her own books. In June, two months before publication date, she had written Jovanovich expressing these views.

> *Life* has rung me here about doing a "Close-Up" story. They sent me some samples this morning, which made me very uneasy. There were Dr. Spock, Rachel Carson, and Dame Edith Sitwell. The first two were not so bad, but Dame Edith was grotesque, and not the less so because of the gushing admiration the *Life* writer expressed for her. It seemed to me the reason for the difference was not simply Edith's nonsense but was inherent in the literary profession. Spock and Rachel Carson belong in *Life* because he is a public health figure and she is a biologist who's fighting for a cause. There's no discrepancy between what they do professionally and a *Life* interview. But it's not so for a poet or a novelist. A picture-story cannot help vulgarizing a writer because the part of himself that writes is invisible by its nature. The best they can do is to make a connection with the writer's exhibitionism, his worst side.
>
> Would you be cast down if I said no?

Jovanovich was disappointed, as "there is no question but what the *Life* article would create tremendous publicity for the book and aid its sale," but, he added, he would never urge her to do anything she was not comfortable doing. She finally did acquiesce to a *Life* story. Jovanovich told her that Harcourt, Brace & World had been getting constant inquiries and wanted to set up interviews that she "might find agreeable." During the summer she herself had received dozens of requests for interviews, pictures, and stories, but she accepted very few of these offers. As she explained to Jovanovich, "Unless it's an extreme emergency, I will not appear on any radio or TV program gratis or give interviews to the press. I say gratis because that is the test as to whether you are appearing to make publicity for yourself or for some legitimate purpose."

McCarthy did accept an invitation to read in November at the Ninety-second Street Y (in New York), where she had read a preliminary chapter of *The Group* several years before. When Jovanovich heard that she would appear at the Y, he cabled: JACK PAAR IS WILLING TO PAY YOU 3000 DOLLARS FOR EXCLUSIVE TAPE INTERVIEW. She cabled her acceptance. Besides the YMHA reading and the "Tonight Show" appearance, she also talked to the Women's Press Club in Washington, where she met one of her nieces, also named Mary McCarthy, for the first time. (Young Mary McCarthy, a student at the Catholic girls' school

Georgetown Visitation, was a daughter of McCarthy's youngest brother, Sheridan, who lived in Chicago. McCarthy rarely saw Sheridan, an insurance executive, or Preston, a banker from Wilmington, Delaware, because she felt she had little in common with them and their worlds. Kevin's acting career, however, was more congenial to her literary interests.) While in Washington, she also attended a Vassar Alumnae Club tea, at which she stated, with characteristic perversity, that if she had a daughter, she would send her to Radcliffe, not Vassar.

Mary McCarthy had first conceived the idea of *The Group* eleven years earlier, just after finishing *The Groves of Academe.* In the fall of 1951 she wrote the John Simon Guggenheim Memorial Foundation about a project that would take, she estimated, "two years, though it might be done in one if there weren't the necessity of doing short stories or journalism concurrently to keep myself alive. At the moment, I am stony broke, not having done any outside writing for more than a year, in order to get finished, and I foresee a repetition of this situation if I concentrate my energies again, which I very much want to do, being full of beans with this new idea." The idea, she explained in the application, was to write a chronicle novel dealing with love and technology from the 1930s to the 1950s. The characters "are a group of newly married couples who emerge out of the Depression with a series of optimistic beliefs in science, engineering, rural electrification, the Aga stove, technocracy, psychoanalysis, planned parenthood, Modernage furniture, the Modern Museum, photography, Bendix washers, the movies as contemporary art form, etcetera. . . . The book is a history of contemporary ideas as well as of social mores, but these ideas are studied only as they impinge on love and family life. In fact, in a certain sense, the ideas are the villains and the people their hapless victims."

She did not get the grant, but she worked on the book anyway, writing three chapters before she "gave up to do something easier and more immediately rewarding." One of the chapters, "Dottie Makes an Honest Woman of Herself," was published in *Partisan Review* early in 1954; it created a furor. No one before had written so openly about contraception. Dottie's visit to the doctor to get a pessary, written so matter-of-factly and with such unflinching detail, shocked nearly everyone, even Peggy Guggenheim. When McCarthy read the story at John Myers's apartment, Guggenheim was struck dumb and never once opened her mouth for the rest of the evening. McCarthy "was a firebrand," says Brendan Gill today, "a pioneer taking big chances, and by doing so, increasing the range of permissible subject matter." "That woman," said

one wit, "has done for the pessary what Herman Melville did for the whale." McCarthy told a 1968 interviewer, "There was a terrible protest about the Dottie-going-to-the-doctor chapter. It was considered the most outrageous thing—that I had betrayed feminine secrets." Years after the story was published, Philip Roth alluded to it in *Goodbye, Columbus*. When the protagonists, Neil and Brenda, talk about getting a diaphragm for Brenda, the following exchange takes place:

> "Neil, how do you think I'd feel lying to some doctor."
> "You can go to Margaret Sanger, in New York. They won't ask any questions."
> "You've done this before?"
> "No," I said. "I just know. I read Mary McCarthy."
> "That's exactly right. That's just what I'd feel like, somebody out of her."

Near the end of the novella, in a hotel where they are pretending to be married, the following exchange takes place:

> "Your heart's pounding," I said to her.
> "I know," she said.
> "Are you nervous?"
> "No."
> "Have you done this before?" I said.
> "I read Mary McCarthy."

In 1959, the same year that *Goodbye, Columbus* was published, Mary McCarthy turned back to *The Group* and applied again for a Guggenheim grant, this time successfully. She described the projected book as "a kind of compendious history of the faith in progress of the nineteen-thirties and forties as reflected in the behavior and notions of [eight] young women—college graduates of the year 1933. . . . No male consciousness is present in the book; through these eight points of view, all feminine, all consciously enlightened, are refracted, as if from a series of pretty prisms, all the novel ideas of the period concerning sex, politics, economics, architecture, city-planning, house-keeping, child-bearing, interior decoration, and art. It is a crazy quilt of *clichés*, platitudes, and *idées reçues*. Yet the book is not meant to be a joke or even a satire, exactly, but a 'true history' of the times despite the angle or angles of distortion."

She held firmly to her original conception, although she kept shortening the time span of the novel, which, in the final version, begins with the wedding of Kay Leiland Strong in June 1933 and ends with her funeral in July 1940. Her story is the focal point for the activities and preoccupations of the book's eight other Vassar graduates. One reason McCarthy abandoned the twenty-year span had to do with the nature of comedy, as she saw it. Interviewed by the *Paris Review* in 1960, she remarked that "these girls are all essentially comic figures, and it's awfully hard to make anything happen to them"; and later, in a letter to Doris Grumbach, that "the capacity to learn from experience or instruction is what is forbidden to all comic creations and what is comic in you and me." Since the girls, to be comic, could not grow wiser in the course of the book, her original time span, from Roosevelt's inauguration to Eisenhower's, seemed too long; she therefore reduced the period during which she had to deal with them. She told an interviewer that she was "awfully mean to those girls. I stopped writing . . . three or four times over those eleven years. I felt that I was just whacking those girls over the head and making them parrot this terrible nonsense. Not that they didn't, in reality, parrot a lot of nonsense."

The characters are presented more sympathetically than their creator realized. In a letter to Dwight Macdonald, Nicola Chiaromonte endorsed what he saw as an unwonted compassion. "Mary's sarcastic attitude to her characters, which made her previous novels (with the exception of *The Company*) quite unbearable to me, has mellowed, and become real novelistic interest." Macdonald agreed and added that "the odd thing is that most of the intellectuals I've talked to, or read, about *The Group* think it is the old Mary, cold and bitchy and superior, and don't at all see—as you do—that, while she does 'put down' les girls, on occasion and perhaps habitually, she also strikes often a quite new note of sympathy and concern." What he did not like was the style; although he understood perfectly that it was meant to be written in the vernacular of the characters, Macdonald missed "Mary's own well-groomed, witty style."

The novel consists of chapters written from the viewpoint and in the language of eight girls who have roomed together in their last year at Vassar and of Norine Schmittlapp, also class of 1933. McCarthy's own voice is almost completely silent; *The Group* is as far as she could go in ventriloquism, she has said. Since everything is written in the characters' voices, everything is dramatized. The characters do little besides talk, and their conversations effectively characterize them. This method requires that McCarthy confine herself to noting the trivia of their social milieu—appearances, dress, eating habits, furniture, small talk, and manners—and this enormous detail came from her memory. "I have a belief," she has said, "that the only documentation that is any good is that which remains in the memory."

The only exceptions to the mimicry of *The Group* are the author's commentary and narration, which are kept to a minimum. McCarthy told a translator that the author speaks only in the first chapter, when she introduces the characters—"Dottie's cough, 'like a perpetual scruple,'" or 'Elinor was always convinced of other people's hypocrisy since she could not believe that they noticed less than she did'"—and in the novel's last sentence—"where the same voice that set the scene at the beginning now pronounces a valedictory on Harald, as he starts thumbing a ride back to New York." Narration is restricted to an indication of simple actions—"Dottie turned restlessly in bed"; "Libby's eyes protruded"; "Lakey started the car"; "Helena looked around the apartment."

William Abrahams, one of the few critics who realized that the novel was written in the "chirp, twitter, gasp, and gabble" of the group, wrote that "Miss McCarthy's mastery of intonations and vocabulary of what one might call 'educated-banal' is a remarkable *tour de force,* sustained as it is for almost four hundred pages. Only very rarely does she falter in her discipline: then the *author* enters, and one hears—'Her eyes, which were a light golden brown, were habitually narrowed, and her handsome blowzy face had a plethoric look, as though darkened by clots of thought.' At such moments one is forcibly reminded of what has been sacrificed to obtain the virtuoso style-that-is-no-style of *The Group.*" Many reviewers said she wrote in clichés, without seeing that the clichés were there on purpose. "What I was trying to say," McCarthy told the Women's National Press Club in Washington, "was that for these girls clichés precede experience. Experience is turned into manufactured clichés before it happens. This is a consumer society and the girls in 'The Group' are trainees for this society. They think of everything under brand names: eating is turned into recipes, sex into contraceptives, and child-bearing becomes the question of nursing or bottle feeding."

The way the girls in the group are drawn irresistibly to the latest fad, whether breast feeding or modern furniture, is very funny, and nothing is funnier in *The Group* (which is, above all else, a wonderfully comic novel) than the confrontation in chapter 6 between sensible, refined Helena Davison, who sees things for what they are and who can speak bluntly, and left-wing, literal Norine Schmittlapp, who champions all the latest theories on everything in the most sweeping generalizations. The very furnishings of Norine's apartment, in which the girls' meeting takes place—books like *Das Kapital* and *Ten Days That Shook the World,* Alfred Stieglitz photographs of New York City slums, Diego Rivera prints of

Mexican slums—"seemed to be saying something, asserting something, pontificating." Norine, who is not a member of the group, lights a cigarette and announces that her husband, Putnam Blake, is impotent.

"Oh," said Helena, slowly. "Oh, Norine, I'm sorry." "It's not your fault," said Norine hoarsely. Helena did not know what to say next. She could still smell Put's tobacco and see his pipe in an unemptied ashtray. Despite the fact that she had had no sexual experience, she had a very clear idea of the male member, and she could not help forming a picture of Put's as pale and lifeless, in the coffin of his trousers, a veritable *nature morte.* . . . "We got married in June," Norine enlarged. "A couple of weeks after Commencement. I was a raw virgin. I never had a date till I knew Put. So when we went to this hotel, . . . I didn't catch on right away. Especially since my mother, who hates sex like all her generation, told me that a gentleman never penetrated his bride on the first night. I thought that for once Mother must be right. . . .

"Finally," she continued hoarsely, "I faced the truth. I went to the Public Library. They've got a Viennese woman there in Information— very *gemütlich.* She drew me up a reading list on impotence."

Norine then accounts for Put's impotence—"He's got a mother tie," she tells Helena.

"He'd had all his early sex experience with whores and factory girls in Pittsfield, it turned out. They'd pull up their skirts, in an alley or a doorway, and he'd ejaculate, sometimes at the first contact, before he got the penis all the way in. He'd never made love to a good woman and never seen a woman naked. I'm a good woman; that's why he can't make it with me. He feels he's fornicating with his mother. That's what the Freudians think; the Behaviorists would claim that it was a conditioned reflex."

Norine continues, itemizing the various techniques she has employed to uncondition Put and then suddenly gets to the point of her confession— that Harald, Kay's new husband, "had become a sort of male potency symbol" for her. Ingenuously, she adds, "I wouldn't want to wreck [Kay's] marriage." "Then don't," Helena answers abruptly. Norine, however, admits that she and Harald have been lovers for quite a while.

"It undercuts Harald that she works to support him. He has to assert his masculinity. You saw what happened last night—when he burned his play. That was a sort of immolation rite, to propitiate her; he was making a burnt offering of his seed, the offspring of his mind and balls." At these words

Helena's normal droll self assumed command again. "Oh, Norine!" she protested. "Do come down to brass tacks." . . . "What is it," [Norine] wondered, eyeing Helena, "that makes you want to puke at the imponderables?"

Helena uncharacteristically explodes.

Her voice, though she strove to maintain its careful drawl, began to tremble. Norine, staring, slowly put out her cigarette. "You say your husband can't sleep with you because you're a 'good woman.' I suggest you enlighten him. Tell him what you do with Harald. And about the progressive-school teacher with the wife and six children. That ought to get his pecker up. And have him take a look at this apartment. And at the ring around your neck. If a man slept with you, you'd leave a ring around him. Like your bathtub." . . . Helena gulped; she had not spoken so fiercely since she was a spunky child and angry with her mother. . . . She did not know, now, what had possessed her to fly off the handle—a defensive loyalty to Kay or to a canon of honesty.

When Norine asks her what she "needs to do to change" her life, Helena says:

"I'd start with a little 'elbow grease.' . . . I'd get some toilet paper. There isn't any in the bathroom. And some Clorox for the garbage pail and the toilet bowl. And boil out that dishcloth or get a new one. . . . I'd unchain the dog and take him for a walk. And while I was at it, I'd change his name." "You don't like Nietzsche?" "No," said Helena, dryly. "I'd call him something like Rover." Norine gave her terse laugh. "I get it," she said appreciatively. "God, Helena, you're wonderful! Go on. Should I give him a bath to christen him?" Helena considered. "Not in this weather. He might catch cold. Take a bath yourself, instead, and wash your hair in the shower. . . . And buy some real food—not in cans. If it's only hamburger and fresh fruit and oranges." Norine nodded. "Fine. But now tell me something more basic."

Helena's simple concreteness is lost on Norine, who is so in love with ideas that she is blind to real things, to what is valuable in life. The scene is really the whole novel in miniature. What went wrong with this generation, McCarthy is saying, was its attempt to live life by abstractions, by recipes, by formulas. That Norine takes this to such an extreme is what makes her such a great comic character.

On the whole, the reviews of *The Group,* both pro and con, were milder than those for McCarthy's previous books. William Jovanovich characterized them as innocuous. "I'm intrigued by the apparent desire of most reviewers not to be wrong about the book," he wrote McCarthy two weeks after publication. "It is as if they were afraid that they had missed the point and that someone would accuse them of not being bright enough or sensible enough to see it. And again I don't find any real trace in these reviews of what was common talk in the office before publication, namely, that women would not like the book and men would. As literary criticism, the reviews are pretty punk, but they *are* selling reviews." Jovanovich was right. Arthur Mizener's review on the front page of *The New York Times Book Review* was essentially a plot summary, and Granville Hicks's piece that accompanied a picture of Mary McCarthy looking like the Virgin Mary on the cover of the *Saturday Review* consisted of six noncommittal paragraphs. Even when a reviewer seemed not to like the book, he said something that was likely to attract potential readers: "the book is 95-per-cent feminine gossip" that is "very funny" *(America);* "a gem of American social history" *(The Nation);* "surface reproduction of the thirties is vivid" *(The New Republic);* the second-chapter seduction is "so prolonged and so microscopic in detail that the author seems to have written it for burial in a time capsule against the day when sex is a forgotten activity" *(Newsweek);* "an interminable catalogue of facts about food, furniture, clothes, birth-control . . . especially among the rich . . . a mastery of social detail" *(New Statesman).*

Norman Mailer's review, which filled the first three pages of *The New York Review of Books,* was one of the few that was not noncommittal. Although he claimed to have found only "little glints of gold in a ton of clay," he saluted McCarthy for conceiving such an ambitious collective novel. But he concluded, she failed in execution.

> She failed out of vanity, the accumulated vanity of being over-praised through the years for too little and so being pleased with herself for too little; she failed out of profound timidity—like any good Catholic-born she is afraid to unloose the demons; she failed out of snobbery—if compassion for her characters is beginning to stir at last in this book, she can still not approve of anyone who is incapable of performing the small act exquisitely well.

But this novel, Mailer wrote, showed promise of greatness to come. "Does anyone know where society will end," he asked, "if the heroine of *The Company She Keeps* should encounter Julien Sorel?" Dwight Macdonald said privately what Norman Mailer had pronounced so publicly. "Mary tried for something very big, a collective novel," Macdonald wrote Chiaromonte, "but didn't have the creative force to weld it all together, so that it falls apart into a series of disparate episodes, some weak, some strong, but not adding up to a whole."

Because *The Group* was still number one on the *Times* best-seller list in the new year, the New York *Herald Tribune Book Review* commissioned a front-page story, " 'The Group' on Mary McCarthy," that reported what several women portrayed in the novel thought of Mary McCarthy. She was furious. "I suppose you have seen . . . the horrible nasty piece in yesterday's *Tribune*, which moves me, damn it, to want to sue," she wrote Jovanovich.

> But I'm afraid mere mistakes and malice are not actionable. The thing that makes me most furious is where it says I pursued the original of Dottie into a man's apartment and then into a birth control clinic. I don't know what this means unless it's intended metaphorically. Dottie's defloration is totally fictional and didn't happen to the real Dottie, so far as I know, or to me, as is elsewhere suggested. Furthermore, I can't figure out who the person is that thinks she is Libby MacAusland and says such invidious things about me. . . . Half of Libby is drawn from a girl who did not go to Vassar at all. And the reporter is wrong when she says there's no original for Polly Andrews; there are two. . . . And if that psychiatrist thinks she is not in the book, she ought to have her head examined. . . . And Helena is not three group members but one non-group member. The Group is an idea, not a study of the actual group disguised—a Platonic ideal.

The real-life models for the mercilessly comic fictional portraits McCarthy had drawn did not, obviously, care what her novelistic intentions were. They only saw parts of themselves, and they did not like what they saw. One of those who spoke to Sheila Tobias, the author of " 'The Group' on Mary McCarthy," agreed that "it's all there—our parents, our habits, our prejudices, our illusions." What they said individually about their most famous classmate was not as nasty as McCarthy's letter to Jovanovich suggests: "We had no idea we were making such an impression on our Mary"; "she had that harsh, angular hair-do, the one she still wears today. She may, in fact, be the only Vassar girl not to have changed her hair style in 30 years. Perhaps she takes care of it now, but then there was always some clump of hair out of place." The worst came from the person who bears a strong resemblance to Norine Schmittlapp; she said, "The only thing Mary learned to love at Vassar was the sound of her own voice." This woman was most annoyed that her family name, decorously Anglo-Saxon on both sides, had become the ugly, Germanic Schmittlapp (a name McCarthy used twice, having given it to Henry Mulcahy's laundress in *The Groves of Academe*).

As heady as all the excitement over her first best-seller had been during most of 1963, by the beginning of 1964 she was sick of it. She told William Phillips that "the success of *The Group* goes on and keeps me standing in a pillory" and Robert Lowell that her equilibrium was unsteady owing to "the success of *that book* and all its byproducts. . . . I can scarcely open a book, a newspaper, or magazine without feeling like the president of a personal anti-defamation league. Eventually it will stop; I welcome the sight of John O'Hara grappling up the bestseller list—today he is in third." Still later she wrote Jovanovich that "being an author *is* very hard on one's ego." To her mind, the worst that happened as a result of *"that book"* was Elizabeth Hardwick's parody entitled "The Gang," which appeared pseudonymously under the byline Xavier Prynne in *The New York Review of Books.* Specifically, Hardwick lampooned the chapter about Dottie's defloration. She managed to caricature quite a lot of *The Group* in her short piece—classical allusion ("Maisie had always, rather demurely, thought of the great event as a 'defloration,' for the Late Latin, *defloratio* "); literary allusion, albeit Shaw instead of Shakespeare, ("Remember Bernard Shaw? Something about brief and ridiculous"); the unusual spelling of the hero's name ("Johhn—spelled, oddly enough, with two h's in the Finnish manner" like the "old Scandinavian" spelling of Harald); the heroine's reflections about what mother would think ("Mother would somehow have minded the odious couch more than the 'events' "); the profusion of brand names (after heating a can of Heinz tomato soup, Maisie puts on her "Lord and Taylor biascut cocktail dress"; Johhn gets his clothes at Macy's; a character notices paper carnations in a Kraft cheese glass); and the flaw in Maisie's triumph (Johhn's snoring, which is as worrisome to Maisie as Dick's denial of kisses was to Dottie).

McCarthy was not amused, maybe because she felt, as she had recently written in a review of Kenneth Tynan's *Curtains,* that "no author can be parodied successfully who has not already committed self-parody." When Robert Lowell told her that his wife had done the *New York Review of Books* parody, she became angry. In a New Year's letter to him, she elaborated on her reasons.

> I think it's easier to forgive your enemies than to forgive your friends, and that is not just a remark. With your enemies you don't feel a sense of

betrayal, and what is at the bottom of a sense of betrayal but bewilderment—a loss of your bearings? I would not know how to act with Elizabeth yet; that is, I feel I would start acting falsely.

In a postscript, she added:

You can forgive an enemy because that immediately puts you on a fresh basis with him; the slate is wiped clean. But with a friend, you can't wipe out the past because the past includes your friendship as well as the injury you feel you've been dealt. So you have no basis on which to start again, neither the old one nor a brand-new one. The practical way of coping with this is to revise your opinion of the friend, in a downward direction. In this way you have a new friend. But I don't want to do this with Elizabeth.

Although she still fails to find humor in the incident, she has obviously forgiven Hardwick, since the women are still friends (and neighbors). Today she says it was the conjunction of Hardwick's parody and Mailer's review in successive issues of *The New York Review of Books* that upset her.

I wasn't persuaded at the time of friendly intentions, which was all the more strange to me in that I'd been a friend of the magazine from the beginning, and had written for them for the first number [February 1963], and at the very moment they were publishing the Hardwick parody and commissioning the Mailer review Silvers [Robert Silvers, one of the founding editors] was begging me (by wire, if I'm not mistaken) to write something for him for the very same number, which, on my side, would certainly have looked like condonation. I never could understand why suddenly they had it in for me. Lowell said that it was simply that *The Group* was being such a success. . . . It may be my sense of injury over all this was compounded by Lowell, who was my chief source of information and who could be mischievous when the mood was on him.

On the other hand, McCarthy graciously accepted criticism when it was serious and direct. Katharine White's is a case in point. Although White admitted that she had "galloped through *The Group* with fascinated attention," she deplored its explicit sex scenes, which she thought "went over that thin line of taste 'between candor and shame,'" and she complained about its being "too much a social document and too little a novel." McCarthy thanked her former editor—Katharine White had retired from *The New Yorker*—"for taking all those pains to tell me the truth."

* * *

By the time *The Group* started slipping from the best-seller list in America, it was just coming out in Europe and Australia. It was a commercial success everywhere, but especially in England, where it was a Book Society choice, and in Germany, where it sold a quarter of a million copies. Because of the novel's explicitness, however, it was banned in Italy, Ireland, and Australia, giving rise to expensive lawsuits. Eventually, the lawsuits were dropped, but not before Jovanovich, as McCarthy's primary publisher, had written several letters defending author and book. He also replied to several Americans who had written Harcourt, Brace denouncing *The Group* as "the most vulgar book" and "a public strip-tease." "You'll be amused to know," he wrote McCarthy, "that I have personally written a dozen or so letters to irate readers . . . and have refunded the price to a few." His typical letter said:

> Your comments on Mary McCarthy's book I understand. Obviously this book has repelled and offended you deeply. Yet as I do not question your motives in declaring yourself against the book, I should like to ask you sincerely not to question mine.
>
> Mary McCarthy is a first-rate writer, possibly one of the dozen best writers of our generation, and as her publisher I have had occasion to appreciate the seriousness and dedication she brings to her art. The matter of explicit sexual descriptions in literature is part of our time—Miss McCarthy did not introduce the trend, nor is she the leading example of it—and it has developed from a score of influences and ideas that are difficult to assess, such as Freudianism, the anti-romanticism following the war, etc., etc. As a publisher I cannot ignore serious writing of our own time. I would not consciously publish pornography, and I do not believe *The Group* is this: its purpose is not to titillate the senses nor to induce immoral thoughts, and I believe it does not do either. Actually, on this question alone—of course there is far more to the book than this—it seems to me that *The Group* leaves a reader with a sense that immoral behavior is painful, boring, and stupid. I doubt that you will agree, but this is an opinion shared by some critics.

Not surprisingly, *The Group* was made into a movie. What *is* surprising is that, before the novel was even published, every major film studio had considered it and turned it down. Charles Feldman, an agent turned producer, bought it for $162,500 plus 10 percent of the distributor's gross after break-even point, and then tried to convince the companies that had already rejected the book to finance production. To increase the value of his property, he spent $50,000 on advertising for the novel in the United States, $12,000 in England, and other similar amounts in countries where *The Group* was coming out in translation. He hired Sidney Buchman, a veteran Hollywood writer whose career had severely suffered from the House Un-American Activities Committee hearings, to adapt the book and to serve as producer. The adaptation presented few difficulties because McCarthy had recorded the characters and their relationships, and even their clothes, furniture, and environment, in vivid detail. Buchman stayed close to the novel, inventing dialogue only to transpose characters' thoughts into speech. Although McCarthy had not asked to see the movie script, Buchman sent her a copy. She did not comment on it. Pauline Kael, in a lengthy essay on the making of *The Group,* thought that possibly Buchman's

> fidelity to [McCarthy's] material did not please her any more than infidelity might have; she is, notoriously, a writer given to seeing the faults in *any* course of action. And in this case it was obvious that neither inventiveness nor fidelity could be completely satisfactory. There were huge structural gaps in the book that in dramatic terms (and in terms of fiction also) cried out for invention; yet Buchman must have known that he could not invent in her style. He played it safe, preferring narrative holes to inadequate invention.

Kael wrote that, despite the "narrative holes" and despite the fact that both writer-producer Buchman and director Sidney Lumet had missed the point of *The Group*—namely, that the girls "really are products of the thirties, using fashionable, liberal 'ideas' to explain and falsify what they're doing—the movie was good.

> What gives the movie its vitality—and despite its carelessness and sloppy style, it is one of the few interesting American movies of recent years—is that the talented, fresh young performers are given some material to work with. There's solid observation in Mary McCarthy's writing, and the movie is a considerably more realistic and sophisticated account of modern male-female relationships and what goes wrong in them than we've had on the screen. It deals with the specific experiences of women in our time that Mary McCarthy has always specialized in: how a girl (Dottie) may want to lose her virginity but then feels unwanted and deserted when a casual affair doesn't turn into "love"; how scared virgins may come on as the sexiest teasers (Libby); how a woman's life can be made a ridiculous martyrdom to theories of child care (Priss); how people now "use" analysis in their relationships (Polly and Gus).

The critic of the *Saturday Review* agreed with Kael that the film was "out of the ordinary," but other reviewers were not so complimentary. *Time* called it a "suds opera"; *The New Republic,* "sentimental"; and *Life,* "overlong." Although producer Sidney Buchman had predicted the film would ride on the coattails of the novel's notoriety, it was not a box-office success. Thirty-seventh among 1966's top-grossing movies, it earned less than three million dollars.

The Group was not just McCarthy's first best-seller but an international commercial success. (More than five million copies in hardcover and paperback have been sold worldwide since its initial publication.) There were several reasons for this. The book had been the subject of wide publicity and controversy ever since the publication of the excerpt "Dottie Makes an Honest Woman of Herself" in 1954. *The Group* brought previously unexplored women's experiences into the open. Moreover, it studied the effects of an elite education on a group of privileged girls. The public has always been interested in the doings of those who are perceived to possess unusual advantages. McCarthy was aware of this, having written as early as 1951 that

> like Harvard, [Vassar] is always good for a knowledgeable smile from members of the population who have scarcely heard the name of another college. It signifies a certain *je ne sais quoi;* a whiff of luxury and the ineffable; plain thinking and high living. If a somehow know-it-all manner is typical of the Vassar student, the public has a way of winking that it knows all about Vassar, though the sly wink only intimates that there is something to know.

In addition, the novel recreated a period in American life about which many people were—and still are—curious or nostalgic.

Whatever the importance of these factors, however, *The Group* sold so well mainly because, unlike McCarthy's previous novels, which had centered around intellectuals and their foibles, it dealt with a much broader segment of society. McCarthy herself told an interviewer that the book was not only about a "whole social class, which is upper middle . . . Protestant, educated," but that it was also "a history of a vanishing class. These people don't exist now as they did then in such numbers." This was sad, she thought—and accounts, partly, for her unusually compassionate treatment of her characters. Although earlier she had felt she had been too hard on the girls, she reconsidered this judgment after finishing *The Group.* "This is the first book, I think, where I have any sympathetic characters practically."

Hannah Arendt sensed these departures from her friend's previous novelistic practice. "It is quite different from your other books, at the same time milder and sadder; it reads like a definite statement of that period, but looked at from a perspective, or perhaps rather you have arrived at a point so far removed from your former life that everything can now fall into place. You yourself are no longer directly involved. And this quality makes the book more of a novel than any of your other books." Arendt was right. McCarthy's new life with a decisive and good man who made her very happy, and her removal from New York and its incestuous literary life, changed her fiction. Friends say it became "mellower"—not always an improvement, they hasten to add. Angélique Levi, for example, says that "what she gained in humanity, she lost in strength."

McCarthy now says she did not like the considerable renown that publication of *The Group* brought her. "I hated it when *The Group* got the best-seller treatment; there was a time when I thought it had ruined my life. I didn't like the exposure; it made me into a different kind of person. I had to change my hairdo; I couldn't stand the sight of that bun in photographs. And I hated the whole business of interviews and TV. I felt I'd been corrupted. Not that I was a corrupt person, but that the world which I despised had somehow eaten its way into me. I had been corroded perhaps more than corrupted." She told her brother Kevin, when he interviewed her for *People* in 1979, that she did not like *The Group* anymore. "I think it's a bit coarse."

CHAPTER XIX

STEPMOTHER
(1963–1966)

"I HAVE NEVER been mad about children," Mary McCarthy once told an interviewer, "but certain specific ones I have liked." The only children that show up in her seven novels are the urine-drenched, unkempt Mulcahy offspring, who make a fleeting appearance in *The Groves of Academe.* While this may seem strange in a writer who has focused on so many areas of feminine experience, it is a reflection of her lack of interest in children. Kate McCarthy, Kevin's second wife, says that her husband is a far more "maternal" figure than his sister. Moreover, children of friends claim to be more comfortable with Jim West than with his wife. This is partly because she is so formal in her day-to-day living. It is hard to imagine Mary McCarthy, a devotee of Elizabeth David, fixing peanut butter-and-jelly sandwiches for lunch, and, in fact, she once complained that that was all Dwight Macdonald's children would eat. Yet she has also said that she "enjoyed the experience of being a mother," and in a letter to her uncle Frank Preston, she maintained that she had always wanted more children. (Somewhat inconsistently, and rather offhandedly, she told an interviewer in 1980 that she had "had quite a lot" of abortions.)

In twenty-four books, she has written little about children. The protagonist in *Birds of America* tells children stories "of white wooden houses, ponds, waterfalls, skating, clamming, ice-cream freezers, blueberries, corn-on-the-cob—one of his mother's rules for telling stories to children, which she learned as a child from her father, was always to put in something good to eat." Something good to eat was always the centerpiece of any arrangement or activity McCarthy planned for children—sumptuous picnics, for which she prepared cold lobster, turkey, and rice-and-currant salad, to celebrate a stepson's birthday; treasure hunts for the "summer" children at Bocca di Magra that often yielded an edible harvest; and every Christmas, trees strung with popcorn and cranberries and hung with candy canes and gingerbread men with raisins for faces. In *Memories of a Catholic Girlhood* she wrote that "nothing is more boring to a child than the principle of utility," and in "Everybody's Childhood," a review of Monique Wittig's *The Opoponax,* that "a child is a little robot, and the bad child in a class, like the boy who wants to show his penis to the other children or the girl who pulls a white hair out of the teacher's bun, is a bad robot, while the others are good robots. The idea of children as little individuals is far from the realities of their experience. They are all copycats by choice and necessity—witness their singsong voices, their insistence on *correcting* each other, particularly noticeable in girls.''

These perceptions seem to indicate that McCarthy is looking at children from the outside, and this apparent lack of understanding carries over into her real-life relationships with children, in spite of her having been a good mother to Reuel. Margo Viscusi, one of her two literary executors and a former part-time secretary, reveals something of Reuel's childhood attitude toward his mother when she says: "I know he feels that she was brilliant and entertaining, and probably looked after his education very well. But one feels that he would have liked her to be a little more typical mother. I'm sure she didn't bake chocolate chip cookies when he brought boys home. She probably baked chocolate soufflés because she's such a perfectionist. And they probably didn't eat standing around the kitchen. The table was laid.''

McCarthy enjoys children more when they are almost grown up. Her portrayal of Peter Levi, the likable nineteen-year-old protagonist of *Birds of America,* reveals a real understanding of an adolescent boy, and for this reason, most readers assume he is Reuel. He is not, though most certainly her empathy with the fictional teenager came from her own experience in raising a teenage boy.

When the Wests moved into their rue de Rennes apartment at the end of 1962, McCarthy was fifty years old and the mother of a twenty-four-year-old son who was teaching comparative literature at UCLA. Once again, however, she would have at least partial responsibility for small children—Daniel West was ten, Alison nine, and Jonathan seven. The children were upset at being separated from their father, whom they idolized. What made the situation even more uncomfortable was that their mother, whom they lived with in Paris, frequently made critical remarks about her former husband and his new wife. The children attended the École Alsacienne, a French day school, and two weekends a month they stayed with their father and stepmother. The rue de Rennes apartment was too small to accommodate three children so the Wests rented two successive "weekend" houses, one in the tiny village of Gourville, about an hour from Paris, and the second in Verderone. The Gourville house was small, with a separate building that had once been a bakery, where McCarthy read ghost stories and Sherlock Holmes to her stepchildren. In the winter they were sometimes snowed in, once without so much as firewood, "but we did go tramping through the snow," as McCarthy described the weekend, "making feeding stations for the birds and the children naturally adored it." The Verderone house, "which provided us, among other amenities, with floods in the cellar, heat failures, power failures, plumbing problems, moles in the lawn, short circuits, and telephone blackouts," was quite grand, especially compared with the first one. As Alison West remembers, "It was a very large manor house with a very large enclosed garden out back and high walls surrounding it. There were rows of pine trees—baby saplings—being cared for out back."

Weekends in the country with the children continued for the next five years, until their mother decided to send them to boarding school in England. During these five years in Paris they spent Christmas Day with their father and stepmother, and during the Easter holidays they would travel with them, often to Holland or England. In summer they went to Bocca di Magra, which they loved. Alison West says today that "Bocca di Magra remains one of the most paradisiac memories of my whole childhood. I remember our summers there as moments of absolutely undiluted joy. We would take a boat every morning and go around the point to a beach, and either we'd come back for lunch or have a little picnic on the beach. And every summer we would take a trip to a different city, Florence, or Rome, or Venice." During one of these summers Kevin McCarthy's two daughters spent five weeks in Bocca di Magra. Alison and the younger of the two, yet another Mary McCarthy, had been born on the same day. They became great friends. Mary Dabney McCarthy can recall in detail the sight-seeing trips that were part of the summer. "I remember going to museums with my aunt and her telling us all about everything we were seeing. I was trying to absorb it all."

In the summer of 1964 the Wests skipped Bocca di Magra because of Jim's compulsory home leave. Instead, they went back to Stonington, Connecticut, where they had gone the autumn after their marriage and where they already had frieds—Eleanor Perényi and her mother, Grace Stone (who wrote novels as Ethel Vance), David Jackson, and James Merrill, whose extra apartment McCarthy used for writing.

The Wests rented a house built in 1720 that had once been the village tavern. Being back in New England inspired McCarthy to introduce the children to American culinary art. "I've been having great cooking binges," she wrote Carmen Angleton, "baked beans and watermelon pickle and currant and raspberry jelly and huge cakes and ice-creams turned in the backyard. . . . In my mind, this is all supposed to be very beneficial for the children, opening their eyes to a new way of life." The children loved Stonington, especially the novelty of riding bicycles up and down the town's sidewalks, a pleasure unavailable in Paris or Bocca di Magra; they also enjoyed swimming, sailing, and playing tennis at the Wadawamuck Club. The club, consisting of a small single-story clubhouse, a short stretch of lawn, tennis courts, and a beach that at low tide was mostly slimy rocks, was not particularly exclusive. Even so, two members who had gone to Vassar and who resented *The Group* blackballed Mary McCarthy, thus denying admission to the family. Merrill and Jackson, knowing that McCarthy wanted a membership for the children, finally persuaded the members to let the Wests in. Their initial exclusion put them in good company. Years before, when Franklin Roosevelt was governor of New York, he and Eleanor had arrived on their boat expecting the normal privileges extended to members of similar clubs, but were turned away because one Wadawamuck member insisted they were Communists. In the case of the Wests, the club members might have been better off holding to their original censure. Predictably, McCarthy used Stonington and its inhabitants in her next novel, *Birds of America.* The first two chapters are set in the village, which she calls Rocky Port.

Despite the marvelous weekends and vacations with their father and stepmother, the children felt somewhat ill at ease, according to Alison. This was partly because her mother "did her best," Alison says, "to interfere in her children's relationship with both their father and stepmother" and partly because of their stepmother's "lack of a maternal presence." Alison concedes that "Mary was very, very conscious of the need for order in our lives and planned our holidays extremely conscientiously and made sure we had everything we wanted. And the holidays were wonderful. But I cannot say our home atmosphere was ever warm. Mary does not like little children that much. And we knew it and felt it, and, to a degree, suffered from it because it made the environment rather formal for children." The weekends in the country stopped in 1966, when the children entered boarding school, and the summers in 1968, one year after James West bought a house in Castine, Maine. All three children went to Maine in the summer of 1967, but after that, Margaret West did not allow Alison to return. The boys' summer visits grew shorter and further apart.

One reason for the formality of life in the West household had to do with McCarthy's need for a quiet time in which to work—not on the weekends, perhaps, but certainly during the summers. In Bocca di Magra, the houses available for rental were modest Italian summer homes with bare furnishings. They provided no private place for a writer to work, so Jim West tried to keep the children out of the way for at least a few hours each day. When McCarthy was desperately trying to finish *The Group,* she wrote William Jovanovich:

> I've started work here—on a rigid schedule; otherwise I'd never get anything done. We get up at seven; Jim goes to get bread and we have breakfast at seven-thirty. At ten he goes to the beach with the children; I follow at eleven or so. Then, after lunch, I work from four to six again or sometimes four to seven. All this is running splendidly, except that the children, having been warned so firmly not to bother me during the sacred hours, look at me with wide-eyed alarm, as though I were something—fire or a zoo animal—that they'd been taught not to touch.

In Stonington she rented James Merrill's extra apartment, where she spent part of each day writing. A room of her own away from domestic distraction gave her the time to begin a new novel, but for the most part she wrote reviews during these years when West's children were young. During the 1960s two collections of previously published reviews and essays appeared—*On the Contrary,* published in the United States in 1961 and in England in 1962 (and reprinted in paperback as *The Humanist in the Bathtub* in 1964); *Mary McCarthy's Theatre Chronicles 1937–1962,* published in 1963—and thirteen new reviews and essays came out, ten of them during these years with the children. (They were collected in *The Writing on the Wall,* published in 1970.)

Many people consider McCarthy's essays and criticism to be her best writing. William Shawn, who published many of her literary essays during his tenure as editor of *The New Yorker,* said in a 1981 interview, "I love her nonfiction, and I regard her essays on Venice and Florence as our finest critical pieces. They are really literary pieces as much as her other writing." McCarthy's teachers at Vassar had told her it would be as a critic that she would distinguish herself. She herself, on occasion, has revealed uneasiness about her talent as a fiction writer, even though she thinks of herself primarily as a novelist. She once told Nicola Chiaromonte that "one thing about myself as a fiction writer I've observed . . . is that I think of chapters in a novel as composed like short stories, i.e., tracing a sort of circle. Which is very unnovelistic. In real novels, for instance Dickens, a chapter doesn't come to rest at the end; on the contrary, it leaves you with unfinished business." Recently she said that writing a nonfiction book is easier than writing a short chapter of fiction. "That may mean that I have no natural talent for fiction. It must mean

that, or that it isn't at least as accessible to me as the other. But I prefer, in the end, writing fiction because you're creating something that wasn't there before."

She feels certain, though, that her literary criticism has enabled her to turn out serious fiction. "Criticism teaches you to express yourself clearly, with some pungency. It teaches you to organize your emotions." Yet many critics of her fiction think that the critic in her gets in the way of the novelist. Her novels are essayistic, those critics contend; they are nothing more than dramatized theses. Her career, in Van Wyck Brooks's opinion, has been that of an essayist who also writes novels. William Barrett thinks this is because the intellectual impulse in her fiction "takes such a grip of her that it finally stifles the life out of her characters. This is the only reason to explain why her novels and stories are not greater than they are; they have every other gift—wit, sharp observation, extraordinary intelligence, an unflagging brilliance and elegance of language; they lack only the the simple virtue of feeling."

She herself recognizes a conflict between the novelist, whose job it is to impose shape on a mass of particulars without sacrificing their particularity, and the essayist, who is a synthesizer, eliminating all loose ends. If the critic in her impedes her fiction, the artist in her enchances her criticism. Since she is first of all a novelist, it is natural that she would care about how novels are made. Three essays in *On the Contrary,* "Settling the Colonel's Hash," "The Fact in Fiction," and "Characters in Fiction," state unequivocally her position on how a good novel is made. Its images "belong, as it were to a family," she writes in "Settling the Colonel's Hash," "very closely knit and inseparable from each other; the parent 'idea' of a . . . novel generates events and images all bearing a strong family resemblance. And to understand . . . a novel, you must look for the parent 'idea,' which is usually in plain view, if you read quite carefully and literally what the author says." In "The Fact in Fiction" she argues that "the staple ingredient" of good novels is a "heavy dosage of fact," and in "Characters in Fiction" she deals with the voice-and-point-of-view issue, maintaining that "the power of the author to speak in his own voice or through the undisguised voice" of the hero is what gave nineteenth century fiction its memorable characters, but today, when the author plays the ventriloquist, who speaks in an assumed voice, there is a noticeable "languishing of the characters."

Not only do these pronouncements describe her own method of writing, but they also provide a key to understanding her method of literary analysis. The essays in *The Writing on the Wall* about works by Shakespeare, Nabokov, Salinger, Burroughs, Flaubert, Compton-Bur-

nett, and Orwell, among others, illustrate this method. She gets behind
or underneath the written surface of a book by laboriously mining it for
its meaning. "Everybody's Childhood," her review of Monique Wittig's
The Opoponax (published in France in 1964 and translated into English
in 1966), is an apt sample of her method.

Crucial to an understanding of what Monique Wittig is up to,
McCarthy contends, is a recognition of exactly how she uses pronouns
and verb tenses. *The Opoponax* consists of Catherine Legrand's memories
of her Catholic girlhood from nursery school to high school, revealed
in fragments that convey an immediacy of sensation. Monique Wittig as
Catherine Legrand remembers as a third person indefinite (which has no
equivalent in English), but never as a first or third person singular. In
French, the third person indefinite, *on,* "is impersonal, indefinite, abstract, neutral, guarded," McCarthy writes. "It is myself and everybody
in a given collective at a given time. . . . *On ne fait pas de ski aujourd'hui.
On fait le calcul. On s'ennuie.* There wasn't any skiing today. We did our
arithmetic. It's boring here." In *The Opoponax* the narrative voice lies
between the "I" and the "she," thus avoiding the intimate subjectivity
of one and the distanced objectivity of the other. And, according to
McCarthy, Wittig's

> technical experiment, asking an epistemological question about the nature
> and limits of memory, has led to a genuine finding. . . . Catherine Legrand
> is not a fictional alias or transparent disguise for Monique Wittig: she is
> a conjecture about an earlier Monique Wittig. It is clear that between
> "me" remembering and my previous self, there is a separation, . . . so that
> if I write "I" for both, I am slurring over an unsettling reality.

It was Monique Wittig's inspiration to express that uncertainty in narrative terms with the *on,* the French indefinite pronoun.

Another peculiarity of *The Opoponax,* according to McCarthy, is that
it is written entirely in the present tense, which is different from the
narrative present in English. As McCarthy points out:

> The narrative present in English is used for what the manuals call "vivid-
> ness," and it is probably more American than English. "I come into the
> room. I see this guy with a gun. He jumps me." But we do not use it
> habitually; the French do.

A third peculiarity of Wittig's novel is the absence of any transitions to
show time sequence. This, combined with Wittig's use of the indefinite

pronoun and the present tense, has led to a new insight into childhood. As McCarthy describes it:

> The indefinite pronoun proves to be a key that unlocks more doors than may have been expected on the first try. The *on* not only marks a neutral relation between author and material: it marks a neutral relation of the child to herself. Combined with the static present and the monotone of the run-on paragraphs, it reveals that to be a child is not at all a simple, spontaneous thing. To be a child is something one learns, as one learns the names of rivers or the kings of France. Childhood, for a child, is a sort of falseness, woodenness, stoniness, a lesson recited. Many children are aware of this—that is, aware of being children as a special, prosy condition: "We can't do that! We're *children!*" Playing children is a long boring game with occasional exciting moments. It is obvious that children imitate adults and other children: that is known as learning. But the full force of this has not been shown, at least in fiction or autobiography, until *The Opoponax.*

"Everybody's Childhood" shows why McCarthy's review-essays are at the same time sensible and interesting. When she dissects someone's work, she knows what she is talking about, since she has dissected her own fiction the same way. She told the Danish translator of *The Group* that when she had finished each chapter of the novel, she wrote pages of questions, "asking why this, why that, what does it mean." And later, in an interview with Edwin Newman, she said that any writer has to "try to find out what he is saying. A wrong word or phrase tells you what you are saying is not true, but often it is hard to find out why." So, when she reviews a book, she uncovers another writer's narrative technique as she watches him or her grappling with the same narrative problem she has faced, and, as in the case of *The Opoponax,* she rejoices when a novelist has found an ingenious solution.

It was McCarthy's literary criticism that first attracted writer Doris Grumbach to her. In May 1964 Grumbach wrote an essay for *Commonweal* about why there are no great women novelists, and in it she liberally quoted from McCarthy's "The Fact in Fiction." On the basis of this article, an editor at Coward-McCann asked her to write a book about McCarthy's writing. In October 1965, when she was two-thirds finished with *The World of Mary McCarthy,* as the book was tentatively titled— later, at McCarthy's suggestion, it became *The Company She Kept*—she asked McCarthy for an interview. "My policy has been to stay as far from hearsay, gossip, and the usual bilious tittle-tattle of friends and former friends as I could," she said.

> In fact, I have spoken to no one who knows you or knew you. My aim was, and is, to use what you've written, and what has been written about you and your work (a nice mélange of misinterpretation, misreading, and plain deafness), as evidence of your status as critic and novelist. I had thought it possible, and desirable, to avoid you too, but there are the purely factual questions I can settle or answer in no other way except to ask you.

The women met in early January 1966 at McCarthy's Paris apartment. The Wests, with children, had just gotten home after spending the Christmas holidays at William Mostyn-Owen's castle in Scotland. Grumbach interviewed her subject for a few hours one afternoon, using a tape recorder, and later mailed the transcript of the interview to McCarthy for corrections. Since she wanted to use material from the tapes verbatim, she needed clarification of several subjects they had discussed. Reading the transcripts, McCarthy was alarmed. In the interview, she did what she has so often done before and since: having started talking, she got carried away, revealing more than she intended. She wrote back:

> I must tell you that I am worried about the future destiny of this interview. My understanding was that we were doing it for background for your book. But *not for publication.* It's evident that if it were published, a number of people could sue me for libel (or is it slander on tape?), and in fact could sue you too and your publisher. . . . Other people could be wounded. Having met you, I feel I can trust your discretion . . . trust you, that is, not to quote things that I wouldn't want quoted.

McCarthy drew up a list of imprudent disclosures recorded on the tapes that she did not want to appear in Grumbach's book, and then left it up to Grumbach not to quote "some things I may say later in this letter as well." Having said that, she drew up a year-by-year chronology of her life, including, again, a few more startling revelations. Grumbach wrote back, assuring McCarthy that she had no intention of using anything on the tapes except such innocuous information as publication dates, places of residence, and the like. "Let me rush to put your mind at ease," she wrote. "I have *no* intention of using . . . any of the portions which you feel might be libelous." Although mollified, McCarthy was still uneasy. She wrote Grumbach that it was "strange to have a book written about

yourself in your lifetime. I mean a book that included you as a person, not just a critical analysis of your writings."

Coward-McCann sent McCarthy the page proofs early in September. At the time, she had been shaken by the news of her brother Sheridan's death and by the sudden decision of West's former wife to take her children out of school in Paris and put them in boarding school in England. Although the children's absence would eliminate the necessity of renting a country house for weekends, the move upset both Mary and Jim West. Not until she arrived in Basel for a visit with Hannah Arendt at the end of September did she read the galleys of *The Company She Kept.* She did not like what she read. She was alarmed to find that Grumbach had reported unkind remarks about people that she had made on tape, intimate details of her life and her husbands' lives, and details of her love affair with West, although she admitted to William Jovanovich that she had given Grumbach "a sad mixture of confidences and dry chronology."

She wrote Grumbach immediately. "My biography has lost its specificity, as you recount it; it might as well be the life of Brigitte Bardot, 'as told to . . . ,' the lowdown. And the lowdown is low." But she complimented Grumbach on her literary judgments, especially the long and well-written analysis of *The Group.* "This is certainly the best thing *anyone* has done about it. As for your earlier observation—that Vassar is the heroine—I'm not sure I agree, but it is an arresting thought." McCarthy marked the galleys so that Grumbach and her publisher could see what she objected to as being too personal, and sent them to New York.

Coward-McCann had also sent Edmund Wilson a set of galleys; he became very angry at his former wife. "He calmed down somewhat," McCarthy told Hannah Arendt, "when he learned I had not authorized these revelations. He's hoping to stop publication of those sections of the book that deal with our marriage." Wilson told McCarthy that "it is very dangerous to let people make tape recordings." In October, McCarthy consulted William Jovanovich, who turned the matter over to a lawyer. "I think we must try to use persuasion at this stage," Jovanovich wrote McCarthy. He warned her, though, that "a tremendous lot of damage was done—. . . your unfortunate candor in the course of the interview; your subsequent correspondence, including the long biographical letter; the marking up of the galleys and their return *before* you consulted a lawyer, etc. etc." When the matter was settled, not until the end of the year, only ten or twelve paragraphs in the entire book were changed or eliminated.

The episode illustrates how McCarthy's directness and openness get her in trouble. Once she had agreed to be interviewed, she conversed for four hours with a perfect stranger while a tape recorder preserved every word, and then, despite concern over the disposition of the tapes, supplied a single-spaced eleven-page letter in which she listed exact dates of crucial events in her life, including the specifics of early sexual experience. "Why did she put that in," Grumbach wondered. "Clearly because . . . she considered all precise details, *facts,* necessary for a complete portrait. Page 2 of the chronology, however, warned me that this was as far as she intended to go. 'Here,' she wrote, 'veil drawn sexual history.' Not that she *did.* There is something compulsively frank [about McCarthy]."

There is, indeed, and her frankness no doubt confused Grumbach, who, despite cautionary notes from McCarthy about what not to quote, assumed that if her subject supplied the information, she was free to use it. McCarthy was truly surprised that Grumbach's galleys included remarks about Edmund Wilson's drinking; about McCarthy family members, whom she had no desire to hurt; and about her own extramarital affair with West, whose children, she felt, could be harmed by such a revelation. "You reassured me, after sending the tapes," McCarthy had written Grumbach, "that this material was for 'background' only. Now this background has astonishingly become the foreground. It seems plain to me that you have a high sense of rectitude, so I can only think that you have acted in good faith, though without much judgment." Today McCarthy says she cannot understand "how Grumbach justified what she did in her own eyes." She still maintains that Grumbach explicitly promised not to publish intimate personal remarks from the tapes—indeed, the tapes were to be sealed for twenty years.

Grumbach contended that McCarthy enjoys "confession of the frankest kind. And this she knows about herself. 'I talk too much,' she admitted when she saw the transcript. 'Unfortunately I am not discreet, and I do not seem to learn,' she said when she wrote to tell me how horrified she was with the galleys."

McCarthy does have a need to "get everything down" accurately, a manifestation of the meticulousness and honesty of her nature and of a natural tendency that forbids her to hold anything back. It is this same compulsion that forces Martha Sinnott in *A Charmed Life* to confess to Dolly all her actions and impulses, no matter how incriminating.

> "One more thing," said Martha hurriedly, in an offhand tone but holding her friend's gaze. "About the baby. It occurred to me that the reason I wanted one was because of them." Dolly dropped her eyes. "You mean

the Murphys," she muttered, staring at the floor. Martha nodded. "They have a baby. I want a better one."

This candor—recording the kind of perverse thoughts most people entertain at one time or other, but never give voice to or admit to having had, even to themselves—is one of the characteristics that makes her fiction memorable.

McCarthy's frankness is another trait of the rebel who loves to shock. People who do not know her well, and sometimes even those who do, are often astonished by what she will say about herself. Sometimes, though, she makes a revelation, such as telling Grumbach when she lost her virginity, and then regrets it. She explained why in a letter to Grumbach. "If I tell you, say, that I lost my virginity at the age of fourteen in a Marmon roadster," McCarthy wrote, "this remains at the level of a gossip column unless I tell you more. Which would be too long a story. Unless I were to tell it myself in writing. The bare fact itself is embarrassing; it is, precisely, naked." Nonetheless, she provided this bare, naked fact for a writer writing about her. (Twenty years later, in *How I Grew*, she did tell the story herself.)

The Company She Kept was published in early 1967 to unenthusiastic reviews. Ellen Moers in *The New York Times Book Review* criticized Grumbach for having "made little effort to cross the 'faint line' between biography and fiction. The 'facts' of her portrait are mostly lifted from the McCarthy works, in ample quotation." Grumbach, in an accompanying article entitled "The Subject Objected," defended her book and actions. "The end of the affair . . . came when I realized how highly autobiographical a fiction writer she was, and I felt the need to document this realization."

CHAPTER XX

VIETNAM
(1966–1973)

*T*HE *COMPANY SHE KEPT* had been commissioned because of the runaway success of *The Group*. To McCarthy's mind, Grumbach's book was just another example of the mixed blessings of fame. *The Group*'s notoriety pleased Mary McCarthy in at least one sense, however: it gave her an immense audience that she felt might listen to her about what she saw as the immoral American military presence in Vietnam. She would be disappointed; few of her readers paid attention to her books about the war. Yet years after the last American had left Saigon, she said that when a girl in Harvard Square thanked her for what she had written, "that was a delicious high point of my career."

American involvement in the Vietnam War began under President Eisenhower, was stepped up under President Kennedy, and accelerated under President Johnson until, by the mid-1960s, there were more than half a million American soldiers in a country the size of California. Although escalation of the war brought about unprecedented broad public criticism in the United States, the majority of Americans still supported the administration's policies in Vietnam, including the bombing of North Vietnam when it began in the winter of 1965.

Mary McCarthy was convinced by this time of the war's immorality and futility. She looked for ways to persuade Americans that the government's conduct of the war was wicked. During the duration of the war she conceived of, and rejected, several improbable schemes—prevail upon the pope to intervene, practice tax refusal, convince prominent Americans to go to Hanoi to witness the bombing in order to make the point that civilians were being killed by the American air strikes. But what she could best do as a writer, she realized, was to write. Thus, when Robert Silvers, the editor of *The New York Review of Books,* asked her in the spring of 1966 to go to Vietnam for the magazine, she was fired with the idea of doing *something.* Her husband, officially a State Department officer, although still on loan to the OECD, decided he would have to resign if she went. But he had three children to support; McCarthy refused to go. Three quarters of a year later, Silvers tried again. West reconsidered the need to resign, deciding that the State Department would have to fire him if it objected that strongly.

So it was that McCarthy wrote Carmen Angleton on January 7, 1967, to ask if Angleton would like to go to Saigon. "I've been chafing for nearly a year against a sense of impotence in this emergency, have dreamed of practicing tax refusal and been restrained by the thought of Jim. But he now feels that as a writer and a citizen I have the right to go and see what is going on there, whether I am married to a foreign-service officer or not." Recognizing her journey as "a betrayal of Peter Levi," the hero of *Birds of America,* which she had started in Stonington in the summer of 1964, she wrote William Jovanovich that she would go to Saigon. "You are perhaps not surprised since you must have noticed how agitated I've been about this topic."

The American ambassador to France, Charles "Chip" Bohlen, whom McCarthy knew socially, was helpful to her, although he disapproved of her attitude toward the war. He arranged for her to be issued a passport in her own name so that she would not have to use her diplomatic one; he obtained State Department permission for her to go to North Viet-nam (she would not use this clearance until 1968); he notified American diplomats in Saigon to expect her arrival; he sent a message of introduc-tion to Henry Cabot Lodge, the American ambassador to South Viet-nam; and he suggested that she be briefed on the official American position before she left for Asia. McCarthy wrote about Bohlen's cooper-ation:

> The fact that I was who I was and the wife of a U. S. diplomat (almost like a member of the family) no doubt made a difference but that is the way the world works everywhere. Or not quite. Had I been the wife of a Soviet official, announcing that I was going abroad to criticize Kremlin imperial-ism, my husband would have joined me within a matter of days in a camp or a madhouse.

She was fairly certain that Bohlen "enjoyed the wry humor of harboring a viper in his official bosom. That was very American too."

In preparation for leaving, Mary McCarthy drew up a will. She left jewelry and books—objects of sentiment, really—to those close to her, such as Hannah Arendt, Carmen Angleton, Angélique Levi (now her French translator), Miriam Chiaromonte, Kevin's children, and Jim's children, in a manner that typifies her femininity, her love of friends, and her habit of close observation.

> But I had fun making my will, especially with the bequests of jewelry and art objects. Would the jacinthe and brown topazes be good with Hannah's eyes? And Carmen—the seed-pearl bracelet we had chosen together, with

the little insets of sapphires and diamonds. The fire opal? Anjo. Miriam—
the diamond-and-pearl earrings from Bucellati. My grandmother's diamond wristwatch with the red and blue figures? Perhaps that should stay
in the family. So one of Kevin's daughters? My daughter-in-law, Marcia
[Reuel's wife] would get the Polish lavallière. Jim's daughter, Alison, the
thin Polish bracelet with the sapphires. It was like picking out presents,
which I love doing, and the men as usual were harder.

Most of her "beneficiaries" urged her not to go. She would make a
fool of herself, they said. She disagreed, and anyway, "if I did, it did not
seem to me important either to my career (something I had never cared
about) or to the anti-war movement." Her friends tried other arguments
to dissuade her—it was dangerous; she was not a journalist; professional
newsmen would snub her. She argued that "readers put perhaps not
more trust but a different kind of trust in the perceptions of writers they
know as novelists from what they give to the press's 'objective' reporting
or political scientists' documented and figure-buttressed analyses."
Moreover, "one does what one knows how to do. And I know how to
write, so I do that." Besides, she felt she had an advantage over many
journalists in being fluent in French, which would be especially useful
for what she intended to do, namely, "to describe what is known as the
American presence in Saigon. And meet the South Vietnamese intellectuals, who are French-speaking and hence unreachable by most Americans there."

As it turned out, the newspapermen in Saigon were helpful and
friendly. "The Baltimore *Sun* lent me his army jacket and cap," she
writes in *The Seventeenth Degree;* "the New York *Times* let me take a hot
bath in his bathtub, *Time* organized a meeting with students, *Newsweek*
got me a hotel room and met me at the airport, Agence France Presse
drove me to the airport when I left." Several, Thomas Buckley of *The
New York Times,* William Tuohy of the *Los Angeles Times,* and Jonathan
Randal of *The Washington Post,* became good friends. They marveled
that she was not at all like her reputation; in fact, they found her endear-
ing and "little-girlish" in the way she was always grateful for the least
thing. She frequently had drinks with them on the big porch of the large,
antiquated Continental Palace Hotel, where she stayed, along with many
other journalists.

On the way back to Paris, she stopped off in Cambodia to see the
temple of Angkor Wat and the other temples around Siem Reap. She
said she did not enjoy the trip owing to the immaturity and volatility of
so many Cambodians. "They were very nervous-making to be around,"

she later recalled. "They were always trying to get you to change money on the black market. . . . They'd rush into my room, and one of them went right into the shower, waving, screaming, 'your passport.' . . . The whole thing was fraught with uneasiness on my part caused by their childish hysteria." When she got home, she had been gone a month. The three articles she wrote for *The New York Review of Books* appeared in April and May 1967; Harcourt, Brace & World republished them, plus a fourth, entitled "Solutions," the following November as *Vietnam*. She described no military operations and ignored politics. She wrote instead about the effect of Americans on the South Vietnamese. She depicted in depressing detail the ruin that American soldiers and civilians were inflicting on this tiny country.

> As we drove into downtown Saigon, through a traffic jam, I had the fresh shock of being in what looked like an American city, a very shoddy West Coast one, with a Chinatown and a slant-eyed Asiatic minority. Not only military vehicles of every description, but Chevrolets, Chryslers, Mercedes-Benz, Volkswagens, Triumphs, and white men everywhere in sports shirts and drip-dry pants. The civilian take-over is even more astonishing than the military. . . . New office buildings of cheap modern design, teeming with teazed, puffed secretaries and their Washington bosses, are surrounded by sandbags and guarded by M.P.'s; new jerry-built villas in pastel tones, to rent to Americans, are under construction or already beginning to peel and discolor.

Saigon, she concluded, resembled a gigantic PX. McCarthy met Vietnamese students and intellectuals, and she trekked in baggy fatigues (lent her by one of her husband's former colleagues in the USIA) into refugee villages, hospitals, and a leper colony in Hue. She recounted these experiences in a chilling chronicle studded with gruesome and unforgettable vignettes. One told of a pilot who, while directing a bombing mission, spotted a lone Vietnamese on a bicycle. The Southeast Asian stopped, dismounted, took up a rifle, and fired. The pilot retaliated with a bombload of napalm—"enough for a platoon."

McCarthy wrote that American soldiers were able to act with such brutality because they used language that obfuscated the reality of war. Thus, enemy actions were "atrocities"; American atrocities were "accidents"; Napalm became "Incinder-jell," which made it sound like Jell-O. Worse than these euphemisms was the language of the American political scientists, "who have stamped their vocabulary and their habits of thought on this loony trial of strength in the Asian arena. The worst of all is the terrible removal of morality from the whole affair by this separation of words from their meaning"—observations that Simone Weil and George Orwell had made so eloquently in the 1940s, but obviously with little effect.

> It is peculiar that the academic experts who have been studying guerrilla techniques, Communism, "wars of liberation" for nearly two decades have been unable to face the question of intention in this kind of warfare, where combatants and noncombatants are all but inseparable, while U.S. means of killing and exterminating have been reaching a point close to perfection. Foreknowledge of the consequences of an action that is then performed generally argues the will to do it; if this occurs repeatedly, and the doer continues to protest that he did not will the consequences, that suggests an extreme and dangerous dissociation of the personality. Is that what is happening with the Americans in Vietnam, where words, as if "accidentally," have broken loose from their common meanings, where the Viet Cong guerrilla is pictured as a man utterly at one with his grenade, which fits him like an extension of his body, and the American, on the other hand, is pictured as completely sundered from his precision weaponry, as though he had no control over it, in the same way that Johnson, escalating, feigns to have no option in the war and to react, like an automat, to "moves" from Hanoi?

Finally, McCarthy urged the withdrawal of American troops from Vietnam. Her answer to those who insisted that America must find an honorable exit was simply that there was "no honorable exit from a shameful course of action. . . . The country needs to understand that the war is wrong, and the sole job of the opposition should be to enforce that understanding."

Diana Trilling disagreed, and gave vent to that disagreement in *The New York Review of Books.* The January 18, 1968, cover announced the exchange that took place between the two intellectuals in a heavy black headline: "Diana Trilling vs. Mary McCarthy." Trilling said that withdrawal would "consign untold numbers of Southeast Asian opponents of Communism to their death and countless more to the abrogation of the right of protest which we American intellectuals hold so dear." McCarthy answered by reiterating her position. She concluded that

> if as a result of my ill-considered actions, world Communism comes to power, it will be too late then, I shall be told, to be sorry. Never mind. Some sort of life will continue, as Pasternak, Solzhenitsyn, Sinayavsky, Daniel have discovered, and I would rather be on their letterhead, if they

would allow me, than on that of the American Committee for Cultural Freedom, which in its days of glory, as Mrs. Trilling will recall, was . . . actually divided within its ranks on the question of whether Senator Joseph McCarthy was a friend or enemy of domestic liberty.

But few heeded, or even heard of, McCarthy's protest. Although she understood that at the time she wrote the Vietnam articles "only a minority [was] *interested* in the war," she was unprepared for the silence which followed the publication of *Vietnam.* "My publisher was absolutely thunderstruck," she disclosed on William F. Buckley, Jr.'s "Firing Line." "He had never seen a case of a book on a controversial subject by a well-known author—this was after the success of *The Group*—that received virtually no notice." Buckley suggested the reviewers ignored *Vietnam* because "they thought it was preposterous."

Intellectuals, who did not need awakening, seemed to be the only persons listening to her. The editors of *Tempo Presente,* the Italian magazine sponsored by the Congress for Cultural Freedom, and an Italian publisher, Giangiacomo Feltrinelli, to cite two examples, decided to publish her Vietnam articles; because Nicola Chiaromonte, one of the two *Tempo Presente* editors, translated them, they were to appear in *Tempo Presente* first. But a scandal concerning the magazine's financial backing caused Feltrinelli to withdraw his offer of book publication. *Tempo Presente,* as well as *Der Monat* in Germany, *Encounter* in England, and *Preuves* in France, the best of the magazines sponsored by the Congress for Cultural Freedom, were partly financed by CIA funds, according to a story that had appeared in *Ramparts* in 1966. The Congress for Cultural Freedom, it turned out, was a device for channeling money from the CIA to these journals. The CIA, covertly dispensing money to foundations that subsidized the magazines, gave intellectuals a means of expression. Since the founders of the Congress for Cultural Freedom were anti-Stalinists, their views corresponded in some way to official United States policy. Thus the CIA allowed these intellectuals to publish anything they liked. But when the CIA scandal broke, nearly everyone connected with the magazines, especially their editors, was indignant at having been deceived. Nicola Chiaromonte responded more temperately. "The firm point is (as far as the magazines are concerned) that the editors, insofar as they were in good faith, are responsible for what they did publish or did not publish, and not for anything else: a problem of where the money came from is only relevant if they (the editors) submitted to pressures from the CIA, which I don't think was the case." Mary McCarthy agreed and sent Chiaromonte a letter affirming her solidarity "with *Tempo Pre-*

sente and with its editors, who have published, as I can testify as a subscriber, a magazine of unique independence and freedom of thought, whose policy, far from being dictated by the CIA or any other agency, has been hostile to all the organizational pressures, both political and commercial, of modern western society on the intellectual in its midst." At the same time, her Italian publisher remained adamant; he wanted nothing to do with any magazine financed by the CIA, so if McCarthy published the Vietnam articles in *Tempo Presente,* he would not do a book. She kept faith with Nicola Chiaromonte and *Tempo Presente.*

When Mary McCarthy had finished the articles for *The New York Review of Books* at the end of April, she went back to work on *Birds of America.* William Jovanovich, who stopped in Paris on his way back to New York after five days with Milovan Djilas in Belgrade, was pleased. Later in the spring McCarthy paid a visit to Sonia Orwell in London, and she helped Angélique Levi with the French translation of *A Charmed Life.* At the end of June she and West went to America on home leave. They stayed with Kevin in New York and enjoyed a brief reunion with Kevin and Mary's brother Preston McCarthy at the wedding of a niece, the daughter of their deceased brother, Sheridan. Then the Wests left for Castine, Maine, where they had just purchased a home. "Bit by bit," she wrote later,

> Vietnam had altered the pattern of our lives. Not only had I turned into a part-time itinerant journalist, with longish absences, separation, but our summer holidays were now spent in a new geography. Until Vietnam seized us, we used to go to Italy, on the Ligurian coast. . . . But in 1967 we bought the house in Maine. That was right after I had come back from South Vietnam, and one of our motives was the war: if I was going to take a stand against U.S. policy, I ought to have a piece of U.S. ground under my feet. . . . We always cited it to ourselves as an argument in favor of buying (sight unseen in my case), along with other arguments—that Jim came from Maine and was homesick for it, that he had to have some place to spend compulsory home leave, that the house was beautiful, that he could pass it on to his children—balancing all these against the cost, the distance, the fact that most years we would be able to occupy it for only a month or six weeks. . . . On the Fourth of July, he showed me into the house. . . . It is strange to think that because of our hateful foreign policy I have been, so to speak, repatriated. Now I share with Jim a cemetery lot overlooking Penobscot Bay.

Mary McCarthy was delighted with Castine, which she called "a real Fourth-of-July New England village." Located at the tip of a peninsula formed by the junction of the Bagaduce and Penobscot rivers, Castine had experienced its greatest growth in the early nineteenth century, when most of its Federal homes were built. One of these is the Wests' house, built in 1805 and standing on Main Street, which slopes down to Penobscot Bay. Its clapboard facade, which they painted yellow— "we've struck a bold note on Castine's black and white piano keyboard: the outside, which was white this morning, is turning pale yellow"— boasts a typical Federal Palladian window above a handsome doorway with elaborate fan and sidelights—all framed by a pediment and columns. In the foyer is a dramatic and unusual freestanding bifurcate staircase. "Workmen are swarming all over the house," she wrote William Jovanovich, but "we're restraining ourselves about interior improvements—only the hall and library."

Life in Castine was quiet and pleasant. With the Lowells, who lived nearby, and other similarly inclined summer residents, they formed a little Cercle Français that met every Saturday night to read Pascal or Montaigne or Molière. Inviting houseguests—in this first summer the Jovanovichs and their Stonington friends came—would provide something of the community life they had enjoyed for several years in Bocca di Magra. At the end of September they made a quick trip to Montreal's Expo '67 to visit the OECD Pavilion, then stayed at the Lowells' apartment in New York before sailing for Europe on the *United States.*

In January and February 1968 the Communists launched large-scale attacks in South Vietnam, causing heavy damage and loss of life. The Tet offensive, as this nationwide onslaught came to be called, and the earlier Communist attack on the U. S. marine base at Khe Sanh marked the beginning of the end of American involvement in Vietnam. By mid-February a Gallop poll showed that 50 percent of the public disapproved of President Johnson's war policy, while only 35 percent approved. On February 14 the administration budgeted $32 billion for the war for fiscal year 1969; on the fifteenth the Air Force reported the loss of the eight hundredth aircraft over North Vietnam; on the twentieth the Senate Foreign Relations Committee began public hearings challenging the necessity of the war; on the twenty-second the Army announced the highest weekly total of American combat deaths—543; on the twenty-fifth General Westmoreland requested an additional 206,000 troops. Walter Cronkite, who had been called "the most trusted man in America," said the war was a stalemate and that negotiation was the only way out.

Mary McCarthy avidly followed all the news from Asia and America. "Jim has taken to bringing home *The Guardian,*" she wrote Robert

Lowell, "as well as the *Herald Tribune* and the *Monde* every day, and I feel compelled to read in it the same stories . . . that I have read in the other papers and will read in *Time, Newsweek,* the English weeklies (now including *The Listener*), the French weeklies, and *The New York Review of Books* and *The New Republic.* This appears to me as a kind of duty, like eating raw vegetables, but it's probably a mere vicious habit. On a particularly 'hot' day, like yesterday (U. S. Embassy in Saigon invaded; Air Force bombing Saigon), he also brings home streams of Reuter's teletype from the office." A few days later she wrote Elizabeth Hardwick, "Here the Viet Cong offensive is almost the exclusive topic. Our little Sony TV set has come out of the closet and is staying on the living-room table. . . . I'm uneasy about Khe Sanh; the dangerous position of the Americans there has had too much advance publicity. Some Americans, peaceniks, and other foreigners here are saying that this will be the Army's excuse to introduce tactical nuclear weapons: they have set up the trap for themselves." (Michael Maclear in *The Ten Thousand Day War* states that General Westmoreland had considered using tactical nuclear weapons at Khe Sanh and had even established a secret group to study the possibility, but Washington ordered him to desist.)

Besides reading, talking, even dreaming, about events in Vietnam, McCarthy went to draft-resistance meetings, but was disillusioned by the "mixture of total incoherence and dead clichés" resorted to by the resisters. James Jones assured her that linguistic ineptitude was characteristic of this generation of youth; that was what education had done to them. The principal respite from her Vietnam-related activity was a twelve-day trip to Sicily over New Year's. As she wrote Robert Lowell:

> It's not like Italy at all but more, in a way, like North Africa. All those earthquakes are part of it, and Etna, as though there were fettered titans underneath, . . . in itself looks Arabic or anyway Eastern—so much white and silvery olive trees. Though there are some vineyards, Sicily isn't a grape country: oranges, lemons, prickly pears, almonds, and probably figs in season. Mohammedan fruits. And strange green cauliflowers. . . . In places, it's like a boneyard of past civilizations and geology—so much broken stone in the fields and then the detritus of Greek temples, colossal.

Meanwhile, American deserters and resisters had been flocking to Paris. Few of them spoke French, and even those who learned were unable to get work papers. Most Americans who had been living in the city believed "that Paris will be hell for most of these kids," McCarthy wrote Elizabeth Hardwick.

American firms, who no doubt wouldn't be very sympathetic anyway, are moving out and firing people. The American churches are either supporting the war or disapprove of "illegal" acts of protest, though one minister, faced with some homeless kids, might help. And the French aren't a benevolent or charitable people. Hence consternation. All of this, of course, including my own reaction, has its comic side, ready-made for a satirical play. We may oppose the war but we're not eager to turn our houses into hostels for war-resisters. But with all allowances made for selfishness and hypocrisy in my own concern and alarm, . . . I feel an immense yearning for action.

The chance for action came in March. In the fall of 1967 she had asked the North Vietnamese for authorization to go to Hanoi to write about conditions there. By February 1968 she had despaired of gaining admission. It was frustrating because she had already obtained American permission the year before, when she went to Saigon. Moreover, Harcourt, Brace had offered to finance the trip, even though whatever she wrote would appear in *The New York Review of Books* first. To her delight and astonishment, she received an invitation from Hanoi on March 1. Within days she had made all the necessary preparations, including letters to Chiaromonte to state her reason for the trip, to the Lowells to announce her intention of making Elizabeth one of her literary executors, and to her husband (to be read after she had gone) to give advice to those left behind.

She was going, she told West, to write an account of "what it is like there now" and "to tell the reader of bombing of hospitals, schools, etc. . . . Not being a political authority, I have to use what authority I have, which is that of an observer and narrator. In my opinion, manifestos and demonstrations and marches have become almost counter-productive." (Later, during a television debate with *Daily Mail* columnist Bernard Levin, she would say that Zola's pamphlet "J'accuse," which charged the French government with having framed the Jewish officer Dreyfus, would not have influenced events "if Zola had been signing manifestos every other day like Sartre and Simone de Beauvoir.") "Since this letter is taking on a testamentary character, I'll conclude with a parting piece of advice to the Left. The teach-in principle was good; extend it. Take it into factories and offices. And granges where there are still farmers. It's a very American thing, based on the idea of educability—universal education. . . . Thank you for your love and goodness—the golden fleece of your warm, sweet nature. I wish you well." The tone of this four-page letter is stiff and sermonizing, unlike her usual witty, warm, and informal letter-writing style, indicating a real concern that she would not return from Hanoi. The letter sounds like something she could imagine being printed in a newspaper story of her death by bombing.

The night before departure, the Wests invited novelist James Jones, Princeton professor Joseph Frank, and lawyer David DuVivier and their wives for dinner. The next day the DuViviers drove McCarthy to Le Bourget Airport. After lunch, she took off, "shaking in my boots, almost literally," she wrote Kevin.

The Wests kept in touch by cable and letters. Mary wrote from Athens, only hours after saying goodbye in Paris, that her plane had been grounded by bad weather. She wrote two more letters on the plane from Athens to Phnom Penh, where she was held up once again by bad weather. Time passed agreeably in Cambodia, thanks to two invitations to dinner at the British ambassador's. Finally, she left for Vientiane, Laos, on an old propeller-driven Convair jammed with Poles, Indians, a few Cambodians, and the Yugoslav ambassador to Laos. In Vientiane, the plane was grounded due to a faulty radio before it could go on to Hanoi.

Expecting a protracted delay in Vientiane, she registered at the Million Elephants Hotel, where she ran into one of her husband's colleagues from the American Embassy in Paris. The hotel was full of Americans, including U.S. Air Force pilots who, according to the Laotians, were flying food and supply drops for the U.S. Aid Mission in Laos. The next day, told to return to Phnom Penh at once unless she could secure a visa (her transit pass had expired), she turned to her husband's embassy friend for help. Although it was Saturday, he obtained permission for her to stay. That afternoon she attended a state tennis match in which the Crown Prince participated. "All this is so musical-comedy-like or Shavian in contrast to the bombers pounding just across the border," she wrote West. That night she went to a charity ball given by the French ambassador. The next night she had dinner with the Japanese novelist Seicho Matsumoto, whose daughter was married to a member of the Japanese delegation to the OECD. They ate at a Chinese restaurant on a porch that overlooked the Mekong River, and he told her he had been waiting in Vientiane for three weeks, regularly boarding the plane for Hanoi and then having to turn back.

Mary McCarthy had been away from her husband for a week and had not heard a word from him. "You can't telephone to Europe from Vientiane—only as far as Bangkok. Otherwise I'd have called you long ago," she wrote. No sooner had she mailed this letter than she received a cable from West. She was relieved that news of him had reached her, "bringing with it your warm, gay, virile presence." On March 18, a week and a day after leaving Paris, she went shopping for the West children, buying coins for Jonathan and stamps for Daniel, but finding nothing suitable for Alison. She met the prime minister, Prince Souvanna Phouma, the same day. She had written eleven letters in the eight days she had been gone, and every one of them expressed her love for James West—"love all the pockets in your nature"; "miss you horribly"; "I cling to you"; "so long as you are *there* and I know it, I'm happy"; "I am madly, crazily in love with my husband"; "I love you more all the time."

After four days in Vientiane, she finally got to board the International Control Commission plane on March 19. The ICC plane flew, weather permitting, six times a month between Vientiane and Hanoi. The old Convair circled above darkened Hanoi before getting permission to land. As soon as it touched ground, the pilot instantly doused his lights. Passengers disembarked with the aid of the hostess's flashlight. Surprisingly, the airport was brightly lit. The Vietnamese Peace Committee greeted the passengers with bouquets of snapdragons, pink sweet peas, pale pink roses, larkspur, and daisies. The first air-raid alert came as McCarthy was being driven from the airport to the city. Everyone headed for bomb shelters, which were widespread and easy to locate—in the country they might be simple holes in the ground, but in Hanoi there were large communal shelters, as well as individual cement cylinders, resembling manholes, every few feet. During alerts all foreigners, wearing the steel helmets that were mandatory during these alerts, were hustled to shelters by their guides and interpreters.

During Mary McCarthy's stay in Hanoi there was no bombing near her hotel, the Thong Nhat, although the siren sounded several times in a twenty-four-hour period, sending guests to the hotel's shelter. During the day, alerts had the gaiety of a social gathering, but at night when she heard a siren she would "jerk up from the pillow with my heart pounding, grope my way out of the mosquito netting, find the flashlight in the dark, slippers, dressing gown, et cetera, and stumble, still unnerved, down the stairs and out through the hotel garden, pointing my flashlight down, searching for the entrance to the shelter." Hanoi, "a shady, leafy city," with its lakes, parks, and promenades, reminded her of Minneapolis. It was a clean city, but one obviously at war. "Besides the shelters, the anti-aircraft, the scoreboard of shot-down airplanes, the army trucks, the boys and girls in uniform, there are huge war posters everywhere, graphics of Liberation Front heroes, slogans." Hanoi was also a drab city;

the people dressed in somber colors, usually in black trousers with a white shirt or blouse, and the women wore no makeup. There was nothing to buy in the stores, and the old French residential quarter had been left to fall into ruin.

Every other day Mary McCarthy sent her husband a cable so that he would know she was safe. On March 22 she entrusted a letter to an Englishwoman. "I don't want to tempt fate by saying it's not dangerous here, but I *can* say honestly that it's not scary. I was much more frightened in Vientiane, waiting to go. There have been up to now about three alerts a day." One day she had met the Danish ambassador to Peking in the hotel shelter, she continued. Everyone noticed and speculated about why the American bombing seemed to have moderated in the last few days, not only in Hanoi but all over the north. However, she reported, even without the bombing and constant alerts,

> Hanoi is extremely noisy—a cacophony of honking horns, shifting gears, spluttering of motor bikes, motors accelerating. This makes it hard to sleep and gives an old-fashioned pitch to the life here. . . .
>
> We are having a round of ceremonial visits, as in any *bloc* country: Journalists' Union, Writers' Union, Museum of the Revolution, art museum. Great consumption of little cups of tea, cookies, candies; at Journalists' Union, Hanoi beer, which is good. Food in general not bad at all; at celebratory dinners excellent. . . . This morning a visit to a cooperative village in the suburbs—rather idyllic; fish ponds, model pig sty. . . , experimental chicken-breeding, fruit-tree grafting, weaving. . . . I smelled the lemon blossoms, and saw litters of newborn piglets, air raid shelters in the fields, a watchman on a tower, . . . a militia unit . . . with a machine-gun pointed skyward. In the commune reception-center pictures of Marx, Engels, Ho, Lenin, Stalin. . . . We're driven in Russian cars. The main problem is that we're constantly with our guides. They've asked us not to go out walking in the streets without them, in case of an alert. . . . My *dear* Jim, thank you for staying so close by cable. I love you beyond anything.

Jim West had sent wonderful cheering cables, which his wife called "newsbulletins," every other day.

> YOU UNEXCELLED CORRESPONDENT. NATHALIE [Sarraute] LIZZIE [Hardwick] MARIO [Levi] DOZEN OTHERS SEND LOVE. KOT [Jelenski] TO NEW YORK TODAY. . . . GOOD FLIGHT MY DEAREST.

DELIGHTED YOUR LETTERS AND ARRIVAL TELEGRAM. BOBBY AND ROCKY WILL RUN. MONIQUE [Wittig] AND NOOTEBOOM [Cees Nooteboom] SEND LOVE. ALL OF MINE FOREVER.

ROCKY NOT RUNNING. WESTY [Westmoreland] LEAVING. YESTERDAY SIXTY PERCENT OF SEVENTY THOUSAND VOTERS NASSAU COUNTY VOTED PAUSE NOW. . . . EXPECT CHILDREN TODAY. . . . ETERNAL RESPECT AND LOVE FROM ME.

In the United States, President Johnson had to choose between escalation and retreat. Clark Clifford, his Secretary of Defense and formerly a committed hawk, now urged the president to get out of Vietnam. On March 22, Johnson announced that General William Westmoreland, who had just a month earlier requested an additional 200,000 troops, was to leave Vietnam by June, and on March 31, a gaunt president faced the television cameras in his oval office and addressed the nation. He took everyone by surprise, even close associates, when he said, "I shall not seek, and I will not accept, the nomination of my party for another term as your president." Mary McCarthy heard the speech live, over the Voice of America, at nine o'clock on the morning of April 1 in Hanoi. She was listening with several reporters in the hotel room of an Australian journalist for the London *Daily Express.* Everyone present, she recalled,

> dancing, kissing, hugging each other, took a bit of the credit. . . . A plump French photographer was doing a sort of proud jig with a flower-pot on his head. . . . We had helped bring the war to an end—for that of course was our expectation as we drank a toast in a horrible Bulgarian alcohol. It could not last much longer. So it had been worth it, I thought. Jim in Paris . . . would have just turned off the radio and would know that the bombing had stopped at least in the part of North Vietnam we were in. He would be rejoicing, and we could both assure ourselves, with a great relieved sigh, that I had done the right thing. Three weeks ago, waiting in Laos for the . . . plane to take us on the last leg of the long journey to Hanoi, I had had awful doubts.

The optimism did not last long. She wrote William Jovanovich a few weeks later that she began

> to wonder whether it was not an April Fool, after all. The shock when we heard that very day that Thanh Hoa was being bombed up near the 20th

parallel; I hoped at first that Hanoi was imagining it. Then the Pentagon confirmed.

McCarthy left Hanoi on April 2 on the ICC plane to Vientiane. From there she flew to Hong Kong and then to Tokyo to meet her husband, who had come there on OECD business. "Tokyo was all right, but it seemed unreal after Hanoi," she reported to Jovanovich "—all those geishas and the elderly tourists and the lively prosperity."

In Paris by mid-April, she started writing *Hanoi,* which would appear first as four separate articles in *The New York Review of Books.* Realizing that only a handful of Americans would get the chance to see Hanoi for themselves, she concentrated on depicting the North Vietnamese and their culture. They were dedicated and driven, she wrote, by a goal bigger than, and outside of, themselves—"Their ethic is in the service of the state." Their heroic effort and single-mindedness in pursuit of this ethic made them an ascetic people, so much so that the American peaceniks who came to Hanoi were put off and amused "by the local habits of courtesy, refinement, respect for age, sexual abstinence, decorum." The society attracted Mary McCarthy, making an impression not unlike that which the Sacred Heart convent in Seattle had made on her as a child. She described its appeal in a letter to Nicola Chiaromonte, concurring with a statement he had made about socialism's being possible only in an aristocratic society, and in a letter to Dwight Macdonald, writing that North Vietnam is "the only 'people's democracy' I've ever seen that's run on aristocratic principles and largely by aristocratic persons with a traditional code of manners and morals."

The shared determination of all citizens imparted a sense of community, which McCarthy also found appealing. "The feeling that Vietnam is a close community or family is sometimes quite strong in Hanoi, as when our guides of the Peace Committee appeared all dressed up in their best suits one afternoon because we were going to visit the National Liberation Front and that was like visiting your most important relations." But what really captivated Mary McCarthy about the North Vietnamese was their respect for limit.

> Vietnamese socialist planning has been based on an idea of limit. This is the originality, emphasized by Pham Van Dong, of the Vietnamese "way." By refusing outside help in the form of troops, they have succeeded in limiting the war. Fearful of a population explosion, they have limited births. . . . thanks to the bombing, they have been able to reverse modern demographic trends and actually reduce the population of cities.

In a letter to Nicola Chiaromonte, whose governing principle was the concept of limit, she wrote that

> they . . . have a contempt for the consumer society, including the version found in Russia and the bloc countries. Pham Van Dong, I thought, was sincere when he said they didn't want North Vietnam to industrialize in a big way. The idea seemed to fill him with horror and disdain. You couldn't exactly say they had (your words) "a certain contempt for power," since after all they're exercising power in the form of dictatorship. And yet one felt, even there, a kind of tentativeness and respect for limit. Scorn, an aristocratic emotion or sentiment, is one of their great weapons in rhetoric.

McCarthy's admiration for the dedication, solidarity, and restraint of the North Vietnamese, coupled with the depth of her feeling against the war, led her to overlook some shortcomings in the North Vietnamese. She herself admitted that she found it "somehow impolite" to ask certain questions.

> The cat sometimes got my tongue during long car rides with my friends of the Peace Committee, and when we conversed I tried to bypass subjects that would oblige me to say "the Americans" or "we" while they were saying "the neocolonialists" or "the Johnson-McNamara clique." Instead, I asked them about the flora and fauna of the regions through which we were driving. In that way, I learned something about the native trees, flowers, birds, folk remedies, how the rice seedlings were transplanted, the difference between Vietnamese tea and Chinese tea. . . . My companions probably thought me quite a strange person—superficial—and indeed I felt myself that to be so concerned about the names of flowers and trees . . . was a luxury typical of a capitalist author, who could afford the pedantry of nomenclature.

Partly because she could not ask pointed questions and partly because she had been in North Vietnam only two and a half weeks, she described the people and their government as "unoffending," thereby underestimating the role that North Vietnam played in maneuvering the war in the south. She could not believe that the North Vietnamese were capable of mistreating American prisoners, feeling certain they were making a careful distinction between the person and his crime. She partly disregarded the special treatment she was getting, which was meant to influence her judgments. While she criticized the misdeeds of Americans in Vietnam, she ignored the atrocities committed by the other side, prompting her friend, Richard Rovere, to wonder "why compassion led her to celebrate virtue and strength of character in Hanoi that she had never discerned elsewhere—not in Saigon, not in New York or Paris, not on Cape Cod or in the groves of academe."

McCarthy was not, however, totally blind to the faults of the North Vietnamese. In a letter to Dwight Macdonald she remarked on "the shortage of freedom and the awful art" and the difficulty of breaking through the shell of official Communist language. People hid behind slogans like "U.S. Imperialist Aggressors," "People's Liberation Army," "War of Destruction." Although the North Vietnamese people treated their visitors with excessive fuss and ceremony, their flat language indicated, she feared, a people lacking in sensibility or, worse, an authoritarian populace dedicated to the official truth. Just before leaving for Hanoi, she wrote her husband she was neither "pro-Viet Cong [nor] pro-North Vietnamese, except in the sense of being naturally inclined to pull for the weak and the outnumbered. . . . If North Vietnam were at peace, I would sympathize with whatever elements in its society were for an extension of freedom. The war has brought about an extraordinary decentralization there, and it may be that this could be the basis, after the war, for a less monolithic control. That's what I hope. I don't accept the thesis that socialism leads 'inevitably' to unfreedom, more controls, more depersonalization. Nobody has ever seen what a Marxist state would behave like if it were free of external interference." This ideal of decentralized socialism explains, more than anything else, her partiality for, and reluctance to find fault with, the North Vietnamese.

Overall, *Hanoi* was a plea to Americans to see the Vietnam War as a moral problem. McCarthy undercut abstract notions—saving the free world from Communism, the domino theory—with descriptions of concrete reality. As she described North Vietnamese hospitals, factories, grade schools, and war museums, she set forth her own inner life as it responded to all this.

> The private tumults and crises I have been undergoing . . . involved the omnipresence, the ubiquity of God. . . . Being an unbeliever made no difference. I had swallowed Him too many times as a child at the communion rail, so that He had come to live inside me like a cherry stone growing or like Socrates' unshakable companion and insistent interlocutor: oneself.

The book was, as William Jovanovich wrote, "a superb blending of observation of a terrible, awesome circumstance and observation of yourself watching it." *Hanoi,* like *Vietnam,* was almost totally ignored by the critics.

Castine and a lengthy visit from Sonia Orwell provided a respite from McCarthy's total immersion in the war. But when she returned to Europe in the fall, she resumed antiwar activity. In October, for the *Sunday Times,* she covered an antiwar demonstration in London. It was a relatively peaceful protest against American involvement in North and South Vietnam and against England's support of that involvement, even though the "sole active British contribution was training police dogs to track down Viet Cong." *The New York Review of Books* published her account on December 19 as "Letter from London: The Demo." In November she went on a lecture tour in Italy for the Italian Cultural Association. She addressed local groups (in Italian) in Turin, Genoa, Rome, Milan, and Bari, principally on how American writers (including herself) reacted to, and wrote about, Vietnam. She spoke most frequently, however, about Norman Mailer's *Armies in the Night* and *Miami and the Siege of Chicago.* In Genoa she encountered an elderly right-wing audience that attacked her for her position on Vietnam. Although they were angry with her, they ended up fighting among themselves.

During most of 1969 Mary McCarthy worked on *Birds of America,* with weekend jaunts to London and the Dordogne, an Easter vacation in Germany and Holland with Jim and the children, a trip to Switzerland in June to see Hannah Arendt, a stay in Castine during July and August, a television appearance on "The Dick Cavett Show" in August, a visit to the DuViviers in East Hampton, and an unexpected trip to New York in November for emergency dental work—"a descending scale," she wrote the Lowells. "I used long ago to come to New York to see a lover, then to see a psychoanalyst, then an editor or publisher, then a lawyer, and finally the dentist. I can't quite make this work out to the Seven Ages of Man." At the end of the year—at the invitation of Associated Television (the commercial network)—Mary McCarthy flew to London just before Christmas to nominate Ho Chi Minh, who had died in September, as the Man of the Decade. "I *like* Ho," she wrote Nicola Chiaromonte, "or at least the idea of him. In my [television] talk I said he had something in common with Pope John. Among other points of similarity, the fact that admirers of Ho, like admirers of Pope John, are reluctant to see either as organization men who made it in a tough international bureaucratic hierarchy. . . . Yet both made an impression quite genuine, I think, of simplicity and 'goodness.' "

During 1970 and early 1971 McCarthy turned most of her attention to *Birds of America,* the novel she had started in 1964 but had put aside to write about the war. Even so, she continued to be occupied with the Vietnam conflict into the 1970s, in particular with the court-martial trials of Lieutenant William Calley and Captain Ernest Medina, which arose from the incident known as the My Lai Massacre. On March 16, 1968, Charlie Company of the U. S. Eleventh Infantry Brigade killed several hundred old men, women, and children in My Lai, a Vietnamese hamlet. Captain Ernest Medina, the company commander, who thought that My Lai was held by the Viet Cong, ordered Lieutenant Calley to clean out the village. Instead of Viet Cong, Calley and his men found defenseless citizens, whom they killed, although it took all day. A few soldiers refused to participate in the killing, calling it point-blank murder. The first man to do something about My Lai had not even been there and did not hear about it until a month later. He was Ronald Ridenhour, who had been with Charlie Company before the incident. He learned about the massacre from his comrades. A year later, as a returned veteran, Ridenhour wrote an account of what had apparently happened and mailed twenty-three copies of it to President Nixon, key congressmen, and officials in the Pentagon and the State Department. The Army opened a full-scale inquiry into the slaughter. On September 5, 1969, the day before Calley was scheduled to be discharged, he was formally charged with the murder of 109 Vietnamese civilians. He was tried and, on March 21, 1971, found guilty.

When the Calley trial started, Mary McCarthy was finishing *Birds of America;* when the guilty verdict came, she was reading page proofs. After Calley's conviction, Captain Medina was court-martialed for his part in the My Lai killings. Calley's trial had raised the larger question of accountability: Who was ultimately responsible for My Lai? McCarthy wrote William Shawn to ask if she could cover the Medina trial in order to explore this issue further and to revive the public's waning interest in Vietnam. Shawn said yes and published her twenty-five-thousand-word essay, entitled "Reflections: A Transition Figure" in June 1972. William Jovanovich followed with an eighty-seven-page paperback pub-lication, *Medina,* the first of McCarthy's books to appear under the publishing house's new name: Harcourt Brace Jovanovich. (Harcourt, Brace & World became HBJ in January 1970.)

Jovanovich had not wanted McCarthy to waste her time and effort on the trial. "The whole question of guilt and responsibility has become talked out and vulgarized by the Calley case," and besides, he added, hundreds of articles had already appeared in *Time, Newsweek,* and *Life;* and *Look* planned to devote full issues to the controversy. "It will be a

popularly worn subject by autumn." Anyway, he concluded, neither the Calley nor the Medina trial would "serve to bring attention once again to the main question of our getting out of Vietnam."

McCarthy disagreed. She attended the trial in August 1971 at Third Army Headquarters, Fort McPherson, Georgia. (Although Calley's case had been tried at nearby Fort Benning, the Army decided, in the interests of efficiency and economy, to try all further cases related to My Lai at Fort McPherson.) McCarthy disliked downtown Atlanta, where she stayed, because it "did not look as if anybody lived there: they just held salesmen's conventions all year round"; it consisted, she found, of "parking lots, multi-level garages, motels with swimming pools and free ice-dispensers in a simple cadre of insurance-company skyscrapers." Worse, the trial was dull, mainly because, she thought, the government wanted the public to lose interest. The trial was over by the end of September; Medina was acquitted. McCarthy did not finish the full report of the trial until February 1972. Apologizing for the long delay, she assured Shawn that since "what I'm sending you is not at all what we projected, I won't be hurt if you can't use it." He did.

Medina contends that the public should have brought pressure on the military and the government to pursue the prosecution to the fullest extent possible. McCarthy argues that if Medina had been convicted, as he ought to have been, it would have been far more difficult for the military to acquit or release from criminal charges those higher up the chain of command—the generals and the nation's political leaders. "Medina was a transition figure between the war-makers and the 'animals' (as the airmen in Vietnam called the infantry), and his acquittal halted a process that might have gone up the ladder of responsibility." Nor are ordinary citizens free of blame. U.S. policy in Vietnam is criminal; the My Lai Massacre was detonated, after all, by search-and-destroy operations. Although the people did not make this policy, McCarthy concludes, they failed to act like good citizens in holding their government accountable.

The American presence in Vietnam was lessening when the Wests invited Elizabeth Hardwick to spend Christmas of 1972 with them in Paris. The day of their annual Christmas party, however, President Nixon resumed bombing over North Vietnam. They thought of canceling the party but did not. Instead, McCarthy hatched the idea of organizing a group of twenty prominent Americans, full of conscience and from different walks of life, including some Republicans, who would go to Hanoi and "live under the bombs as witnesses." She drew up lists of names; telephoned Washington and New York dozens of times seeking advice and suggestions; spoke to former attorney general Ramsey Clark, whom she did not know but who agreed to the plan, provided she cleared it with the North Vietnamese in Paris and made no public announcement until visas had been definitely promised. Although the Wests had planned to leave for Amsterdam the morning of December 21, she delayed their departure to contact the North Vietnamese delegation in Paris to explain the project. "When I mentioned the number twenty, Mr. Phan, an old friend of mine from North Vietnam, sounded aghast. He doubted that Hanoi could accommodate so many. But that was the point, I told him. The travel of three or four would not have sufficient 'impact.' The number had to be in scale to the bombing."

Elizabeth Hardwick thought the scheme "was both funny and typical of Mary," she said later. "I thought it was wonderful. It's pure Jeanne d'Arc; bring me my troops. It's also very girlish, and extraordinarily ladylike and bourgeois and suburban at the same time. This is what makes her unique: these tremendous gestures which are well thought through. She has definite ideas and she's very serious about what her thoughts are; she's not at all loose in any kind of political activity or thought."

Her husband did not find her newest antiwar scheme so amusing. McCarthy recorded their conversation about it in *The Seventeenth Degree.*

> "Do you want people to think you have a suicide urge?" he burst out late one afternoon.
> "I don't care," I said.
> "Do you care if *I* think it?"
> "Yes, of course. But you're wrong. Honestly, I don't want to be killed."
> "But if you go out there and don't get killed, what's the point? You have to be killed to make your point."
> "I don't follow that."

Later she realized he was right. "Suppose none of . . . the twenty got killed, what would we eventually do? Go home. And tell the public the bombs were falling?"

The three friends drove to Amsterdam, arriving at their hotel late at night owing to the delay in leaving Paris. Elizabeth Hardwick was miserable with the flu; and McCarthy, with her husband's opposition. "It seemed to me days since I had been able to coax a smile from him," she later wrote. "I could hardly have expected him to be enthusiastic about a proposition that involved a high risk of my death; yet I am someone who needs enthusiasm. Probably I even demand it. When now it was not forthcoming, I began to wilt like an untended plant." They spent Christmas in Amsterdam with Cees Nooteboom, a Dutch writer whom McCarthy had met ten years before at the Edinburgh conference that Sonia Orwell had directed.

On December 27 Hardwick flew to New York and the Wests took the ferry from The Hook of Holland to Harwich to make another tour of English cathedral towns. They were in the town of Lincoln when they heard that the bombing in Vietnam had stopped.

Back in Paris in mid-January 1973, McCarthy wrote friends urging them to make "a little anti-war effort" by "writing to the B-52 pilot who'd had enough at Christmastime." She referred to Captain Michael Heck, the first pilot—at least on public record—who had refused to fly bombing missions. She also visited the North Vietnamese Paris delegation; they "were incredulous that there had been so little reaction to the bombing in the United States. They could hardly take it in and asked me for an explanation." Only a few days later, on January 27, 1973, a cease-fire agreement was signed. After eight years of combat and twenty years of "guidance," American military involvement in Vietnam was over. In March the last of the GIs boarded flights for home.

American intervention had been a mistake of the greatest magnitude, and McCarthy wrote about what she saw as one of the reasons for it in her review of David Halberstam's *The Best and the Brightest,* a study of the men who had made the critical decisions that got America into Vietnam and kept her there for so long. McCarthy was irritated by Halberstam's thesis that "an aristocracy of brains came to Washington with the Kennedys." To the contrary, she wrote:

> Kennedy's academic advisors, with the exception of Galbraith (who was also exceptional in giving some sensible advice), far from being "men of towering accomplishments" [Halberstam's words], were mostly pale fish out of university think tanks. Whatever their actual field of knowledge, they were considered to be adepts of political science—a pseudo discipline of "ruthless" thinking about political "realities" that had developed in the universities under Cold War pressure. . . . What came to Washington was not brains and birth but packaged ideology, a form of overweening stupidity generated in university departments of Political Science and Government. . . . The gross stupidities and overconfidence of the Kennedy-Johnson advisers, not to mention their moral insensitivity, issued

from a sectarian faith in the factuality of the social sciences, which is not by any means the religion of an elite. The use of computers and input from the "scientists" of the Rand Corporation increased the reverence of the faithful for this crass body of beliefs.

In the summer of 1966, before she had written a word about Vietnam, she had told Edwin Newman, who interviewed her in Paris for television, that "if Americans do not act against the war, put down some real stake, our case would not be so different from the 'good' Germans under Hitler who claimed to have disagreed with the Final Solution, offering as proof the fact that they had taken no active part in it." Between 1967 and 1973 Mary McCarthy published three small books on Vietnam. In 1974 these essays, along with an autobiographical piece that discloses why she wrote about the war, and "Sons of Morning," her review of *The Best and the Brightest,* were published in a large volume entitled *The Seventeenth Degree.* This work summarizes her six-year attempt to awaken the American public to the human realities of Vietnam, realities that are movingly represented in a photograph of a ten- or eleven-year-old Vietnamese girl that is part of McCarthy's picture collection of family and friends. The little girl lies on a bed, looking straight ahead with big black frightened eyes. And no wonder: her body is emaciated, its rib cage entirely visible; her skin from her toes to her neck is burned and pockmarked from napalm; and her long fingers are little more than bones covered by what looks like the wrinkled and sagging skin of a very old person.

On June 12, 1975, forty-three days after the fall of Saigon to Communist North Vietnam, *The New York Review of Books* published a special supplement on "The Meaning of Vietnam." "The wistful idea (in which I have fitfully shared) of a 'use' to which the Vietnam experience could be put," Mary McCarthy wrote, "shows that our faith remains a naive, mechanical utilitarianism, which has no room in it for death in private life or tragedy in politics." In 1979 she told an interviewer how much the grim events subsequent to the American withdrawal had upset her, and how she had "contemplated writing a real letter to Pham Van Dong asking him, 'can't you stop this'; how is it possible for men like you to permit what is going on?" She never wrote that letter, too discouraged, perhaps, by the political and human tragedy that continues in Vietnam.

CHAPTER XXI

DOMESTIC VIRTUES
(1970–1972)

BIRDS OF AMERICA, which Mary McCarthy had begun in 1964 but had put aside three times to write about Vietnam, was published in 1971. Although the war is present in the background, the primary theme of *Birds of America* is the pernicious way this century's culture has come to be dominated by technology. "The key, the little germ idea, the seed" of *Birds of America,* McCarthy told an interviewer, came to her in 1962, two years before she started writing.

> There was a boy we knew in Paris. He was the son of people of my generation, academics, whom we knew slightly. He used to come around and see us. He had this terrible apartment. I never was in it, but heard his description of it, and I can well imagine what the room was like, how dark it was. And he bought a plant. And he used to take this plant for WALKS, and that was really the germ of the book. . . . You start with something like that because it's alive. And you don't question what that means. It's like a little germ culture you put on glass, and then it starts developing. It's only after you've written a chapter that's sort of sprung out of it that you begin to know what it means. You *have* to know before you can get much further.

As it happens, this image of an American boy taking his plant for walks does not show up in the novel until chapter five.

> The plant-seller had warned Peter [Peter Levi, the main character] that the Fatshedera did not like too much light—which should have made it an ideal tenant for his apartment. But after a month's residence there, looking out on the air shaft, it had grown long, leggy, and despondent, like its master. Its growth was all tending upward, to the crown, like that of trees in the jungle. The leaves at the base were falling off, one by one, and though he had been carefully irritating the stem at the base to promote new sideward growth, it had been ignoring this prodding on his part and just kept getting taller, weed-like, till he had finally had this idea of taking it for walks, once or twice a week, depending on the weather. It did not seem to mind drafts, and the outdoor temperature on a sunny day in late November was not appreciably colder than the indoor temperature *chez* him. He thought he was beginning to note signs of gratitude in the invalid

for the trouble he was taking; a little bump near the base where he had
been poking it with his knife seemed about to produce a stalk or pedicel,
and there was a detectable return of chlorophyll, like a green flush to the
cheeks of the shut-in.

From that "little germ idea" to the finished manuscript, eight long
years would pass without a published Mary McCarthy novel. Of course,
there would be several essays and the three Vietnam books, which
occupied much of her working time; but it was McCarthy's perfectionism
more than anything that accounted for the interval between *The Group*
and *Birds of America*. She had started writing during the summer that she
and West and his three young children lived in a rented house in Stonington, Connecticut, which, as the fictional Rocky Port, became the
setting for the first two chapters of *Birds of America*. A year and a half
later she wrote William Maxwell, a *New Yorker* writer and editor, that
"this novel has been dragging along . . . ; I have worked and reworked
chapters you saw." Early in 1970 she told Hannah Arendt that she had
"some crazy hope still of finishing it by the end of March. . . . I feel
stirrings of life in it, but that's usually toward the end of a day's work,
and the morning brings pessimism in the form of dissatisfaction, so that
I start undoing the web I thought I was spinning. The truth is, I have
no idea how I'm going to end it, and this is what I have to learn—
. . . which for me comes with this endless rewriting." She did not finish
by March. In April she wrote William Jovanovich that "it's been a grind,
fearfully depressing. Writing the same few pages over and over. . . . The
awful thing is that I've not been idling but working very hard. And so
little to show for it."

She had been working hard, some days putting in ten to twelve hours
on *Birds of America*. But she also did quite a lot of traveling—to London
in March, Holland and Japan in April, New York in May, Switzerland
in June, and Castine in July for the rest of the summer. Because West's
children did not spend their customary summer with their father and
stepmother (to Mary and Jim's regret), McCarthy made steady progress
on *Birds of America*. For this reason, and because there were fewer guests,
the summer of 1970 in Maine was unusually quiet. Jonathan, West's
youngest child, came for two weeks, and Reuel, who had just finished
two years of teaching at UCLA, came with his wife (he had married in
1963) and two-year-old son on his way to a teaching job at the University
of Western Ontario. "Jay is enchanting," McCarthy wrote Edmund Wilson about his grandson, "remarkably bright and quick and with delicate
gleams of wit and humor unusual in a child his age." McCarthy left

Castine for a few days in August to attend a conference in Aspen on technology and the environment, a subject she dealt with in *Birds of America*.

By the time she got back to Paris in the fall, the novel was almost complete. She made a quick trip to Rome to revisit the Sistine Chapel, the scene of a chapter, and in November she was back in America to attend Heinrich Blücher's funeral. The novel was finished by December 1. To celebrate, she went to London while Jim West visited his sons at school on the Isle of Wight and then his daughter, who was now at Sherborne in Dorset.

William Jovanovich published the first chapter of *Birds of America* as a small fifty-seven-page book that he sent as Christmas greetings to two thousand people. "Winter Visitors," as the chapter is titled, starts in Rocky Port in the summer of 1964. Peter Levi and his mother, the twice-divorced harpsichordist Rosamund Brown, return to the village they had lived in off-season four years earlier. The chapter is mainly Peter's memory of that happy fall of 1960. Peter loves Nature, which for him is the New England countryside with its interesting birds. His mother loves cooking "real" food, which to her means turning out dishes from an old Fannie Farmer cookbook; but because everything available in the stores is either prepackaged or frozen, she can find neither the implements nor the ingredients she needs. The extravagant energy she expends in searching for them and in browbeating local shopkeepers into stocking them is genuinely comic.

At least one Stonington resident liked what McCarthy had done with the village. James Merrill wrote:

> It whets the appetite for the next course. (One can't but fall into metaphors of eating, with all the glorious meals you write about; plus stirred memories of past occasions here in Rocky Port. . . .) It's all so beautifully done. I can't think *when* the family romance has been frosted with such fine sugar and such strong Kirsch; you do take the cake! No, but truly, I felt throughout your handling of Peter and his mother the eeriest analogies with that stage of my own life, when my father had left, and everything conspired to keep my mother and me not as unhappy as we should have been, in our New York version of your rented cottage. . . . Bless you for being so wise *and* so magical.

Merrill, in whose Stonington apartment she had written much of what he praised, was in Paris early in 1971. So, too, were the Chiaromontes and Sonia Orwell and dozens of other friends, old and new, who habitually "passed through" Paris. This is why, other than Christmas in Rome, a trip to London for a BBC appearance on behalf of medical aid to North Vietnam, and ten glorious days in Sicily (with Hannah Arendt and the DuViviers) to celebrate their tenth wedding anniversary, the Wests stayed close to home. By April "interviewers, photographers, and miscellaneous strangers with requests," including "a girl from *Time,* flown in from New York for three days to do a piece," began besieging the rue de Rennes apartment. *Birds of America* was not to be published for another month, but because it was McCarthy's first novel since *The Group* and because it had been selected by the Literary Guild, prepublication flurry was inevitable. She was even persuaded to make an appearance on "The Dick Cavett Show."

Both Mary McCarthy and William Jovanovich believed *Birds of America* promised to do as well as *The Group.* Harcourt Brace Jovanovich launched the novel with an extensive promotional campaign. Immediately before publication, the company ran ads for several days in a row in the *Atlanta Journal-Constitution,* the *Chicago Tribune, The Washington Post,* the *Los Angeles Times,* the *Boston Globe,* the *San Francisco Chronicle, The New York Times,* and *Publishers Weekly;* and immediately after publication, in *The New York Review of Books, The New Yorker,* the daily *New York Times,* with full-page ads in *The New York Times Book Review.* The first print run was 50,000 copies. Not surprisingly, *Birds of America* appeared on the best-seller list right after it came out, but it fell off almost as precipitously. McCarthy blamed her reviews for killing sales.

"My breath was taken away by the unfavorable quality of the reviews," she told an interviewer at this time. In the *Saturday Review,* John Aldridge, who had condemned her pre-*Group* fiction as "those stiff, claustrophobic little studies of the intellectual life," and who characterized *The Group* as "imaginatively constipated" and "dead at the center," said of this novel that "her tone is no longer strident or shrewish"; but he described her ideas as silly. According to Aldridge, she equated the scarcity of certain food with the collapse of Western civilization; her method, moreover, was to make lists instead of discoveries. Helen Vendler, in *The New York Times Book Review,* under the headline "Mary McCarthy again her own heroine—frozen foods a new villain," asserted that she "is ruthlessly circumscribed by her own lived experience." Others called McCarthy a brilliant snob who cut down others only to make herself look good, as well as "our leading bitch intellectual."

"They are reviewing me, not my book," McCarthy wrote William Jovanovich. She wondered "if the book reviewing profession is made up of personal enemies."

Of course, not all the reviews were negative. As McCarthy told an interviewer from *Publishers Weekly* at the end of July 1971, her magazine and newspaper reviews had been "29 favorable, 24 unfavorable, and 9 middling." And the book sold well, though not nearly so well as *The Group,* but Harcourt Brace Jovanovich sold 48,500 of its first printing of 50,000 copies; the Literary Guild sold 129,528 copies; and New American Library sold 199,441 of its paperback edition. In addition, there have been subsequent editions published by The Franklin Library and by Avon Books.

It is surprising, though, that such a gentle book—the least "social" of all her books—elicited so many hostile reactions. Hannah Arendt had her own explanation. "Some of the reasons for the reaction are clear—no one expected you to write this kind of book. . . . And in this book it is your whole person that speaks as author." Whether this explained reviewers' reactions or not, Arendt was right that in *Birds of America* McCarthy's person speaks as author. This does not mean that the novel is written in her voice—she chose again to speak primarily in the voice of a character, in this case Peter Levi—but that the old-fashioned domestic virtues so dear to McCarthy permeate the book.

As a food purist (she refuses today to own a food processor or even to use an electric coffee grinder, because it heats as it grinds), she found American domestic life in the 1960s and 1970s appalling. The trend away from the kitchen toward frozen, prepackaged, and already-cooked food was quite advanced by the time she started *Birds of America.* Good cooking, she predicted in a letter to William Maxwell, "will soon become 'gourmet' cooking." As she worked on the novel, she often reported on the prevalence of "the Rocky Port syndrome" in letters to William Jovanovich and Carmen Angleton. She complained that everything in Stonington and Castine was frozen and filleted; that "there doesn't seem to be a live chive in Stonington—only frozen in jars," or a live hen or turkey—only frozen, "like the people"; that there was not a cake rack or muffin tin in the village; that "most people are too lazy to grow flowers, except the old perennials they can't stop from coming up"; that "everybody lives on 'gourmet' foods that are tinned, even the sandwiches for a small party are frozen"; that she could not buy a whole fish in either of these seaside villages. " 'We don't get any call for that' is the merchant's slogan. The children, who don't share the adult taste for frozen lasagne casseroles and canned lobster newburg with pre-saffroned rice, live on hamburgers and hot dogs, but in a year or so they will be eating dog or cat food, I think. And *loving* it." All of the preparing, shopping, and cooking she had done for her stepchildren during the summer they were in Stonington shows up in *Birds of America:*

> His mother turned everything she did into a game—with rules, of course. The rules of the Rocky Port kitchen were that every recipe had to come out of Fannie Farmer, had to be made entirely at home from fresh or dried or salted ingredients. . . . Mixes . . . were out, as well as frozen foods. . . . The game was not as easy as it sounded, since the Rocky Port market leaned heavily on its frozen-food chests, and there were no fresh vegetables to be had, even in the supermarket in the neighboring town. . . . Getting fresh fish was a problem despite the fishing fleet. It was easier for a gull. . . . Peter hated it when she sent him around to borrow muffin tins or cake racks or a flour sifter. Nobody had them; nobody used them any more. . . . In the very first days she had drawn attention to herself by giving Mrs. Curtis a list of things that were missing in their kitchen that she considered *essential,* underlining the word, such as pie tins and a breadboard. . . . Their landlady, a Goldwater stalwart, had taken offense; she refused to supply any more kitchen stuff unless his mother restored the historical notice to the house front. The situation was deadlocked. His mother said that a house without a griddle or a strainer, not to mention pie tins and so on, had no claim to an historical placard.

When a neighbor gives Rosamund an old wooden ice-cream freezer with a rusty crank, she decides to make ice cream at once. When she finds rock salt in the hardware store, the owner wants to know what she needs it for. After all, "folks here used it winters, to melt the ice on their sidewalks." When she makes currant jelly, she cannot find jelly glasses. "The storekeeper shook his gray head emphatically. 'Don't get any call for them.' . . . With jelly glasses, naturally, parafin had gone. And Mason jars with rubbers. 'Haven't had a call for them in years.' " She makes watermelon pickle, which necessitates using every available pan and cover to store the rinds. Then she has to drive ten miles to get the most essential ingredient—calcium oxide—from a druggist. " 'Mind if I ask what you want it for, lady?' 'Why? Is it poison?' 'No, 'tain't that. I was just wondering. Haven't had a call—' 'I know,' she said."

McCarthy's most routine errand or meeting in Stonington furnished copy for the novel. And it was no different in Maine. Three years later she would report: "The Peter Levi problem, or rather his mother's problem, is very acute up here. No fish, though there are plenty in the sea; . . . no green vegetables (virtually); scarcely a curl of parsley. Man in Bar Harbor fish market: 'If you want a whole fish with bones in it, you have to get it shipped from Boston.' " Obviously, Mary McCarthy drew from her own experience to express in the novel her regret over the disappearance of old-fashioned domesticity, and of much else in America, owing to the "improvements" of technology. "I must say, America is a shock," she wrote Dwight Macdonald from Castine.

> Even to the children. There is this weird business of technology turning into its opposite, as if in some Midas fable: no trains, scarcely a bus, whereas forty years ago there were all sorts of carriers that took visitors to Castine, including a night boat from Boston that steamed into the harbor, loaded with summer trunks. No farming any more, except industrialized potato-growing, no fish, frozen bread; apparently people drive for miles to attend cake sales. It is all very pathetic. I must stop and go call up the paperhanger—another all but extinct craft. We're going to have to import him from Bar Harbor. Practically like colonial times.

Her decidedly domestic nature has prompted many interviewers to ask what she thinks of the women's movement. Besides the fact that McCarthy does not feel comfortable with any movement, she particularly dislikes the self-pity and shrillness she sees in the women's movement. "As for Women's Lib, it bores me. Of course I believe in equal pay and equality before the law and so on, but this whole myth about how different the world would have been if it had been female-dominated, about how there would have been no wars—and Women's Lib extremists actually believe these things—seems a complete fantasy to me. I've never noticed that women were less warlike than men. And in marriage, or for that matter between a woman and her lover or between two lesbians or any other couple, an equal division of tasks is impossible—it's a judgment of Solomon. You really would have to slice the baby down the middle." Of course, there is no "woman" problem in the circles she moves in, nor have any of her husbands been anything but generous in supporting her in her work. McCarthy, understandably, is happy in the feminine sphere—marriage, domesticity ("I myself don't object to the idea of serving"), pretty clothes, gardening, and, above all, cooking. Having taught herself to cook, she has always taken great care with whatever she prepares, making everything from scratch and never resorting to electrical shortcuts in the kitchen—a fact that amuses, and sometimes annoys, friends. In *Birds of America,* McCarthy has portrayed the way she acts in her own kitchen. *Birds of America* is her favorite among her own novels—"I like the hero. I like the ideas. Well, it's close to my heart."

Although friends sometimes smile at her purism, her protagonist,

Peter Levi, understands the deeper issues involved in his mother's quest for buckwheat flour and whole fresh fish with heads and bones. He is his mother's child in his sensitivity to the quality of life (his love for the natural and the beautiful), yet this, he finds, conflicts with his firmly entrenched belief in justice (his acceptance of democracy and egalitarianism). It is this opposition that provides the "movement" of the novel and is embodied in Peter's encounter, on the boat train to Paris, with the American schoolteachers, whom he sees as kind and neighborly but ignorant and vulgar as well; in his struggle to keep the public toilet clean in his Parisian lodgings; and in his dislike of the hordes of tourists who get in the way of his enjoyment of the Sistine Chapel. Peter's dilemma— he believes in equality, yet he is revolted by the tourists and even proposes that art-appreciation examinations be given for admission to the Sistine Chapel—illustrates the difference between his social idealism and the reality of society.

At the same time McCarthy was working on *Birds of America,* she was reading and writing about Ivy Compton-Burnett's novels. In her essay "The Inventions of I. Compton-Burnett," she explains Peter's dilemma in different terms:

> "I wonder who began this treating of people as fellow-creatures," says a character in *Manservant and Maidservant.* "It is never a success."
> "Once begun, it is a difficult thing to give up," another character answers.
> "It seemed such an original idea," a third says, as if with a sigh.
> "We can see how unnatural it is by what comes of it," the first retorts.
> But, once introduced, the idea of equality does appear natural, not only as a "self-evident" proposition in political philosophy but by the very fact of having entered a number of minds. At the same time, social equality does not seem to square with the facts of life, some of which are the facts of Nature as well.

These ideas, McCarthy has said, are really what *Birds of America* is about. "I have thought for years that once this egalitarian notion was discovered, say sometime in the eighteenth century, there's been a continual flight from it. . . . At the same time, any person with a child's fairmindedness cannot help thinking that equality's a good idea." Peter Levi, the novel's hero, writes a long letter to his mother in which he expresses his theory of equality—that it is not such a good idea but that once it was thought of, there was no getting rid of it.

"A Touch of Nature" is another essay McCarthy wrote during the time she worked on *Birds of America.* This and "The Inventions of I. Compton-Burnett" may be read as glosses on the novel. In "A Touch of Nature" she regrets the fact that technology has replaced nature in people's sense of the scale of man.

> To the extent that Nature has to be defended from man . . . instead of being intrinsic to his species-existence, it is simply a backdrop, a photogenic setting, and has nothing to say, one way or another, in determining values or revealing truth. Indeed, the notion, still harbored by every reactionary heart, including my own, that Nature is itself a value, has become subject to opinion. . . . Nature is no longer the human home. It cannot be a coincidence that modern physics, by interfering with Nature, has for the first time posed a threat to the species and perhaps to most other forms of organic life on earth. . . . Technology, originally associated with the civilizing arts of building and weaving, has replaced Nature as the Number One opponent of human society.

In *Birds of America,* when Peter spends his Christmas holiday in Rome contemplating the beauties of the Sistine Chapel and the seventeenth-century architect Borromini—and here, a perceptive critic has said, McCarthy "hardly bothers in moments of high feeling to strain herself through the sensibilities of the 19-year-old lad"—he accidentally encounters his academic advisor from the Sorbonne. The meeting crystallizes Peter's objections to American capitalism and technology. Mr. Small, with his smug technocratic belief in this best of all possible worlds, is a spokesman for the wonders of contemporary American civilization. "I can't think of a more challenging time to be alive for an American," he says. "All the options are open. No society in history before our own has given so-called mass man such opportunities for self-realization." He scorns Peter's elitist rejection of technology. That people in an egalitarian world will defile the environment more than people in a hierarchical one strikes Mr. Small as elitist, yet it seems obvious that the sheer number of consumers of art, education, and travel, for example, will be far greater in an egalitarian society than in a hierarchical one. The uglification produced by technology and mass society is thereby increased exponentially. Peter's position, however, is made more difficult by his respect for a kindly Italian radical, Arturo Bonfante (based on Mario Levi), who reminds Peter that the picturesque simplicities he wants to preserve actually constrict people's lives.

At the end of the novel, Peter, who has gone to the zoo in despair over the bombing of North Vietnam, is wounded by an angry swan. Afterward, in the hospital (where technology in the form of penicillin, to which he is allergic, almost kills him), he has a dream of being visited by Kant, who announces that "Nature is dead." McCarthy believes that nature is dead or at least dying; in an interview at the time of the novel's publication, she explained the implications of this.

> If Nature—in the beautiful form that we normally think of it: that of the outdoors, plants, farms, forests—if this were to disappear, which it is doing, there'd be nothing stable left to stand on, no ground for ethics. Then you'd really be in a Dostoevskian position: Why shouldn't I kill an old pawnbroker—because there's no longer a point of reference or a court of appeals. . . . And if this is gone then we are lost.

This view—that man needs to respect the natural world and listen to its laws because it is a foundation of ethics—comes, in large part, from McCarthy's reading of Shakespeare. She has remarked that the characters in Shakespeare's work who are drawn to nature, to the instinctive and the concrete, like the rustics, the clowns, and the fools, usually get the last word. The characters who are attracted to abstraction, on the other hand, are somehow bested, like the young men in *Love's Labour's Lost*, or like Angelo, Lear, Coriolanus, and Shylock. Even those characters who do listen to the messages of the natural world and yet seem to be defeated in the end are actually ennobled. Ophelia, Desdemona, Emilia, Imogen, and Cordelia are examples. "In all these young women there is a sense of being wronged," McCarthy has written, "of bewilderment, and at the same time a kind of acceptance, not of being wronged, but of the unjust nature of experience itself. They bow to life without yielding, and out of that they get their dignity." Thus, to destroy nature is to impair man's moral faculty, which, according to McCarthy, is a regulatory instinct that keeps him in balance with the natural things of the world.

Partly, it is technology that is killing nature. Owing to market forces of worldwide dimensions, resources, including the land itself, are seen as commodities. As a result, people enjoy less rapport with nature. McCarthy concedes some technological blessings—the vacuum cleaner, for instance—but in general, she sees deterioration in every area of life. Taking air travel as an example of an "absolutely ruinous" technological advance, she told an interviewer, "Aside from getting us into wars, it distorts our relationship with Nature. And I think our perception of the world and our values stem absolutely from the possibility of some reasonably true perception of Nature—which is gradually disappearing, and will soon become impossible."

And partly, it is the idea of equality that is killing nature. The faster men attain their egalitarian dream, the more surely they debase the environment, and not only the environment: food is frozen and becomes tasteless; entertainment becomes standardized through television; education is universalized by a "watering-down" process. As Irvin Stock, McCarthy's most perceptive critic, has said, *Birds of America* shows that if "men are to share equally in all life's goods—including those of the mind, . . . these goods must be stripped of the particulars that limit their accessibility. They must be 'processed' into easily reproducible and portable approximations of the real thing." Egalitarianism is a fine idea, but to live wholly by an idea, McCarthy has been saying since *The Oasis,* is to deny reality.

While *Birds of America* is a serious book, its tone is lighthearted and affectionate. While writing it, McCarthy often accompanied her Newport friend Nicholas King, who lived in Paris at the time, on bird walks, and the novel is full of real birds—from the dead Great Horned Owl in the first chapter to the ill-tempered swan whose bite puts Peter in the hospital in the last. In between are flocks of birds, real and metaphorical. Peter's mother is like the rose-breasted grosbeak; neighbors in Rocky Port are retired birds; the hard-drinking admiral has the hoarse voice of a seabird; the migratory species, the tourist-bird, is all over Europe. Peter goes bird watching in the Buttes-Chaumont Park with *les jeunes ornithologistes de France.* He also attends a Thanksgiving dinner hosted by a general attached to NATO, who is appalled because a guest, a vegetarian, refuses to eat turkey, "the sacred fowl." The general gives her some anyway. However, she

> had not succumbed to the appetizing slice of breast in its casing of crisp brown skin. Instead, she was eating carefully around it: the onions, the rutabagas, the sweet potatoes, the Ocean Spray cranberry jelly. She avoided the mashed potatoes polluted with gravy and the stuffing contaminated by animal fat and juices during its stay in the oven. [Peter] followed the progress of her fork as it constructed fortifications against the giblet gravy, which ran between the banks of vegetables, lapped at the base of the tottering tower of jelly, divided into rivulets, and finally congealed.

Details like this abound in this comic novel, which, by identifying moral
issues in minutiae, gives a sense of what is happening to contemporary
culture.

Much of McCarthy's attitude toward contemporary culture had
evolved out of her discussions with Nicola Chiaromonte, which had
begun on Cape Cod in the mid-1940s and which had continued during
Chiaromonte's New York years and on through a decade of summers
in Bocca di Magra to the visits and correspondence between the Wests
in Paris and the Chiaromontes in Rome. Thus when Chiaromonte, at
sixty-seven, dropped dead of a heart attack on January 18, 1972, in an
elevator in the Italian Radio Building after having delivered a broadcast,
McCarthy lost a gifted friend whom she greatly admired and who was
in many ways her mentor. The next day she wrote Hannah Arendt.

> Jim and I are going down this afternoon for the funeral (tomorrow)
> with Carmen, who happened to be here. The Levis will be on the same
> plane. Anjo [Angélique Levi] is very broken up (it was she who told me)
> and is saying that she can't go on, what can she do, and sobbing in a
> distracted way. I think of it as antique Jewish mourning, remembering my
> grandmother when she screamed at Aunt Rosie's death. Miriam's compo-
> sure is a contrast; she seems to be trying to console others, like a mother.
> To cut short the contagion of sobs.

Hannah Arendt answered immediately.

> Mary, look, I think I know how sad you are and how serious this loss is.
> . . . As far as Anjo and Miriam are concerned (I sent Miriam a cable):
> Miriam is quite in tune with Jewish mourning. Women were not admitted
> to funerals according to orthodox rites *because* they were likely to scream.
> I looked up once more the Jewish death prayers: they, that is, the *kaddish,*
> are a single praise of God, the name of the dead one is not even men-
> tioned. The underlying notion is what is inscribed on all Jewish funeral
> homes: The Lord hath given, the Lord hath taken away, blessed be the
> Lord. Or: Don't complain if something is taken away that was given you
> but which you did not necessarily *own:* And don't forget, to be taken away,
> it had first to be given. If you believed you owned, if you forgot that it
> was given, that is just too bad for you. Not that Anjo is not also quite
> Jewish. Jews are also one of the Mediterranean peoples, and that means
> they are expressive, demonstrative, and know how to lament. And lamen-
> tations (of which I am perhaps no longer capable) are what we owe the
> dead ones precisely because we go on living.

Soon after the funeral McCarthy set about organizing friends to send a letter to the Agnelli Foundation for a grant to subsidize the publication of Chiaromonte's uncollected writings and correspondence. "That letter went through as many variants as a long poem," McCarthy wrote Hannah Arendt, "getting more and more marmoreal as it was worked on by more and more hands, finishing with expressions like 'lo Scomparso' (the Departed One). There was also the question of who should sign and who shouldn't and who would and who wouldn't—the criterion of the first being that the signer's name should be known to Gianni Agnelli and at the same time that he should be a friend of Nicola's. All this kept Miriam's phone busy with local and long-distance calls. Mine too. And the phone of a girl who had slept with Gianni Agnelli and was considered the final authority, though not, alas, on the text (hers, rather simple and impetuous, was the best). Anyway it looks now as if the grant will come through, thanks probably to a command from Agnelli." In his lifetime Chiaromonte had published only two books—*The Dramatic Situation,* a collection of his writings on the theater, and *The Paradox of History,* essays on the novel and the ideas of history developed in it that were first delivered as the Christian Gauss Lectures at Princeton. Owing partly to McCarthy's efforts, Harcourt Brace Jovanovich posthumously published *The Worm of Consciousness and Other Essays* (1976), which Chiaromonte's widow, Miriam, edited and for which McCarthy wrote an introduction; and the University of Pennsylvania Press reissued *The Paradox of History* (1985) with an afterword by McCarthy. She also wrote the essay "Nicola Chiaromonte and the Theatre" (1975) for *The New York Review of Books.* In summing up her feelings for him, she wrote, "Anyone who knew and loved Chiaromonte will recognize that an intransigent and fearless honesty was a basic trait of his character." Plainly, it was her own love of honesty that had responded so avidly to Chiaromonte's.

CHAPTER XXII
LIVES OF
THE MIND
(1972–1979)

Mary McCarthy turned sixty on June 21, 1972, and celebrated at a dinner party given by her husband at Prunier's. In recognition of this milestone, the producers of French television's "Variances" taped a special thirty-minute interview. A newspaper commentator, recalling an earlier television interview during which she had called Paris "a city of notaries and concierges" where "love and youth are as short-lived as the mating season of birds," marveled at her present amiability. He called her "a new Mary McCarthy," a "mellowed, smiling woman who talked for half an hour without drawing a drop of blood." No blood was drawn, he wrote, chiefly because the interviewer asked few questions. McCarthy, "left to carry the ball pretty much by herself," seemed more interested in making points about technology and its dehumanization of human existence than in assailing current or past writers. In fact, she had nothing but praise for the writers she mentioned, especially Tolstoy, whose view of technology, she said, coincided with her own. When the interview aired, she was in Castine.

It was a glorious summer, with visitors from America and Europe and forty-two guests (some from Castine) for her annual lawn party. West's children, however, did not come at all that summer. Danny, the oldest, was in London; Jonathan, the youngest, was in Paris with his mother; and Alison was a student at New York University, majoring in the history of art and Russian. McCarthy worked most of July and August on a nine-thousand-word review of Aleksandr Solzhenitsyn's *August 1914* for the *Saturday Review.* "I found that a terribly hard job," she wrote William Jovanovich. "I had to read the book through twice, in the interests of my mental clarity, and keep poring over the Britannica, 12th and 13th editions, with a magnifying glass bent on the map of East Prussia provided there. I also resorted to Churchill's *The Unknown War* and filled a notebook with my reconstruction of the military chronology, the names and numbers of army corps, regiments, divisions, with identification of their commanders."

What troubled her about *August 1914* was Solzhenitsyn's views of history and technology, which were diametrically opposed to Tolstoy's. "[Solzhenitsyn] disagrees with Tolstoy's contention in *War and Peace* that great men cannot influence the course of events but at best can only swim along with it and await a countercurrent or the turning of the tide. Solzhenitsyn holds that leadership is determining in war. . . . Whoever is right—Solzhenitsyn or Tolstoy—about the course of history and the sense or lack of sense it makes does not matter so much." McCarthy, however, devoted an exhorbitant amount of time and energy to show that no matter what Solzhenitsyn professes, his novel, which, after all, had to follow the outlines of the story history had already written, actually "confirms" Tolstoy. Ever since her conversations with Nicola Chiaromonte on Cape Cod in the 1940s, Tolstoy has been the historical figure she empathizes with most.

Mary McCarthy was back in Paris by the middle of September, having stopped en route at Kevin's New York apartment. She had been home less than two months when she crossed the Atlantic again, this time to join Hannah Arendt for a three-day conference on Arendt's work in Toronto.

During 1973 Mary McCarthy made ten transatlantic crossings, several to report on the Ervin committee's hearings on the Watergate break-in for *The Observer* of London. She wrote six articles for *The Observer.* These, plus three that she wrote for *The New York Review of Books,* became the nine chapters of *The Mask of State: Watergate Portraits,* which Harcourt Brace Jovanovich published in June of 1974.

For the first time McCarthy found something beneficent about technology. Granted, she saw aspects of the Watergate affair—the "dirty tricks," the burglarizing of Daniel Ellsberg's psychiatrist's office, the installation of the White House monitoring system—as "advanced technology enlisted in the service of patriotism"; but when it was accidentally discovered that Nixon had been bugging his own office and that "the case would resolve, once and for all, the same way it had started, by an inadvertence of technology," she could write, "Technology had come to the country's rescue with those marvelous tapes." Just as ironic was the Nixon administration's "infatuation with the latest technology," which "went hand in hand with a passion for secrecy." As a result, Nixon, a "television creation" who distrusted print journalism, was using the "wrong medium for a public suddenly hungry for facts, not images and stage props," in trying to tell his story. For "television, with its half hour nightly news summary larded with commercials and rather fatty comment, was not up to the job of telling the tale, . . . and the newspapers, rising to the emergency, had come into their own, as though Marshall McLuhan had never been thought of and we were back in the Gutenberg Galaxy." As McCarthy explained to her English readers, with an unusual display of patriotic pride, most Americans seemed to be taking part in this "fascinating event," mastering all the crucial dates, the intricacies of laundered money, the ITT subplot of Dita Beard and Howard Hunt, the Vesco interlude, and the complicated relationships among the ever-widening cast of characters.

The Ervin committee hearings were televised twice daily, once live and once rerun on educational television. So many Americans tuned in that it was like a gigantic, countrywide town meeting, which McCarthy found exciting. "Here television shows its real usefulness," she said. "Yet without the supplement of the daily newspaper and the weekly news magazines, it is doubtful whether the public would have been up to the televised spectacle." The English, like many other Europeans, could not understand why Americans were so aroused by Watergate. And McCarthy, like many other Americans, felt compelled to tell them. At first, she mused about the possibility that Watergate represented an American need for atonement for its sins in Vietnam. But no matter how much she wanted to believe this, later she came to see it as a revival in the belief in the Constitution as a "practical political instrument."

> In me this brought on like a fierce intoxicant a rare fit of national pride. . . . Nixon's objective, I believe (insofar as he had gone beyond simple self-perpetuation in office), was to dismantle the Constitution, not only its rights and guarantees but its essential tripartite structure. In his view, warmly shared by his associates, as transpired from the Senate Watergate Committee hearings, the Constitution was a crazy, rattletrap antique, too simplistic to merit attention from a contemporary mind. And, by a nice reversal, it was the Constitution that undid him, not *Washington Post* reporters Bob Woodward and Carl Bernstein and their absurd stoolie, "Deep Throat," but the judiciary and legislative branches of the government rounding on the monstrous trespassing executive.

The Mask of State: Watergate Portraits was published in June 1974. Only two reviews of it, Richard Goodwin's in *The New York Times* and Harold Rosenberg's in *The New York Review of Books,* were positive. Both reviewers credited McCarthy with masterful analyses of the main characters and concurred with her belief that character was the key to Watergate. "By elimination," she wrote in February 1974, half a year before Nixon resigned, "we arrive at the only suspect who had the power to authorize Watergate and the character traits to match."

Other reviews were negative, ranging from the commonplace— "Mary McCarthy dips her typewriter into vinegar before she starts to

write"—to the meanspirited—"She is one of those ladies who follow the hunt at a distance, eyes agleam and spurs clapped to the horse's side, passionate in their enthusiasm for the moment when the hounds will reach the fox. . . . She tells us little except what happens when emotion rides the mind." The most disagreeable, to McCarthy's mind, was James Fallows's thirteen-page review in *The Washington Monthly* entitled "Mary McCarthy, The Blinders She Wears." Because Fallows believed that "Mary McCarthy's importance as a political writer [was] no longer to be overlooked," he undertook a painstaking analysis of *The Mask of State.* According to him, "she obviously [enjoyed] being on the scene of the political story of the day," but not when it interfered too onerously with her private life. To illustrate this point, he wrote that "she dropped out of the Ervin hearings early because it was time to return to Paris." Even Harold Rosenberg, whose positive review was principally a rebuttal of Fallows's, agreed that she "missed a vital element . . . through being out of the country when Patrick Buchanan took the witness stand," because, Rosenberg said, "Nixon's speech writer openly affirmed the strategy of seizure of power by his minority group and keeping hold of it permanently by incapacitating popular opposition." Fallows concluded, in a section subtitled "Glued to Her Seat," that she was an impudent outsider who did insufficient legwork. (McCarthy herself had admitted being an outsider. In a letter to William Jovanovich on Watergate Hotel stationery, she complained that "the press group here is a very competitive group, not welcoming or helpful to outsiders," unlike the friendly journalists she had encountered in Saigon.)

"Perhaps I should finish my life as a translator" was McCarthy's facetious reaction to the reviews in a letter to William Jovanovich. But to Hannah Arendt she disclosed that she was puzzled and hurt, especially that none of her friends had come to her defense.

> If one of my friends had been in *my* place, *I* would have raised my voice. This leads to the conclusion that I am peculiar, in some way that I cannot make out, *indefensible,* at least for my friends. They are fond of me but with reservations. In any case none of this involves you because you were in the hospital and then recovering when it happened, because you weren't in the U.S. and didn't see those unpleasant pieces and because, finally, even if you had been on Riverside Drive and in the peak of condition, you couldn't have helped since people would have said that you were repaying the Eichmann debt, that we had dedicated books to each other, etc. In other words, that you were a tainted witness.

The hospitalization McCarthy alluded to in her letter occurred in Scotland in May 1974. Arendt had been in Aberdeen to deliver one of her Gifford Lectures, which McCarthy had attended. Soon after McCarthy returned to Paris, Arendt suffered a heart attack, and McCarthy went back to Aberdeen for a week. Late in the summer Arendt visited Castine and again at Christmas, the first time the Wests had opened their house in winter. "Great festivities are planned," McCarthy wrote William Jovanovich, "notably reading aloud or acting out English mystery plays—the Shepherd's, the Magi, and Herod; I've procured them from the British Council Library and Jim has had them photostatted." It was a glorious holiday, which the Wests shared with Stonington friends Eleanor Perényi, with her mother and son; Kevin and his daughter Lillah; Alison West, who was now a graduate student in NYU's Institute of Fine Arts, having recently received her B.A. *magna cum laude* from the same institution; the DuViviers; as well as Hannah Arendt. On Christmas day, despite falling snow, forty guests assembled at the Wests'. Like Miss Brayton in Portsmouth, Mary McCarthy covered a table with presents, though hers were purchased in Paris and London. "We were in London last Saturday," McCarthy had written Carmen Angleton earlier in the month, "just overnight, but we devoted our shopping to Castine—food and Christmas decorations and Christmas carol records and Christmas-tree lights and odds and ends for the fish pond (the guests, as I believe you know, pull ribbons and fish a gift)." Elizabeth Hardwick, Penelope Gilliatt, and the Wests' Castine neighbors, the Philip Booths, were there for New Year's.

In the new year, when McCarthy was back in Paris and Arendt in New York, they kept in constant touch with Sunday phone calls and frequent letters. In April 1975 they met in Copenhagen, where Arendt was awarded the prestigious Sonning Prize for her contribution to European civilization. (Previous winners included Winston Churchill, Albert Schweitzer, Bertrand Russell, Karl Barth, Laurence Olivier, and Arthur Koestler.) In June, McCarthy visited Arendt in Marbach, Germany, where Arendt was staying for a month to fulfill her obligations as one of the executors of Karl Jasper's estate. Since Arendt stayed in Europe all summer and McCarthy was in Castine, the two friends did not see each other until September, when Arendt was on her way back to America. She died suddenly of a heart attack on December 4. McCarthy flew to New York for the funeral four days later.

Hannah Arendt had made Mary McCarthy literary executrix of her estate. Though McCarthy had been hard at work on a novel at the time of Arendt's death, she put it aside for nearly two years to focus on

Arendt's thoughts and writings. When she died, she had been working on a book called *The Life of the Mind,* which she envisioned as a three-part work. As projected, volume one was to be about "Thinking." In it she would consider questions such as: What makes us think? What is the 'use' of thinking? Are truth and meaning the same? The first part of volume two was to be about "Willing," and in it she would ponder perplexities of the will: In what sense is it free? Does it exist at all, or is it merely an illusion of consciousness? If it exists, is it not split into two wills? Part three, to be contained in the second volume, was to be about "Judging." Thinking and willing were the subject of Arendt's Gifford Lectures at the University of Aberdeen. "Thinking" had been the focus of the first group of lectures in 1973; McCarthy had attended the first and last lectures of this series. In the spring of 1974 Arendt had delivered the second series, on "Willing." She had planned to conclude with the series on "Judging," to be delivered in 1976. At the time of her death she had written drafts of "Thinking" and "Willing." The first page of her "Judging" manuscript was in her typewriter when she died. Mary McCarthy made this work publishable by editing the "Thinking" and "Willing" sections and by adding an appendix that contained extracts from Arendt's lectures on Kant's *Philosophy of Judgement* given at the New School for Social Research in New York. Harcourt Brace Jovanovich published *The Life of the Mind* in two volumes in 1978.

Mary McCarthy was well suited to the task of editing Arendt. Her meticulousness was invaluable in coping with the extensive quotations and references in Arendt's work, and her familiarity with German—she had been taking lessons for several years—helped her sort out the meaning of Arendt's sometimes convoluted sentences. Most important, she and Arendt had shared ideas for years. As early as 1954, Arendt wrote McCarthy:

> The chief fallacy is to believe that Truth is a result which comes at the end of a thought-process. Truth, on the contrary, is always the beginning of thought; thinking is always result-less. That is the difference between "philosophy" and science: science has results, philosophy never. Thinking starts after an experience of truth has struck home, so to speak. The difference between philosophers and other people is that the former refuse to let go, but not that they are the only receptacles of truth. This notion that truth is the result of thought is very old and goes back to ancient classical philosophy, possibly to Socrates himself. If I am right and it is a fallacy, then probably it is the oldest fallacy of Western philosophy.

And fourteen years later, responding to McCarthy's review of Nathalie Sarraute's *Between Life and Death,* she wrote:

> . . . there is so much in it that is very close to things I have been thinking about in recent years. The whole question of inner life, its turmoil, multiplication, the splitting-into-two (consciousness), the curious fact that I am One only in company, the importance or non-importance these data have for the thinking process, the "silent dialogue between me and myself," etc. . . . The silent dialogue of thought goes on between me and myself, but not between two selves. In thought, you are self-less—without age, without psychological attributes, not at all as you "really" are.

"This convergence of cast of mind," as McCarthy called the similarity of their intellectual viewpoints, was of enormous benefit to Arendt, who had worked on several of her texts with her friend, and had even gone over some of the "Thinking" section of *The Life of the Mind,* in embryonic and advanced stages, with McCarthy. McCarthy had objected to the correct, but now rare, use of the word *thoughtlessness* to mean the disinclination to think (versus its more common denotation of heedlessness or forgetfulness). "It seems to me a mistake," McCarthy wrote Arendt in 1971, "to force a key word in an essay to mean what it doesn't normally, even when the reader understands what you are trying to say with it." One of Arendt's points was that an Eichmann, despite his ordinariness and lack of ideological conviction or evil motive, could do what he did because of thoughtlessness, that is, his refusal to examine whatever happens. Maybe, Arendt reasoned, thoughtfulness might make men abstain from evil. McCarthy also pointed out a lack of clarity in the difference between what Arendt called thoughtlessness and stupidity. She wrote Arendt:

> I would have said that Eichmann was profoundly and egregiously stupid, and for me stupidity is not the same as having a low I.Q. Here I rather agree with Kant (and always have, without knowing that Kant said it), that stupidity is caused, not by brain failure, but by a wicked heart. Insensitiveness, opacity, inability to make connections, often accompanied by low "animal" cunning. One cannot help feeling that this mental oblivion is *chosen,* by the heart or the moral will—an active preference, and that explains why one is so irritated by stupidity, which is not the case when one is dealing with a truly backward individual. A village idiot may be far less stupid than an Eichmann. Hence the old equation between "simplicity" and goodness of soul or heart. An idiot of course can be reflective; he *thinks,* in your sense, probably quite a lot, maybe more than most

people, since his other mental powers are deficient, and he "connects," which is somewhat different from making logical chains of ideas, though I would be hard put to say how the simple meditative associations of an idiot were distinguishable from the processes of normal logic.

A clarification of thoughtlessness and how it differed from stupidity, as well as further elucidation of other points McCarthy had made in her letter, showed up in the final manuscript. Unquestionably, Arendt had profited from McCarthy's suggestions, just as McCarthy was aided in the final editing by having provided advice in the past.

McCarthy's familiarity with the material notwithstanding, putting together *The Life of the Mind* was an enormous task. Since the mid-1960's she had had a part-time secretary who typed and filed correspondence, so McCarthy began by having her secretary type up Arendt's manuscript in triple spacing. "Then I'll go over it," she wrote William Jovanovich, "see how it looks as a whole, and probably retype it or have it retyped once more. It needs quite a lot of work." Part of what it needed was what Hannah Arendt had wryly called "Englishing." Arendt had not learned to write in English until she was thirty-five. As a result, she wrote sentences that were often extremely long, in the German manner, and she frequently misused prepositions and misplaced adverbs. The editing job also involved hunting for references and checking elusive quotations. After five months of steady work on "Thinking," which was to be volume one, McCarthy wrote Carmen Angleton, "I've stayed mostly inside, with all the draperies drawn, surrounded by the *Critique of Pure Reason,* the complete Plato, the complete Greek Drama, two selected Aristotles, Nietzsche, Epictetus, working on Hannah's manuscript. And it is *finished.* I sent it off yesterday. . . . I feel like a heroine but have no one, I perceive, to appreciate me. No one will ever know or ought ever to know the true state of that manuscript, and I must keep quiet about it. . . . And yet I want my toil to be appreciated, damn it. The trouble with being a perfectionist, which Hannah certainly wasn't, is that you expect admiration. Which of course she had no interest in."

Mary McCarthy still had to edit the second volume of *The Life of the Mind,* answer editorial queries on page proofs of the first volume, acknowledge questions about Arendt's literary estate, and work on a version of "Thinking" for *The New Yorker.* Ten months later she was still working.

It has been all Hannah, day after day and even night after night. I haven't touched my novel except for a six-day interim when I did three or four pages—it is hard to get back into after footnotes, Heidegger, and Hegel. . . . I can't describe what has been going on. Some is normal editing and revising, which in Hannah's case is more like translating. But the checkers at Harcourt discovered a frightening chaos in the footnotes and in the citations from other authors.

Not until November 1977, two years after Hannah Arendt's death, did McCarthy's work on *The Life of the Mind* end. Early in the month William Shawn had brought her to New York for final queries for *The New Yorker* series. By the end of the month two installments of *The Life of the Mind* had appeared. "In celebration of my new-found freedom," she wrote a friend, "I started work on my novel again." Of course, her work as literary executrix continued. Dozens of requests from doctoral students and scholars wanting access to Arendt's private papers at the Library of Congress had to be answered. While responding to these and similar queries required judgment, it did not require the same expenditure of time and energy as the editing chores.

Her effort had been, of course, a labor of love, which she discusses in an editor's postface that appears in both volumes.

> It has been a heavy job, which has kept going an imaginary dialogue with her, verging sometimes, as in life, on debate. . . . But it has also been, if not fun, . . . rewarding. I have learned, for example, that I can under-stand the *Critique of Pure Reason,* which I had previously thought impene-trable by me. Searching for a truant reference, I have read some entire Platonic dialogues (the *Theaetetus,* the *Sophist*) that I had never dipped into before. I have learned the difference between an electric ray and a sting ray. I have reread bits of Virgil's Bucolics and Georgics, which I had not looked at since college. . . . Throughout this travail, there have been times of positive elation, a mixture of our school days revisited (those textbooks, late-night discussions of philosophic points), and the tonic effect of our dead friend's ideas, alive and generative of controversy as well as of surprised agreement. Though I have missed her in the course of these months—in fact more than a year now—of work, wished her back to clarify, object, reassure, compliment and be complimented, I do not think I shall truly miss her, feel the pain in the amputated limb, till it is over. I am aware that she is dead but I am simultaneously aware of her as a distinct presence in this room, listening to my words as I write, possibly assenting with her musing nod, possibly stifling a yawn.

Vassar's 1976 commencement address, which McCarthy delivered, bore the marks of her recent preoccupation with Greek thought. In her talk she illustrated her thesis that education should be its own end by focusing her listeners' attention on pre-Socratic and Socratic Athens, periods when "knowledge of nature and the laws of geometry were the earliest objects of study, but with little sense of practical application, of what could be *done* with that knowledge." Among Socrates's students, only Plato was preparing for a career in philosophy. The others talked, discussed, analyzed, for the fun and love of it. And Plato admitted that if philosophy was useful for anything, it was only that it could teach statesmen to govern. But even this was Socratic heresy, McCarthy pointed out. Knowledge was to be pursued for its own sake, not as a means to some other end.

The same year Bard College, the small liberal arts college that tried to put the Socratic ideal into practice, awarded McCarthy an honorary degree. Illness prevented her from accepting in person, but one of her former Bard students read her prepared address. "A final and moving reason for my warmth of gratitude to you for this honor which brings me officially into the Bard community," McCarthy wrote, "is that my friends—Heinrich Blücher, a Bard teacher of genius, and his wife, Hannah Arendt—are here in the graveyard, commemorated by two stones. This fall their collection of books will go to the Bard Library."

McCarthy was now free to work on *Cannibals and Missionaries,* the novel that she had first started thinking about in 1974. At the time of Arendt's death, at the end of 1975, she had finished three chapters; when she turned sixty-five, on June 21, 1977, she was about halfway finished. (Her husband, who always planned momentous occasions for her birthdays, organized a dinner for fifty at the apartment of Jonathan Randal, the *Washington Post* bureau chief in Paris, whom McCarthy had been friends with ten years earlier in Saigon.) She finished the novel in Rome at the American Academy—a residential community for fine arts and humanities scholars, where she had been invited to be scholar-in-residence—early in 1979.

From the time she began the book at the end of 1974 until it was finished in February 1979, she had not published even an essay or a book review of her own. But once free of its burden, she agreed to chair two roundtables, one in English and the other in French, on Hannah Arendt at the American Center in Paris. During April she and her husband met Frank Preston, her eighty-four-year-old uncle, and his second wife, Myrtle, for an Easter tour of Ireland, a country McCarthy had never visited before. She had seen little of her uncle since her college years. His first wife, Isabel, had annoyed the teenage Mary McCarthy because, she wrote recently in *How I Grew,* "she repeatedly interfered with my grandmother's guidance to me on the subject of nail polish, lipstick, silk stockings, and so on, but never in the direction of a greater permissiveness." After Isabel's death, Frank had remarried; and on a European wedding trip in 1962, the newlyweds had seen the Wests in Paris. When Frank Preston got sick a few years later, McCarthy flew to Seattle for three days. Frank Preston died in 1986, the last descendant of Simon Manly Preston to carry the name Preston.

The Wests spent the summer of 1979 in Castine as usual, returning to Paris in September. Less than a month later they both flew to New York, at Harcourt Brace Jovanovich's expense, for the official publication of *Cannibals and Missionaries* on October 15. That night McCarthy read a chapter at the YMHA Poetry Center on East Ninety-second Street. It was a lucky coincidence of dates—the date of the reading, the official publication date, and the feast of Saint Theresa of Avila, for whom Mary Therese McCarthy was named, all of which fell on October 15—that prompted her to come to New York, she said. Elizabeth Hardwick entertained at her West Sixty-seventh Street apartment after the reading. It was a large party, and among the guests were Kevin McCarthy; Frances Fitzgerald, whose book on Vietnam, *Fire in the Lake,* McCarthy had admired; Evelyn Hofer, the photographer for *The Stones of Florence;* Eileen Simpson, whom she had known since the early days of Simpson's marriage to John Berryman; Mary Gordon, whose *Cannibals and Missionaries* review, which had appeared two weeks earlier in *The New York Times Book Review,* McCarthy had liked; Shana Alexander, whose book on Patricia Hearst, *Anyone's Daughter,* had also just come out; and Senator Eugene McCarthy, who had inspired the character of Senator Jim Carey in *Cannibals and Missionaries.* "There's no attempt at disguise," McCarthy told Kevin later. "On the other hand, it's not really supposed to be Gene McCarthy. It's an improvisation on the theme of Gene McCarthy. It was fun—trying to be inside his mind and to be his voice and do his voice."

The Wests stayed with Frani Blough Muser, Mary's Vassar classmate, on East Eighty-sixth Street, and passed a pleasant week enjoying reunions with friends and family—Kevin, his children, and his new wife, Kate, as well as Alison West. McCarthy agreed to do a taped interview for Dick Cavett's television program—an interview that would have dramatic consequences when it was aired the following January. McCarthy was also interviewed by Kevin for *People.*

It had been five years earlier when she sat down at her desk in her book-lined study in Paris to record a "Note to Myself on a Possible Novel." This inchoate yet profitable exercise of two days yielded a design of the most topical and least autobiographical of her novels. As *Cannibals and Missionaries* opens, in 1975, a committee of prominent liberals sets out by air for Iran to investigate torture under the Shah. A party of art collectors on its way to visit Iranian museums and archaeological sites occupies the plane's first-class section. Terrorists hijack the plane over France and divert it to Schiphol in the Netherlands, where they extort a mammoth helicopter from the Dutch government and NATO to take the liberals and millionaires to a deserted Dutch polder (land reclaimed from the sea by dredging and landfill). Most of the novel takes place on the polder, where the terrorists, posing as a television company filming frontier life, have taken over a farm as a hideout. The list of characters who will live in this enforced community include twelve millionaires, whose Cézannes, El Grecos, and single Vermeer are flown in and exchanged for their lives; the five terrorists—two Arabs, a South American, and two Netherlanders, including Jeroen, their leader; and eight liberals—the relentlessly optimistic Episcopalian rector of Saint Matthew's in New York's Gracie Square; a sweet octogenarian bishop; a U.S. senator who is an ex-seminarian and poet; a poisonous president of a prominent women's college; an American journalist; a Dutch deputy; and two professors, one English and the other American.

Much of this was conceived by McCarthy in her "Note to Myself on a Possible Novel," in which she wrote:

> Possibility of a group of kidnappees. Disadvantage: close to *Grand Hotel, Ship of Fools, Bridge of San Luis Rey* formula of diverse figures brought together and held together by chance. This might be obviated if group is traveling together for some reason. . . . To attend a convention? No. They would be too much alike. But what if they are on a peace mission of investigation of torture, say, in some dictatorship—Iran? . . . Most obvious site for kidnapping is an airplane. . . . They would not be the only passengers. As for the hijackers, whoever they are, they will have to speak English. . . . What if the terrorists get to realize that some of their prisoners own fortunes in works of art? A demand that a Giorgione, say, be surrendered in return for its owner's life? But why would the terrorists want the Giorgione, except that it does not have to be fed and cannot escape? Well, for publicity, it has more solid value than inflated currency. A museum starts to assemble in the hideaway compound. . . . The novel is about values—exchange values. What will you give for what? Art as the supreme value. Or as the supreme exchange value? Its scarcity.

The novel questions the modern tendency to see human beings as dispensable but art as irreplaceable, a trend that began, perhaps, during

World War II with the Allied and German understanding not to bomb certain monuments, and continues to the present day, when political leaders discuss up-to-date weapons that will exterminate people but leave buildings intact. It was the theft of Vermeer's painting "Young Lady with a Guitar" by Irish terrorists during the winter of 1974 that set Mary McCarthy pondering this point. The terrorists cut off strips of the painting, sent them to newspapers, and threatened to destroy the masterpiece if their demands were not met. That people were more gripped by this than by the 1973 case of J. Paul Getty's grandson, whose ear was cut off by his kidnappers, fascinated McCarthy. "And the whole question of the value people put on works of art is very interesting, especially for someone who cares about art and beauty in every way as I do," she said in a 1979 interview.

Her musings became the subject of a lecture she gave in the spring of 1974 at the University of Aberdeen on "Art Values and the Value of Art." Hannah Arendt, who was present, said afterwards, "You should draw on that for a novel." Her remark, plus a statement William Jovanovich had made that pictures were now being kidnapped as if they were people, led directly to *Cannibals and Missionaries.* The genesis for the committee of liberals in the novel was a group that an Iranian in Paris had tried to organize to investigate torture under the Shah. "There was this character who came to see me in Paris," McCarthy later explained, "and who stayed on my sofa for about six weeks with his folders, and I was writing all these people like Ramsey Clark and Bishop Paul Moore." The committee that the Iranian talked to her about turned out not to exist.

Her favorite character in the novel is Henk Van Vliet de Jonge, partly modeled on her Dutch friend Cees Nooteboom, who introduced her to several people in Holland—including Hans Van Mierlo, a member of Parliament and political party leader; Joop de Uyl, the prime minister; and Han Lammers, the *Landdrost* (governor) of the new polder complex—and who advised her in choosing Dutch names and in using Dutch words. Certainly, she never had a better time researching a novel. After one trip late in 1975, she wrote William Jovanovich:

> Holland was fun. We drove up to look again at the newest polder—in Flevoland—from a new angle—where and how could a plane land? We found a little flying club and school and learned that its airstrip couldn't take anything bigger than a six-passenger craft, so that was out, which I was glad of, because the flying club, with bar, restaurant, etc., was too tame and civilized for my taste. Our conclusion, with some Dutch guidance:

only two types of bigger aircraft could land on a polder—one a Fokker Friendship and the other a big helicopter, which the Dutch army doesn't possess but which might be borrowed from the German NATO forces. I decided I preferred the helicopter, because it can put down anywhere, while the Friendship would have to land on the highway—wide enough (we *thought;* we practically used a tape-measure) but a little dull. We also recognized that nothing could land at night on the polder, which slightly affects the novel's time-table.

My next step was to visit Parliament, under the wing of a real younger Dutch deputy, Hans Van Mierlo, whom I'd confessed the whole plot to. He set up a visit, so that I could spend the whole afternoon in the Chamber, meet the elderly President (equivalent to the Speaker of the House of Commons) and the Prime Minister. It was rather a large party that descended on the Hague: two Dutch writers (one their leading younger novelist) and a girl who is Holland's musical celebrity, something between a pop star and a *chanteuse.* We are all friends anyway and we had tea with the Speaker. I had an appointment at six with the Prime Minister, which broadened into a dinner invitation for all of us and Van Mierlo. Then the Prime Minister's wife asked to come along. (Jim had gone back to Paris, alas.) This took place in a gay restaurant on the water, and soon I confessed all to the Prime Minister too, who pitched in with everybody else to help with the logistics of the plot. Then, leaving the Prime Minister and his wife, we went to the press bar in the chamber, which was still sitting, and Van Mierlo brought up the Minister of Defense, to discuss the helicopter question. He allowed that he *could* borrow a helicopter big enough to hold thirty persons from the Germans but probably wouldn't if it was to oblige some hijackers. "But if one of the hijackees is a Parliamentarian?" said Van Mierlo. "Oh, then, yes." This exchange was what called for the revisions; Van Vliet de Jonge has to be a *sitting* parliamentarian if I am to get my helicopter, whereas in the version you saw he had lost his seat. (In reality, he couldn't lose it anyway except by resigning; the Dutch vote party slates and the leader of a party couldn't lose his seat in an election unless the whole party was wiped out.)

It was a most amusing, indeed enchanting, adorable evening and day. I am in love with Holland all over again and particularly with Hans Van Mierlo, a good-looking, slightly too fat, poetical deputy, who by mesmerizing coincidence comes from a Catholic family, like my hero Van Vliet de Jonge and, like him, lost his faith young. To relieve your mind—Jim has a slight crush on him too. A sweet note was contributed by the Prime Minister's wife, as we were saying good-bye outside the restaurant: "Oh"—sadly—"aren't you going to have our Queen in your novel?"

The upshot, I fear, will be that everybody in Holland will be informed of the hijacking plot of the story, though all were sworn to secrecy. But, as was agreed at dinner, it will doubtless get deformed in the narration and people will hear that there has been a plot (the other kind) to kidnap a Dutch deputy and hold him for ransom on a polder.

The fact-finding trip, one of several over the next few years, was a product of McCarthy's conviction that there cannot be anything in fiction that flies in the face of fact. One reason she loves *War and Peace* is the veracity of its details. "If Tolstoy had put the battle of Borodino two years before its historical date," she stated in a 1971 interview, "it would be disturbing. Readers ought not to say, 'Oh, it couldn't have happened that way.' " Fiction, she insists, must have a firm substructure. All details must be accurate, even if making them so involves dismantling something already written. For example, a research trip to Holland resulted in a "setback" in chapter 8 of *Cannibals and Missionaries.* In its opening, she had pictured one of the characters watching a soccer game on Dutch television on a Sunday afternoon. But, she learned, telecasting does not normally begin until 6 P.M., with the exception of a late Sunday afternoon Calvinist religious service, and soccer is shown on Wednesdays. In her new version, the character watches a children's Mickey Mouse program on German television.

It was not only trips to Holland that set her undoing the structure she had already fabricated. Once it was a picture of the configuration of seats in a 747 jet. She told William Jovanovich:

> I would not have had to go back all the way to page 63 if a technical— not a literary—problem hadn't stared me in the face when Jim sweetly brought home floor plans of Air France's jumbo jets and I found that I'd described an impossibility—in those planes smokers and non-smokers don't sit in separate sections but in separate cabins—the non-smoking is just behind first class. Also there's a difficulty about the location of the serving pantries. You'd be amazed how difficult and enraging this has been to fix. In comparison, the gross *literary* faults were highly corrigible. The ideal would be to put them in a 707, but Air France has no 707 Sunday to Teheran, and it has to be Sunday because Chapter 1 was Saturday and there is the business about the consulate being closed. There is a 707, Air Iran, at one o'clock from Orly, but I don't see the art collectors taking that or indeed any of the characters taking it because they would have to change airports—well, they *could* do that, but why? Also, I'm not familiar with how the personnel on Air Iran behaves. And besides Air Iran doesn't serve drinks if it can help it—the prophet.
>
> A 747 presents other drawbacks, but that I already knew. It's too big to land on a polder. At least Jim thinks it is, and I shall check that with

the Dutch over the weekend. But probably the hijackers will have to demand to be given another plane in Schiphol. . . .

The moral of all or some of this is the writing-course maxim: Write about what you know. I haven't been in a jumbo jet since this whole smoking and non-smoking nonsense has been instituted, and I thought that each cabin would be divided into non-smoking ahead, smoking behind, as it is in a 707. (It's true I had a few misgivings, which is why I asked for the floor and seating plan.) Anyway, it is now all beautifully schematized, with the characters' places in the cabin marked by initials. When I get back, if I'm satisfied, I'll send you the new pages.

I'm afraid this is terribly boring—I mean, the technicalities—but I have this fanatical obsession with accuracy. The events in my books may be improbable or lightly fantastic, but the characters have to take real airplanes that can be found on a schedule: the schedule in force in January 1975.

Her passion for exactitude prompted her to check and recheck every detail. She questioned Cees Nooteboom countless times about birds in the polder, the time required to get from Amsterdam to the polder, what kind of Dutch police would be called; she asked William Mostyn-Owen of Christie's the market value of various paintings; she sought medical expertise from two doctors; she questioned Nicholas King about New York's "social" names; she checked German words with Werner Stemans, her German teacher, and Dutch words with a colleague of her husband's; she even interviewed someone who had been hijacked. This concern with the accuracy of details is due not only to her belief that the basic ingredient of the novel is a "heavy dosage of fact," but also to the belief that these details enable a writer to create atmosphere. "I think writing should make a strong impression in terms of atmosphere," she has said, "like the strong impression of the heath in *The Return of the Native*."

The atmosphere of *Cannibals and Missionaries* was what troubled her most during the book's planning phase. In her "Note to Myself" she had envisioned a novel that would be "closer to Conrad than, say, to *Middlemarch*. Extreme situations. Are they welcomed or shrunk from as tests? What worries me about this novel is that it doesn't feel particularly like me. . . . I am attracted by the 'small' event. That's how *Birds of America* began. But here is a big event. Reduce it to tiny particulars. The Dutchman collects tiny paintings. Somebody else on the plane carefully pockets sugar, salt, mustard. Holland as a 'miniature country,' or 'pocket' model."

Harcourt Brace Jovanovich printed 50,000 copies of *Cannibals and Missionaries,* but only half that number sold. McCarthy's reading public was shrinking, partly owing to the long intervals between novels—it had been eight years since *Birds of America* and sixteen years since *The Group.* Once again, there were a great many negative reviews. The most enthusiastic reviewer was Mary Gordon, who wrote that *Cannibals and Missionaries* "would have been impossible without [McCarthy's] experience of traveling to Vietnam as a reporter. Many of the details of that experience, particularly those about physical fear and communal bonding, find their way into this novel in the accounts of the passengers' ordeal." But most of the other reviewers, though they praised McCarthy for her extraordinary research and bullwhip wit, found the book boring, especially the long-drawn-out business of ransoming the rich hostages and their paintings. The novel is tedious in parts probably because McCarthy deals with more than two dozen characters who are confined to a severely limited space. All they can do is think and talk; and with McCarthy playing the ventriloquist again, they do so in their own voices. Even though the characters in *Cannibals and Missionaries* have more interesting minds than those of the Vassar girls in *The Group,* the reader grows weary of all the switching back and forth among them. Yet what this novel illustrates more than anything else is the author's keen ear for naturalistic dialogue, passing as it does from one voice to another without warning, like an oral Daumier. Two reviewers thought she failed on this point too. Benjamin DeMott wished "the author were less class-bound," and Margaret Wimsatt asked, "Why do all those wealthies speak like Vassar girls, *circa* 1934?"

Getting the voices right was McCarthy's most formidable task in creating *Cannibals and Missionaries.* She described the effort in a letter to Hannah Arendt:

> I find I am steering down a channel with some familiar landscape on either side. On the one hand [the Episcopal minister] keeps sounding like the girls in *The Group* and on the other side like Peter Levi. Scylla and Charybdis.
>
> It is sad to realize that one's fictions, i.e., one's "creative" side, cannot learn anything. *I* have learned, I think, but they, or it, haven't. The reason for this would be interesting to discover, if one only had the time. These confining boundaries, I suppose, are set by my life-experience, which lies in vaguely upper-middle-class territory lying between those girls and Peter. My mental experience is broader, but that doesn't seem to count for the imagination. And if I went and worked in a factory, would the

"hands" in a novel I wrote afterwards think like Vassar B-minus students of forty years ago or else be half-Jewish, thoughtful, and given to humor? I am going to have a Jewish character, a young woman in this novel, and already I am feeling the temptation to make her *half*-Jewish, in the belief that I cannot fully imagine, from the inside, the outlook of a Jewish girl. It all leads to the awful recognition that one *is* one's life; God is not mocked.

CHAPTER XXIII
"INCLUDING 'AND' AND 'THE'"
(1980–1984)

ON JANUARY 25 and 26, while McCarthy was in London to deliver a series of lectures, the two-part interview she had taped with Dick Cavett the previous October aired in the United States. During the program, Cavett asked McCarthy to name contemporary writers she thought were "overrated and we could do without, given a limited amount of time." "I don't think we have those anymore," she answered, meaning, she said, that today's books were either popular successes that usually dealt with sensational violence or sex, or serious or witty publications that had at least some merit. Surprised by her response, Cavett repeated his question, as if he could not believe what he had heard. "We don't have the overpraised writer anymore?"

"At least I'm not aware of it," McCarthy replied. "The only one I can think of is a holdover like Lillian Hellman, who I think is tremendously overrated, a bad writer, and a dishonest writer, but she really belongs to the past."

"What is dishonest about [her]?" Cavett asked.

"Everything," McCarthy responded. "I said once in some interview that every word she writes is a lie, including 'and' and 'the.'"

Lillian Hellman, alone in her Park Avenue apartment, saw the broadcast. She was furious. After the show, she telephoned several people, including Cavett, to give vent to her anger. Cavett offered to let her rebut McCarthy's attack on his show. She refused. Two weeks later she sued Mary McCarthy, Dick Cavett, and the Public Broadcasting System's New York affiliate, Channel 13, which had broadcast the show, for two and a quarter million dollars on the grounds that her reputation had been damaged—one and three-quarter million for pain and anguish and half a million for punitive damages for what she charged were McCarthy's libelous remarks about her.

McCarthy first learned of the lawsuit when Herbert Mitgang of *The New York Times* telephoned her in London to ask for her reaction. She "made no effort to modify what she said about Miss Hellman during the broadcast," Mitgang wrote in the February 16 *Times*. After the phone call, McCarthy went to a party at the DuViviers' and told them about the lawsuit, which she found amusing. But when she returned to Paris ten days after Mitgang's call and read clippings from the New York newspapers that friends had sent her, she began to take Hellman's action more seriously. On February 26 she wrote William Jovanovich:

> . . . until yesterday, incredibly, not a single item of newsprint had reached us. . . . Till then we didn't know what was in the complaint, what in fact I'd *said* on the Cavett Show (so many months ago), nor that the sum demanded was two and a quarter million dollars—I'd understood that it was two, not that, from my perspective of $63,000 in savings, the difference is perceptible.

McCarthy was soon corresponding with Benjamin O'Sullivan, who had been her lawyer for many years; the litigation department of his firm, Holtzmann, Wise, and Shepard, began preparing McCarthy's defense. O'Sullivan, who was not himself a libel specialist, acted as an adviser during the suit.

The lawsuit provoked a great deal of gossip and opinion, some of which appeared in newsprint and nearly all of which deplored both McCarthy's gratuitous statement and Hellman's litigious response. Even Kevin McCarthy, in the unpublished part of a taped interview with his sister for *People,* asked what she had against Lillian Hellman. "You really gave her a terrific slam," he said. Most New York intellectuals believed that Hellman's lifelong Stalinism was what irked McCarthy. "It's not just two old ladies engaged in a cat fight," said *Dissent* editor Irving Howe. "The question involved—of one's attitude toward communism—is probably the central political-cultural-intellectual problem of the 20th century. I think for many of us those disputes were the formative passions of our lives—for good or bad, it's made people what they are today." Lillian Hellman told *The New York Times* that she, too, assumed politics was responsible for what McCarthy said about her. "I think she has always disliked me. It could go back to the Spanish Civil War days, in November or December of 1937, after I had returned from Spain."

It was not surprising that Hellman thought this. She had, after all, met McCarthy only two times, and on both occasions McCarthy had been quite sharp with her over the issue of the Spanish Civil War. The first meeting, in 1937, was at a dinner party to which Hellman had come with Louis Kronenberger, at the time working for *Fortune.* McCarthy remembers that she recognized Hellman as the author of *The Children's Hour.* "I'm not sure I knew at first that she was a Stalinist but in the discussion of Spain it became evident and I spoke out, perhaps rather fiercely." (A dinner party similar to the one at which she met Lillian Hellman was described in "The Genial Host," a chapter of *The Company She Keeps,* as

Hellman biographer William Wright points out in *Lillian Hellman; The Image, The Woman.* Though the protagonist of the story accuses the Stalinists present of being unpaid Russian agents, McCarthy did not do so on this occasion, as Wright reports, nor was the party destroyed when she spoke out.)

The second encounter between Hellman and McCarthy occurred in 1948, also at a dinner party. Harold Taylor, the president of Sarah Lawrence, where McCarthy was teaching at the time, had invited Hellman, McCarthy, Stephen Spender, and several students for dinner at his house. When McCarthy arrived, Hellman was talking to the students on a sun porch. She was telling them that John Dos Passos had turned against the Spanish Loyalists during the Spanish Civil War because of his stomach: he was disappointed by the food in Madrid. McCarthy told O'Sullivan:

> She was alone in Taylor's sun parlor, with her wide-eyed converts and, when I came in, she paid no attention to me, taking me (I suppose) for a student, because I looked quite young then, or for a younger faculty person of no importance. At any rate she went on talking to the girls, as though she could not guess that there was anyone in the room capable of giving her the lie. Which I then did, suggesting that if the girls wanted to know his real views, they should read *Adventures of a Young Man* on the subject, published nine years before. He had not "turned against the Loyalists" then, only against the Communists who were running the show and murdering Trotskyites, Poumists, and Anarchists. His immediate motive (I think I may have said) was not the food in war-time Madrid but the murder of Andrés Nin, who had been his friend. Well, I won't expand on the incident, but I remember that on her bare . . . arms she had a great many bracelets, gold and silver, and that they all began to tremble—in her fury and surprise, I assumed, at being caught red-handed in a brainwashing job. I have never seen her since, but it is true that this incident stuck in my memory. I was no longer close to Dos (I didn't agree with his political "evolution"), but Edmund, and he and I had been friends, and I couldn't bear to hear those lies so smoothly applied to him, as if they were coming out of a dispenser tube. She wasn't *openly* hostile to him (which might have tipped the girls off), but smiling, knowledgeable, tolerant of his weaknesses—"He did love his food." To me, that was wickedness.

Although it was evident that the antagonism between the two women went back many years, McCarthy insisted that she was not grinding a political ax with her remarks on the Cavett show. She told O'Sullivan:

What has happened, obviously, is that the whole business as seen by the press has been a lining-up of political sides. This is really *her* doing. In fact my remark on the Cavett Show wasn't political, overtly or covertly. To me the woman is false through and through. It's not just the fresh varnish she puts on her seamy old Stalinism. In one of those "autobiographical" volumes she tells some story about "Dash" and a pond on her property full of turtles; I no more believe that than I do her account of her House un-American performance. This isn't true of all old Communists and fellow-travelers. I imagine Howard Fast is fairly truthful, for instance, and Arthur Miller, in contrast to Hellman, behaved very straightforwardly during the un-American affair. I wish that somehow Stalinism or anti-Stalinism wouldn't be allowed to figure in [our answer to Hellman]. She wouldn't have inserted it if she didn't feel it was to her advantage; she wants it to look as if I'm persecuting her for her "brave" support of progressive causes.

In fact, it was the Spanish Civil War, although indirectly, that brought Hellman's name to McCarthy's mind the day Dick Cavett asked his fateful question. Hellman, without knowing it, was the cause of a dispute among the board members of Spanish Refugee Aid. Spanish Refugee Aid had been founded by Nancy Macdonald in 1953 to help needy Spanish refugees from the civil war who had chosen to live in France rather than under a fascist regime in their homeland. In addition to being one of its charter members and making yearly donations (including, one year, the manuscript of *The Group*), McCarthy had at one time been chairman of Spanish Refugee Aid. But it was during Dwight Macdonald's tenure as chairman that the Hellman trouble erupted. Periodically, prominent people were asked to become sponsors in the hope that their names would attract donations. When such a person agreed to become a sponsor, his or her name was printed on SRA stationery, along with the names of other sponsors. Dwight Macdonald had asked Lillian Hellman to be a sponsor; she said yes. Gabriel Javsicas, a board member, was furious and persuaded other board members to rescind Macdonald's invitation. Macdonald, who had missed the meeting at which Hellman was discussed, convinced board members to reconsider. Javsicas resigned from the board, taking James Farrell and Mary McCarthy with him. Dwight Macdonald then persuaded McCarthy not to resign; Javsicas sued Spanish Refugee Aid in small claims court. When McCarthy appeared on the Cavett show, Javsicas was threatening to write all the sponsors to ask if they wanted to be on a list with such a person as Lillian Hellman. Had there not been the minitempest at Spanish Refugee Aid, McCarthy said, she would not have thought of Hellman when Cavett asked her to name overpraised writers. "She is not much present to my consciousness," she told O'Sullivan.

McCarthy's writing—personal correspondence as well as published work—certainly bears this out. She has been a prolific letter writer in the fifty years since the Spanish Civil War, yet until the lawsuit, not once did she mention Hellman's name in her correspondence. Moreover, when her lawyers asked her to list every instance of a written statement she had made that related to Hellman, she could find only four in all her published work—surprising, in a way, since she had been a drama critic when Hellman was a practicing playwright. The first allusion to Hellman, and an indirect one at that, occurred in an essay on movies. In 1944, for *Town and Country,* she wrote "A Filmy Version of the War," in which she deplored the overromantic and unrealistic portrayal of World War II in the current crop of Hollywood movies. In one of these movies, *North Star,* "the Soviet Union appears as an idyllic hamlet with farmhouses and furniture in a style that might be labeled Russian Provincial and put in a window by Sloane." Although Lillian Hellman had written the script for *North Star,* McCarthy did not identify her as its author (nor did she identify the scriptwriters of any of the other movies she discussed). The second allusion to Hellman was in a 1946 review of *The Iceman Cometh,* the first sentence of which reads, "To audiences accustomed to the oily virtuosity of George Kaufman, George Abbott, Lillian Hellman, Odets, Saroyan, the return of a playwright who—to be frank—cannot write is a solemn and sentimental occasion." The third, in 1947, was in another review. "Except in the neighborhood of Moss Hart and Lillian Hellman, there is everywhere in the theatre this season a sense of restored dignity." The fourth and last time McCarthy had mentioned Hellman was in "The Reform of Dr. Pangloss," a review of the 1956 musical version of *Candide.* "Miss Hellman and her collaborators have elected to play it safe. Anything in the original that could give offense to anyone—Jews, Arabs, or Holy Church—has been removed. . . . A bowdlerized *Candide,* a *Candide* that cannot afford to be candid, is a contradiction in terms."

Hellman's bringing suit against McCarthy was widely deplored by other writers and by civil libertarians. But once begun, the suit could not be easily dismissed. Libel laws exist to protect people from false and defamatory statements, and McCarthy's statement that *every* word Hellman wrote was a lie was false, literally speaking, and it was certainly defamatory. McCarthy's lawyers did not make a motion to dismiss the suit, since they could have won only if what McCarthy had said could *not* be interpreted as defamatory. However, the expression of opinion, as opposed to the false expression of fact, is protected under the First Amendment. McCarthy's lawyers, therefore, opted to make a motion for summary judgment, asking the court to resolve the case on purely legal grounds: in this instance, on the constitutional question of whether McCarthy was exercising her First Amendment right of freedom of speech and freedom to criticize a public figure. Questions of law are resolved by judges, so the motion for summary judgment is made to the judge only. (Questions of fact on which there is conflicting evidence—such as whether Hellman was truthful—must be decided by juries.)

Accordingly, O'Sullivan wrote McCarthy that she had two defenses as a libel defendant: "One is that the statement alleged to be defamatory was in the nature of 'rhetorical hyperbole.' The other is that the allegedly defamatory statement was an expression of opinion, rather than a statement of fact." Prior cases, notably *National Association of Letter Carriers* v. *Austin* and *Greenbelt Cooperative Publishing* v. *Bresler* upheld the right of hyperbole. Moreover, Hellman, as a public figure, could not win a judgment unless she could prove either that McCarthy knew what she said was not true, or that she said it with reckless disregard for whether it was true or not. This theory—that public figures are people who have chosen to lead highly visible lives and therefore have voluntarily sacrificed much of their protection from adverse commentary—comes from the 1964 decision in *New York Times* v. *Sullivan*. Public figures, the judge in the Sullivan case reasoned, have ample opportunity to publicly rebut any false allegations. But Hellman contended that she was not a public figure.

Before filing the motion for summary judgment, the lawyers for the contending parties took them through the process known as discovery, which consists of document production, of interrogatories (defendants and plaintiff write questions and answers for each other) and of depositions (they take each other's testimony under oath, with a court reporter present). The discovery process is always time-consuming, and in this case, with several sets of defendants and lawyers, (McCarthy, Cavett, and the Public Broadcasting System were all represented by different firms), it took more than three years.

McCarthy was deposed by Ephraim London, Hellman's lawyer, on August 12, 1981, at Holtzmann, Wise and Shepard's Fifth Avenue offices. London had already deposed Cavett, and his questioning was mild in tone and avoided "hard" questions. His questioning of McCarthy lasted only one hour and twenty minutes and was again mild.

The "hardest" question McCarthy had to answer was what she meant by saying "everything" Hellman wrote was dishonest. McCarthy replied, "I will probably make matters worse. Again it is a rhetorical exaggeration, that nothing in her writings rings true to me. That does not mean that her writing is made up of literal lies. And I don't mean *literally* nothing when I say 'nothing in her writings rings true.' . . . Of course, say perhaps seventy percent of factual statements are probably true. I don't mean they aren't. I mean the general tone of unconvincingness and falseness."

"And that was your intent in making the statement?" London said.

"To point to this trait in her work."

"The trait in the work, or your opinion of the trait in her work?"

"It is the same. When I give it as my opinion, I am pointing to this trait in her work, that is, to what I see as this trait in her work."

"But not that all of her writing was in fact lies," London concluded.

"I would say no."

The motion for summary judgment was filed in June 1983. In May 1984 Judge Harold Baer, Jr., in an eighteen-page opinion, denied McCarthy's motion to dismiss suit. He wrote that "to call someone dishonest, to say to a national television audience that every word she writes is a lie, seems to fall on the actionable side of the line—outside what has come to be known as the 'marketplace of ideas.'" Judge Baer accepted Hellman's argument that she was not a public figure. According to Baer, in addition to "general notoriety" a public figure must be a person who is involved in a "public issue, question or controversy."

An appeal was immediately launched by all remaining defendants (the action against Cavett was dismissed on grounds that he was not involved in the preparation or editing of the program). Because if the appeal did not succeed McCarthy would face the staggering costs of going to trial to prove Hellman a habitual liar, Holtzmann, Wise and Shepard brought in Floyd Abrams to augment their team of defense lawyers for the appeal. An eminent attorney with a celebrated record in First Amendment cases, he had successfully argued in the United States Supreme Court against the government's attempt to suppress publication of the Pentagon papers. He was to argue for McCarthy before an intermediate-level appellate division consisting of a panel of five judges. But just a few weeks later, before the appeal could be tried, Hellman died. In August, Ephraim London announced the termination of the suit.

The lawsuit was a financial strain for McCarthy, and indeed many people thought that Hellman's intent was to punish McCarthy financially. McCarthy's pretrial costs mounted to almost $25,000. When the suit ended, she still owed money to Holtzmann, Wise and Shepard and to Floyd Abrams. Robert Silvers talked about starting a defense fund, but an "angel" appeared who gave her a check for $25,000, which paid for Abrams's preliminary work and for what she then owed O'Sullivan's firm. Even after "the angelic intervention," as she described her financial deliverance, she was still out of pocket "something over $20,000."

Hellman was not hurt financially, since London took no legal fees from her. But the suit had damaging consequences for her. It may have cost her little financially, but it cost her a great deal of credibility as a nonfiction writer. It is true that before the lawsuit many readers—Diana Trilling, Allen Weinstein, Sidney Hook, William Phillips, William Buckley, and William O'Neill among them—had pointed out misrepresentations in Hellman's memoir *Scoundrel Time,* especially her account of her appearance before the House Un-American Activities Committee. They exposed a number of false statements: that, contrary to her claim, she was not the first witness to offer HUAC only partial cooperation, that she made Alger Hiss look innocent by altering facts about Whittaker Chambers's cache of microfilms of State Department documents, that she called James Wechsler a friendly witness (when, in fact, he was openly hostile to HUAC), and that she accused those connected with *Partisan Review* and *Commentary* of not speaking out against Senator Joseph McCarthy. Yet most readers paid little attention, dismissing the charges against Hellman as ideologically inspired, if they noticed at all.

After Hellman brought suit, however, the issue of her veracity was widely discussed. Many people stepped forward and offered McCarthy examples of Hellman's dishonesty. McCarthy wrote O'Sullivan that an old Hungarian lady claimed that Hellman "stole *The Little Foxes* from her playwright husband, now deceased, whose agent had submitted the manuscript to Hellman's friend and producer Shumlin." She also told O'Sullivan that Walter Goldwater, the treasurer of the defunct Europe-America Groups, had written to tell her that Hellman had attempted to break the will of Dorothy Parker. Although Parker had left her money to the NAACP, Hellman, who was Parker's executrix, "tried to say that DP was not quite in her right mind, and tried to get permission to give the money to SNCC or CORE or some other organization closer to Hellman's heart." Renata Adler told McCarthy that *Time* writer Stefan Kanfer had collected a great many instances of Hellman's lying and misstatements when he was preparing a book on blacklisting and the McCarthy period. At the time, McCarthy wrote O'Sullivan, Kanfer "was persuaded by friends not to include this damaging stuff" on Hellman, but since she had filed the lawsuit, McCarthy said, "this has been on his conscience and he is eager to supply it for my defense." Jonathan Randal recalled for McCarthy a conversation about Hellman that he had had with Martha Gellhorn, Hemingway's third wife, about Hellman's treatment of the Spanish Civil War in her memoirs *Unfinished Woman* and *Pentimento*. According to Randal, Gellhorn insisted that every word of Hellman's account of her own activities in Madrid was a lie.

In fact, Gellhorn was at that time preparing an article for the *Paris Review* on the subject. Her twenty-two-page article, which appeared in Spring 1981, matched Gellhorn's own notes and newspaper articles (she had been a foreign correspondent in the 1930s and 1940s) against Hellman's memoirs to demonstrate that the latter were frequently at variance with the facts. Gellhorn's article, a digest of which appeared in *The New York Times,* was followed by other reports that found Hellman guilty of lying in print, most notably Samuel McCracken's article "Julia and Other Fictions by Lillian Hellman," which concluded that the image Hellman had created of herself as a "ruthlessly honest writer" was far from deserved.

In the same period, the publication of *Code Name Mary,* the memoirs of Muriel Gardiner Buttinger, further undermined Hellman's credibility. The memoir, as well as the testimony of contemporaries, demonstrated virtually beyond doubt that Muriel Gardiner had been the original of "Julia," the close friend who has such an important role in Hellman's memoir *Pentimento*. But Hellman had never met Gardiner, which strongly implies that "Julia" is a fiction.

McCarthy herself, in the course of the lawsuit, naturally had to scrutinize the veracity of Hellman's writings. "I'll have to work up a dossier of her crimes against the truth," she wrote William Jovanovich early in the proceedings. She went about the task with her usual thoroughness. This was her dissection of one page in *Pentimento:*

> In *Pentimento,* p. 183, [Hellman] embarks on an explanation of why she would not consent to Tallulah Bankhead's desire to give a performance of *The Little Foxes* to benefit Finnish refugees during the Russian invasion of Finland in World War II. "I had been in Helsinki in 1937 for two weeks," she begins and tells how there were giant posters of Hitler on the side wall of her hotel and how a member of the U.S. Olympic team, a man of Finnish descent, took her to a Nazi rally there, where the raised-arm salute was given, the Horst Vessel song sung, and admiring speeches delivered in Finnish, which the Olympics man translated for her. Now I am willing to believe that most of the above statements are true, that there were big posters of Hitler on the wall of her hotel, that she went to a Nazi rally, that she was in Finland for two weeks. Yet these truths do not add

up (as she implies) that Finland was a fascist country, which would justify
the Russian invasion, which in turn would justify Hellman's refusal to give
a benefit for victims of the invasion. The fact that she does not *say* in so
many words that Finland was a fascist country makes it a worse lie, because
more specious and evasive, than a lie direct.

There are many examples of this kind of misrepresentation strewn
through her "autobiographies."

McCarthy's examples of misrepresentations amounted to twenty-two
typed pages.

In examining Hellman's work, McCarthy distinguished between misrepresentations of truth, like the misleading picture of Finland she cited,
and outright false statements. One example of many of the latter is the
"Willy" chapter in *Pentimento.*

> *Pentimento,* pp. 53–98, "Willy." An informant writes me that what pur-
> ports to be the story of a relation by marriage of Plaintiff's is really the
> story of Samuel Zemurray, a very well-known New Orleans figure, and
> the United Fruit Company in Honduras. Uncle Willy's gun-running to
> Costa Rica is like the thinly disguised fictional equivalent of that traffic,
> recognizable, he says, to any old-time resident of New Orleans. There
> would be no harm in that if it were called fiction. If this tip is to be used,
> it will have to be fleshed out with a lot more research—into New Orleans
> history. One lead that could be followed up in a newspaper morgue is the
> obit of Willy mentioned on p. 98; he had died in an automobile accident
> together with two other men who had been riding with him in the car;
> shortly before that, he had gone into bankruptcy. So if Willy actually
> existed, one could find the newspaper story on the fatal accident, on his
> links with the "big company," his own "Guacosta Fruit Import Com-
> pany," on the bankruptcy scandal and his marriage to Plaintiff's great-aunt
> Lily. Plaintiff's name surely would be listed among those surviving this
> picturesque figure. By that time she was a celebrity; as she tells us, she had
> a long-distance call from a New Orleans newspaper asking for a comment
> on Uncle Willy for the obit. The trouble, as so often, is the haziness, not
> to say murk, of the chronology. What year is Willy supposed to have had
> his car crash in? Some time after Plaintiff and Hammett have moved to
> Hollywood for four or five months, she indicates, which ought to place
> it in the Forties, while she and Hammett were still drinking; they seem
> to have stopped around 1950. So one would have to comb through
> newspaper files of between 1941, say, and 1950. Only to find nothing?

McCarthy did hire a researcher to go through microfilms of the *Times-
Picayune* between 1941 and 1950. The search revealed that Hellman had

indeed lied about her own family in what purports to be a real-life memoir. Willy, whose real name is Charles Weinberger, is her great-uncle by marriage. His wife, Rose Weinberger (Lily in Hellman's memoir), is her maternal grandmother's sister. Hellman turned her uncle into a swashbuckling, romantic gunrunner and tycoon who lived in a mansion with ten servants, drove fast cars, and had a hundred-foot yacht, an apartment at the old Waldorf, and a hunting lodge on Jekyll Island, when in real life he was a potentate of the Shriners. She worked a similar transformation on her great-aunt. According to Hellman, the aunt took morphine, slept with her chauffeur, and never spoke to her husband. None of this was true. Hellman changed the Weinbergers' only child, daughter Amelie, into a psychotic son who tried to rape Hellman when she was a child. Charles, Rose, and Amelie Weinberger were dead when *Pentimento* was published, and thus unable to dispute her story.

As William Wright says in his biography of Hellman, "By suing Mary McCarthy, Hellman forced one of the country's sharpest and most energetic minds to pore through the entire Hellman *oeuvre* in search of lies." It was not surprising that Hellman requested the papers in her proceeding be sealed. But Cavett's lawyers persuaded the court to reject this request, so McCarthy's interrogatories are filed with the court records and are available to anyone. Indeed, as Wright suggests, they may have been drawn on by some of the writers who later wrote pieces discrediting Hellman.

McCarthy spent a great deal of time and effort, as well as many thousands of dollars, on the Hellman lawsuit. But she is quite unrepentant today. "If someone had told me, don't say anything about Lillian Hellman because she'll sue you, it wouldn't have stopped me. It might have spurred me on. I didn't want her to die. I wanted her to lose in court. I wanted her around for that."

McCarthy had gotten into the fracas in the first place by speaking out spontaneously and impulsively on national television. It is not unusual for her to say something startling, giving no thought to the consequences, and it is not unusual for her to get into trouble for such outspokenness. She probably could have stopped the whole affair in its first stirrings by saying something conciliatory toward Hellman, such as, "It was an obvious exaggeration made for laughs." But she did not. Once the suit got going, she would not back down. Told that Hellman would stop the suit if she would publicly apologize, McCarthy replied, "But that would be lying."

CHAPTER XXIV

LOOKING BACKWARD
(The 1980s)

WHEN NEWS of the Lillian Hellman lawsuit broke, on February 15, 1980, Mary McCarthy was at the University of London, delivering the Northcliffe Lectures. On April 2 she mailed the typed manuscripts of the four lectures to William Jovanovich. He read them, responded enthusiastically, and promised to publish them in February 1981. Because of the lawsuit, however, she and her lawyer, Ben O'Sullivan, wanted an earlier publication date.

> It would help me, I think, legally, and I know morally, if some critical writing of mine could appear and be talked about. Ben is very firm on the point that this is not a dispute or "feud" between two authors (as Mailer presented it just now in the *Times Book Review*) but a legal attack by an author on a critic. He maintains that I was exercising my function as a critic when I made the remark on television and would feel, I suppose (I haven't asked him), that it would do me good to be seen currently in that light and, as some friends say, in top form during the exercise. I do feel that myself; it would hearten me to see something of mine in print that shows me exercising my power of judgment. In principle, I could write some book reviews, but that wouldn't be the same as writing about the great men and women of letters. And anyway where would I get the time? . . . The lawsuit is already a time-devourer . . . and will decidedly get worse.

Jovanovich published the lectures in a 121-page book entitled *Ideas and the Novel* in October of 1980. If McCarthy's purpose was to remind readers that she is as respected for her criticism as for her novels, she succeeded. Many reviewers disagreed with her thesis that the greatest novels (written in the nineteenth century) are those that have dealt with matters like religion, politics, public issues, whereas today, owing to the influence of Henry James, such novels are not written because "ideas are held not to belong in the novel," and factual exposition or moral instruction are avoided. But often they concluded that it was not necessary to agree with McCarthy to admire her book. One such reviewer, John Romano in *The New Republic*, wrote that although he found her "crucially and centrally wrong," he was "grateful for the chance to read an armful of masterpieces over her shoulder." In only one major review, in *The Times Literary Supplement,* was her credibility as a critic questioned. The reviewer called *Ideas and the Novel* "a tattered rag-bag of undeveloped impressions," and thought McCarthy "should get on with writing good novels." Apparently this reviewer missed McCarthy's pronouncement in another London newspaper that *Cannibals and Missionaries* was her last novel. "Something I've observed is that one loses one's social perceptions," she told Miriam Gross of *The Observer;* "they get blunted and dimmer as one gets older—it's partly a matter of eyesight. You can continue writing poetry and essays and so on, but to be a novelist you have to have this alert social thing."

In June 1980 McCarthy had been afflicted with shingles, a viral infection that causes high fevers as well as painful blisters and sores on the skin along the path of sensory nerves. The disease has no cure or predictable duration, but in McCarthy's case it went into remission late in 1980. At the same time, however, she was experiencing a loss of equilibrium that often occurred when she stood or started walking. Because this unsteadiness or uncertainty of gait started at the same time the shingles struck, she assumed at first it must be the result of the medicine prescribed for the infection. After it was discontinued and the dizziness persisted, she underwent test after test to find out what was really wrong. Finally, her doctors decided it was ataxia, a loss of control of the motor activities ascribed to a shrinkage of the cerebellum.

Not until the summer of 1984, four years after the shingles and dizziness began, did she get relief—from an operation performed at New York Hospital. Acting on a hunch that her balance problem might be caused by hydrocephalus, a doctor had suggested a shunt, a procedure that surgically creates a passage to drain fluid from inside the skull, thereby eliminating pressure on the brain. But this relief proved to be temporary, as she was back in the hospital in the late fall for another operation, "supposedly corrective of the first." A third operation in 1985 seems finally to have worked.

Despite almost continuous health problems during the first half of the decade, McCarthy continued her usual activities, adding swimming to them on the advice of a doctor. Her traveling even increased somewhat, owing mainly to her husband's retirement from the OECD at the beginning of 1980. From that time until the present, the Wests have regularly spent half a year in Paris and half a year in Castine. During their six months in Europe they make frequent trips throughout France and to London and Rome; and in America they go to the many college campuses where McCarthy is a frequent lecturer. Since 1986, when

McCarthy accepted the Charles Stevenson Chair of Literature at Bard College, they live in Annandale-on-Hudson during the fall. Their children come to Castine when they can. Reuel, who is divorced from his first wife, is married to a Japanese musicologist. He has a six-year-old girl named Sophia; his first child, Jay Wilson, is now twenty. Daniel West is married and living in California; Alison, who was married briefly, is living in New York; and Jonathan is married and living in Poland.

As always, the focus of McCarthy's energies is writing. She continues to turn out reviews and essays, chiefly for *The New York Review of Books* and for *The New York Times Book Review.* In 1985 Harcourt Brace Jovanovich published a collection of these pieces as *Occasional Prose.* The book also includes obituary portraits of her friends Philip Rahv, Nicola Chiaromonte, Hannah Arendt, and F. W. (Fred) Dupee; political reporting; several prefaces and afterwords to other people's books; a retelling of *La Traviata* commissioned by the Metropolitan Opera Guild (McCarthy is an ardent opera fan); and a biographical sketch of her Portsmouth neighbor, Miss Alice Brayton. Of the twenty-one pieces that comprise *Occasional Prose,* eleven were written in the 1980s.

Reviewers were uncommonly kind to the collection when it appeared, perhaps because of McCarthy's septuagenarian status. "Miss McCarthy . . . has mellowed considerably. We miss, in these remarkably unvituperative essays, her impressive ferocity," opined Jeffrey Meyers in the *National Review.* Diane Johnson in *The Times Literary Supplement* complimented McCarthy for having "the tact to present her opinions wittily," surely the first time any reviewer has called McCarthy tactful. The warmest and most interesting review was Jacqueline Austin's in *The Village Voice: "Occasional Prose* does not wound, it braces. There is no undeserved mockery here, but much wisdom, honest thought, strong writing. . . . The very brilliant child has grown up." Only Julian Moynahan in *The New York Times Book Review* detected something of the "old" Mary McCarthy when he wrote, "Everywhere in *Occasional Prose* appear bracing opinions tartly expressed—Americans are slow, tedious talkers; big-time art collectors are not very nice people; the word 'drugget' must never be used for stair carpeting; everybody misuses prepositions because nobody studies Latin in school anymore. . . . May she continue to call us to attention ('No slumping in the back seats!'), showing us the world of her imagination."

The work on which McCarthy has lavished the most time and energy in the last few years is her intellectual autobiography. As early as 1973, William Jovanovich suggested she write such a book, which has now grown to a projected three volumes. The first, *How I Grew,* appeared in the spring of 1987. It covers her life through graduation from Vassar, with an emphasis on the teenage years in Seattle. Volume two, she thinks, "will probably take me up only to my marriage to Edmund, though Jim wonders whether this will be far enough. Still, those years cover the Spanish Civil War, my *Partisan Review* period, my writing for *The Nation* and *The New Republic,* besides my marriage to Johnsrud, divorce, living in the Village, and so on; this in fact is a period in New York that people now always ask questions about."

How I Grew is a disappointment because McCarthy's usual elegant, lively, taut, and witty way with words is in short supply. Granted, the memoir is peppered throughout with that McCarthy trademark, the stingingly apt verbal thrust, like her evocation of the Chapin girls in her freshman class at Vassar:

> There were also in Davison, among the freshmen, some New York society girls, mainly from Chapin, whose deaf-sounding voices were constantly calling to each other in corridors, out the windows, across the dining-hall. "Cum-Cum!" they called, for Comfort Parker, "Rosil-l-la!" for Rosilla Hornblower, "A-lye-dah!" for Alida Davis. A whole bevy of them, trilling and cawing, lived in Davison and behaved as if no one else did.

Yet *How I Grew* sometimes reads like stream-of-consciousness with sign-posts:

> But I am digressing in the middle of a digression, piling Ossa on Pelion, we Latinists would say.

McCarthy even employs the old-fashioned convention of addressing the reader, a device she has never used so directly and insistently before.

> Not to leave you in suspense, Reader, I did it.

> Weep with me, Reader.

> As you can see, Reader, I do not care for that side of myself.

And most surprising of all, there are a few lapses in her usual practice of turning out highly polished sentences:

> The center of my life, though, during that second term in Annie Wright's new buildings, gabled, dormered, casemented, and beginning to be

creeper-covered, with a cloister to walk in on rainy days, which had a camellia tree blooming beside it, was not a man or a boy but Mary Ann Lamping, a senior.

McCarthy seems self-absorbed in *How I Grew,* sometimes even self-satisfied, yet she is not a self-satisfied person—far from it. Self-recriminations abound in her books, and in this memoir she is unusually hard on herself. During the planning stage of *How I Grew,* she wrote William Jovanovich about how she envisioned her story.

> In the garden, reflecting on the autobiography, I thought of a grisly title: *Excuse Me for Living.* That gives a hint of what I have, at least partly, in mind: a catalogue of my sins, both of commission and omission. I suppose one can't arrive at my time in life without a consciousness of failure and a wondering as to what went wrong. This is perhaps a biological matter, the reckoning of a decaying organism looking back on its plenitude. I remember laughing one day hearing B. B. up in Vallombrosa announcing that he was a failure and being joined by K. Clark and Johnnie Walker of the National Gallery; what would a *real* failure have thought, listening to the three of them? And yet now I see that they weren't necessarily insincere.

The problem with *How I Grew* is that in covering roughly the same years as *Memories of a Catholic Girlhood,* but trying hard not to repeat previous material, McCarthy avoided the more dramatic incidents and characters that had made that book engaging. She was forced to rewrite chapter 1 after *The New Yorker* had turned it down because it seemed too close to the earlier memoir. Upon re-submission, she wrote:

> Of course, even with the changes it may seem to you to be too close to *Memories of a Catholic Girlhood.* That can't be helped, since life dealt out a single, unchangeable set of events—my parents' death, Uncle Myers, Catholic piety. I can't avoid mentioning these things, even if they're meant to serve only as background to the birth of some sort of mind in me. . . . The third chapter is likely to have some duplication, too, since it will contain quite a lot about my Episcopal boarding-school, which was amply treated in *The New Yorker.* Obviously I'll try to make it as different as possible, writing about other teachers and girls, but the Principal will still be there and something of the atmosphere.

Making it as different as possible is precisely the trouble; this accounts for the long stretches of trivia told in fatiguing detail, conveying a sense that everything the author thought in passing, everything she did, everything she saw, smelled, touched, heard, and felt, and especially everything she read is of great importance because she is important.

Many reviewers, of course, pointed to this, and none of them too kindly. "Well, aren't we special?" was the refrain of James Wolcott's lengthy *New Republic* review, and Rhoda Koenig complained about "the trivia and theatrics of this book" and its "tacky" style. Even Wilfrid Sheed, who wrote a positive review, mentioned "the self-importance problem" that is "endemic to all autobiography." He made the point, though, that the best way to read *How I Grew* is in conjunction with *Memories of a Catholic Girlhood.*

> In "Memories" we meet a younger Mary McCarthy who is in process of becoming a Sacred Heart convent-school girl, and to this day her older self still reminds me more of one of those than of any of the other selves latent in this newer narrative. The fixed smile, the unflagging ladylikeness, the Grace Kelly coolness and the mind of a nun forever correcting papers—these were, if not standard issue at Sacred Heart schools, common enough; and if one imagines such a cool customer strolling gracefully (shoulders back, and appear to glide) through the events of this book, it brings them to a vivid and quite startling new life, supplying us with the one missing face and making of the combined memoirs something of an event in itself; that is to say, a genuine artwork as original as any of her fiction, while containing all the facts even a McCarthy could want.

When the intellectual autobiography is finally finished, McCarthy hopes to write a book on Gothic architecture, a project she started in 1971 but one she has put aside many times to do other work. She told an interviewer then that she thought her Gothic book would be similar in structure to *The Stones of Florence.* "I have seen almost everything Gothic in France," she added. In 1973 she wrote William Jovanovich that the book was under way. "I've started the Gothic book which I carried to page 2, then, as usual, like one of those insects climbing a wall in an algebra problem, immediately fell back to p. 1. But at least something is on paper, which means the book is real."

In December of 1973 she delivered a Johan Huizinga Lecture (named for the author of *The Waning of the Middle Ages,* the classic study of French and Dutch life, thought, and art in the fourteenth and fifteenth centuries) at Leyden University. Her topic, "Can There Be A Gothic Literature?" bemused her audience.

Tonight, just before I came to talk to you, a Dutch friend told me that in Holland my title had been a source of mystification: in Holland, the word "Gothic" was applied only to buildings. This news was rather shattering and yet I was glad to hear it. Glad to know that in this clear-headed country at any rate my lecture was otiose, unnecessary: nobody had ever thought that there *could* be a Gothic literature.

Elsewhere, however, *Gothic* as applied to literature is a recognized term in any critic's vocabulary. McCarthy's purpose in the lecture was to discover what this term means when applied to medieval literature.

Since the Gothic period was one characterized by a single faith and by great cathedral building, there ought to have been a Gothic literature. But she detected nothing of the forms of Gothic architecture in the mystery plays, the stories, or the poetry of the period. She found that only *The Divine Comedy,* the product of a country with no fully understood Gothic architecture, qualified as "a strongly architectural work, with three superimposed levels, each containing corridors and gradations, and the final movement is vertical, flowing and streaming, like the gravity-defying slender Gothic columns, toward the heavenly light of Paradise described with an almost scientific exactitude." She also detected something of this architectonic impulse in Chaucer. She went on to explain to her Dutch audience the evolution, beginning in the eighteenth century, of the special meaning of the term *Gothic* when applied to a literary work. She concluded where she began—that there is little evidence of architectonic structure in the literature of the Gothic age.

The Huizinga Lecture has been printed as a pamphlet by an Amsterdam publisher, but nothing else has come of her research, which included dozens of trips to study cathedrals, sculpture, and drawings. However, McCarthy has compiled considerable notes and part of a chapter, which are filed away for the book she plans to write on Gothic architecture.

Mary McCarthy first appeared in print fifty-five years ago. Since then she has continuously turned out work of an extremely high caliber. "This amazing woman could ride through earthquake and thunder, pass through the most dire upheavals in her personal life, from which another woman might have collapsed in hysteria," William Barrett wrote in *The Truants,* "and her typewriter would go on indefatigably tapping. There are, of course, hacks who go on pounding it out no matter what, but Miss

McCarthy is of another class; the energy of her writing always came out unwearied, buoyant, and polished."

She has imitated no one. The order in her life shows up in her impeccable syntax; the perfectionism, in her obsession with moral distinctions; the honesty, in her passion for naturalistic detail; the wit, in her abundant use of sentence fragments, which hit the reader like the timing of a first-rank comedian; the dramatic flair, in her characterization of people with dialogue and in her tendency (in her criticism) to pen apt one-liners; and the high expectation she has of her reader in her insistence on using uncommon words and long paragraphs, even refusing to separate dialogue according to speaker.

In recent years many belated honors have been bestowed on her—First Distinguished Visitor at Vassar (an honor conferred on graduates of outstanding achievement and contributions), the Ingram-Merrill Award, the National Medal of Literature, the Edward MacDowell Medal, the Charles Stevenson Chair at Bard College, and honorary degrees from Bard, Syracuse University, the University of Hull, the University of Aberdeen, the University of Maine, and Bowdoin College. She has been a judge for several fiction awards—the Prix Formentor, the Booker Prize, and the National Book Award. She has been writer-in-residence at the American Academy in Rome and at the University of Maine. And she has been a member of the American Institute of Arts and Letters since 1960. But she has never been accorded the status many critics think she deserves. Her work is less widely discussed in American colleges and universities than that of some of her contemporaries. Critic Irvin Stock thinks this is because she is a neoclassicist in a country of romantics. "The sprightliness and detachment of her prose, her preference for sense over sensibility, her satirical eye for the hidden ego in our intellectual pretensions," he says, "are qualities we are not comfortable with in this country. They may amuse, but they also antagonize."

McCarthy herself has admitted that she has "always sought to proselytize," yet Elizabeth Hardwick has remarked that "if Mary McCarthy is a scourge, she is a very cheerful one, light-hearted and even optimistic. I do not see in any of her work a trace of despair or alienation but instead rather romantic expectation. She always expects better of persons and of the nation." And, in the same spirit, Benjamin DeMott has called McCarthy one of the "most original and most readable Puritans this country has produced."

Her passion is for strict truth, even, or especially, about herself. "Self-deception remains in my book a major sin or vice," she writes in *How I Grew.* Her childhood, with its sudden reversals, made the possibility of starting over unusually real to her, and when one starts over, one invents a new self, thereby increasing the likelihood of self-deception. Even so, as an orphan she used her will and imagination not to hide from reality but to forge the person she became and is today.

The process began when the pampered, highly intelligent, and impetuous child suddenly became an orphan "rudely set down in a place where beauty was not a value at all." So bleak was the new household in Minneapolis that she strove to be first in sports, studies, and saintship at an ugly parochial school, and in so doing she learned, as she writes in *How I Grew,* "how to exercise power over my circumstances." Back in her grandparents' home in Seattle, she was exposed to the graciousness that is possible in daily life, reflected today in her own fine and expensive tastes; and to books, which she had been starved for in Minneapolis and which were now available at her grandparents' house, at the library (she got her first card at this time), and from friends. From Dorothy Atkinson, who taught her English at Annie Wright, she got the idea of going to Vassar, though it was a four-day train trip away. Finally, settling in New York led to what she has called a watershed, a turning point. The day James Farrell put her name on the Committee for the Defense of Trotsky changed everything; the resulting political awareness affected the people she met, the places she went, and the pieces she wrote.

Of course, she was unaware of its significance at the time, just as she did not see the impact Nicola Chiaromonte had on her until long after the fact. Chiaromonte's reverence for Tolstoy became an integral part of McCarthy's outlook. In 1980 she wrote: "[Tolstoy] did not care for saviors in whatever shape they presented themselves. As is indicated in *Anna Karenina,* it is enough if a man is able to save his own soul by living for it, which is the same thing as living for God—the rest will take care of itself. This is the Tolstoyan message, which went through various stages but did not really change." Substitute "ideology" for "saviors" and the titles of her twenty-four books for *Anna Karenina,* for a summation of Mary McCarthy's life and work.

McCarthy has summed up her own life and work rather too modestly. In the early 1970s Philip Rahv interviewed her for his short-lived journal, *Modern Occasions.* He asked her what they, as early anti-Stalinists, had accomplished.

> Almost nothing that I can see. When I say "we," I mean the group of Trotskyites and Trotskyite sympathizers or fellow-travelers around *Partisan Review.* We fought the good fight against Stalinism when we were very

much outnumbered and outweighed, materially speaking. And most of us did not "sell out" on the ideological plane to the various New Deals and New Frontiers or join the conservative fringe. But that was a rather negative accomplishment, and as for our battle against Stalinism, we were losing until U.S. foreign policy finally hardened into anti-Communism after its wartime vacillations. Then suddenly most of the old Stalinist fellow-travelers turned in our direction. . . . Some of us (you and me included) were OK on McCarthy, but again history took care of that and I would not like to claim that our disputes . . . had any influence on events. Meanwhile, like most American writers, professors, and editors, we were getting richer. And less revolutionary. Not just because we had more money, but because we were getting older, and because, according to our analysis, it was not "a revolutionary situation." That was doubtless true, but just here our clear-mindedness perhaps did us a disservice. We were *writers,* not organizers or revolutionary cadres, but, looking back, it seems to me that I personally might have done a little more than write books.

William Phillips thinks McCarthy is wrong about the effect their group had on current affairs, and recent historians of the period, such as William O'Neill and Alan Wald, agree. At the very least, the early anti-Stalinists broke the monopoly that Stalinism had on liberal-left minds. Moreover, they probably changed the opinion of many writers and intellectuals, and they may even have had some influence on changing the opinion of the country about Russia.

More recently, in a speech at the MacDowell Colony, McCarthy said:

Why should I care that I have lived my life as a person and writer in vain? We all live our lives more or less in vain. That is the normal common fate, and the fact of having a small *name* should not make us hope to be exceptions, to count for something or other.

But Mary McCarthy "counts for" more than she realizes or acknowledges. Alison Lurie, reviewing *How I Grew,* summed up her status among the current generation of intellectual women. "Her achievement was to invent herself as a totally new type of woman who stood for both sense and sensibility; who was both coolly and professionally intellectual and frankly passionate." More than twenty-five years ago Elizabeth Hardwick speculated about why McCarthy came to mean so much to other women, her antifeminist disclaimers notwithstanding.

A career of candor and dissent is not an easy one for a woman; the license is jarring and the dare often forbidding. Such a person needs more than confidence and indignation. A great measure of personal attractiveness and a high degree of romantic singularity are necessary to step free of the mundane, the governessy, the threat of earnestness and dryness. . . . With Mary McCarthy the purity of style and the liniment of her wit, her gay summoning of the funny facts of everyday life, soften the scandal of the action or the courage of the opinion.

And the result, Hardwick concluded, is that it is "hard to think of any writer in America more interesting and unusual than Mary McCarthy." But above all else, to McCarthy's steadfast readers, she has, to use her own words of more than thirty-five years ago, "made a . . . contribution to sanity in our times."

The reader will find citations in the notes for the books, articles, and letters that I consulted and the interviews that I conducted. Therefore, I have omitted a formal bibliography. I have listed here, however, the twenty-four McCarthy books I refer to in the text. I have cited first editions whenever they were available to me; any title for which I have had to use another edition is indicated with an asterisk.

FICTION

*The Company She Keeps, New York: Harcourt Brace Jovanovich/Harvest, 1970.

The Oasis, New York: Random House, 1949.

The Groves of Academe, New York: Harcourt, Brace and Company, 1952.

*A Charmed Life, New York: Avon Books, 1981.

The Group, New York: Harcourt, Brace & World, Inc., 1963.

Birds of America, New York: Harcourt Brace Jovanovich, 1971.

Cannibals and Missionaries, New York: Harcourt Brace Jovanovich, 1979.

Cast a Cold Eye, New York: Harcourt, Brace and Company, 1950.

The Hounds of Summer and Other Stories, New York: Avon Books, 1981.

NONFICTION

Sights and Spectacles: Theatre Chronicles 1937–1956, New York: Meridian Books, 1957.

Venice Observed, Paris: G. & R. Bernier, 1956.

*Memories of a Catholic Girlhood, New York: Harcourt Brace Jovanovich (paper), n.d. [1957].

The Stones of Florence, New York: Harcourt, Brace and Company, n.d. [1959].

On the Contrary, New York: Farrar, Straus and Cudahy, 1961.

Mary McCarthy's Theatre Chronicles 1937–1962, New York: Farrar, Straus and Company (The Noonday Press), 1963.

Vietnam, New York: Harcourt, Brace & World, 1967.

Hanoi, New York: Harcourt, Brace & World, 1968.

The Writing on the Wall, New York: Harcourt, Brace & World, 1970.

Medina, New York: Harcourt Brace Jovanovich, 1972.

The Seventeenth Degree, New York: Harcourt Brace Jovanovich/Harvest, 1974.

The Mask of State: Watergate Portraits, New York: Harcourt Brace Jovanovich, 1974.

Ideas and the Novel, New York: Harcourt Brace Jovanovich, 1980.

Occasional Prose, New York: Harcourt Brace Jovanovich, 1985.

How I Grew, New York: Harcourt Brace Jovanovich, 1987.

A Note on Abbreviations

For brevity, I have used abbreviated versions of the titles of certain works by McCarthy, and a few periodicals, after their first appearance in the Notes; I have also used the initials of some individuals in citing unpublished correspondence or interviews. These abbreviations are listed below.

Individuals

CA	Carmen Angleton
HA	Hannah Arendt
BB	Bernard Berenson
NC	Nicola Chiaromonte
DG	Doris Grumbach
EH	Elizabeth Hardwick
WJ	William Jovanovich
DM	Dwight Macdonald
MM	Mary McCarthy
WP	William Phillips
ASJ	Arthur Schlesinger, Jr.
EW	Edmund Wilson
RW	Reuel Wilson

Periodicals

NYT	*The New York Times*
NYTBR	*The New York Times Book Review*
NYRB	*The New York Review of Books*

Works by Mary McCarthy

BA	*Birds of America*
CL	*A Charmed Life*
CM	*Cannibals and Missionaries*
CSK	*The Company She Keeps*
Group	*The Group*
GA	*The Groves of Academe*
HIG	*How I Grew*
Ideas	*Ideas and the Novel*
MCG	*Memories of a Catholic Girlhood*
MMTC	*Mary McCarthy's Theatre Chronicles 1937–1962*
MS	*The Mask of State: Watergate Portraits*
OC	*On the Contrary*
SD	*The Seventeenth Degree*
SF	*The Stones of Florence*
VO	*Venice Observed*
WW	*The Writing on the Wall*

PREFACE

Page

xi   *"crammed with cerebration."* John Aldridge, *The Devil in the Fire,* New York: Harper's Magazine Press Books, 1972, p. 217.

xi   *"her approach to writing."* Paul Schlueter, "The Dissections of Mary McCarthy," in *Contemporary American Novelists,* ed. Harry T. Moore, Carbondale: Southern Illinois University Press, 1964, p. 55.

xi   *"Mary, our saint." New York Review of Books,* October 17, 1963, p. 1.

xi   *"God bless you."* Dwight Macdonald to Fred Dupee, 11/11/65, Dwight Macdonald Papers, Box 14, Folder 255, Sterling Library, Yale University, New Haven.

xii   *"being on the receiving line."* MM to Hannah Arendt, 9/30/74.

xii   *"dared too early."* William Jovanovich to MM, 2/25/71.

xii   *"belongs to that group." Mary McCarthy's Theatre Chronicles, 1937–1962,* New York: Farrar, Straus and Company (The Noonday Press), 1963, pp. 81, 82 (hereafter cited as *MMTC*).

xii   *"if art." MMTC,* p. 134.

xii   Arendt's view. HA to MM, 5/28/71.

xiii   *"I had heard."* Author's interview with William Tuohy, London, March 1982.

xiii   *"Mary is full of life."* Author's interview with Countess Anna Maria Cicogna, Venice, April 1982.

xiii   *"Mary had a good time."* Nicola Chiaromonte to DM, 3/9/65, Macdonald Papers, Box 10, Folder 244.

xiii   *"I would date."* MM to Doris Grumbach, 9/26/66.

xiii   *"The care she takes."* Author's interview with Eleanor Perényi, Stonington, Conn., August 1982.

xiii   *"I like labor-intensive implements."* Edward MacDowell Medal award ceremony, 8/26/84.

xiv   *"Mary's so tenacious"* and *"Yes. Pure in her food."* Author's interview with Kate and Kevin McCarthy, Sherman Oaks, Calif., March 1982.

xiv   *"Winning is the key."* Author's interview with Angelique Levi, Paris, April 1982.

xiv   *"a normal person."* MM to HA, 8/17/59.

xiv   *"Well, that's all Mary needs."* Author's interview with Eileen Simpson, New York, August 1982.

xiv   *" 'I like your shells.' "* Mary McCarthy, *A Charmed Life,* New York: Avon Books, 1981, p. 76 (hereafter cited as *CL*).

xiv   *"wish to play a part."* Mary McCarthy, *Memories of a Catholic Girlhood,* New York: Harcourt Brace Jovanovich, 1957, p. 125 (hereafter cited as *MCG*).

xiv   *"I do not seem."* MM to EW, 10/n.d./66. Edmund Wilson Papers, Beinecke Library, Yale.

xv   *"I am not discreet."* MM to DG, 9/26/66.

xv   *"honesty."* Author's interview with Stanley Geist, Paris, April 1982.

xv   *"no one was speaking."* Doris Grumbach, *The Company She Kept,* New York: Coward, McCann, 1963, p. 148.

xv   *Jim is checking off."* MM to William Jovanovich, 1/18/65, courtesy William Jovanovich.

xv   *"deliberately, to the gallery."* MCG, p. 101.

xv   *"apart from the run of people."* Mary McCarthy, *The Company She Keeps,* New York: Harcourt Brace Jovanovich/Harvest 1970, p. 155 (hereafter cited as *CSK*).

xv   *"trying to do."* Elizabeth Niebuhr interview with MM, "The Art of Fiction," *Paris Review,* Winter–Spring 1962, p. 67.

xv   *"pity this woman."* William Barrett, *The Truants,* New York: Anchor Press/Doubleday, 1982, p. 66.

xv   *"all style."* Author's telephone interview with William Barrett, January 1982.

xvi   *"I think."* Mary McCarthy, *Vassar Views,* April 1982, p. 2.

xvi   *"among those writers."* Irvin Stock, *Fiction as Wisdom: From Goethe to Bellow,* University Park: The Pennsylvania University Press, 1980, p. 185.

PROLOGUE

Page

1   Kevin McCarthy's question. Kevin McCarthy's interview with his sister for *People Weekly,* October 1979, unpublished portion.

1   Epidemic. The 1918 flu epidemic was technically a pandemic, a term meaning occurrence in most people in a country or several countries.

1   *22 million people.* This figure is only an estimate, as in many places in Africa and Asia no death records exist. But the American epidemiologist Edwin Oakes Jordan (*Epidemic Influenza,* 1927), computed mortality at 21,642,274.

1   *Northern Pacific train.* Mary McCarthy wrote in *How I Grew* that the family probably took the Chicago, Milwaukee, and St. Paul because it "was anchored on St. Paul" (p. 236), whereas the Northern Pacific was "anchored on Chicago." The McCarthy cousins to whom author spoke insist it was the Northern Pacific the family traveled on.

2   *"Waving good-bye."* MCG, p. 35.

2   Doctor, nurse. Author's interview with Blanche McCarthy Michaels, Minneapolis, August 1981.

2   Death of Roy and Tess. A unique aspect of this flu was that half the deaths occurred in the twenty-to-forty age group. Usually, it is the very young and the very old who are hardest hit.

CHAPTER I

5   Family history. McCarthy family history is based on Louis
      McCarthy's research and records made available to me by his
      daughters, Mary Louise McCarthy McKissick and Cynthia
      McCarthy Sandberg, and on copies of baptismal and mar-
      riage certificates made available by various members of the
      family, principally Blanche McCarthy Michaels.

5   *"I was a natural rebel."* Mary McCarthy, "The Novels That
      Got Away," *NYTBR,* November 25, 1979, p. 102.

6   William Sheridan. 1806–1893.

7   Years in Dakota. Charles McCarthy's history of the origin of
      McCarthy Brothers Company.

8   Facts about Roy's family. Louis McCarthy's notes written
      shortly after his brother's death; and author's interviews with
      James McCarthy, Mary Lou McCarthy McKissick, Cynthia
      McCarthy Sandberg, Charles McCarthy, Blanche McCarthy
      Michaels, Eleanor McCarthy, and Daniel Woolsey in Min-
      neapolis, August 1981; Kevin McCarthy in Los Angeles,
      March 1982; Preston McCarthy in Annapolis, November
      1981; and Judy McCarthy Knickerbocker in Point Clear,
      Ala., August 1982.

8   Interior of house. Photographs in possession of Cynthia
      McCarthy Sandberg.

9   Anti-Catholic text. John T. Kane, *Catholic and Protestant Con-
      flicts in America,* Chicago: Regnery, 1955, p. 40.

10   "Religion of Beauty." *MCG,* p. 21.

10   *"Sour baleful doctrine."* Ibid, p. 21.

10   *"bloodcurdling Catholicism."* Ibid, p. 50.

11   *"I refuse to."* Ibid, p. 15.

11   *an old manager.* Author's interview with Preston McCarthy.

11   Texas. "My grandmother," Mary McCarthy writes in *Memo-
      ries of a Catholic Girlhood,* "but recently passed away, had left
      a fund to erect a chapel in her name in Texas, a state to which
      she had no known connection" (p. 80). The two-thousand-
      dollar bequest she made toward the building of Saint Eliza-
      beth's Church in Pflugerville, Texas, is a consequence of this
      trip.

12   Alden Partridge. Partridge was appointed in 1805 to the
      newly established U.S. Military Academy at West Point. On
      receiving his commission as first lieutenant of engineers in
      1806, he was assigned to duty at the academy as an instructor

and remained there until 1817, when, after two years as acting superintendent, he was sentenced to be cashiered for refusing to relinquish his post to a successor. He was allowed to resign in 1818. Norwich University, which he founded in 1819, was one of the first institutions in the U.S. to offer college-level instruction in engineering and agriculture.

12–13   Preston's various ranks. *Heitman Register of Army Officers* (Francis B. Heitman Historical Register and Dictionary of U.S. Army, vol. for 1903, p. 806).

13   Revenue collections. *Annual Report of the Commissioner of Internal Revenue,* Washington: Government Printing Office, 1874; and letter from Elizabeth Knauff, manager of Information Services Division, Department of Treasury, to author: "Aggregate revenue collections for the First District declined from $576,102.12 in 1868 to $57,321.70 in 1869. In 1872 aggregate collections were less than $17,000."

13   *"While Collector."* Simon Preston to W. A. Ellis, 9/3/97, Special Collections, Norwich University Library, Northfield, Vt.

14   Harold Preston's education. Front-page obituary, *Seattle Times,* January 2, 1939.

14   Information about the Morgensterns. Author's phone interviews with Elizabeth Morgenstern Greenebaum (Elkan's daughter), December 1982.

14   *"Roy was quite," "charming, attractive."* Zella Steele to MM, 12/8/55, 1/11/56.

15   *Roy's bank books.* First deposit of $1,100 made November 24, 1911.

CHAPTER II

Page
16–19   Family life. All information, except when specifically noted, is from a calendar pad kept by Roy McCarthy from October 14, 1914, to October 28, 1918, in the possession of Kevin McCarthy, who provided author a Xerox of the original pad. Louis McCarthy's family provided a typed copy of the calendar plus appended comments made by Louis shortly after Roy's death.

17   Kevin waking Pomps. Roy McCarthy to Louis McCarthy, 8/28/18.

17   *plates full of plump peaches.* Author's interview with Kevin
            McCarthy, Los Angles, March 1982.

17   Discipline of children. Harry McCarthy to MM, 3/8/52.

18   *"the young rascals."* Roy McCarthy to Louis McCarthy in
            France, n.d., courtesy Kevin McCarthy.

18   *eight days later.* Sacred Heart (Forest Ridge) House Journal,
            1907–1913.

19   *closed all schools.* October 6, 1918.

19   Ink and fire. Harry McCarthy to MM, 3/8/52.

                              CHAPTER III

Facts about the years 1918–1923 come from interviews with
Mary McCarthy, Kevin McCarthy, Preston McCarthy, Mrs. Sheridan
McCarthy, Frank Preston, Eleanor McCarthy (widow of Louis),
Cynthia McCarthy Sandberg (youngest child of Louis), Mary Lou
McCarthy McKissick (oldest child of Louis), Blanche McCarthy Michaels
(Roy's first cousin), James McCarthy (son of Esther), Daniel Woolsey
(son-in-law of Esther), and Judy McCarthy Knickerbocker (daughter of
Harry).

Page

20   *the Prestons wanted to take.* Zella Steele to MM, 1/11/56.

20   *disputed this.* Author's interview with Frank Preston, Seattle,
            February 1982.

20   *"get some of us."* Author's interview with MM, Paris, April
            1982.

20   J. H.'s arrangements. Louis McCarthy's papers.

21   *Kevin and Preston remember.* Author's interviews with Preston
            McCarthy, Annapolis, November 1981, and Kevin
            McCarthy, Los Angeles, March 1982.

22   *Kevin is certain.* Author's interview with Kevin McCarthy.

22   *"Up to the time."* Mary McCarthy, *The Company She Keeps,*
            New York: Harcourt Brace Jovanovich/Harvest, 1970, pp.
            262, 263 (hereafter cited as *CSK*).

23   *was let go.* Harry McCarthy to MM, 3/8/52.

23   *"Our ugly church."* MCG, p. 18.

24   Judy McCarthy and Zula. Author's interview with Judy
            McCarthy Knickerbocker, Fairhope, Ala., August 1982.

24   *"Mary's always got."* Author's interviews with James
            McCarthy, Minneapolis, August 1981, and Judy McCarthy

Knickerbocker, Fairhope, Alabama, August 1982, Mary McCarthy's first cousins; Blanche McCarthy Michaels and Charles McCarthy, Minneapolis, August 1981, more distant cousins.

25   Time with grandmother. Author's interview with MM, Paris.

25   *"Uncle Myers and Aunt Margaret."* Mary McCarthy, *How I Grew,* New York: Harcourt Brace Jovanovich, 1987, p. 16 (hereafter cited as *HIG*).

25   *an Ursuline boarding school.* Author's interview with MM, Paris.

25   Harry's "loan." Author's interviews with Blanche McCarthy Michaels and Charles McCarthy.

26   *an excited conference.* Author's interview with MM, Paris.

26   *"I was sitting."* MCG, p. 79.

CHAPTER IV

Page

27   *"a crude box."* MCG, pp. 55–56.

28   *Chesapeake retriever.* Author's interview with Frank Preston, Seattle, February 1982.

28   *"should have been lit."* Richard Simonton to MM, 4/23/57.

28   *"recall that she ever spoke."* Ibid.

28   *"Mrs. Preston was."* Zella Steele to MM, 12/8/55.

29   *"All those old things."* MCG, p. 204.

29   *"looked almost as young."* Zella Steele to MM, 12/8/55.

29   *"those big lumps."* Harry McCarthy to MM, 3/8/52.

30   Facts about Preston's career. Harold Preston's front-page obituary, *Seattle Times,* January 2, 1938.

30   *"the injustices."* MCG, p. 167.

30   *"I think one of Mary's."* DM to NC, 12/10/59, Dwight Macdonald Papers, Box 10, Folder 242, Sterling Library, Yale University, New Haven.

31   *"old arthritics."* Harry McCarthy to MM, 3/8/52. Harry's unique spelling and punctuation have been left unchanged.

34   *"I don't remember."* MM to Harry McCarthy, 4/5/52.

35   *"much more admirable."* Carole Corbeil, "The Unsinkable Mary McCarthy," *The Globe and Mail,* October 23, 1982, p. ET1.

35   *flying in one door.* Author's interview with Frank Preston.

36   *"I was fresh."* MCG, pp. 103–104.

37   *"Unlike them."* HIG, p. 26.

38   *"I don't believe in God."* Miriam Gross, "A World Out of Joint" (interview with Mary McCarthy), *Observer,* October 14, 1979.

38   Retreat and grandfather story. Eileen Donahoe (a Sacred Heart classmate) to author, 7/7/82.

39   Garfield grades. High school transcript, Vassar College files.

39   *"conscious for."* HIG, p. 31.

39   *"It was I, I, I."* Author's interview with Mrs. Benjamin Hibshman (Till Rosenberg), Seattle, February 1982.

39   *"allowed as to how."* Author's interview with Jess Rosenberg, Berkeley, February 1982.

39   *"Miss Atkinson symbolized."* Elizabeth Daniels's interview with MM, Vassar, February 1982, courtesy Elizabeth Daniels; and Mary McCarthy, "The Vassar Girl," *Holiday,* May 1951, p. 49.

40   *"I was an intellectual."* HIG, p. 38.

40   *"Mary was pretty shocking."* Author's interview with Mrs. Harold Williams (Jean Eagleson), Seattle, February 1982.

40   *"she was involved."* Mrs. S. J. Harcharik (Beth Griffith), quoted in "A Surprising Survivor Among Girls' Schools," *Seattle Sun,* November 27, 1977.

40   *"She was a braggart."* Author's interview with Mrs. Benjamin Hibshman (Till Rosenberg).

41   *"a transparent little pouch."* HIG, p. 78.

41   *"He did not invite me."* Ibid, p. 155.

42   *cultural trips.* Barbara Dole Lawrence to MM, 2/21/81.

42   *"regarded Annie Wright."* HIG, p. 162.

42   Story about prostitute. MM's files, Paris (now her archives at Vassar).

42   *Wuthering Heights* paper. MM's files.

43   *praised Mary's aptitude.* Ethel Mackay recommendation, 6/20/29, Vassar files.

43   *"made Miss Marjorie Atkinson cry."* HIG, p. 136.

43   *"a girl with a terrific I.Q."* Mrs. S. J. Harcharik, quoted in *Seattle Sun.*

43   Comment about wig. Author's interview with Mrs. Stuart Frazier (Elinor Perkins), Seattle, February 1982.

43   *"sometimes lacking."* Adelaide B. Preston evaluation, 6/12/29, Vassar files.

44   *"Dr. H. N. MacCracken," "just graduated."* D. E. Skinner to H. N. MacCracken, 6/18/29, Vassar files.

44   *"We wanted Cornish."* HIG, p. 83.

CHAPTER V

Page

47   *"I should like."* MM to Helen Sandison, 4/29/29, Vassar files.

47   *college board scores.* Mary McCarthy to Ted Rosenberg, 11/1/29, courtesy Jess Rosenberg.

47   *"threshold," "a cornucopia."* Mary McCarthy, "The Vassar Girl," *Holiday,* May 1951, p. 49.

48   *"The scenery is nice."* MM to Ted Rosenberg, 11/1/29.

48   *"bucolically set."* McCarthy, "Vassar Girl," p. 49.

48   *liked little.* MM to Ted Rosenberg, 11/1/29.

48   *"a ridiculous subject," "a very aesthetic creature."* Ibid.

48   *"just vapored on."* Elizabeth Daniels's interview with MM, Vassar, February 1982, courtesy Elizabeth Daniels.

48   *"a timid little bird."* Ibid.

48   *"The English teacher."* MM to Ted Rosenberg, 11/1/29.

49   "Contrasts." Mary McCarthy's paper in *Sampler,* November 21, 1929, pp. 4–5, Vassar College Library, Special Collections.

50   *"the best thing."* Daniels interview.

50   *"Miss Kitchel had noticed."* Mary McCarthy, *The Group,* New York: Harcourt, Brace & World, 1963, p. 193 (hereafter cited as *Group*).

50   *"If there was any single course."* Daniels interview.

50   *"Aside from Christian doctrine."* Miriam Gross, "A World Out of Joint" (interview with Mary McCarthy), *Observer,* October 14, 1979, p. 35.

51   *"I love reality."* Mary McCarthy, *Birds of America,* New York: Harcourt Brace Jovanovich, 1971, p. 67 (hereafter cited as *BA*).

51   *"You have only your will."* Mary McCarthy, *Cannibals and Missionaries,* New York: Harcourt Brace Jovanovich, 1979, p. 350 (hereafter cited as *CM*).

51   *"I still punctuate."* Daniels interview.

51   *"My family sent for catalogs."* MM to admissions committee, 4/29/29, Vassar files.

51   *"radicalized."* HIG, p. 262.

51   *"I fell madly in love."* Mary McCarthy, "Politics and the Novel," *Occasional Prose,* New York: Harcourt Brace Jovanovich, 1985, pp. 201, 202.

52   *"felt more than ever."* McCarthy, "Vassar Girl," p. 53.

52	Radicals and prom. Eunice Clark Jessup, "Memoirs of Literature and Socialists 1929–1933," *Vassar Quarterly,* Winter 1979, p. 16.
53	*"Ah. So this." HIG,* p. 179.
53	*"I a 'lowly' freshman."* Ibid, p. 210.
53	*A Vassar classmate remembers.* Author's interview with Frani Blough Muser, New York, October 1982.
54	*"I knew some of the names." HIG,* p. 253.
55	*"thrown her over."* Ibid, p. 251.
55	*"over-prominent."* Ibid, p. 222.
55	*"no longer represented." Group,* p. 183.
55	*"Most of us."* Elizabeth Spires, "An Afternoon With Elizabeth Bishop," *Vassar Quarterly,* Winter 1974, p. 8.
56	Huxley review. "Two Crystal-Gazing Novelists," *Con Spirito,* February 1933, Vassar College Library, Special Collections.
56	*"I'm not starving." HIG,* p. 263.
56	*"in a mixed-up way."* Mary McCarthy, "My Confession," *On the Contrary,* New York: Farrar, Straus and Cudahy, p. 78 (hereafter cited as *OC*).
56	*"The Vatican doors."* "In Pace Requiescamus," *Con Spirito,* April 1933, Vassar College Library, Special Collections.
56	*"she had a group."* Author's interview with Eunice Clark Jessup, Wilton, Conn., October 1982.
57	*"Thousands and thousands." HIG,* p. 216.
57	*"it was a rich joke."* Ibid, p. 217.
57	*"all those mornings."* Ibid, p. 214.
57	*"There was never a word."* Ibid.
57	*"it delighted me."* Ibid, p. 265.
58	*"I spent Christmas."* MM to Ted Rosenberg, 1/13/30.
58	*"I haven't minded."* MM to Frani Blough, 12/26/31, courtesy Frani Blough Muser.
58	*"nice, sweet battered soul."* MM to Frani Blough, 7/22/32.
59	*"to have a look," "I have been having."* Ibid.
59	*"I just couldn't stand." Vassar Views,* April 1982, p. 4.
59	Familiar cartoon. Jean Anderson and Anne Cleveland, *The Educated Woman,* New York: E. P. Dutton & Co., 1960.
59	*"a dab of this."* MM to Dean Thompson, 12/15/30, Vassar files.

60   *"the idea of* using.*"* Mary McCarthy's Vassar commencement address, June 1976, Vassar College Library, Special Collections.

60   *"the staple ingredient."* "The Fact in Fiction," *OC,* p. 251.

60   *"its concern."* Ibid.

60   *"a wistful respect."* Doris Grumbach, *The Company She Kept,* New York: Coward-McCann, 1967, p. 49.

60   *"bright wild girl."* *HIG,* p. 200.

CHAPTER VI

Page

61   *"It was June."* *Group,* p. 3.

61   Description of wedding. MM to Frani Blough, 7/21/33, courtesy Frani Blough Muser.

61   *"I knew, too late."* *HIG,* p. 267.

61   *"why he decided."* MM to DG, 7/22/66.

61   *"John's character."* MM to Frani Blough, 7/21/33.

62   *"The immediate reaction."* Harold Johnsrud to Frani Blough, 4/13/34.

62   *"We have had."* MM to Frani Blough, 9/23/34.

63   *Capitol Elevator dividends.* Trustee payments made to Mary McCarthy when married to Johnsrud:
12/16/33 $300.52
5/1/34   300.52
8/10/34   300.00
8/15/34   309.74
11/27/34 150.00
7/26/35   100.00
8/30/35   594.08

63   Christmas presents. MM to Frani Blough, 1/3/35.

63   *a low opinion.* Kevin McCarthy's interview with his sister for *People,* October 1979, unpublished portion.

63   Reviews in *Nation.* Gubsky (5/30/34, p. 626), Graves (6/13/34, p. 680), Sheehan (3/6/35, pp. 282, 284), Zara (6/19/35, p. 718), Vinogradov (3/13/35, p. 312).

64   Reviews in *Nation.* Boyle (12/26/34, p. 747), Hilton (1/30/35, p. 138), Graves (4/10/35, p. 434), Bessie (9/4/35, pp. 278–279), Gingrich (3/27/35, p. 366), Cronyn (7/17/35, p. 82), Johnson (8/21/35, p. 221), Linklater (6/19/35, p. 720), Young (8/8/34, p. 167),

Olivier (8/15/34, pp. 194–195), Burnett (10/10/34, p. 417).

64   McCarthy did most reviews. Author's interview with MM, Castine, Maine, August 1984.

64–66   Book critics series. Mary McCarthy, "Our Critics, Right or Wrong," *Nation:* Part I (10/23/35, pp. 468–469, 472), Part II (11/6/35, pp. 542–544), Part III (11/20/35, pp. 595–596, 598), Part IV (12/4/35, pp. 653–655), Part V (12/18/35, pp. 717–719).

66   *"Saint Valentine's massacre." Time,* June 1, 1942, p. 84. (in a review of *CSK*).

66   Drama critics series. Mary McCarthy, "Our Actors and the Critics," *Nation,* May 8, 15, 1937.

66   *"so decorated."* Mary McCarthy, "Versions of Shakespeare," *Partisan Review,* February 1938, p. 35.

66   *"increasingly social-minded."* Mary McCarthy, "Murder and Karl Marx," *Nation,* March 25, 1936, pp. 381–383.

67   *"wild with hunger."* Author's interview with MM, Castine.

67   Rousuck. Obituary, *NYT,* October 14, 1970; and author's interviews with Kevin McCarthy, Los Angeles, February 1982; Brendan Gill, New York, August 1982; John Myers, Brewster, N.Y., August 1982; and MM, Castine.

68   *"outlaw side." HIG,* p. 248.

68   Filching manuscript. Author's interviews with MM, Castine, and John Richardson, New York, August 1982.

68   *"a sardonic twist."* "My Confession," *OC,* p. 81.

69   *"The Johnsruds came."* Julia Denison Rumsey to author, 8/26/83.

69   *"very chic."* Granville Hicks, *Part of the Truth,* New York: Harcourt, Brace & World, 1965, pp. 140, 141.

69   Successful run of *Winterset.* MM to DG, 7/22/66.

69   Facts about Porter. MM to Eleanor Perényi, 7/26/67; and author's interview with E. P., Stonington, Conn., August 1982.

69   *"very cut up."* MM to DG, 2/22/66.

69   *"Private cohabitation." CSK,* p. 8.

70   Reno facts. MM to author, 7/22/83.

70   *"embarrassingly sentimental."* MM to Eleanor Perényi, 7/26/67.

CHAPTER VII

Page

73   *his father's adversities.* "My Confession," *OC,* p. 81.

73   *"the atmosphere."* Ibid, p. 84.

73   *glowing piece.* Mary McCarthy's review of Sylvia Townsend Warner's *Summer Will Show* in *Nation,* August 15, 1936.

73   "Circus Politics in Washington State." Mary McCarthy's article in *Nation,* October 17, 1936, pp. 442–444.

73   *"While my grandparents."* "My Confession," *OC,* p. 93.

74   *"Those rascals in Russia."* William Manchester, *The Glory and the Dream,* New York: Bantam Books, 1975, p. 56.

74   Capitol Elevator trustee payments:
9/23/36 $150.00
10/1/36 329.98

74   *twenty-five dollars a week.* John Simon Guggenheim Foundation Fellowship application, 1943.

74   *Covici had wanted to publish.* John Chamberlain, *A Life With the Printed Word,* Chicago: Regnery Gateway, 1982, p. 5.

74   *"she was just waiting."* Author's interview with Cleo Paturis, New York, January 1982.

75   Farrell/McCarthy dialogue. "My Confession," pp. 95, 96.

76   *"fellow-traveling liberals," "infuriated."* Ibid, p. 99.

76   *"monstrous."* Ibid.

76   *"the defendant, Pyatakov."* Ibid, p. 100.

76   *"a blow."* Philip Rahv, "The Great Outsider," *NYRB* vol. 1.

76   Trotsky commission, Coyoacan. Alice Ruhle-Gerstel, "Trotsky in Mexico," *Encounter,* April 1982, pp. 27–47.

77   Invitations. *News Bulletin* published by American Committee for the Defense of Leon Trotsky, March 16, 1937, Dwight Macdonald Papers, Box 53, Folder 1283, Sterling Library, Yale University, New Haven.

77   *"For my generation."* Mary McCarthy, *The Seventeenth Degree,* New York: Harcourt Brace Jovanovich/Harvest, 1974, p. 313 (hereafter cited as *SD*).

77   *"I knew you were."* MM to James Farrell, 10/25/57, Farrell Papers, University of Pennsylvania, Philadelphia.

77   *The change was evident.* "My Confession," p. 103.

77–78 *"Like Stendhal's hero."* Ibid, p. 77.

78   Meeting Rahv. MM to DG, 2/22/66.

78   *"an intransigent."* Mary McCarthy's introduction, Philip
      Rahv, *Essays on Literature and Politics, 1932–1972,* New
      York: Houghton Mifflin Company, 1978, pp. vii–x.

78   *"Helena was."* Delmore Schwartz Papers, Beinecke Library,
      Yale University, New Haven, quoted in James Atlas, *Delmore
      Schwartz: The Life of an American Poet,* New York: Farrar,
      Straus and Giroux, 1977, p. 99.

79   Kaltenborn book. MM to author, 7/22/83.

79   *"While necessarily confining."* Robert Brooks's review of *Kal-
      tenborn Edits the News* in *Saturday Review,* September 25,
      1937, p. 24.

80   Silone, Levin, etc. Philip Rahv to DM, Macdonald Papers,
      Box 42, Folder 1030.

80   *"Fred and I."* Philip Rahv to DM, 8/4/37.

80   *"The whole region."* MMTC, p. viii.

81   *"The magazine had accepted me."* Ibid, p. ix.

81   *"And I remained . . . absolutely bourgeois."* Elisabeth Niebuhr,
      "The Art of Fiction" (interview with Mary McCarthy), *Paris
      Review,* Winter–Spring 1962.

81   *"There is nothing."* Author's interview with WP, New York,
      December 1981.

81   *"It was something."* MMTC, p. x.

81   *"most lively."* William Barrett, *The Truants,* New York: An-
      chor Press/Doubleday, 1982, p. 65.

82   *"As a writer."* Mary McCarthy, *Sights and Spectacles: Theatre
      Chronicles, 1937–1956,* New York: Meridian Books, 1957,
      p. xiii.

82   *Partisan Review* editors. Dwight Macdonald and L. K. Morris
      left in 1943. Philip Rahv was editor until his death, and
      William Phillips is still editor.

82   Director of Gauss Lectures. Author's interview with Joseph
      Frank, Princeton, October 1981; and letter to author dated
      11/3/81: "Mary McCarthy gave a single Gauss seminar on
      'Current Realism in the American Theater' during the aca-
      demic year 1956–57." Mary McCarthy remembers this diff-
      erently: "I don't think 'The American Realist Playwrights'
      could have been the subject; more likely it was something to
      do with the novel. 'The American Realist Playwrights' was
      one of the three lectures I gave on my State Department trip
      to Poland, Yugoslavia, and England." (MM to author, 12/
      19/83.)

82   *"were still committed to Marxism."* *MMTC,* p. ix.

83   *"T. S. Eliot's ideological conservatism."* William Phillips, "What Happened in the 30s," *Commentary,* July 1962, p. 207.

83   *"We wanted to be."* *MMTC,* p. ix.

83   *first editorial. Partisan Review,* December 1937, p. 3.

83   "So far as." Leon Trotsky to DM, 1/20/38, Macdonald Papers, Box 53, Folder 1283.

83   *"Given the narrow."* Philip Rahv to Leon Trotsky, 2/20/38.

84   *"His letter."* Philip Rahv to DM, 8/4/37, Macdonald Papers, Box 42, Folder 1030.

84   *"Tonight I am having."* MM to EW, 12/1/37, Edmund Wilson Papers, Beinecke Library, Yale University, New Haven.

85   *"About Delmore Schwartz."* MM to EW, 12/3/37.

85   *"his violet eyes," "prudish about sex."* James Atlas, *Delmore Schwartz: The Life of an American Poet,* New York: Farrar, Straus and Giroux, 1977; and author's interview with James Atlas, New York, October 1981.

CHAPTER VIII

Page

86   Meeting Wilson. Author's interview with MM, Castine, Maine, August 1984.

86   *"All my habits of mind."* *MMTC,* p. ix.

87   *"the happenings of the weekend."* MM to EW, 11/29/37, Edmund Wilson Papers, Beinecke Library, Yale University, New Haven.

87   *"I am still shaken up."* MM to EW, 11/30/37.

87   *"I am still* distraite.*"* MM to EW, 12/1/37.

87   Wilson's response. EW to MM, 12/2/37.

88   *"The train was awful."* MM to EW, 12/7/37.

88   *"Here is something funny."* MM to EW, 12/14/37.

89   *"very merry inside."* MM to EW, 12/30/37.

89   *"It was so damned unexpected."* MM to EW, 1/2/38.

89   *"it will be trying."* MM to EW, 1/19/38.

89   *"must be a little."* MM to EW, 1/19/38.

89   *"He was terribly upset."* Author's interviews with Nancy Macdonald, New York, November 1981 and August 1982.

90   *"once we get him."* Dwight Macdonald Papers, Box 42, Folder 1030, Sterling Library, Yale University, New Haven.

90   *"Before we married."* Deposition taken 2/23/45, McCarthy Archives, Vassar College Library.

90   *"child-like side."* Edmund Wilson, *The Thirties,* New York: Farrar, Straus and Giroux, 1980, p. 704.

91   *"a bourgeois family man."* MM to ASJ, 2/13/55, courtesy Professor Schlesinger.

91   *she was too bohemian.* Author's interviews with WP, New York, December 1981, and Mrs. John Jessup, Wilton, Conn., November 1981.

91   *"Directly after our marriage."* Deposition taken 2/23/45.

91   *"How could you?"* Author's interview with MM, Paris, April 1982.

91–92 Fight and Payne-Whitney. Author's interview with MM, Paris.

92   *"Sitting there in lobby."* Group, pp. 315–316.

93   *"about the pregnancy."* EW to MM, 6/17/38, MM files, now at McCarthy Archives, Vassar College Library.

94   *the diagnosis.* Wilson Papers.

94   *Reuel Kimball Wilson was named for.* Author's interview with RW, London, Ontario, February 1982.

94   *"As my family."* Edmund Wilson to Christian Gauss, October 27, 1938, in *Letters in Literature and Politics 1912–1972,* ed. by Elena Wilson, New York: Farrar, Straus and Giroux, 1977, p. 313.

94   *"social interpretation of Taine."* Edmund Wilson to Christian Gauss, March 3, 1939, in *Letters in Literature and Politics,* p. 317.

95   *"the university is something fantastic."* Edmund Wilson to John Dos Passos, July 16, 1939, in *Letters in Literature and Politics,* pp. 15–16.

95   Students' reactions. Author's telephone interview with Mark Ashin, a former student of Wilson's, Chicago, 1981.

95   *"He had lectured on Flaubert."* HIG, p. 260.

95   Apartment and fights. Author's interview with Professor and Mrs. Walter Blair, Chicago, August 1981.

95   *"How cute."* EW to MM, 7/31/39, MM files, now at McCarthy Archives, Vassar College Library.

96   *"I've been getting bored,"* EW to MM, 8/13/39, MM files, ibid.

96   *"I miss you."* EW to MM, 8/16/39, MM files, ibid.

96   *"I'll be glad."* EW to MM, 8/19/39, Wilson Papers.

CHAPTER IX

Page
98   *five-thousand-dollar loan.* Author's interview with RW, Well-fleet, Mass., August 1982.

99   Title to *The Boys in the Back Room.* Author's interview with Adelaide Walker, New York, October 1981.

99   *"The style with long."* Mary McCarthy's review of John Dos Passos's *Adventures of a Young Man* in *Partisan Review,* Summer 1939, p. 114.

99   *"has written about your book."* Edmund Wilson to John Dos Passos, July 16, 1939, in *Letters in Literature and Politics 1912–1972,* New York: Farrar, Straus and Giroux, 1977, p. 320.

99   *"straight off."* Quoted in Doris Grumbach, *The Company She Kept,* New York: Coward-McCann, 1963, p. 86.

99–100 *"About halfway."* Elisabeth Niebuhr, "The Art of Fiction" (interview with Mary McCarthy), *Paris Review,* Winter-Spring 1962, p. 65.

100   *"the performance of."* Review of CSK in *Books,* May 24, 1942, p. 8.

100   *"I've thought."* EW to Fred Dupee, 5/16/40, Dupee Deposit, Butler Library, Columbia University, New York.

100   *"Mary is well toward."* Edmund Wilson to Christian Gauss, September 8, 1941, in *Letters in Literature and Politics,* p. 343.

100   *"Actually she doubted." CSK,* p. 6.

101   *"her whole way of life."* Ibid, p. 84.

101   *"There was an air."* Ibid, p. 110.

101   *"it was a kind of detail."* MM to Edwin Newman for WNBC interview, 12/4/66.

101   *"poor, loveless." CSK,* p. 163.

102   *"therapeutic lie."* Ibid, p. 302.

102   *"unusual quality."* Malcolm Cowley's review of CSK in *New Republic,* May 25, 1942.

102   *"a splendid thing."* Vladimir Nabokov to Edmund Wilson, in *The Nabokov-Wilson Letters, 1940–1971,* ed. Simon Karlinsky, New York: Harper & Row, 1979, p. 61.

102   *"furious debate."* Review of CSK in *Time,* June 1, 1942, pp. 82, 84.

102   *"not a likeable."* Malcolm Cowley's review of CSK in *New Republic,* May 25, 1942, p. 737.

102   *"full of contradictions."* Review of CSK in *NYT,* May 24, 1942, p. 7.

102   *"Miss McCarthy."* Review of *CSK* in *New Yorker,* May 16, 1942, p. 73.

102   *"I came down."* EW to MM, 8/10/42, MM's files, now at McCarthy Archives, Vassar College Library.

103   RKO and rights. Author's telephone conversation with Charles Schlessiger, Brandt and Brandt, 2/5/87.

103   *"that is what sent."* Maria Leiper is quoted in a letter (12/3/82) to the author from Peter Schwed, chairman emeritus of the Editorial Board, Simon and Schuster. Mary McCarthy: "I don't remember my separation from Simon and Schuster that way at all. . . . It seems a bit unlikely to me that Bernice Baumgarten, who had an eye on the contract as my literary agent, would have let an inequitable contract be accepted. [McCarthy was *not* Baumgarten's client on July 1, 1942, the time of the RKO contract. Brandt and Brandt's first sales slip in her file is dated October 28, 1942.] It seems to me, too, that the movie sale took place *after* I left Simon and Schuster. The reasons for that, in my memory, were more emotional than businesslike. Dick Simon, who I thought was quite a nice man, rather more musical than literary, took my literary situation very much to heart, was greatly worried about my financial future, and frightened by what seemed to him my carefreeness or irresponsibility. I cannot remember what the spark was that set all this off, but it may have been a new contract, perhaps covering several books that he wanted me to sign with them after *The Company She Keeps,* and I suspect I behaved in an airy way, refusing to be pinned down. At that point, . . . he shouted something like, 'I can't stand this! Go get yourself an agent!' Calming himself, he recommended Bernice to me. I obeyed, and from then on was her client." (MM to author, 4/11/83.) The records at Brandt and Brandt and Edmund Wilson's August 10 letter indicate that Maria Leiper's memory in this matter is more accurate than Mary McCarthy's.

103   *"not a realistic novel."* John Simon Guggenheim Memorial Foundation files.

104   Returned advance. Charles Schlessiger, Brandt and Brandt.

104   "The Company Is Not Responsible." Mary McCarthy's article in *New Yorker,* April 22, 1944, pp. 77–80.

104   *"at the beginning."* Niebuhr, "Art of Fiction," p. 75.

105   *"For lunch."* Edmund Wilson, *The Forties,* New York: Farrar, Straus and Giroux, 1983, pp. 27–28.

106   *"Our life."* Edmund Wilson, *The Thirties,* New York: Farrar, Straus and Giroux, 1980, p. 704.

106   *"The fault was mostly Wilson's."* Author's interview with Adelaide Walker.

106   *"When I inherited."* Carol Brightman, "Mary, Still Contrary," *Nation,* May 19, 1984, p. 616.

106   *"he didn't like to feel."* Author's interview with Adelaide Walker.

107   *"Over the years."* Adelaide Walker to EW, 9/12/47, Edmund Wilson Papers, Beinecke Library, Yale University, New Haven.

107   *faculty members.* Professor and Mrs. Walter Blair, Mark Ashin.

107   *"Don't I know!"* Author's interview with John Myers, Brewster, N.Y., August 1982.

107   *"Edmund certainly had."* Author's interview with Adelaide Walker.

108   *"A tyrant and paranoid."* Brightman, "Mary, Still Contrary," p. 615.

108   *"Edmund is pathetic."* MM to ASJ, 11/13/55, courtesy Professor Schlesinger.

108   "It may be." EW to MM, 6/13/44, McCarthy Archives, Vassar College Library and quoted in *New York Times,* May 1, 1985, p. B8.

108   *"I've drawn."* MM to ASJ, 11/13/55.

108   *"He casts a long shadow."* Mary McCarthy, *A Charmed Life,* New York: Avon Books, 1981, p. 91 (hereafter cited as *CL*).

108   *"We had about."* Mary McCarthy's testimony during divorce proceedings, 2/23/45.

108   "The Weeds." Mary McCarthy's story in *New Yorker,* September 16, 1944, pp. 25–43.

109   "Dear Edmund." Note to Wilson, n.d. McCarthy Archives, Vassar College Library and quoted in *NYT,* May 1, 1985, pp. B1–B8.

109   *"The only husband."* Kevin McCarthy's interview with his sister for *People,* November 1979, unpublished portion.

CHAPTER X

Page

113   Depositions. Copy of depositions in McCarthy Archives, Vassar College Library and quoted in *NYT,* May 1, 1985, p. B8.

113   *behaved neurotically.* Edmund Wilson, *The Thirties,* New York: Farrar, Straus and Giroux, 1980, p. 704.

113   Support. Letters from Hunt, Hill and Betts and from Baer and Marks, Edmund Wilson Papers, Beinecke Library, Yale University, New Haven.

114   *"He thought it was a crazy notion."* Katy Dos Passos to John Dos Passos, 3/8/45, Dos Passos Papers, Accession 5950, Box 20, University of Virginia, Charlottesville.

114   *"though, as you probably know."* EW to John Dos Passos, 6/3/45, Dos Passos Papers, Accession 5950, Box 1.

114   Wilson's claims. Authors interviews with Adelaide Walker, New York, October 1981; DM, New York, October 1981; Eunice Clark Jessup, Wilton, Conn., October 1981; and MM, Paris, April 1982.

114   *"Alienation."* What people now call a psychiatrist was called an alienist in the 1940s. The alienist tried to cure patients of a sense of alienation.

114   *"his insistence."* Author's interview with DM.

114   *"I would, of course."* Adelaide Walker to EW, 9/12/47, Wilson Papers.

115   *"I am in bed."* Katy Dos Passos to John Do Passos, 11/8/45, Dos Passos Papers, Accession 5950, Box 20.

116   Washing machine incident. Author's interview with Adelaide Walker.

116   *"Well, Dwight."* Author's interview with DM, New York, October 1981.

116   Schwartz story. Delmore Schwartz Papers, Beinecke Library, Yale University, New Haven, quoted in James Atlas, *The Life of an American Poet,* New York: Farrar, Straus and Giroux, 1977.

117   *"The city is full."* EW to RW, 7/7/45, MM files, Paris (now at Vassar).

117   *"which have arms."* EW to RW, 7/29/45, MM files, now at McCarthy Archives, Vassar College Library.

117   *"I remember."* Mary McCarthy, "The Fact in Fiction," *OC,* p. 267.

117   *"Toward the end of the war."* Elisabeth Niebuhr, "The Art of Fiction" (interview with Mary McCarthy), *Paris Review,* Winter-Spring 1962, p. 75.

118   *"America, I think."* Adrienne Clarkson's interview with MM for CBC, Vassar, October 1968.

118   *"We talked about Tolstoy."* Carol Brightman, "Mary, Still Contrary," *Nation,* May 19, 1984, pp. 611–619.

119   Nicola Chiaromonte. Author's interviews with Miriam Chiaromonte, Rome, April 1982; Irma Brandeis, Annandale-on-Hudson, N.Y., August 1982; Eileen Simpson, New York, January 1982; DM, New York, October 1981; Joseph Frank, Princeton, November 1981.

119   *"a transient love affair."* Author's interview with MM, Castine, Maine, August 1984.

120   *"in times of crisis."* Nicola Chiaromonte, "The Mass Situation and Noble Values," *The Worm of Consciousness and Other Essays,* New York: Harcourt Brace Jovanovich, n.d., p. 237.

120   *"was a radical in thought."* Nicola Chiaromonte, "Social Law After Proudhon," *politics,* January 1945, p. 27.

120   *"In the last analysis."* Nicola Chiaromonte, "On the Kind of Socialism Called Scientific," *politics,* February 1946, p. 40.

120   McCarthy's views of psychoanalysis. Kevin McCarthy's interview with his sister for *People,* October 1979, unpublished portion.

121   *"His ideas did not fit."* Mary McCarthy's preface, Chiaromonte, *Worm of Consciousness,* p. xv.

121   *"is not concatenation."* Nicola Chiaromonte, *The Paradox of History,* London: Weidenfeld & Nicholson, n.d., p. 119.

121   *"One can foresee."* Quoted in "My Confession," *OC,* p. 105.

121   *"rationality is present."* Chiaromonte, *Paradox of History,* p. 19.

121   *"The faith in History."* Mary McCarthy, "The Unresigned Man," *NYRB,* February 14, 1985, p. 27.

122   *"If we could get to know."* Ibid.

123   "The Iliad, or the Poem of Force." Simone Weil's essay, trans. Mary McCarthy, *politics,* 11/45, pp. 221–231.

124   *"a watershed."* MM to DG, 2/22/66.

124   *"Nicola, I've long wanted."* MM to NC, 3/6/68, MM's files, Paris (now at Vassar).

124   *"She creates."* Author's interview with Miriam Chiaromonte.

124   *"Fisherman's shingled cottage."* Mary McCarthy, "The Novels That Got Away," *NYTBR,* November 25, 1979 p. 9.

125   *"It is not my idea."* MM to EW, 7/18/45, Wilson Papers.

CHAPTER XI

128   *"happy tradition of eccentricity."* Ibid.

128   *"tall, soft-bellied."* GA, p. 13.

129   "The Unspoiled Reaction." Mary McCarthy's story in *Atlantic Monthly,* March 3, 1946, pp. 98–101.

129   Bowden Broadwater. Bowden Broadwater preferred not to be interviewed. My descriptions of him and the marriage are based on dozens of interviews with those who know him, including: John Richardson, New York, January 1982; Nicholas King, New York, November 1981 and January 1982; Eve Gassler Stwertka, Frani Blough Muser, New York, November 1981; Niccolò Tucci, New York, October 1981; Reverend F. Q. Shafer and Margaret Shafer; Irma Brandeis; Arthur Schlesinger, Jr., New York, January 1982; Barbara Anderson Dupee; Sir Harold Acton, Florence, April, 1982; Emilia Sartori, Florence, April 1982; Countess Cristina Rucellai, Florence, April 1982; Carmen Angleton, Rome, April 1982; and John Myers, Brewster, N.Y., August 1982.

129   *"He worked on her."* Author's interview with John Myers.

129   *was pleased by her decision.* Author's interview with Barbara Anderson Dupee.

129   *"there was something."* Quoted in Doris Grumbach, *The Company She Kept,* New York: Coward-McCann, 1963, p. 127.

131   *monthly expenses.* MM to EW, 1/46, Edmund Wilson Papers, Beinecke Library, Yale University, New Haven.

131   *"His Saint Bernard's preparation."* MM to EW, 11/5/45, Wilson Papers.

132   *"I haven't gone yet."* MM to RW, 8/18/46, Wilson Papers.

132   *"everything that Europe."* Mary McCarthy, "Lausanne," *Town and Country,* November 1946, pp. 130, 262, 267, 270.

133   *"quite wonderful."* MM to EH, 1/48, Robert Lowell Papers, Houghton Library, Harvard University, Cambridge, Mass.

133   *"mustard plaster."* McCarthy, "Lausanne."

133   *"suddenly remembered," "He got us moved."* Jacqueline Bograd Weld, *Peggy, The Wayward Guggenheim,* New York: E. P. Dutton & Co., 1986, p. 352.

133   Facts about Guggenheim's career. (pamphlet) *Peggy Guggenheim Collection,* New York: Solomon Guggenheim Foundation, n.d.

133   *"I wore one."* Peggy Guggenheim, *Out of This Century,* New York: Universe Books, 1979, p. 3.

134   "The Cicerone." Mary McCarthy's story in *Partisan Review,* February 1948, pp. 151–176.

135   *"The Elevated concealed."* Bowden Broadwater, "Ciao," *Paris Review,* Winter 1961, pp. 41–51.

135   *"I am enclosing a check."* EW to MM, 10/25/46, MM files, Paris (now at Vassar).

135   *"We haven't found."* MM to EW, 12/11/46, Wilson Papers.

135   Lutheran officiated. MM to EH, 7/20/49, Lowell Papers.

CHAPTER XII

Page

136   *"The morning of February 18."* Bowden Broadwater, "Ciao," *Paris Review,* Winter 1961, p. 41.

136   Wanted to be writer. Author's interview with RW, London, Ontario, February 1982.

136   *"reverted to a hermit's diet."* MM to EH, Robert Lowell Papers, Houghton Library, Harvard University, Cambridge, Mass.

137   Bowden good husband. Author's interview with DM, New York, October 1981.

137   *"Bowden has at last."* DM to NC, 5/11/47, Dwight Macdonald Papers, Box 10, Folder 241, Sterling Library, Yale University, New Haven.

137   *"with deer, snakes."* MM to DM, 6/21/47, Macdonald Papers, Box 31, Folder 779.

137   *"Papa dear."* RW to MM, 5/25/47, MM's Paris files, now at McCarthy Archives, Vassar College Library.

138   *"that entirely different things."* EW to MM, 7/1/47, ibid.

138   *"I'm afraid."* EW to MM, 8/25/48, ibid.

139   *"funny to have."* Randall Jarrell, *Randall Jarrell's Letters,* ed. Mary Jarrell, Boston: Houghton Mifflin Company, 1955, p. 383.

139   *"Gertrude Johnson was."* Randall Jarrell, *Pictures from an Institution,* London: Faber and Faber, n.d., pp. 12, 51, 73, 143, 197.

139   *"The only points."* MM to author, 11/17/84.

139   *"After the war."* Elisabeth Niebuhr, "The Art of Fiction" (interview with Mary McCarthy), *Paris Review,* Winter-Spring, 1962, p. 77.

140   *"We are a group."* Manifesto courtesy Miriam Chiaromonte.

140   *Partisan Review* contributes nothing. MM to Walter Goldwa-
          ter, 9/3/82.

140   *five hundred dollars.* Miriam Chiaromonte remembers this
          figure, but Mary McCarthy and Elizabeth Hardwick think it
          was higher.

140   Inheritance. Exact amount: $23,251.71.

140   Fund-raising activities. EAG minutes, 4/11/48, courtesy
          Miriam Chiaromonte.

141   Special meeting. EAG minutes, 4/11/48.

141   *two thousand dollars. politics,* Summer 1948, p. 204.

141   *"They planned to be."* MM to Walter Goldwater, 9/3/82.

141   *"I became very busy."* Ibid.

141   *"the faces of Hook."* Ibid.

141   *"We are having."* MM to DM, n.d., Macdonald Papers, Box
          31, Folder 779.

141   *"dear Mary."* NC to MM, 7/9/48.

141   *"My preliminary impression."* MM to DM, 7/n.d./48, Mac-
          donald Papers, Box 31, Folder 779.

142   *"Hook and the PR boys."* DM to NC, 12/10/48, Macdonald
          Papers, Box 10, Folder 241.

142   *"No one wants."* Ibid.

142   *EAG's last gasp.* DM to NC, 4/14/49, Macdonald Papers,
          Box 10, Folder 242.

143   Worked in shed. Author's interview with Augusta Dabney
          Prince, New York, October 1981.

143   *"For years."* MM to Adrienne Clarkson, CBC, Toronto, 10/68.

143–145   Quotes from *Oasis.* Mary McCarthy, *The Oasis,* New York:
          Random House, 1949: *"a network,"* p. 29; *"ten years before,"*
          p. 8; *"Facts of any kind,"* pp. 35, 36; *"Agreeing in principle,"*
          p. 31; *"ostracism,"* p. 12; *"was it to follow,"* p. 13; *"cavalcade,"*
          p. 30; *"a strong will,"* 70.

145   *"the only one that aimed."* MM to DG, 2/22/62.

145   *Oasis: "an absolutely."* Brendan Gill, *New Yorker,* August 20,
          1949, p. 65; *"mild entertainment":* Clorinda Clarke, *Catholic
          World,* November 1949, p. 58; *"small rewards":* Denham
          Sutcliffe, *Christian Science Monitor,* August 23, 1949, p. 14;
          "a philosophical disquisition": Iris Barry, *Herald Tribune,* Au-
          gust 14, 1949, p. 3; *"sins":* Henry Rago, *Commonweal,* Sep-
          tember 9, 1949, p. 536; *"Miss McCarthy is":* Gorham
          Munson, *Saturday Review,* August 20, 1949, p. 12; *"of cheerful
          assent":* Gill, *New Yorker; "the 'satire' contains":* T. J. Ross,

New Republic, August 18, 1949, p. 25; *"toothlessness":* Paul Goodman, *Furioso,* Winter 1950, pp. 77–78.

145   *"more serious consideration."* Edmund Wilson, *Furioso,* Spring 1950, p. 88.

146   *Rahv went to a lawyer.* Author's interview with DM.

146   *"I thought."* Author's interviews with EH, New York, October 1981 and January 1982.

146   *"talked too freely."* William Barrett, *The Truants,* New York: Anchor Press/Doubleday, 1982, p. 42.

146   *"For a while."* Barrett, *Truants,* p. 68.

146   *"That book."* Author's interviews with EH.

147   *"I'm the man."* Author's interview with Walter Goldwater, New York, August 1982.

147   *"Bellow and I."* Harold Kaplan to Philip Rahv, Macdonald Papers, Box 42, Folder 1030.

147   *"It might be."* Philip Rahv to DM, 3/24/49, Macdonald Papers, Box 42, Folder 1030.

147   *"Have you read."* DM to NC, 4/7/49, Macdonald Papers, Box 10, Folder 241.

147   *"true to some extent."* Ibid.

148   *"Mary's story has caused."* NC to DM, 4/11/49, Macdonald Papers, Box 10, Folder 241.

148   *"Mary's story: yes."* DM to NC, 4/14/49, Macdonald Papers, Box 10, Folder 242.

148   *"the English magazine."* Barrett, *Truants,* p. 67.

148   *"has no qualms."* Margaret Marshall, *Nation,* September 17, 1949, p. 281.

148–150   Waldorf conference. William O'Neill, *A Better World, The Great Schism: Stalinism and the American Intellectuals,* New York: Simon and Schuster, 1982, p. 103 ff.; William Barrett, "On the Horizon: Culture conference at the Waldorf," *Commentary,* April 1949, pp. 487–493; Irving Howe, *A Margin of Hope,* New York: Harcourt Brace Jovanovich, 1982, p. 156 ff., and "The Culture Conference," *Partisan Review,* May 1949, pp. 509–511; and Joseph Lash, "Weekend at the Waldorf," *New Republic,* April 12, 1949, pp. 10–14.

149   *"He just laughed."* Author's interview with MM, Castine.

149   Americans for Intellectual Freedom. Americans for Intellectual Freedom was also called American Intellectuals for Freedom and Ad Hoc Committee for Intellectual Freedom. Sidney Hook had organized a Committee for Cultural Freedom in 1939, its purpose being to oppose dictatorships of the

left and the right. In his memoir *Out of Step* (Harper & Row, 1987), Hook tells how he decided to resurrect this committee (it had become dormant during World War II) in order to counter the propaganda being released to the media from the organizers of the Waldorf conference. He summoned as many members of the 1939 committee as he could reach to Dwight Macdonald's apartment. He writes, "I initially held out for calling our group the Committee for Cultural Freedom in order to stress our continuity with the earlier embodiment of our position, but in view of the fact that there were so many fresh accessions to our ranks, I yielded on that point" (p. 385).

149   *"I don't think."* Author's interview with MM, Castine.

149   *"with umbrellas."* Ibid.

149   *"You goddamned intellectuals."* Ibid.

CHAPTER XIII

Page

153   *"I am tempted."* MM to ASJ, 2/7/49, courtesy Professor Schlesinger.

153   *"The Oasis is a gem."* Elisabeth Young-Bruehl, *Hannah Arendt: For Love of the World,* New Haven: Yale University Press, 1982, p. 196.

153   *"How can you."* Ibid.

153   *"We two think."* Ibid.

154   *"She was a beautiful woman."* Mary McCarthy in *NYT,* December 9, 1975, Section 1, p. 44.

154   *"What distinguishes her."* HA to Guggenheim Foundation, 2/2/59, Hannah Arendt Papers, Library of Congress, Washington.

156   *"frugal, foursquare."* MM to Katharine White, 7/20/49, *New Yorker* files, courtesy William Shawn.

156   *"Everything is."* MM to EH, 6/24/49, Robert Lowell Papers, Houghton Library, Harvard University, Cambridge, Mass.

156   *"You must find."* EW to MM, 2/5/47.

156   *"camping out."* MM to Kevin McCarthy, 6/2/49, courtesy Kevin McCarthy.

156   *"painters and plumbers."* MM to DM, Dwight Macdonald Papers, Box 31, Folder 779, Sterling Library, Yale University, New Haven.

156   *"The first day."* MM to EH, 6/24/49, Lowell Papers.

157   Colors, decoration. MM to EH, 7/8/49, 7/20/49, Lowell
        Papers.

157   *a large number of antiques.* MM's introduction to Nancy Mac-
        donald's *Homage to Spanish Exiles,* New York: Human
        Sciences Press, 1987, p. 21.

157   *"Dearest Reuel."* MM to RW, n.d., Edmund Wilson Papers,
        Beinecke Library, Yale University, New Haven.

158   *"myriads of birds."* MM to DW, n.d., Macdonald Papers, Box
        31, Folder 779.

158   *"B. and I."* MM to EH, 8/22/49, Lowell Papers.

158   *"a kind of circuit-rider."* Ibid.

158   *"all part of."* MM to EH, 11/8/51, Lowell Papers.

159   *"strange woman."* MM to EH, 7/20/49, Lowell Papers.

159   *"quite commercial."* MM to Robert Linscott, 8/8/49, Special
        Manuscript Collections Random House, Butler Library, Co-
        lumbia University, New York.

159   *"One weekend."* MM to EH, 7/7/49, Lowell Papers.

160   *"The Newportians behaved."* Mary Meigs, *Lily Briscoe: A Self-
        Portrait,* Vancouver: Talonbooks, 1981, p. 146.

160   *"This letter."* MM to Macdonalds, 11/20/49, Macdonald
        Papers, Box 31, Folder 779.

160   *"we are a little depressed."* MM to EH, 12/13/49, Lowell
        Papers.

160   *"very strapped."* MM to EW, 2/20/50, Wilson Papers.

161   *"Reuel and Mike."* DM to MM, 7/11/49.

161   *like her manager.* Author's interviews with Nicholas King and
        Barbara Anderson Dupee.

161   *"Greenwich Village at night."* Ten-part series. Ran in *New York
        Post* from February 20 to March 3, 1950.

161   *"The Man in the Brooks Brothers Shirt."* January 15, 1950.

161   *"Lesbian in the Brooks Brothers Shirt."* MM to ASJ, 2/20/50,
        courtesy Professor Schlesinger.

162   *"VERY bad."* DM to NC, 12/21/50, Macdonald Papers,
        Box 10, Folder 242.

163   *"who couldn't make much."* Author's interviews with Nicholas
        King, New York, October 1982 and January 1983.

163   *"It looks really."* MM to Robert Linscott, 8/8/49, Special
        Collections, Columbia.

164   *"Why doesn't Random House."* MM to Robert Linscott, 8/13/
        49, Special Collections, Columbia.

164   McCarthy's change of publisher. Author's telephone inter-
        view with Robert Giroux, 3/24/87.

165   "Miss McCarthy's eye." Review of Mary McCarthy's *Cast a
        Cold Eye* in *NYT,* 9/24/50, p. 9.

165   "Bowden doesn't do much." DM to NC, 12/21/50, Macdonald
        Papers, Box 10, Folder 242.

165   "a little dazed." MM to EH, 10/17/51, Lowell Papers.

166   "I really wanted." Elisabeth Niebuhr, "The Art of Fiction"
        (interview with Mary McCarthy), *Paris Review,* Winter
        1961–Fall 1962, p. 67.

166   "a rare talent." Review of GA in *Atlantic Monthly,* April 5,
        1952, p. 86.

166   "a stunning." Alice Morris's review of GA in *NYT,* February
        24, 1952, p. 7.

166   *affinity with Molière.* Robert Halsband's review of GA in *Sat-
        urday Review,* March 8, 1952, p. 13.

166   "my intention." John Simon Guggenheim Memorial Foun-
        dation files, submitted 11/1/48.

167   "The whole question." Niebuhr, "Art of Fiction," p. 90.

167   "Now the normal way." "Characters in Fiction," *OC,* p. 286.

168   "Mary seemed to want." Meigs, *Lily Briscoe,* p. 152.

168   "probably has something." Mary McCarthy, "Everybody's
        Childhood," *The Writing on the Wall,* New York: Harcourt,
        Brace & World, 1970, pp. 102, 103 (hereafter cited as
        WW).

169   "with full powers." Mary McCarthy, *Ideas and the Novel,* New
        York: Harcourt Brace Jovanovich, 1980, p. 30 (hereafter
        cited as *Ideas*).

169   "a lack of." MM to NC, 9/25/62, MM's files, Paris (now at
        Vassar).

169   "imposed on any artist." MM to author, 4/1/87.

169   "the common world." "Characters in Fiction," p. 292.

169   "However, I like Mary's mind." NC to DM, 2/27/52, Mac-
        donald Papers, Box 10, Folder 242.

169   "McCarthy's fiction." Author's interview with DG, Washing-
        ton, D.C., November 1982.

170   "her characteristic tone." John Aldridge, *Time to Murder and
        Create,* New York: David McKay Co., 1966, p. 103.

170   *two principal flaws.* DM to NC, 2/14/52, Macdonald Papers,
        Box 10, Folder 242.

171   "Racine is." *CL,* p. 141.

171   *"I cannot account."* MM to DM, n.d., Macdonald Papers, Box 31, Folder 779.

171   *"Miss Brayton's views."* MM to EH, 8/22/49.

CHAPTER XIV

173   Congress for Cultural Freedom. Author's interview with Kot Jelenski, Paris, April 1982.

173   *"Intellectual freedom."* NYT, June 30, 1950, p. 6.

173   American Committee for Cultural Freedom. William O'Neill writes in *A Better World* (Simon and Schuster, 1982) that "this was not the same group organized by Sidney Hook in 1939 to fight the Popular Front. It was new, growing out of a Congress for Cultural Freedom held in West Berlin in June 1950" (p. 277). Sidney Hook writes in *Out of Step* (Harper & Row, 1987) that "formally, the American Committee for Cultural Freedom was organized in 1951, although it existed informally before then [i.e. as A. I. F.]" (p. 420). But, according to Hook, it did not grow out of the Congress for Cultural Freedom. "The American Committee was the only national committee that had been formed and was functioning *before* the congress was organized. It was, strictly speaking, an independent affiliate of the congress and continually on the verge of disaffiliating with it" (p. 423).

174   *"ill-aimed."* NYT, March 30, 1952, p. 47.

174   *"The term 'cultural freedom.'"* "No News, or What Killed the Dog," OC, pp. 32, 34, 41. This article is the text of Mary McCarthy's address at the Waldorf.

174   *"on the fringes."* MM to EH, 10/17/51, 2/25/52, Robert Lowell Papers, Houghton Library, Harvard University, Cambridge, Mass.

175   *"that the legal position."* Peter Duval Smith, "Mary McCarthy Said," *Vogue,* October 15, 1963, p. 98.

175   *"the sort of thing."* Prospectus written by Mary McCarthy, courtesy Mrs. Richard Rovere.

175   *"The truth."* Mary McCarthy, "The Menace to Free Journalism," *Listener,* May 14, 1953, pp. 791–792.

176   *"would fix its attention."* MM to Richard Rovere, ASJ, et al., 12/4/52, courtesy Professor Schlesinger.

176   Magazine format. Prospectus, courtesy Mrs. Richard Rovere.

177   All facts and quotes concerning fund-raising, meetings, etc.,
        unless otherwise noted, are from letters from MM to ASJ:
        12/4/52, 12/15/52, n.d./52, 3/3/53, n.d./53, 3/20/53,
        4/17/53, 4/21/53, 5/3/53, 6/9/53, 10/28/53, courtesy
        Professor Schlesinger.

177   *"that was not the view."* MM to author, 4/1/87.

178   *autobiographical story.* Mary McCarthy, "Artists in Uniform,"
        Harper's, March 1953, pp. 41–49.

178   a habit Bowden disliked. Author's interview with Margaret
        Shafer, Annandale-on-Hudson, N.Y., 1982.

179   *"There were no symbols."* Mary McCarthy, "Settling the Colo-
        nel's Hash," *Harper's,* February 1954, pp. 68–75.

179   *A friend.* Helvetia Perkins.

179   *"Secluded corner," "Minster was feeling."* Mary McCarthy, "Ap-
        palachian Revolution," *New Yorker,* September 11, 1954, p.
        52.

180   Elena Wilson *refusals.* Author's interview with Adelaide
        Walker, New York, October 1981.

180   Montgomery Clift. Author's interview with Augusta Dabney
        Prince, New York, October 1981; and Patricia Bosworth,
        Montgomery Clift, New York: Harcourt Brace Jovanovich,
        1978, p. 257.

180   *"John Sinnot cut."* CL, p. 1.

181   *"fell in love."* Mary Meigs, *Lily Briscoe: A Self-Portrait,* Vancou-
        ver: Talonbooks, 1981, p. 146.

181   *"Mary McCarthy."* Ibid, p. 145.

181   *"was in a delicate situation," "She and John."* CL, pp. 2, 13.

181   *"There are a number."* Mary McCarthy, "Letter from Portu-
        gal," *New Yorker,* February 5, 1955, pp. 83–102.

182   Labor cheap. MM to DM, 4/9/55, Macdonald Papers, Box
        31, Folder 780, Sterling Library, Yale University, New
        Haven.

182   *The talk.* Mary McCarthy, "Thoughts of an American in En-
        gland," *Listener,* June 17, 1954, pp. 1041–1042.

182   *"writing," "in the little front room."* Meigs, *Lily Briscoe,* p. 148.

183   *read his completed manuscript.* Author's interview with ASJ,
        New York, January 1982.

183   *"I love it here."* MM to HA, 12/8/54, McCarthy Papers, now
        McCarthy Archives, Vassar College Library.

183   *"Capri is."* MM to DM, 4/9/55, Macdonald Papers, Box 31,
        Folder 780.

183   *"Latest, a spinach gnocchi."* MM to ASJ, 5/16/55, courtesy Professor Schlesinger.

183   Reaction to Pompeii. MM to DM, 4/9/55.

183   *"I am pregnant."* MM to HA, 6/14/55, McCarthy Papers, now McCarthy Archives, Vassar College Library.

184   *"did a good deal."* MM to Katharine White, 8/15/55, *New Yorker* files.

184   *"a mystery to me," "on very poor terms."* Doris Grumbach, *The Company She Kept,* New York: Coward-McCann, 1967, p. 180.

184   Broadwater marriage. Author's interviews with Irma Brandeis, Annandale-on-Hudson, N.Y., August 1982; Barbara Anderson Dupee, New York, September 1981; William Mostyn-Owen, London, March 1982; James Merrill, New York, December 1981; Eileen Simpson, New York, January 1982; RW, London, Ontario, February 1982; John Myers, Brewster, N.Y., August 1982; John Richardson, New York, December 1982; and Rosamond Bernier Russell, New York, August 1982.

184   *"Mary's tongue."* Meigs, *Lily Briscoe,* p. 145.

184   *"Mary's smile."* Author's interview with DM, New York, October 1981.

184   *"She would say."* Author's interview with Rosamond Bernier Russell.

184   *"Bowden was invited everywhere."* Author's interview with Margaret Shafer.

184   *"so bitchy."* Author's interview with John Richardson.

185   *"Being an artist."* Mary McCarthy's Vassar commencement address, June 1976.

185   *suffocated by the marriage.* DM quotes MM in letter to NC, Macdonald Papers, Box 10, Folder 243.

185   *"Daunted and somewhat abashed."* MM to Katharine White, 8/3/54, *New Yorker* files.

186   *"I really think."* MM to ASJ, 11/13/55.

186   *"You always were."* CL, p. 97.

186   *"He's not really meant."* MM to ASJ, 11/13/55.

187   *"What I really do."* Elisabeth Niebuhr, "The Art of Fiction" (interview with Mary McCarthy), *Paris Review,* Winter–Spring 1962, p. 67.

187   *"The relation between life."* "The Inventions of Ivy Compton-Burnett," *WW,* p. 141.

187   *"was no doubt sick."* "On Madame Bovary," *WW,* p. 73.

187   *"The others fear."* "Hanging by a Thread," *WW,* p. 182.

188   *"was fraught with."* "On Madame Bovary," p. 76.

188   *"I had a long call."* Phyllis Given to John Dos Passos, 12/14/55, John Dos Passos Papers, Accession 5950, University of Virginia, Charlottesville.

188   *"It was as though."* Meigs, *Lily Briscoe,* p. 153.

188   *Even McCarthy admitted.* MM to DG, 7/22/66.

188   *"either there was."* CL, pp. 121, 122, 123.

189   *"Icebox out of order."* MM to DM, 6/27/51, Macdonald Papers, Box 31, folder 779.

189   *"were offered a martini."* MM to Augusta McCarthy, 10/26/51, courtesy Kevin McCarthy.

189   *"were the best-liked couple."* CL, p. 24.

189   *"I can't stop myself."* Adrienne Clarkson's interview with MM for CBC, Vassar, October 1968.

189   *"It pains me."* MM to Mary Meigs, 1/20/82, MM files, now McCarthy Archives, Vassar College Library.

190   *"Mary picks up."* Author's interview with Angélique Levi, Paris, April 1982.

190   *"a naughtiness."* Author's interview with Miriam Chiaromonte, Rome, April 1982.

190   *"a strange," "only spoke."* CL, p. 8.

190   *"There may be something wrong."* Niebuhr, "Art of Fiction," p. 86.

190   *"a book I don't much like."* MM to NC, 6/8/67.

CHAPTER XV

Page

191   *"We figured."* Author's interview with Rosamond Bernier Russell, New York, August 1983.

191   *"Mr. Bernier seems."* MM to CA, 9/2/55, courtesy Carmen Angleton.

191   *"I'd never heard."* Elisabeth Niebuhr, "The Art of Fiction" (interview with Mary McCarthy), *Paris Review,* Winter 1961–Fall 1962, p. 92.

191   *"a very straight."* MM to CA, 9/2/55.

192 *"all quite charming."* Ibid.

192 *" 'when you are out.' " Venice Observed,* Paris: G. & R. Bernier, 1956, p. 28 (hereafter cited as *VO).*

192 " 'Permesso.' " Ibid, p. 33.

192 *"the Signora takes her aside."* Ibid, p. 165.

192 *"Your glasses."* Ibid.

192 *"the entire family."* Ibid.

193 *"I've seen."* MM to CA, 9/2/55.

193 *"I've been having."* Ibid.

193 *"still indignant."* Ibid.

193 Meeting with Berenson. Author's interviews with Anna Maria Cicogna, Venice, April 1982, and William Mostyn-Owen, London, March 1982.

194 Dinners at Europa. Author's interview with MM, Castine, Maine, August 1984.

194 *"a regular old Volpone."* MM to HA, 9/22/55.

194 *"I've been reading Burckhardt."* MM to CA, 9/14/55.

195 Dinners and learning Italian. Author's interviews with Francis Haskell, Oxford, March 1982, and Carmen Angleton, Rome, April 1982.

195 *"a rather nice apartment."* MM to CA, 4/21/56.

196 *"It seems to me."* MM to BB, 2/25/57, I Tatti files.

196 "a commercial people." *VO,* p. 37.

197 *"from the beginning."* Ibid, p. 120.

197 *"The absence of fanaticism."* Ibid, p. 126.

197 *"frisks among my possessions."* Ibid, p. 165.

198 *"an allegory."* Ibid, p. 37.

198 *"which captivate the eye."* Ibid, p. 113.

198 *"are disappointing."* Ibid, p. 114.

198 *"frail shell."* Ibid.

198 *"a charming book."* Author's interview with Anna Maria Cicogna.

198 *"both numbers."* MM to William Shawn, 7/20/56, *New Yorker* files.

198 *"some amusing," "written with."* Sacheverell Sitwell's review of *VO* in *NYTBR,* November 18, 1956, p. 1.

198 *"The presentation."* MM to BB, 2/25/57, I Tatti files.

199 *"We really didn't want."* Author's interview with Rosamond Bernier Russell.

199 "The Tempest" description. *VO,* p. 134.

200 *"Maybe I should."* Niebuhr, "Art of Fiction," p. 93.

200 *"everything in Venice."* Ibid.

CHAPTER XVI

Page

201 *black Chevrolet sedan.* MM to CA, 4/21/56.

201 *the drive was somewhat perilous.* Author's interview with Carmen Angleton, Rome, 1982.

201 *"I had an accident."* Author's interview with MM, Castine, 1984.

201 *"It seems to me."* MM to BB, 1/20/58, I Tatti files.

202 John Davenport. Author's interviews with Lord Weidenfeld, London, April 1982; Karl Miller, London, April 1982; John Russell, New York, August 1982; and Francis Haskell, Oxford, April 1982.

202 Letters and postcards to Davenport. Author read at Maurice F. Neville Rare Books, Santa Barbara, California, March 1982.

202 *an enormous apartment.* MM to CA, 8/9/56.

203 *"Present: Schiaparelli."* MM to BB, 8/28/56.

203 *"to come and share."* MM to CA, 8/9/56.

204 *"This record lays claim."* MCG, pp. 4–5.

204 *"How typical."* Author's interview with Kot Jelenski, Paris, April 1982.

204 *"And it is also obvious."* J. W. Simons's review of *MCG* in *Commonweal,* July 12, 1957, p. 379.

204 "MM wanted to lie." This review was quoted in *Time to Murder and Create,* New York: David McKay, 1966, p. 114.

205 *"This memory goes back."* MCG, p. 5.

205 *"Miss McCarthy, who writes."* W. T. Scott's review of *MCG* in *Herald Tribune Book Review,* May 26, 1957, p. 3.

206 *"A cough and a tobacco stain."* MCG, pp. 152–153.

206 *"Like all truly intellectual women."* Ibid., p. 93.

206 *"some quality."* Ibid., p. 175.

207 *"Though I often stood first."* Ibid., pp. 108, 109.

207 *"felt for once."* DM to NC, 3/21/52, Dwight Macdonald Papers, Box 10, Folder 242, Sterling Library, Yale University, New Haven.

208	*"What was the point?"* 5/21/57, McCarthy Archives, Vassar College Library.
208	*"but the* padrona *comes."* MM to DM, 5/20/57, Macdonald Papers, Box 31, Folder 780.
208	*"supply of fresh energy."* Ibid, 5/30/57.
209	*"forbidding solitude."* MM to BB, 6/7/57, I Tatti files.
209	*"last year."* MM to DM, Macdonald Papers, Box 31, Folder 780.
209	*"lots of new people."* MM to BB, 6/24/57.
209	Countess Rucellai. Author's interview with Countess Rucellai, Florence, May 1982.
209	Sir Harold. Author's interview with Harold Acton, Florence, May 1982. He has donated his villa to NYU.
210	*"trying to understand."* MM to CA, 9/23/57.
210	*"Relations with the Berniers."* MM to Janet Flanner, 8/4/57, Collections of Manuscript Division, Library of Congress, Washington.
211	*no one would buy it.* Author's interview with Rosamond Bernier Russell, New York, August 1983.
211	*"never sorry for having done."* MM to Janet Flanner, 8/4/57, Collections of Manuscript Division, Library of Congress.
211	*"very hard, too hard."* MM to BB, 3/22/58, I Tatti files.
211	*Her only respites.* MM to BB, Ibid.
212	*"She has made New York."* MM to BB, Ibid.
212	*"Beaton book."* MM to BB, 1/20/58.
212	*it rained for days.* Mary McCarthy, "Brunelleschi's Dome," *Harper's Bazaar,* September 1959, p. 234.
212	*"the photographic situation."* MM to William Shawn, 6/15/58, *New Yorker* files.
212	*"Taking photographic notes."* "Brunelleschi's Dome," p. 235.
213	*"What lovely things!"* Ulrich Middeldorf to MM, 9/12/58, courtesy Professor Middeldorf.
213	*"Some of the best."* Review of Mary McCarthy's *The Stones of Florence* in *Nation,* December 12, 1959, p. 450.
213	*"it would take an octopus."* MM to BB, 1/29/58.
214	Difficulties with photographs. Author's interview with Ulrich Middeldorf (now deceased), Florence, May 1982; and correspondence between MM and Middeldorf, Middeldorf files: Middeldorf to MM, 9/12/58; MM to Middeldorf, 9/30/58, 11/16/58, 3/5/59.

214   *"I shall never."* MM to William Shawn, 6/15/58.

214   *"If I ever get."* MM to BB, 1/20/5.

214   *"but it is tremendously difficult."* MM to Katharine White, 8/7/57, *New Yorker* files.

214   *"I felt that through."* Elisabeth Niebuhr, "The Art of Fiction" (interview with Mary McCarthy), *Paris Review,* Winter–Spring 1962, p. 93.

215   *"is a species of wisdom."* Mary McCarthy, *The Stones of Florence,* New York: Harcourt Brace Jovanovich, [1959,] p. 75 (hereafter cited as *SF).*

215   *"Florence is a manly town."* Ibid., p. 4.

216   Berenson's view. MM to CA; and author's interviews with Harold Acton, Francis Haskell, Countess Rucellai, Countess Cicogna, Venice, April 1982, and Emilia Sartori, Florence, April 1982.

216   *"But, my dear."* McCarthy, "Brunelleschi's Dome," p. 234.

216   "Took Mary McCarthy." Bernard Berenson, *Sunlight and Twilight; From the Diaries of 1947–1958,* ed. Nicky Mariano, New York: Harcourt Brace Jovanovich, 1963, p. 435.

217   *"Because of the darkness." SF,* p. 112.

217   *"The artists of Florence."* Allen Temko's review of *SF* in *New York Herald Tribune Book Review,* January 3, 1960, p. 6.

217   *"the faculty of eliciting." SF,* pp. 112, 113.

217   *"It could be very elegant."* Berenson quoted in a letter from MM to CA, 9/23/57.

218   *"white, black, grey, dun." SF,* p. 20.

218   *Hannah Arendt called it superb.* HA to MM, 8/28/59.

218   *William Jovanovich was pleased.* WJ to MM, 6/2/59.

218   *"far too much insider snobbishness."* DM to NC, 10/19/59, Macdonald Papers, Box 10, Folder 242.

218   *"many questionable ideas."* NC to DM, 11/15/59, Macdonald Papers, Box 10, Folder 242.

218   *"It has eight heroines," "starts in the 1930s."* MM to BB, 11/16/58 and 2/10/59, I Tatti files.

219   *"which brought a lot."* MM to BB, 2/10/59, I Tatti files.

219   *"We have a vast sweep of view."* MM to Nicky Mariano, 8/21/59, I Tatti files.

219   *"abandoned mines."* MM to EH, 10/17/51, Lowell Papers, Houghton Library, Harvard University, Cambridge, Mass.

219   *"strict isolation ward."* DM to NC, 10/19/59, Macdonald Papers, Box 10, Folder 242.

219–221 Stay in Tripoli. Author's interview with Countess Cicogna; Harold Acton, *Memoirs of an Aesthete,* New York: Viking Press, 1970, pp. 350, 351; NC to DM, 12/19/59; MM to Lowells, 11/18/59; MM to WJ, 11/17/59; DM to NC, 10/19/59.

219 Tripoli villa. The family kept returning until the Six-Day War in 1967. Colonel Muammar El Qaddafi seized power, as well as Countess Cicogna's villa, in 1971.

CHAPTER XVII

Page

225 *"None of my other husbands."* Quoted in Doris Grumbach, *The Company She Kept,* New York: Coward-McCann, 1967, p. 184.

226 *"not only one of them."* MM to EW, 3/30/61, Edmund Wilson Papers, Beinecke Library, Yale University, New Haven.

226 *"a direct actionist," "a very nice man."* MM to Frank and Isabel Preston, 4/1/61, courtesy Frank Preston.

226 State Department tour. Author's phone interview with Yale Richmond (cultural affairs officer, American Embassy, Warsaw, 1960), June 1982, and interview with ASJ, New York, January 1982.

226 *"You didn't know."* Grumbach, *Company She Kept,* p. 181.

226 "The Fact in Fiction." *Partisan Review,* Summer 1960, pp. 438–458. "Characters in Fiction," *Partisan Review,* March-April 1961, pp. 171–191. "Americans, Realists, Playwrights," *Encounter,* July 1961, pp. 24–31.

226 *"One catches."* Katharine Whitehorn, "Meeting Mary McCarthy," *Observer,* p. 6.

227 *"doctrinaire functionaries."* SD, p. 227.

227 "paleface"-"redskin" lecture. Author's interview with MM, Castine, August 1984.

228 *"barnstorming actors."* MM to Nicky Mariano, 4/21/60, I Tatti files.

228 *her official itinerary.* McCarthy Archives, Vassar College Library.

228 *"Bowden has taken this."* MM to Nicky Mariano, 4/21/60, I Tatti files.

228 *"all sorts of funny rumors."* Ibid.

228 *"her habit of leaving."* BA, p. 19.

228   *"a veritable dust bowl."* MM to Carmen Angleton, 4/20/60.

228   *"not as easy."* MM to Nicky Mariano, 4/21/60, I Tatti files.

228-229   Difficulties in getting divorce. MM to WJ, 5/12/60; MM to
           CA, 8/20/60, 8/28/60, 12/5/60; HA to MM, 5/30/60,
           5/18/60, 9/16/60, 11/11/60.

229   *"waiting and trying to write."* MM to Nicky Mariano, 4/21/
           60, I Tatti files.

230   *"broke apart."* MM to HA, 8/30/60.

230   *"never been so happy."* MM to HA, 6/29/60.

230   *"Michelangelo, like some."* SF, p. 20.

230   *"The White Rock."* Mary McCarthy, "The Hounds of Sum-
           mer," *The Hounds of Summer and Other Stories,* New York:
           Avon Books, 1981, pp. 199, 200.

231   *"Not at all a deluxe life."* Adrienne Clarkson's interview with
           Mary McCarthy for CBC, Vassar, October 1968.

231   *"twice, the children."* MM to CA, 8/20/60.

231   *"really most happy."* MM to DG, 2/22/66.

231   *"Twelve sit down."* MM to CA, 8/20/60.

231   *"Campari and soda."* Ibid.

232   *"We've passed."* MM to CA, 12/5/60.

232   *"Love apart."* MM to HA, 10/7/60.

232   *"would not leave Poland."* JW quoted in letter from MM to
           HA, 11/23/60.

233   *"He likes life in Cracow."* MM to EW, 3/30/61, Wilson Pa-
           pers.

233   *"Reuel seems to be."* MM to HA, 11/23/60.

233   *"We didn't fight once."* MM to Kevin and Augusta McCarthy,
           3/13/61, courtesy Kevin McCarthy.

234   *"Mary acted."* NC to DM, 5/9/61, Macdonald Papers, Box
           10, Folder 243, Sterling Library, Yale University, New
           Haven.

234   *"more deeply in love"* MM to Nicky Mariano, 4/21/60, I Tatti
           files.

234   *"fighting through."* MM to DM, 3/29/61, Macdonald Papers,
           Box 31, Folder 780.

235   *"I've wished so often."* MM to CA, 4/2/61.

235   Paris wedding. Author's interviews with Carmen Angleton,
           Rome, April 1982; Rosamond Bernier Russell, New York,
           August 1983; Stanley Geist, Paris, April 1982; Kot Jelenski,
           Paris, April 1982; DM, New York, November 1981; RW,

London, Ontario, February 1982, and Wellfleet, August 1982; Gloria Jones, New York, December 1981.

236   *"I really did develop."* Carol Brightman, "Mary, Still Contrary," *Nation,* May 19, 1984, p. 611.

236   *"My love for Jim."* MM to HA, 5/15/60.

236   *"I think Jim West."* Author's interview with Rosamond Bernier Russell.

236   *McCarthy's English publisher.* Author's interview with George Weidenfeld, London, March 1982.

236   *she had found Mr. Right.* DM to NC, 4/6/61, Macdonald Papers, Box 10, Folder 243.

236   *"the impulses that cause."* Whitehorn, "Meeting Mary McCarthy," p. 6.

237   *"everything is offered."* MM to HA, 5/29/60.

237   "fête champêtre." DM to NC, 4/23/61, Macdonald Papers, Box 10, Folder 243.

237   *"I had no doubt."* NC to DM, 5/9/61, Macdonald Papers, Box 10, Folder 243.

237   *occupying government housing.* Author's telephone interview with William Buell, June 1982, Washington, D.C.

237   *an impossible duplication.* Author's interview with Mary Brady, Washington, D.C., November 1981.

238   *"faintly ambulant."* MM to WJ, 6/27/61.

239   *"an organization."* MM to CA, 8/29/61.

239   *thirty-nine signatures.* Author's interview with Signora Biso, Bocca di Magra, May 1982.

240   Stonington background. Author's interviews with James Merrill, New York, December 1981, and Eleanor Perényi, Stonington, August 1982.

240   *"Jim watched."* MM to CA, 2/5/61.

240   *"That was when."* BA, p. 8.

240   *"most of the houses."* Ibid., p. 7.

240   *"when you go."* MM to CA, 8/2/64.

241   *"he was in good spirits."* MM to EW, 12/28/61, Wilson Papers.

241   *"a single, large room."* MM to CA, 2/5/62.

241   Party (January 28, 1962). MM to CA, 2/5/62; and author's interviews with Kevin McCarthy, Los Angeles, March 1982; WJ, New York, November 1981 and January 1982; and Lady Caroline Freud Lowell, London, April 1982.

241   *"Life has got."* MM to CA, 2/5/62.

242   West on loan. MM to author, 7/22/83.

242   OECD information. OECD brochures; and author's inter-
        view with Francis Cassavetti, Press Offices, OECD, Paris,
        April 1982.

242   Apartment. Author's interview with Margo Viscusi, New
        York, October 1981 and January 1982; and visit to apart-
        ment, April 1982. Cost: $33,000 plus renovations. Mary
        McCarthy, sold stock inherited from grandmother to pay for
        purchase.

242   *"I discovered last Saturday."* MM to CA, 12/14/82.

243   *"Jim . . . doesn't get home."* MM to WJ, 7/27/67.

243   "The Hounds of Summer." Mary McCarthy's story in *New
        Yorker,* September 14, 1963, pp. 47–50.

243   *"New eyesores."* MM to CA, 8/8/62.

243   "A Bolt from the Blue." Mary McCarthy's review of Vladi-
        mir Nabokov's *Pale Fire* in *New Republic,* June 4, 1962, pp.
        21–27.

244   "General Macbeth." Mary McCarthy's essay in *Harper's,*
        June 6, 1962, pp. 34–39.

244   "Salinger's Closed Circuit." Mary McCarthy's essay in
        Harper's, October 1962, pp. 46–48.

244   "I like Shawn." Clarkson CBC interview.

244   *"your best course."* WJ to MM, 8/6/62.

244   *"Is there any way."* WJ to MM, 8/23/62.

244   *"I had a fancy luncheon."* WJ to MM, 12/13/62.

245   *"a new life."* MM to CA, 12/14/62.

CHAPTER XVIII

Page
246   *"Hannah has got hold."* MM to WP, 1/9/64, *Partisan Review*
        files, courtesy William Phillips.

247   "What made you do it." MM to Philip Rahv and WP, 9/25/
        63.

247   Phillips's defense. William Phillips, *A Partisan View,* New
        York: Stein and Day, 1983, pp. 108–110.

247   *"My first reaction."* MM to HA, 9/13/63.

248   *"As I see it."* HA to MM, 9/20/83, Library of Congress,
        Washington.

248   *"a densely argued letter."* Letter from Elisabeth Young-Bruehl, author of biography of Arendt, to author, n.d.

248   "Division of antagonists." *A Partisan View,* p. 109.

248   *"to make the criminal."* Mary McCarthy, "The Hue and Cry," *Partisan Review,* Winter 1964, pp. 82–94.

249   *"this is going to make."* MM to WJ, 1/9/64, courtesy William Jovanovich.

249   *"I've lost all perspective."* MM to HA, 3/13/63.

249   *"We are proceeding."* WJ to MM, 2/14/63.

249   *"strongly that it is."* WJ to MM, 2/20/63.

250   *"I'm very much excited."* MM to Julian Muller of Harcourt, Brace & World, 5/20/63.

250   *"I'm beginning to get."* MM to WJ, 7/1/63.

250   *"the book has gotten off."* WJ to MM, 9/15/63.

250   *"the sales are stupefying."* MM to WJ, 9/23/63.

250   "The Group *number one."* WJ to MM, 9/30/63.

251   *"Life has rung me."* MM to WJ, 6/20/63.

251   *"Unless it's an extreme emergency."* MM to WJ, 9/23/63.

251   *"Jack Paar is willing."* WJ to MM, 10/2/63.

252   *"two years."* MM to Henry Moe of the John Simon Guggenheim Memorial Foundation, 9/25/51, Guggenheim files.

252   *"gave up."* MM to Henry Moe, 1/28/59, Guggenheim files.

252   *"firebrand."* Author's interview with Brendan Gill, New York, August 1983.

253   *"There was a terrible protest."* Adrienne Clarkson's interview with Mary McCarthy for CBC, Vassar, October 1968.

253   " 'Neil, how do you think,' " " 'Your heart's pounding.' " Philip Roth, *Goodbye, Columbus,* New York: Bantam Books, 1959, pp. 58, 89.

253   *"a kind of compendious history."* MM's Guggenheim application, 1/28/59.

254   *"these girls are all."* Elisabeth Niebuhr, "The Art of Fiction" (interview with Mary McCarthy), *Paris Review,* Winter–Spring 1962, p. 88.

254   *"the capacity to learn."* MM to DG, 7/22/66.

254   *"awfully mean."* Joan Kufrin, *Uncommon Women,* New York: New Century Publishers, 1981, pp. 84, 85.

254   *"Mary's sarcastic attitude."* NC to DM, 10/5/63, Macdonald Papers, Box 10, Folder 243, Sterling Library, Yale University, New Haven.

254   *"the odd thing is."* DM to NC, 10/9/63.

254   *"I have a belief."* Clarkson CBC interview, 1968.

255   *author's commentary and narration.* Mary McCarthy, "Letter to a Translator," *Encounter,* July-December, 1964, pp. 69–71, 74–76.

255   *"What I was trying to say."* Judith Manners, "She Wouldn't Send Daughter to Vassar," *Washington Post,* November 15, 1963.

256   *" 'Oh,' said Helena."* Group, p. 129.

256   *" 'He'd had all his early.' "* Ibid., p. 130.

256   *"had become a sort."* Ibid., p. 132.

257   *" 'It undercuts Harald.' "* Ibid., p. 133.

257   *"Her voice."* Ibid., p. 138.

257   *" 'I'd start.' "* Ibid., p. 139, 140.

258   *"It is as if."* WJ to MM, 9/15/63.

258   *"little glints of gold."* Norman Mailer, "The Mary McCarthy Case," *NYRB,* October 17, 1963, p. 3.

259   *"Mary tried."* DM to NC, 10/9/63.

259   *a front-page story.* Sheila Tobias, "The Group on Mary McCarthy," *Herald Tribune Book Review,* January 5, 1964, pp. 6–9.

259   *"I suppose you have seen."* MM to WJ, 1/9/64.

260   *"the success of* The Group.*"* MM to WP, 1/9/64, courtesy William Phillips.

260   *"the success of* that book.*"* MM to Robert Lowell, 1/9/64, Robert Lowell Papers, Houghton Library, Harvard University, Cambridge, Mass.

260   "being an author." MM to WJ, 3/2/64.

260   Hardwick parody. Xavier Prynne (Elizabeth Hardwick), "The Gang," *NYRB,* September 26, 1963, p. 22.

260   *"I think it's easier."* MM to Robert Lowell, 1/9/64.

261   *"I wasn't persuaded."* MM to author, 7/22/83.

261   Katharine White's Criticisms. Quoted in Linda Davis's *Onward and Upward: A Biography of Katharine S. White,* New York: Harper & Row, 1987, p. 209.

261   *"For taking pains."* Ibid.

262   *"You'll be amused."* WJ to MM, 12/18/63.

262   *"Your comments on."* WJ to Mrs. Harry E. Sanford, 3/25/65.

263   *"fidelity to," "narrative holes," "really are," "What gives."* Pauline Kael, "The Making of *The Group,*" *Kiss, Kiss, Bang, Bang,* Boston: Little, Brown, 1968, pp. 67–100.

264   *"Like Harvard."* Mary McCarthy, "The Vassar Girl," *Holiday Magazine,* May 1951, and in *OC,* p. 195.

264   *"a whole suicide class."* Adrienne Clarkson's interview with MM for CBC, Vassar, October 1968.

264   *"This is the first book."* Ibid.

265   *"It is quite different."* HA to MM, 9/16/63.

265   *"I hated it when."* Miriam Gross, "A World Out of Joint," *Observer,* October 14, 1979.

CHAPTER XIX

Page

266   *"I have never."* Carol Brightman, "Mary, Still Contrary," *The Nation,* May 19, 1984, pp. 616.

266   *"enjoyed the experience."* Ibid.

266   *"had quite a lot."* Ibid.

266   *"of white wooden houses."* BA, p. 162.

266   *"nothing is more boring."* MCG, p. 26.

266   *"a child is a robot."* WW, p. 106.

267   *"I know he feels."* Author's interviews with Margo Viscusi, New York, October and December 1981.

267   *snowed in.* MM to WJ, 9/15/66, courtesy William Jovanovich.

268   *"which provided us."* MM to WJ, 9/15/66.

268   *"It was a very large."* Author's interview with Alison West, New York, August 1982.

268   "Bocca di Magra remains." Ibid.

268   *"I remember going."* Author's interview with Mary Dabney McCarthy, San Francisco, March 1982.

268   House in Stonington. Author's interview with Alison West.

269   Stonington. Author's interviews with James Merrill, New York, January 1982; David Jackson and Eleanor Perényi, Stonington, Conn., August 1982.

270   *"I've started working here."* MM to WJ, 8/8/62.

270   *"I love her nonfiction."* Author's interview with William Shawn, New York, October 1981.

270   *"one thing about myself."* MM to NC, 9/25/62.

270   *"That may mean."* Michiko Kakutani, "Our Woman of Letters," *NYTM,* March 29, 1987, p. 74.

271   *"Criticism teaches."* Interview with Mary McCarthy in Toronto *Globe and Mail,* October 23, 1982, p. ETI.

271   *"takes such a grip."* William Barrett, *The Truants,* New York: Anchor Press/Doubleday, 1982, p. 65.

271   *"belong, as it were."* *OC,* p. 237.

271   *"the staple ingredient."* Ibid., p. 251.

271   *"languishing of the characters."* Ibid., p. 292.

272   *"is impersonal."* *WW,* p. 105.

272   *"technical experiment."* Ibid., p. 104.

272   *"The narrative present."* Ibid., p. 105.

273   *"The indefinite pronoun."* Ibid., p. 106.

273   *"asking why this."* Mary McCarthy, "Letter to a Translator," *Encounter,* November 1964, p. 76.

273   *"try to find out."* Edwin Newman interview, "A Conversation with Mary McCarthy," filmed and recorded in Paris, broadcast on WNBC-TV, New York, December 4, 1966.

273   *"My policy has been."* DG to MM, 10/23/65.

274   *"I must tell you."* MM to DG, 2/22/66.

274   *"Let me rush."* DG to MM, 3/2/66.

274   *"strange to have."* MM to DG, 7/4/66.

275   *"a sad mixture."* MM to WJ, n.d.

275   *"He calmed down."* MM to HA, 10/11/66.

275   *"it is very dangerous."* EW to MM, 10/3/66.

275   *"I think we must try."* WJ to MM, 10/31/66.

276   *"Why did she."* Doris Grumbach, "The Subject Objected," *NYTBR,* June 11, 1967, p. 36.

276   *"You reassured me."* MM to DG, 9/26/66.

276   *"how Grumbach justified."* MM to author, 1/27/85.

276   *"confession of the frankest kind."* Grumbach, "Subject Objected," p. 36.

277   *"Unfortunately, I am not discreet."* MM to DG, 9/26/66.

277   *" 'One more thing.' "* *CL,* p. 98.

277   *"made little effort."* Ellen Moers, "Fictions and Facts," *NYTBR,* June 11, 1967, p. 7.

CHAPTER XX

Page

278   *"that was a delicious."* MM at MacDowell Colony, 8/26/84.

279   *"a betrayal of Peter Levi."* MM to WJ, 1/30/67.

279   *"The fact that I was."* *SD,* pp. 15, 16.

279   *"But I had fun."* Ibid., p. 18.

280   *"readers put."* Ibid., p. 27.

280   *"one does what."* Interview with Mary McCarthy in *The Montreal Gazette,* September 29, 1967, p. 19.

280   *"to describe what."* MM to CA, 1/7/67.

280   Newspapermen and hotel. Author's interviews with William Tuohy, London, March 1982; Jonathan Randal, Paris, April 1982; Thomas Buckley, New York, October 1981; Philippe Franchine, Paris, April 1982; William Corson, Washington, D.C., June 1982 (phone interview); Alan Glyn, London, March 1982 (phone interview); Barry Zorthian, Washington, June 1982.

280   *"They were very nervous-making."* Kevin McCarthy's interview with his sister for *People,* October 1979, unpublished portion.

281   *"As we drove."* SD, pp. 64, 65.

281   *"enough for a platoon."* Ibid., p. 93.

281   *"who have stamped."* Ibid., p. 122.

282   *"It is peculiar."* Ibid., p. 146.

283   *"only a minority."* Ibid., p. 185.

283   *"My publisher," "they thought it preposterous."* Transcript of "Firing Line" telecast, August 8, 1971, p. 9.

283   Congress for Cultural Freedom. Author's interview with Kot Jelenski, Paris, 1982; and American Committee for Cultural Freedom Papers, Tamiment Library, New York University.

283   *"The firm point is."* NC to DM, 6/25/67.

283–284   *"with Tempo Presente."* MM to NC and Ignazio Silone, 6/8/67.

284   *"Bit by bit."* SD, p. 42.

284   *"a real Fourth-of-July."* MM to WJ, 7/12/67.

285   *"we've struck a bold note."* MM to WJ, 8/2/67.

285   *"Jim has taken."* MM to Robert Lowell, 2/1/68, Robert Lowell Papers, Houghton Library, Harvard University, Cambridge, Mass.

286   *"Here the Viet Cong."* MM to EH, 2/6/68.

286   Tactical nuclear weapons. Michael Maclear, *The Ten Thousand Day War,* New York: St. Martin's Press, 1981, pp. 195–196.

286   *"mixture of total incoherence."* MM to Robert Lowell, 2/7/68.

286   *"It's not like Italy."* MM to Robert Lowell, 2/1/68.

287   *"American firms."* MM to EH, 2/6/68.

287   *"what it is like."* MM to JW, 3/10/68.

287   *"if Zola had been signing."* Transcript of preshow interview of telecast, Nederland Televisie Stichting, 5/14/68.

288   *The night before.* Author's interviews with Mr. and Mrs. David DuVivier, Princeton, November 1981, and Mrs. James Jones, New York, November 1981.

288   *"shaking in my boots."* MM to Kevin McCarthy, 3/6/68.

288   *"You can't telephone."* MM to JW, 3/17/58 (afternoon).

289   *"bringing with it."* MM to JW, 3/17/68 (evening).

289   *"love." "miss." "I cling." "so long." "I am." "I love."* MM to JW, 3/16/68, 3/17/68, 3/18/68, 3/19/68.

289   *"jerk up from the pillow." SD,* p. 205.

289   "a shady, leafy city." *SD,* p. 197.

289   "Besides the shelters." Ibid, p. 217.

290   *"I don't want."* MM to JW, 3/22/68.

290   *"Hanoi is."* MM to JW, 3/22/68.

290   *"You unexcelled correspondent."* JW to MM, 3/18/68.

291   *"Delighted your letters."* JW to MM, 3/21/68.

291   *"Rocky not running."* JW to MM, 3/23/68.

291   *"dancing, kissing." SD,* p. 31.

291   *"to wonder whether."* MM to WJ, 4/16/68.

292   *"Tokyo was all right."* Ibid.

292   *"Their ethic." SD,* p. 316.

292   *"by the local habits."* MM to NC, 12/29/69.

292   *"the only 'people's democracy.' "* MM to DM, 8/13/69, Macdonald Papers, Box 31, Folder 780, Sterling Library, Yale University, New Haven.

292   *"The feeling that." SD,* p. 309.

292   *"Vietnamese socialist planning."* Ibid., p. 307.

293   *"They . . . have a contempt."* MM to NC, 12/29/69.

293   *"the cat sometimes." SD,* pp. 269, 270.

294   *"why compassion led her."* Richard Rovere, *Final Reports: Reflections on Politics and History in Our Time,* New York: Doubleday, 1984, p. 223.

294   *"the shortage of freedom."* MM to DM, 8/13/69, Macdonald Papers, Box 31, Folder 780.

294   *"pro-Viet Cong."* MM to JW, 3/10/68.

294   *"The private tumults." SD,* pp. 315, 316.

294   *"a superb blending."* WJ to MM, 8/11/68.

295   *"sole active British contribution."* Mary McCarthy, "Letter from London: The Demo," *NYRB,* December 19, 1968, p. 6 (republished *Observer* account).

295   *"I like Ho."* MM to NC, 12/29/69.

296   *revive the public's waning interest.* MM to WJ, 4/1/71.

296   *"The whole question."* WJ to MM, 4/7/71.

297   "did not look." *SD,* p. 383.

297   *the trial was dull.* MM to William Shawn, 9/2/71.

297   *"what I'm sending you."* MM to William Shawn, 2/2/72.

297   *"Medina was a transition figure."* SD, p. 384.

298   *"when I mentioned."* SD, p. 47.

298   *"was both funny and typical."* Author's interview with Elizabeth Hardwick, New York, October 1981 and January 1982.

298   Wests' conversation. *SD,* p. 49.

298   *"It seemed to me."* Ibid, p. 51.

299   *"a little anti-war effort."* MM to WJ, 1/15/73.

299   *"were incredulous."* MM to HA, 1/15/73.

299   *"Kennedy's academic advisors."* SD, pp. 428–430.

300   *"if Americans did not act."* Edwin Newman interview, "A Conversation with Mary McCarthy," filmed and recorded in Paris, broadcast on WNBC-TV, New York, December 4, 1966.

300   *"The wistful idea."* Mary McCarthy in "The Meaning of Vietnam," *NYRB,* June 12, 1975, pp. 25–26.

300   *"Contemplated writing."* "The Dick Cavett Show," October 1979.

CHAPTER XXI

Page

301   *"The key."* Joan Kufrin, *Uncommon Women,* New York: New Century Publishers, 1981, p. 82.

301   *"The plant-seller."* BA, pp 160–161.

302   *"this novel."* MM to William Maxwell, 12/2/66.

302   *"some crazy hope."* MM to HA, 1/25/70.

302   *"it's been a grind."* MM to WJ, 4/1/70.

302   *"Jay is enchanting."* MM to EW, 9/15/70.

303   *"It whets the appetite."* Quoted in letter from MM to WJ, 1/20/71.

304   *"My breath."* Publishers Weekly, July 26, 1971, p. 29.

304   *"her tone is no longer."* John Aldridge's review of BA in *Saturday Review,* May 8, 1971, p. 21.

304   *"Mary McCarthy again."* NYTBR, May 16, 1971, p. 1.

304   *"They are reviewing me."* MM to WJ, 5/17/71.

305   *"Some of the reasons."* HA to MM, 5/28/71.

305   *"will soon become."* MM to William Maxwell, 12/2/66.

305   *"the Rocky Port syndrome."* MM to WJ, 8/2/67.

305   *"there doesn't seem."* MM to CA, 7/23/64.

306   *"His mother." BA,* p. 32.

306   *"The Peter Levi problem."* MM to WJ, 7/12/67.

307   *"I must say."* MM to DM, 8/6/67, Dwight Macdonald Papers, Box 31, folder 780, Sterling Library, Yale University, New Haven.

307   *"As for Women's Lib."* Carol Brightman, "Mary, Still Contrary," *Nation,* May 19, 1984, pp. 614–615.

307   *"I like the hero."* Kufrin, *Uncommon Women,* p. 82.

308   *"I wonder who began." WW,* p. 132.

308   *"I have thought."* Quoted in Jean-François Revel, "Miss McCarthy Explains," *NYTBR,* May 16, 1971, p. 2.

309   *"To the extent." WW,* p. 212.

309   *"hardly bothers."* Dorothy Parker, an editor at Atheneum Publishers, in *Christian Science Monitor.*

310   *"If Nature."* Revel, "Miss McCarthy Explains," p. 2.

310   *"In all these young women."* Mary McCarthy, "Mary McCarthy Ad-Libs About Shakespeare's Women," *Show,* February 1964.

310–311 *"Aside from getting."* Brightman, "Mary, Still Contrary," p. 619.

311   *"men are to share equally."* Irvin Stock, *Fiction as Wisdom, From Goethe to Bellow,* College Station: Pennsylvania State University Press, 1980, p. 189.

311   *"Had not succumbed." BA,* pp. 197, 198.

312   *"Jim and I."* MM to HA, 1/19/72.

312   *"Mary, look."* HA to MM, 1/22/72.

313   *"That letter went through."* MM to HA, 4/5/72.

313   *"Anyone who knew."* Mary McCarthy, "Nicola Chiaromonte and the Theatre," *NYRB,* February 20, 1975, p. 28.

CHAPTER XXII

Page
314   "a new Mary McCarthy," *"Left to carry the ball."* Irving Marder, "The Face Was Familiar," *International Herald Tribune,* August 30, 1972.

314   *"I found that."* MM to WJ, 8/30/72.

314   *"[Solzhenitsyn] disagrees."* Mary McCarthy, "The Tolstoy Connection," *Saturday Review,* September 16, 1972, p. 95.

315   *"advanced technology."* Mary McCarthy, *The Mask of State: Watergate Portraits,* New York: Harcourt Brace Jovanovich/ Harvest, 1974, p. 27 (hereafter cited as *MS*).

315   *"the case would resolve."* Ibid., p. 73.

315   *"infatuation."* Ibid., p. 153.

315   *"television creation."* Ibid., p. 5.

315   *"wrong medium."* Ibid., p. 4.

315   *"television, with its."* Ibid., p. 3.

316   *"Here television shows."* Ibid., p. 8.

316   *"In me."* Mary McCarthy, "Watergate Over the Dam," *NYRB,* July 15, 1982, p. 44.

316   *"By elimination."* *MS,* p. 140.

316   *"Mary McCarthy dips."* Review of *MS* in *Best Seller,* June 15, 1974, p. 36.

317   *"She is one,"* Review of *MS* in *Listener,* July 18, 1974.

317   *"Mary McCarthy's importance."* James Fallows's review of *MS* in *Washington Monthly,* May 1974, p. 7.

317   *"missed a vital element."* Harold Rosenberg's review of *MS* in *NYRB,* October 31, 1974, pp. 16–18.

317   *"the press group."* MM to WJ, n.d.

317   *"Perhaps I should finish."* MM to WJ, 6/24/74.

317   *"If one of my friends."* MM to HA, 9/30/74.

318   *"Great festivities are planned."* MM to WJ, 12/16/74.

318   *"We were in London."* MM to CA, 12/11/74.

319   *"The chief fallacy."* HA to MM, 8/20/54.

320   *". . . there is so much."* HA to MM, 8/8/69.

320   *"This convergence."* Mary McCarthy's editor's postface, Hannah Arendt, *The Life of the Mind,* New York: Harcourt Brace Jovanovich, 1978, p. 221.

320   *"It seems to me."* MM to HA, 6/9/71.

320   *"I would have said."* Ibid.

321   *"Then I'll go over it."* MM to WJ, 4/6/76.

321   *"I've stayed mostly inside."* MM to CA, 7/7/76.

321   *"It has been all Hannah."* MM to Eleanor DuVivier, 11/25/77, courtesy Mrs. DuVivier.

322   *"In celebration."* MM to Eleanor DuVivier, 11/25/77.

322   *"It has been a heavy job."* McCarthy postface, *Life of the Mind,* pp. 223, 225, 226.

323–324   *"she repeatedly interfered."* HIG, p. 187.

324 Saint Theresa. "I'm more likely named for some blend of the Little Flower (Saint Thérèse of Lisieux) and my mother." (Author's interview with MM, Castine, Maine, August 1984.) But to Kevin McCarthy she said, "The reason I came . . . was in fact the coincidence that my official publication date was October 15, which by the way, Kevin, I've learned is the day of Saint Theresa of Avila." Kevin replied, "Ah, Mary Therese!" She said, "Yes! . . . The Poetry Center of the YMHA asked me to read on October 15. . . . So I thought this was a happy coincidence." Kevin McCarthy's interview for *People,* October 1979, unpublished portion. Saint Theresa of Avila (1515–1582) was Spanish. She was a Carmelite of the reformed order, and her feast day is October 15. Saint Thérèse of Lisieux (1873–1897) was French. She is called the Little Flower of Jesus and is known for her piety, simplicity, and patience. Her feast day is October 3.

324 *"There's no attempt at disguise."* Kevin McCarthy's interview with his sister for *People,* October 1979, unpublished portion.

324 *"Note to myself on a Possible Novel."* Written 11/13, 14/74.

326 *"And the whole question."* Miriam Gross, "A World Out of Joint," *Observer,* October 14, 1979, p. 35.

326 *"You should draw on that."* CM, 1979, p. xii.

326 *"There was this character,"* Carol Brightman, "Mary, Still Contrary," *Nation,* May 19, 1984, p. 612.

326 Cees Nooteboom's help. Author's interview with Cees Nooteboom, Amsterdam, April 1982.

326 *"Holland was fun."* MM to WJ, 11/21/75.

327 *"If Tolstoy."* Paul Ress, "The Underpinning of *Birds of America,* An Interview with Mary McCarthy," *Vogue,* June 1971, p. 92.

327 *"setback" in chapter 8.* MM to WJ, 5/23/78.

327 *"I would not."* MM to WJ, 10/21/75.

329 *"I think writing."* MM to Ann Terry, who asked preinterview questions for Dick Cavett.

330 *"would have been impossible."* Mary Gordon's review of CM in *NYTBR,* 9/30/79, p. 1.

330 *"the author were less class-bound."* Benjamin DeMott's review of CM in *Saturday Review,* December 19, 1979, p. 53.

330 *"Why do all."* Margaret Wimsatt's review of CM in *Commonweal,* December 21, 1979, p. 727.

330 *"I find I am."* MM to HA, 2/17/75.

CHAPTER XXIII

332   Cavett-McCarthy exchange. Transcript of "The Dick Cavett Show."

332   *"I said once in some interview."* The interview she referred to had appeared in *Paris Metro,* a short-lived biweekly primarily for Americans living abroad. Joan DuPont, "Mary McCarthy, Portrait of a Lady," *Paris Metro,* February 15, 1978, pp. 15, 16, 33.

332   Hellman phoned Cavett. Cavett deposition. ("Cavett testified about a telephone conversation he had with Hellman after the broadcast." Robin Fitelson of Daphne Productions, Cavett's company, to MM, 4/13/81.)

332   *"made no effort."* Herbert Mitgang, *NYT,* February 16, 1980, p. 12.

332   DuVivier party. Author's interview with Eleanor and David DuVivier, Princeton, N.J., November 1982.

333   *". . . until yesterday."* MM to WJ, 2/26/80.

333   O'Sullivan advice. Author's interview with Benjamin O'Sullivan, New York, December 1983.

333   *"It's not just."* Michiko Kakutani, "Hellman-McCarthy Libel Suit Stirs Old Antagonisms," *NYT,* March 19, 1980, p. C21.

333   *"I think she has,"* Lillian Hellman quoted in *NYT,* February 16, 1980, p. 16.

333   *"I'm not sure I knew."* MM to author, 1/15/87.

334   Wright's account of party. William Wright, *Lillian Hellman: the Image, the Woman,* New York: Simon and Schuster, 1986, p. 388.

334   *"She was alone."* MM to Benjamin O'Sullivan, 8/23/80. She also wrote, "The Spenders' memory of my Sarah Lawrence meeting with Hellman is different from mine. They say that it was at their home, not Harold Taylor's, that I arrived punctually and she arrived late and that two separate, hostile groups at once formed. Whatever was said between her and me they think they did not hear; this jibes with my memory in that my version there was nobody present but her and me and the Sarah Lawrence girls. But the variance nevertheless worries me. They're so sure, and so had I been. It almost makes me think that there were two occasions, close together, the first maybe at Harold Taylor's and the second at the Spenders'. (Taylor, the Spenders say, definitely had a sun parlor and they didn't.)"

335   *"What has happened."* MM to Benjamin O'Sullivan, 3/21/80.

335   Spanish Refugee Aid crisis bringing Hellman to mind. Author's interview with MM, Paris, April 1982.

336   *"She is not much present."* MM to Benjamin O'Sullivan, 4/21/80.

336   *"the Soviet Union appears."* Mary McCarthy, "A Filmy Version of War," *Town and Country,* April 1944, p. 112.

336   *"To audiences."* Mary McCarthy, "Dry Ice," *Partisan Review,* November–December 1946, p. 577.

336   *"Except in the neighborhood of."* Mary McCarthy, "Gerontion," *Partisan Review,* January–February 1947, p. 63.

336   *"Miss Hellman."* Mary McCarthy, "The Reform of Pangloss." *New Republic,* December 17, 1956, p. 383.

337   *"one is that."* Benjamin O'Sullivan to MM, 6/13/80.

338   *"to call someone dishonest."* NYT, May 11, 1984.

339   *"the angelic intervention."* MM to author, 1/15/87.

339   *London took no legal fees.* Carl Rollyson, *Lillian Hellman: The Legend and the Legacy,* New York: St. Martin's Press, 1988.

339   *"stole* The Little Foxes.*"* MM to Benjamin O'Sullivan, 3/18/80.

339   *"tried to say that DP."* Quoted in ibid.

339   *"was persuaded by friends."* MM to Benjamin O'Sullivan, 4/18/80.

340   *"ruthlessly honest."* Samuel McCracken, "Julia and Other Fictions by Lillian Hellman," *Commentary,* June 1984, p. 43.

340   *"I'll have to work up."* MM to WJ, 5/15/80.

340   *"In* Pentimento.*"* Interrogatory 15.

341   *"Pentimento, pp. 53–98."* Material for answering interrogatory 15.

342   *"By suing Mary McCarthy."* Wright, p. 395.

342   *"If someone had told me."* Samuel Freedman, "McCarthy Is Recipient of MacDowell Medal," *NYT,* August 27, 1984, p. 15.

342   *"But that would be lying."* Author's interview with Benjamin O'Sullivan.

CHAPTER XXIV

Page
343   "It would help me." MM to WJ, 5/15/80.

344   *"a tattered rag-bag."* Phyllis Grosskurth's review of *IN* in *Times Literary Supplement,* March 6, 1981, p. 252.

344   "Something I've observed." Miriam Gross, "A World Out
        of Joint," *Observer,* October 14, 1979, p. 35.

344   *"supposedly corrective of the first."* MM to author, 1/25/85.

345   *"Miss McCarthy . . . has mellowed."* Jeffrey Meyers's review of
        OP in *National Review,* September 6, 1985, p. 55.

345   *"the tact to present."* Diane Johnson's review of *OP* in *Times
        Literary Supplement,* January 31, 1986, p. 111.

345   "Occasional Prose *does not wound."* Jacqueline Austin's re-
        view of *OP* in *Village Voice,* June 4, 1985, p. 47.

345   *"the 'old' Mary McCarthy," "everywhere."* Julian Moynahan's
        review of *OP* in *NYTBR,* May 5, 1985, p. 15.

346   *"will probably take me up."* MM to author, 1/15/87.

346   *There were also."* HIG, p. 197.

346   *"But I am digressing."* Ibid, p. 8.

346   *"Not to leave you."* Ibid, p. 169.

346   *"Weep with me."* Ibid, p. 172.

346   *"As you can see."* Ibid, p. 237.

346   *The center of my life."* Ibid, p. 88.

347   *"In the garden."* MM to WJ, 8/16/79.

347   *"Of course."* MM to Charles McGrath, 4/27/82, *New Yorker*
        files.

348   *"Well, aren't we special."* James Wolcott's review of *HIG* in
        New Republic, May 11, 1987, pp. 34–37.

348   *"the trivia," "tacky."* Rhoda Koenig's review of *HIG* in *New
        York,* April 20, 1987, pp. 81, 82.

348   *"In 'Memories.'"* Wilfrid Sheed's review of *HIG* in *NYTBR,*
        April 19, 1987, pp. 5, 6.

348   *"I have seen."* Publishers Weekly, July 26, 1971, pp. 19–21.

348   *"I've started."* MM to WJ, 1/29/73.

348   The Huizinga Lecture. Mary McCarthy, *Can There Be A
        Gothic Literature,* Amsterdam: Leendert Stafbergen, 1975.

349   *"This amazing woman."* William Barrett, *The Truants,* New
        York: Anchor Press/Doubleday, 1982, pp. 68–69.

349   *"The sprightliness."* Irvin Stock, *Fiction as Wisdom: From Goethe
        to Bellow,* University Park: The Pennsylvania State University
        Press, 1980, p. 156.

349   *"always sought to proselytize."* HIG, p. 135.

349   *"if Mary McCarthy."* Elizabeth Hardwick's presentation ad-
        dress on the occasion of McCarthy's getting the MacDowell
        Medal, 8/26/84.

349   *"most original."* Benjamin DeMott in *Harper's,* October
        1963, p. 102.

350   *"Self-deception." HIG*, p. 104.

351   *"rudely set down." MCG*, p. 17.

351   *"how to exercise." HIG*, p. 132.

351   *"[Tolstoy] did not care." IN*, p. 77.

351   *"Almost nothing."* Philip Rahv, "The Editor Interviews Mary McCarthy," *Modern Occasions*, n.d., p. 22.

352   William Phillips thinks. Author's interview with WP, New York, December 1981.

352   *"Why should I care."* MacDowell Medal award ceremony, 8/26/84.

352   *"Her achievement."* Alison Lurie's review of *HIG* in *NYRB*, June 11, 1987, p. 19.

352   *"A career of candor."* Elizabeth Hardwick, *A View of My Own, Essays in Literature and Society*, New York: Farrar, Straus and Cudahy, 1962, p. 35.

353   *"made a . . . contribution."* Mary McCarthy, "Artists in Uniform," *OC*, p. 58.

Index

Abel, Lionel, 80, 120, 247, 248
abortion, xv, 93, 107, 266
Abrahams, William, 255
Abrams, Floyd, 338, 339
acting, *see* theater
Acton, Harold, 209–210, 216, 218
Adler, Ellen, 130
Adler, Renata, 339
Adventures of a Young Man (Dos
    Passos), 99, 334
Agee, James, 175
Agence France Presse, 280
Age of Roosevelt, The (Schlesinger),
    182–183
Agnelli, Gianni, 313
Agnelli Foundation, 313
Aiken, Conrad, 117
Alberti, Count, 208–209
Alberti, Leon Battista, 209
Alden, Hortense, 74
Aldrich, Margaret Chandler Astor, 57
Aldridge, John, xi, 170, 304
Alexander, Shana, 324
Alsop, Joseph, 177, 209
Altoona, S.D., 7
America, 258
American Academy (Rome), 323, 350
American Center (Paris), 323
American Committee for Cultural
    Freedom, 173–174, 283
American Committee for the Defense
    of Leon Trotsky, 75–77, 351
"American Realist Playwrights, The"
    (McCarthy), 226, 229
Americans for Intellectual Freedom,
    149–150, 173
A. M. Heath and Company, 250
Anderson, Barbara, 130
Anderson, Jean, 59
Anderson, Maxwell, 62, 69, 130
Anderson, Sherwood, 74, 95
Angleton, Carmen, 133, 183,
    191–195, 201, 202, 213, 228,

Angleton, Carmen (*cont.*)
    231, 235
  McCarthy's correspondence with,
    191–194, 203, 231, 232, 235,
    238–243, 245, 268, 278–279,
    305, 318, 321
  in McCarthy's will, 279–280
Angleton, James, 133
Angoff, Charles, 64
animals, 67
Anna Karenina (Tolstoy), 351
Annie Wright Seminary, 39–44, 351
Anrep, Alda, 201
Anti-Climax (Johnsrud), 62
anti-Communism, 77–78, 149–150
  McCarthyism and, 166, 174
Anti-Defamation League of B'nai
    B'rith, 247
"Anti-Intellectuals, The" (McCarthy
    and Marshall), 65
anti-Semitism, 32, 35, 155, 178
anti-Stalinism, 75–84, 121, 148–150,
    173, 283, 333–334
  accomplishments of, 351–352
antiwar movement, 280, 286–287,
    295, 297–298
"Appalachian Revolution, The"
    (McCarthy), 121, 123, 179–180,
    243
architecture, 118, 198, 215, 348, 349
Arendt, Hannah, xiv, 118, 153–156,
    174, 175, 203, 218, 219, 240,
    275, 295, 304, 315
  Birds of America and, 154, 302, 305
  Chiaromonte's death and, 312, 313
  Eichmann in Jerusalem and, 244,
    246–249
  heart attack and death of, 317–323,
    345
  McCarthy as literary executrix of,
    318–322
  McCarthy as viewed by, xii–xiii,
    153, 154, 265

350   *"Self-deception." HIG,* p. 104.
351   *"rudely set down." MCG,* p. 17.
351   *"how to exercise." HIG,* p. 132.
351   *"[Tolstoy] did not care." IN,* p. 77.
351   *"Almost nothing."* Philip Rahv, "The Editor Interviews Mary McCarthy," *Modern Occasions,* n.d., p. 22.
352   William Phillips thinks. Author's interview with WP, New York, December 1981.
352   *"Why should I care."* MacDowell Medal award ceremony, 8/26/84.
352   *"Her achievement."* Alison Lurie's review of *HIG* in *NYRB,* June 11, 1987, p. 19.
352   *"A career of candor."* Elizabeth Hardwick, *A View of My Own, Essays in Literature and Society,* New York: Farrar, Straus and Cudahy, 1962, p. 35.
353   *"made a . . . contribution."* Mary McCarthy, "Artists in Uniform," *OC,* p. 58.

Index